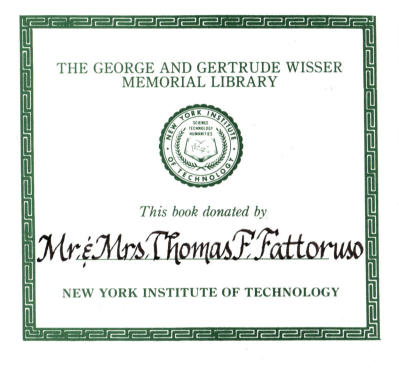

CORPORATE
AND COMMERCIAL
FREE SPEECH

CORPORATE AND COMMERCIAL FREE SPEECH

First Amendment Protection of Expression in Business

EDWIN P. ROME *and*
WILLIAM H. ROBERTS

Quorum Books
Westport, Connecticut • London, England

Library of Congress Cataloging in Publication Data

Rome, Edwin P.
    Corporate and commercial free speech.

    Bibliography: p.
    Includes index.
    1. Advertising laws—United States.   2. Corporation
law—United States.   3. Freedom of speech—United States.
I. Roberts, William H., 1945–   . II. Title.
KF1614.R65   1985   343.73'0786591   84–26496
ISBN 0-89930-041-3 (lib. bdg.)   347.303786591

Library of Congress Catalog Card Number: 84-26496
ISBN: 0-89930-041-3

First published in 1985 by Quorum Books

Greenwood Press
A division of Congressional Information Service, Inc.
88 Post Road West
Westport, Connecticut 06881

Printed in the United States of America

10   9   8   7   6   5   4   3   2   1

Copyright Acknowledgments

Grateful acknowledgment is given for permission to reprint the following:

To Mark Tushnet for the excerpt from his essay "Corporations and Free Speech" in
The Politics of Law, ed. David Kairys, Pantheon Books, New York, 1982.

To the President and Fellows of Harvard College for the excerpt from Zechariah
Chafee, Jr.'s *Free Speech in the United States*, Atheneum, New York, 1969.
Originally published by Harvard University Press. Copyright 1941 by the President
and Fellows of Harvard College, © renewed 1969 by Zechariah Chafee III. Reprinted
by permission.

To Harper & Row for the selection from Alexander Meiklejohn's *Political Freedom*
published by the Oxford University Press, New York, 1965, by arrangement with
Harper & Row, Publishers. Copyright 1948, © 1960 by Harper & Row, Publishers,
Inc. Reprinted by permission of Harper & Row, Publishers, Inc.

Contents

Preface

The topics addressed in this book result from the clash of two conflicting ideas. The first is the conviction that speech which originates with corporations and other commercial organizations is sufficiently different in its content, expressive value, purposes, effects, and utility to society from expression by individuals that corporate or business expression should either not be protected by the First Amendment of the United States Constitution at all or, if it is to be protected, that it merits a lesser degree of constitutional protection than expression by individuals. This conviction seems to arise from a persistent suspicion and distrust of large aggregations of wealth and economic power and of their tendencies and effects on the political and social life of a democratic nation. Or it may arise from spiritual revulsion against the encroaching commercialization of the world and human life in it or from moral antagonism for the values inculcated by the commercial spirit and the political solutions that result from general acceptance of those values.

The second impulse derives from the recognition that protection of every species of expression under the First Amendment not only is protection of the right of the speaker but in a broader sense is protection of the speech itself and that this protection of speech and expression is, at least in part, for the benefit of the listeners or recipients. In the case of political speech of corporations and other business entities, failure to extend constitutional protection might result in the truncation of the public's access to opinion, viewpoint, and information which might be important in making sound judgments on questions of public policy or in selecting political leaders. In the case of commercial speech, the failure to extend constitutional protection may result in lack of information that may cause market failures and market imperfections that defeat the smooth and efficient allocation of resources by the free market economy, which in the democratic capitalist system generates by "invisible hand" mechanisms the fundamental societal decisions on allocation of resources, production and distribution of goods, and the distribution of income. Consumers deprived of relevant commercial information may, by reason of censorship of their sources of commercial information, make unwise, ill-considered, and suboptimal economic decisions. These decisions, in the aggregate, may be suboptimal for a society generally.

The constitutional status of what has come to be known as "corporate advocacy advertising," corporate "image" advertising, and speech of a purely commercial nature is a subject of growing interest to corporate management and to the advertising industry. It is a subject of particular importance to business executives who are involved daily with the advertising of products and services, and it is of interest to corporate directors of public affairs, who operate in the marketplace of ideas, where information important to public opinion formation is disseminated and where public policy can be significantly influenced. Attorneys and judges faced with novel questions of compliance with federal, state, and local regulation of the time, place, manner, content, and financing of commercial speech and image advertising, and corporate speech addressed to public issues, also fall within the audience for which this book is intended. Although we have tried to make our summary of the law detailed enough to serve as an introduction for those who may not be familiar with the controlling judicial decisions in this field and their antecedents, we have also tried to make the book comprehensive enough to be of some use as a sourcebook and overview for lawyers who are already familiar with the precedents.

Little attempt is made here to examine sociological or political aspects of the doctrine of "commercial speech" and of the doctrines conferring constitutional protection on corporate speech. But a remarkable ideological inversion has occurred in these fields. Expansive and traditionally liberal concepts underpinning the constitutional protection of speech have been put to use, sometimes over the opposition of those Supreme Court justices with whom such liberal views have been associated, to extend constitutional protection to commercial and political speech by corporations.

Indeed, Mark Tushnet, one of the penetrating voices of the Critical Legal Studies movement in contemporary American legal thought, has said:

Since 1970, the question of corporate speech has become a central issue of constitutional law. Until then governments had been allowed to regulate corporate speech—for example, by banning cigarette advertising on television—without serious hindrance. Within a relatively short period of time, the constitutional picture has changed dramatically so that today governments find it extremely difficult to regulate corporate speech. In 1980, the Supreme Court held that a state could not prohibit a heavily regulated electrical utility from engaging in advertising that would promote the use of electricity, despite the acknowledged interest in controlling energy use, nor could it prohibit utilities from using mailings to customers as a forum for advocating increased reliance on nuclear energy.

The example above suggests one source of the new concern for corporate speech. With few exceptions, before the 1970s governments had regulated only the speech of corporate actors well outside the core of capitalist enterprise; it mattered little that advertising by fly-by-night sales operations might be prohibited or regulated. The consumer and antinuclear movements of the 1970s, coupled with popular revulsion at corporate involvement in the crimes of the Nixon administration and in overseas bribery, contributed to occasional legislative successes that cut more deeply into the heart of monopoly capitalism. Following a well-worn path, corporations moved from the legislative arena, in which they had lost, to the judicial arena, where they succeeded in persuading the judges to rule that constitutional interests were at stake.

But we cannot understand the development of constitutional protection for corporate speech in any simple conspiratorial way. One indication of the complexity of the issue is that Justice William Rehnquist, the present Court's most reactionary member, has consistently opposed the new developments, while the Court's liberals, Justices William Brennan and Thurgood Marshall, have supported them, albeit with some misgivings. Of course, justices who are conventionally called liberal need not be antibusiness. Indeed, one interpretation of "liberal" jurisprudence is precisely that it has had the effect of shoring up the foundations of American capitalism, sometimes against the strenuous objections of many American capitalists. This interpretation, though, is usually most plausible when capitalism has been threatened enough to require some modest ameliorative steps. In contrast, protection of corporate speech has directly conferred obvious benefits on corporations, which is not what we would ordinarily expect of reforms designed to quell protests against corporate power.[1]

This ideological inversion might make fascinating study by itself, but the practical constraints of time and space required that this book be confined to a description of the current constitutional doctrines in this field, *i.e.*, a systematic, historical account of the relevant judicial decisions and a sketch of the impact of these decisions in a number of distinct fields of law. Of course, the judicial decisions alone do not exhaust this subject, and, when it seemed important to the consideration of the main topics, reference has been made to specific legislation touching these issues.

Broadly speaking, Part I of this book is devoted to the evolution and current status of the "commercial speech" doctrine. Part II is devoted to some of the important constitutional issues presented by decisions such as *First National Bank of Boston v. Bellotti*, 435 U.S. 765 (1978), defining the extent of constitutional protection of corporate participation in public debate on political, social, and economic issues.

We have also tried to provide a sufficiently detailed index, a bibliography, and a table of cases to facilitate the use of the book as a reference work.

Even at the present early stage of development of the constitutional guarantees respecting corporate and commercial speech, it has been necessary to omit for reasons of space several areas which are already adequately dealt with in existing studies. Libel and slander and the law of unfair competition are two examples. Other important areas unquestionably could be added to this list.

We wish to acknowledge the debt owed to Curtis H. Barnette, Esq., Vice President, Law and General Counsel of Bethlehem Steel Corporation, who encouraged some of the work that ultimately led to this book. We would also like to acknowledge the able assistance of Sheilah F. Green and Janet Stuart, who helped us in preparing the manuscript, and Alon Kapen, John Monsees, and Elizabeth Minott, who assisted in the preparation of the bibliography and table of cases.

NOTE

1. M. Tushnet, "Corporations and Free Speech," in D. Kairys, *The Politics of Law* (1982), pp. 253–254 (emphasis added).

CORPORATE AND COMMERCIAL FREE SPEECH

Introduction

The First Amendment provides that "Congress shall make no law . . . abridging the freedom of speech, or of the press." Unquestionably, this amendment was designed by the framers of the Constitution to protect from congressional interference speech concerning political affairs, the form of government, legislation, law enforcement, judicial conduct, and the qualifications of public officials. What the Congress is forbidden by the First Amendment from doing, the executive and judicial branches of the federal government are likewise prohibited from doing. What the federal government may not do, the states are forbidden to interfere with in the field of expression.

Protection of political expression from undue interference by the legislative, executive, and judicial branches of government is the core of the First Amendment. "Speech concerning public affairs," the Supreme Court has said, "is more than self-expression; it is the essence of self-government," *Garrison v. Louisiana*, 379 U.S. 64, 74–75 (1964). Controversies have arisen in the courts and among constitutional scholars, however, over how much further First Amendment protection extends beyond political expression. Few theorists would deny its protection to aesthetic creations, poetry, drama, film, imaginative literature; philosophical, social, economic, and scientific researches; biographical and historical inquiries; and the fruits of the other established branches of learning. The Supreme Court's decisions bring such examples of expression clearly within the scope of the First Amendment.

The extent to which paid advertising, or "commercial speech," enjoys this privileged constitutional status, however, has provoked disagreement among commentators and has resulted in a wavering course of judicial precedent. Whether it derives from the commercial or profit motive of the speaker or from the commercial nature of the content of speech, which proposes a commercial transaction, or from the fact that the speech, in the form of a book, pamphlet, flier, or film, is sold, the commercial element in speech has been regarded by some as justifying a lesser degree of protection for commercial speech than for speech that is not thus "tainted." Indeed, the Supreme Court itself initially held that "purely commercial advertising," in the form of a handbill advertising a public display for which an admission price was charged, was entitled to no protection. In *Valentine v. Chrestensen*, 316 U.S. 52 (1942), the Court held that, although the states and municipalities "may not unduly burden or prescribe" the exercise of the freedom of communicating information and disseminating information in the public streets, the Constitution "imposes no such restraint on government as respects purely commercial advertising." For more than thirty years thereafter, the *Valentine* decision was authority for what was known as the "commercial speech exception"—the principle that purely commercial advertising or commercial speech is completely unprotected by the First Amendment.

In a series of decisions during the 1970s, however, beginning with *Pittsburgh Press Company v. Pittsburgh Commission on Human Relations*, 413 U.S. 376 (1973), and culminating in *Virginia Pharmacy Board v. Virginia Citizens Consumer Council*, 425 U.S. 748 (1976), the Supreme Court reconsidered the commercial speech exception to the First Amendment and utilizing traditional judicial techniques narrowed the *Valentine* holding. The Court distinguished on their facts cases where the exception might have applied and by implication narrowed the scope of the exception. In subsequent decisions, the Court effectively redefined the scope of the exception and, in effect, limited the *Valentine* decision to its facts. Finally, the Court abolished the exception altogether and reformulated it as a rule providing limited constitutional protection to a category of expression which had previously enjoyed no protection at all.

Thus, the commercial speech exception to the First Amendment survives, but in a different form. Commercial speech enjoys some constitutional protection against governmental regulation and proscription but nonetheless is not accorded the full degree of protection which political expression receives.

The commercial speech doctrine, as the Supreme Court has redefined it, remains an anomaly in First Amendment jurisprudence. As the Court has interpreted it, the First Amendment prohibits nearly absolutely governmental interference with protected speech solely on the basis of the content of the speech. Yet, in the area of commercial speech, the commercial content of a message triggers differential treatment by the government. The Supreme Court has even acknowledged this anomaly. As the Court said in *Central Hudson Gas & Electric Corp. v. Public Service Commission*, 447 U.S. 557, 564 n.6: "In most other contexts, the First Amendment prohibits regulation based on the content of the message." The commercial speech doctrine singles out for special differential treatment a category of speech solely on the basis of its content; thus by its very existence in constitutional jurisprudence, the commercial speech doctrine raises the fundamental question whether the First Amendment itself should be interpreted to distinguish between categories of protected expression based solely on content—in this instance between commercial and non-commercial speech. True, certain categories of speech are wholly unprotected by the First Amendment,

such as (1) "fighting words," *Chaplinsky v. New Hampshire*, 315 U.S. 568 (1942); (2) obscenity, *Roth v. United States*, 354 U.S. 476 (1957); (3) libel and slander, *Gertz v. Robert Welch, Inc.*, 418 U.S. 323 (1974); (4) incitement to violence, *Brandenburg v. Ohio*, 395 U.S. 444 (1969); and (5) speech so closely "brigaded" with action that the speech and the act are one, as the false shouting of "Fire!" in a theatre, in Justice Holmes's famous example, *Schenck v. United States*, 249 U.S. 47 (1919) or as in *Giboney v. Empire Storage Co.*, 336 U.S. 490 (1949). The Court has also devised special standards of constitutional protection where speech is mixed with elements of conduct, *United States v. O'Brien*, 391 U.S. 367 (1968). The commercial speech doctrine, however, appears to be the only principle so far to have commanded a Supreme Court majority that singles out, solely by its content, an entire category of protected speech for the purpose of affording some protection, but less than the full degree.[1]
Cf. *Dun & Bradstreet, Inc. v. Greenmoss Builders, Inc.*, _____U.S. _____, 53 U. S. L. W. 4866 (1985) (Powell, J.) (suggesting a broader category of speech that does not address "a matter of public concern").

The doctrine is a major step in constitutional evolution and as might be expected has proven to be problematic in other ways. The Supreme Court has said that the "application of First Amendment protection to speech that does 'no more than propose a commercial transaction' . . . has been recognized generally as a substantial extension of traditional free-speech doctrine which poses special problems not presented by other forms of protected speech," *Friedman v. Rogers*, 440 U.S. 1, 10 n.9. The Court has pointed out that "commercial speech is linked inextricably to commercial activity: while the First Amendment affords such speech 'a limited measure of protection,' it is also true that 'the state does not lose its power to regulate commercial activity deemed harmful to the public whenever speech is a component of that activity,' " *id*. Because of the special character of commercial speech and the relative novelty of First Amendment protection, the Court has adopted a cautious approach toward integrating it into the existing body of First Amendment doctrine. The Court has said that its "decisions dealing with more traditional First Amendment problems do not extend automatically to this as yet uncharted area," *id*. Modes of regulation that are impermissible when applied to non-commercial expression may nonetheless satisfy the somewhat different constitutional standards applicable to commercial speech.

One of the principal purposes of Part I of this book is to delineate as far as possible, in a general way, that "limited measure of protection" to which commercial speech is entitled under the First Amendment and to illustrate those specially developed principles in the recurrent concrete contexts in which these issues have arisen to date. This examination of the commercial speech doctrine begins in chapters 1 through 5 with an analysis of the leading Supreme Court decisions from *Valentine v. Chrestensen* to the most recent rulings. Chapter 5 sums up the current standards and analyzes the controlling principles, including the definition of commercial speech. It addresses the question whether there is some single, definable characteristic of commercial speech which is not found in other kinds of speech which receive the full degree of protection under the First Amendment. Is there some set of characteristics that defines commercial speech? Is the definitional question itself governed by an *ad hoc*, case-by-case balancing of interests depending on the interests and motives of the speaker, of the publisher, of the distributor, of the reader, and depending on the content of the speech or on whether it is sold? Notwithstanding the importance to First Amendment jurisprudence of defining any category of speech that either receives no First Amendment protection or, as in the case of commercial speech, is afforded some lesser degree of protection, the courts have not yet provided clear answers to these questions.

This review is followed in chapter 6 with various applications of the commercial speech doctrine. In contrast with the theoretical discussion, these chapters provide separate treatments of what appear to be the principal areas where questions of the scope of the commercial speech doctrine have so far arisen and have been considered in judicial decisions. The great variety of subjects—antitrust, securities law, advertising, civil rights, liquor and cigarette distribution, labor relations, and others—gives some sense of the breadth of the impact that the changes in this field have already had and may continue to have.

Part II takes up the problems associated with First Amendment protection of corporate political activity. Although it deals with the problems arising under the Federal Election Campaign Act, insofar as the act and its amendments and other laws touch on the question of corporate expenditures to publicize corporate positions on public issues, ballot referendum issues, and candidates, the focus here largely skirts both the separate statutory issues raised by corporate political contributions, campaign contribution limits, separate segregated funds, and the comprehensive regulation of money and in-kind contributions under federal and state legislation (such as the Federal Election Campaign Act and the regulations, decisions, and advisory opinions of the Federal Election Commission). Many comprehensive articles, treatises, and reporter systems adequately cover these technical areas of election campaign financing law. Instead, the book provides a concise introduction to and essential background for some of the main constitutional questions involved in governmental control of the use of corporate treasury funds to make independent ''expenditures''—as contrasted with money ''contributions'' to candidates—to finance the dissemination of information and opinion on political issues, policy questions, and the voting records and political positions and qualifications of candidates for public office and of elected and appointed officials. The constitutional questions raised by government regulation of corporate political contributions are outside the scope of our study.

NOTE

1. In Young v. American Mini-Theatres, 427 U.S. 50 (1976) and in Erznoznik v. City of Jacksonville, 422 U.S. 205 (1975), some of the opinions reflect acceptance of

the notion that courts need not afford full constitutional protection to non-obscene but sexually oriented films, where the government regulation is accomplished through zoning of adult book stores into particular areas of town. Ordinarily, however, even ''offensive'' speech enjoys full constitutional protection, Lewis v. City of New Orleans, 415 U.S. 130 (1974) (utterance of vulgar epithet); Hess v. Indiana, 414 U.S. 105 (1973) (utterance of vulgar epithet); Cohen v. California, 403 U.S. 15 (1971) (wearing of clothing inscribed with vulgar remarks); Brandenburg v. Ohio, 395 U.S. 444 (1969) (utterance of racial slurs); Kingsley International Pictures Corp. v. Regents, 360 U.S. 684 (1959) (alluring portrayal of adultery as proper behavior).

PART I

Commercial Speech

1

The Origin of the "Commercial Speech Exception" to the First Amendment

THE PRE-*VALENTINE* JEHOVAH'S WITNESS CASES: SALE OF RELIGIOUS HANDBILLS AND BOOKS

In *Valentine v. Chrestensen*, 316 U.S. 52 (1942), which is discussed here in detail, the Supreme Court held in a unanimous, three-page opinion that "purely commercial advertising" is not entitled to the protection of the First Amendment. The "commercial speech" exception, as this doctrine has come to be known, survived virtually unexplained for more than thirty years as an important limitation on the protection afforded by the First Amendment. The case involved local governmental interference with the distribution of a two-sided handbill advertising the display of a privately owned submarine at the docks in New York City, for which an admission was charged, and on the other side protesting the policies of the city of New York concerning use of the city's docks.

The Court's holding in *Valentine v. Chrestensen* was not the inexplicable appearance of a new rule and is properly viewed in its context with a number of prior decisions. These antecedents include evangelistic activities, such as handbilling, door-to-door solicitation, and sale and distribution of religious literature, by members of the Jehovah's Witness sect, sometimes known as the Watch Tower Bible and Tract Society, a religious sect which disseminates its teachings and its interpretation of the Bible through the hand distribution of literature by full- and part-time members. Members of this sect cited the example of Saint Paul, teaching "publicly, and from house to house" (Acts 20:20), and interpreted literally the New Testament injunction: "Go ye into all the world, and preach the gospel to every creature" (Mark 16:15). Like *Valentine*, these Jehovah's Witness cases tested the constitutionality of local anti-handbilling ordinances of various kinds, which typically required local licenses and the payment of license fees prior to door-to-door distribution of literature. Some of these decisions addressed the constitutionality of such mandatory licensing procedures. Others examined the constitutionality of the flat prohibition of certain types of handbilling activities. The Supreme Court's attention was drawn in these cases to the allegedly commercial aspects of this form of proselytizing, which sometimes involved attempts to sell brochures, magazines, and books of a religious nature in the course of the Jehovah's Witnesses' door-to-door canvassing in communities throughout the country. Ultimately, the Court was led to adopt a commercial speech exception, which it enunciated for the first time in *Valentine*.

In *Lovell v. Griffin*, 303 U.S. 444 (1938), the Supreme Court reversed the conviction of Alma Lovell, a member of the Jehovah's Witness sect. Acting in the belief that she had been sent "by Jehovah to do this work" and that compliance with the local ordinance requiring prior local approval would have been "an act of disobedience to his commandment," Lovell distributed a pamphlet and a magazine called *The Golden Age*, in the nature of religious tracts, setting forth the gospel of the Kingdom of Jehovah, without first obtaining the written permission from the City Manager of the city of Griffin, Georgia, required by local ordinance. The Griffin ordinance applied to "the practice of distributing, either by hand or otherwise, circulars, handbooks, advertising, or literature of any kind, whether said articles are being delivered free, or whether same are being sold," 303 U.S. at 447. The Griffin ordinance covered "literature" in its broadest sense without specification of content and, as the Court observed, was not limited to "literature that is obscene or offensive to public morals or that advocates unlawful conduct," *id*. at 451. The Griffin ordinance also applied to every manner of distribution "either by hand or otherwise." It prohibited "the distribution of literature of any kind at any time, at any place, and in any manner without a permit from the city manager," *id*. at 451. No license fee was imposed, and the ordinance was comprehensive in its application to distribution of literature, whether money was charged or whether the literature was provided free. Since the permit requirement applied uniformly to both the distribution of commercial handbills and to non-commercial literature, no commercial element was relevant to the Court's ruling. The Supreme Court unanimously invalidated the Griffin ordinance on grounds of its repugnance to the speech and press clause of the First Amendment, without addressing the issue of freedom of religion, which petitioner had also raised in the lower Georgia courts.

In 1939, a year and a half later, the Court decided four cases which reached the Court as companion cases and involved anti-handbilling ordinances of Irvington, New Jersey; Los Angeles, California; Milwaukee, Wisconsin; and Worcester, Massachusetts. In one of these decisions, *Schneider v. State of New Jersey, Town of Irvington*, 308 U.S. 147 (1939), the Court reversed the conviction of Clara Schneider, a Jehovah's Witness who had been convicted in the Recorder's Court of Irvington, New Jersey, for failing to secure, in advance of distribution, a written permit from the chief of police authorizing her to call from house to house in the town to distribute religious literature and to proselytize. Schneider had shown a testimony and identification card of the Society, stating that she would leave some booklets discussing problems affecting the person interviewed. She told the residents she visited that by contributing a small sum, they would make possible the printing of more booklets which could be placed in the hands of others and spread the teaching. She did not apply for or obtain a permit in advance because she conscientiously believed that to do so would have been an act of disobedience to a command of God.

In *Young v. California, City of Los Angeles*, one of the companion cases, the petitioner was convicted of violation of a Los Angeles ordinance that made it unlawful to "distribute any handbill to or among pedestrians along or upon any street, sidewalk or park, or to passengers on any street car, or throw, place, or attach any handbill in, to or upon any automobile or any other vehicle," 308 U.S. at 154. Young was arrested while he was engaged in distributing to pedestrians on a public sidewalk a handbill which bore a notice of a meeting to be held under the auspices of "Friends of Lincoln Brigade," at which speakers would discuss issues relating to the war in Spain.

Snyder v. Milwaukee, 308 U.S. 147 (1939), which was decided at the same time as *Schneider* and *Young*, involved a picket who stood in front of a meat market distributing to passing pedestrians handbills relating to "a labor dispute with the meat market." The handbill set forth "the position of organized labor" with respect to the manner in which the market conducted its business and labor relations and "asked citizens to refrain from patronizing it"—conduct which had been held to constitute a violation of a Milwaukee ordinance that made it unlawful "to circulate or distribute any circular, handbills, cards, posters, dodgers, or other printed or advertising matter in or upon any sidewalk, street, alley, wharf, boat landing, dock or other public place, park or ground within the City of Milwaukee." Some of the handbills Snyder was distributing had been discarded on the sidewalk by pedestrians to whom Snyder had handed them. The ordinance in the *Snyder* case imposed no license requirement. It simply prohibited an entire class of activities.

A fourth case, *Nichols v. Massachusetts, City of Worcester*, 308 U.S. 147 (1939) involved the conviction of Nichols and others under an ordinance making it unlawful to "distribute in, or place upon any street or way, any placard, handbill, flyer, poster, advertisement or paper of any description." Nichols was arrested for distributing in a street of Worcester, Massachusetts, leaflets announcing a protest meeting in connection with "the administration of State unemployment insurance," 308 U.S. at 156.

Each of these decisions during 1939 involved the distribution of literature of a political or religious nature or of literature relating to the economic interests of members of labor organizations of a type often equated with quasi-political literature. None, except possibly the *Schneider* case, involved specifically the solicitation of funds or proposals for a commercial transaction. The Supreme Court reversed the judgments in all four cases over the lone dissent of Justice McReynolds. The four states unsuccessfully attempted to defend the sweeping prohibition of speech and expressive conduct in these ordinances as indirect measures to prevent street littering, although none of the ordinances was drafted so narrowly as to apply only to persons who actually throw papers on the streets. The four decisions were crucial precursors of the commercial speech exception because in each case the Court touched on commercial aspects of the "transaction."

In its discussion of the Irvington ordinance, the Court drew a distinction between commercial and non-commercial speech. The Court pointed out that the Irvington ordinance was "not limited to those who canvass for private profit," suggesting thereby the validity of a distinction between those with a profit motive and those without a profit motive:

> If [the ordinance] covers the petitioner's activities it equally applies to one who wishes to present his views on political, social or economic questions. *The ordinance is not limited to those who canvass for private profit*; nor is it merely the common type of ordinance requiring some form of registration or license of hawkers, or peddlers. 308 U.S. at 163 (emphasis added)

The Court also singled out for special comment the element of "commercial soliciting and canvassing" in the *Schneider* case:

> *We are not to be taken as holding that commercial soliciting and canvassing may not be subjected to such regulation as the ordinance requires.* Nor do we hold that the town may not fix reasonable hours when canvassing may be done by persons having such objects as the petitioner. Doubtless, there are other features of such activities which may be regulated in the public interest without prior licensing or other invasion of constitutional liberty. We do hold, however, that the ordinance in question, as applied to the petitioner's conduct, is void, and she cannot be punished for acting without a permit. 308 U.S. at 165 (emphasis added)

The germ of the *Valentine* holding was present in the Court's dictum in *Schneider* that commercial soliciting and canvassing is distinguishable from the kinds of political and religious soliciting and canvassing involved in these cases and in the implication that, had the case involved only commercial soliciting and canvassing, the constitutionality of the Irvington ordinance might have been upheld as applied to such literature.

Six months after deciding *Schneider v. Irvington, supra*, and its three companion cases, the Supreme Court decided *Cantwell v. Connecticut*, 310 U.S. 296 (1940). *Cantwell* involved the conviction of Newton Cantwell and his two sons, Jesse and Russell, who were members of the Jehovah's Witness sect, for violations of Connecticut General Statutes §6294, and for the common law offense of inciting a breach of the peace. Section 6294 made it unlawful for any person to "solicit money, services, subscriptions or any valuable thing for any alleged religions, charitable or philanthropic cause, from other than a member of the organization for whose benefit such person is soliciting or within the county in which such person or organization is located unless such cause shall have been approved by the secretary of the public welfare council." The law set forth certain specific criteria of *bona fide* status, "efficiency" and "integrity" which local licensing authorities were empowered by the Act to evaluate prior to the issuance of the certificates that were required as a precondition of lawful solicitation.

At the time of their arrest, the Cantwells were engaged in going singly from house to house on Cassius Street in New Haven, Connecticut, equipped with bags containing books and pamphlets on religious subjects, portable phonographs, and sets of records, each of which when played introduced and described one of the books. One of the records, which described a book entitled *Enemies*, included an attack on the Catholic religion. At the time of their arrest, the defendants were calling at private homes in a neighborhood in which about 90 percent of the residents were Roman Catholics and were requesting residents' permission to play the records. If permission was granted, they played the record and then asked the resident to purchase the book described. The commercial element arose from this solicitation to purchase the book. If the resident declined to purchase the book, the canvasser solicited a contribution toward the publication of the pamphlets. If the resident made a contribution, the canvasser provided the resident with a pamphlet if the resident promised that it would be read. The defendants had not applied for or obtained the certificate approval from New Haven's public welfare council that the law required.

The Supreme Court invalidated the Connecticut statute on the ground that it required and permitted the secretary of the public welfare council, as a condition to the issuance of a permit, to determine what causes are "religious" causes, and thus infringed the First Amendment free exercise of religion clause as a prior restraint.

The Court also reversed the defendants' convictions for the common law offense of inducing others to breach the peace. The Court held that the defendants' conduct did not involve assault or threatening of bodily harm, truculent bearing, intentional discourtesy, or personal abuse, and in the absence of a statutory prohibition against specific conduct giving rise to a "clear and present menace to public peace and order," the convictions for the common law offense could not stand. The Court in this case did not mention the commercial character of some of the solicitations.

VALENTINE v. CHRESTENSEN: COMMERCIAL HANDBILLS

The commercial features present in these cases were suddenly crystalized in *Valentine v. Chrestensen*, 316 U.S. 52 (1942). The background of this landmark decision can be concisely summarized. F.J. Chrestensen, a Floridian, purchased a U.S. Navy submarine S-49 and made a business of exhibiting the submarine in various cities for an admission charge. In 1940, Chrestensen applied to the city of New York for permission to dock at city-owned docks off Battery Park. When the city denied him permission to dock at the city's docks, he secured permission to dock at a state-owned pier in the East River. Chrestensen prepared an advertising handbill containing a diagram of the submarine, depicting its location, and advertising and inviting the public at large to take 25¢ guided tours through the torpedo compartment, the sleeping quarters, the kitchen, and other compartments of the craft. The New York police later informed him that they considered his distribution of this commercial handbill to be illegal under Section 318 of the New York City Sanitary Code. New York's handbill ordinance specifically permitted distribution of handbills containing information of a public protest. The section stated that it was "not intended to prevent the lawful distribution of anything other than commercial and business advertising matter."

Acting on this advice, Chrestensen revised the handbill, preserving much of the original material. Chrestensen eliminated the references to the sale of tickets and the ticket price and the invitation to "see" the submarine. In their place, Chrestensen caused to be printed on the bill the statement "the only submarine used for exhibition in the world." On the reverse side of the revised handbill, however, Chrestensen caused to be printed a spirited "protest" against New York City's refusal to permit the docking of the submarine at the city-owned piers—a protest that concluded with the observation that the submarine could be reached in about two minutes at the less convenient state-owned pier. Chrestensen's revised handbill thus mixed commercial elements with non-commercial elements. Nonetheless, New York City police officials informed Chrestensen that distribution of the revised handbill would also be illegal and restrained his effort to distribute it.

Chrestensen brought suit in federal court under the federal civil rights statute, 42 U.S.C. § 1983. The district court declared the New York City ordinance unconstitutional as applied, granted a preliminary injunction, and later granted permanent injunctive relief, preventing New York City's enforcement of the regulation against Chrestensen.

A divided panel of the Court of Appeals for the Second Circuit (Swan and Clark, C.J., with Frank, J., dissenting) affirmed the judgment, *Chrestensen v. Valentine*, 122 F.2d 511 (2d Cir. 1941). Although the majority of the Court of Appeals said that "absolute prohibition of commercial handbills seems . . . of doubtful validity," the court chose not to reach that broader question. Instead, it ruled only that the New York ordinance's prohibition of handbills "cannot extend to a combined protest and advertisement not shown to be a mere subterfuge," 122 F.2d at 516. Judge Clark's thoughtful majority opinion remains instructive. It addressed many constitutional issues involving commercial speech that are still unresolved. Tracing the Supreme Court's decisions involving the validity of municipal prohibitions against distribution of handbills in streets and public places, including *Lovell v. Griffin*, 303 U.S. 444 (1938); *Schneider v. State*, 308 U.S. 147 (1939); *Hague v. CIO*, 307 U.S. 496 (1939), Judge Clark concluded that "a handbill containing advertising matter, even a schedule of admission charges, is not in itself rendered outside the pale of protection against such an absolute and complete prohibition," 122 F.2d at 514. The court rested this conclusion primarily upon *Young v. California*, which was a companion case the Supreme Court decided when it decided *Schneider v. State, supra*. In

Young, the Supreme Court had invalidated a state anti-handbill regulation which had been used to suppress the distribution of a handbill giving notice of a meeting sponsored by a political association. Judge Clark found it significant that the Friends of Lincoln Brigade handbill in the *Young* case had contained the notation, "Admission $.25 and $.50." The Supreme Court had nonetheless held that this commercial element in the handbill did not defeat the protection afforded by the First Amendment. According to the court, Chrestensen's "combined protest and advertisement"—even one that contained a schedule of admission charges— enjoyed the full protection of the First Amendment. Its distribution could no more be absolutely proscribed than could the distribution of purely political or religious tracts that were involved in the Supreme Court's handbill cases.

Judge Clark next disposed of the police commissioner's contention that the ordinance did not apply unless the handbill in question was "primarily" com- mercial and the contention that a commercial advertisement is distinguishable from a non-commercial advertisement—what the court characterized in terms of its content and underlying speaker motivation as matter "exclusively or primarily calculated to attract the attention and patronage of the public to a non-commercial enterprise, *i.e.*, one entered into primarily for considerations other than pecuniary gain," 122 F.2d at 515. The court concluded that a legal standard that made constitutional protection depend on nothing more than a classification of a hand- bill as primarily commercial simply could not suffice. A constitutional standard that required a determination whether a handbill was primarily commercial would inescapably involve the weighing of the author's motive and intent. It would confer upon local police officials what, in effect, would amount to a standardless discretion to weigh the author's motives. The court said, " 'Concrete operation' here will pretty surely result in prohibiting freedom of expression in ways and to an extent quite unconnected with problems of city sanitation," 122 F.2d at 516. The court went on to consider and reject the obvious, mechanical means by which "primary motive" might be plausibly estimated. The majority con- cluded that the detection of "sham" non-commercial motive cannot be accom- plished by reference to "[s]heer numbers of words" devoted respectively to the protest and to the commercially motivated aspects. Nor can it be determined solely by reference to the "[s]pacing and display" of the respective elements of the communication. A motive-based test would simply defy precise definition, 122 F.2d at 516.

There were two commercial elements in Chrestensen's handbill—an economic motive for the protest against the city's refusal of docking privileges and the profit motive reflected in the implied invitation to buy an admission and to tour the submarine. The first, a protest of governmental action that directly frustrated Chrestensen's business interests and impaired his ability to make a profit, focused public attention on specific governmental actions and policies regarding the use of New York City docks. The second, a written statement that, at most, solicited the public's patronage of his business, was not designed to invite consideration of the wisdom of governmental policy or action. That Chrestensen's motive for

protesting New York's policy against docking of private ships offering entertainment may have been his own concrete business interests did not defeat the
constitutional protection to be afforded to his protest, in Judge Clark's view.
That motivation alone, if sincere, would have sufficed to guarantee the protection
of the First Amendment, according to the majority. Even if the handbill were
interpreted as expression intended at least in part to invite public patronage at
the submarine display, the sincerity of Chrestensen's beliefs in protesting the
city's docking policies could not serve as the touchstone for determining whether
the "combined protest and advertisement" were constitutionally protected, 122
F.2d at 515.

In summary, Judge Clark said: "[P]erhaps we should say that, while absolute
prohibition of commercial handbills seems to us of doubtful validity, yet we
need decide no more here than that at least it cannot extend to a combined protest
and advertisement not shown to be a mere subterfuge," 122 F.2d at 516. The
court thus found it unnecessary to define the circumstances in which there might
be sufficient evidence of "mere subterfuge," and it held that in this context an
inquiry into the sincerity of views on public policies was impermissible. The
court also expressed its puzzlement about how such an inquiry into Chrestensen's
sincerity might be conducted: "[I]f intent and purpose must be measured, how
can we say that plaintiff's motives are only or primarily financial? Is he just
engaged in an advertising plot, or does he really believe in his wrongs?" 122
F.2d at 516.

Judge Clark's discussion did not permit the "sham motivation" issue to obscure the fundamental questions. Those issues include these questions: (1) Is
speech that is motivated by commercial interests, speaking subjectively, but in
objective content critical of governmental action or governmental policies, to be
deprived of any constitutional protection simply because of its subjective commercial motivation? (2) Is speech that does no more than propose, solicit, or
invite a commercial transaction deprived of constitutional protection because the
speech is commercial in content and motivated by commercial interests? (3)
Where speech that is purely commercial in its content and motivated only by
commercial interests is intermixed with non-commercial speech, even if the
speaker's only reason for the communication is the speaker's commercial interests, does the presence of these commercial elements deprive the communication
of the full constitutional protection that is otherwise afforded to the discussion
of governmental policy or actions?

Judge Clark's discussion now seems an auspicious beginning to an intelligent
constitutional standard. The court was justifiably wary, that is, of the proposed
distinction between commercial and non-commercial speech. Judge Clark's majority opinion also began the complicated task of disentangling the many different
senses in which expression may be said to be commercial, the ways in which
its commercial nature is totally irrelevant to its protected status, and the senses
in which its commercial nature may possibly be of some constitutional relevance.
Using the basic conceptual scheme underlying Judge Clark's discussion, speech

may be (1) commercial in content and commercial in its motivation, or (2) commercial because of the nature of the speaker's motivation, but political or non-commercial in its content, *e.g.*, critical of governmental action, but occasioned by government action that impinges on the private, economic interests of the speaker, or (3) non-commercial in its motivation and non-commercial in its content, *e.g.*, classical political comment concerning abstract ideological issues, or (4) non-commercial in its motivation but commercial in its content, *e.g.*, the handbill in *Young v. California*, giving notice of a Friends of Lincoln Brigade meeting concerning the war in Spain, but containing a schedule of admission charges for the meeting. The court decided only that if the speech is commercial in motivation, its objective, non-commercial content suffices by itself to warrant full constitutional protection.

Judge Clark's opinion is praiseworthy for its clarity in the initial confrontation with the complex issues of commercial speech and the First Amendment. The same cannot be said of the Supreme Court's cursory, three-page opinion reversing the Second Circuit, *Valentine v. Chrestensen*, 316 U.S. 52 (1942). Indeed, Justice Douglas, a member of the Court that decided *Valentine*, was later to say: "The ruling was casual, almost offhand. And it has not survived reflection," *Cammarano v. United States*, 358 U.S. 498 (1959) (concurring opinion).

After reciting the facts, Justice Roberts simply announced the rule:

This Court has unequivocally held that the streets are proper places for the exercise of the freedom of communicating information and disseminating opinion and that, though the states and municipalities may appropriately regulate the privilege in the public interest, they may not unduly burden or prescribe its employment in these public thoroughfares. *We are equally clear that the Constitution imposes no such restraint on government as respects purely commercial advertising.* 316 U.S. at 54 (emphasis added)

The Court abruptly dismissed the idea that Chrestensen was "engaged in the dissemination of matter proper for public information," that is, a *bona fide* public protest of New York's docking policies, stating that "[i]t is enough for the present purpose that the stipulated facts justify the conclusion that the affixing of the protest against official conduct of the advertising circular was with the intent and for the purpose, of evading the prohibition of the ordinance," 316 U.S. at 55.

The Court's rough-and-ready resolution of the factual question of the "sincerity" of Chrestensen's protest against New York's docking policies raises important and persistent questions concerning the judicial standard for assessing the constitutional status of mixed commercial and non-commercial expression to which we will return in chapter 5. The Court was content, however, to consider the constitutional question of the status of Chrestensen's handbill on the basis that the case involved what the Court described as "purely commercial advertising," and, on that premise, the Court held that distribution of the handbill was not protected by the First Amendment. The Court's holding amounted to little more than *ipse dixit*. The Court cited neither judicial precedent nor historical evidence in support of its conclusion that "purely commercial advertising" is outside the First Amendment's guarantee. It provided no reasoned basis for supporting its holding. The ruling is stark and unexplained. The Court left completely undefined the new category of unprotected expression it referred to as "purely commercial advertising" and provided no guidelines or criteria by which the lower courts could identify what constituted "purely commercial advertising." The Court ignored the political protest on the reverse side of the handbill on the basis of its conclusion that the record was sufficient to support the factual inference that it was placed there for the purpose of evading the ordinance. The Court was also content to make this finding of "constitutional fact" by itself, rather than simply reviewing for sufficient factual basis a finding made by the lower courts, *compare Bose Corp. v. Consumers Union of United States*, 104 S. Ct. 1949, 1965 (1984); *Bender v. Williamsport Area School District*, 741 F.2d 538 at 542n.3 (3d Cir. 1984), *cert. granted*, 105 S. Ct. 1167 (1985); *Block v. Potter*, 631 F.2d 233, 241 (3d Cir. 1980)(appellate court free to draw own inferences from record on "constitutional facts"). In making the speaker's intent to evade the touchstone of the First Amendment status of Chrestensen's handbill, the Court adopted a test that the lower courts subsequently expanded. One court later formulated the speaker's predominant intent rule so expansively that it held that information of public interest and concern was not protected if "it was wholly incidental and subordinate to" the commercial promotion, *New York State Broadcasters Assn. v. United States*, 414 F.2d 990, 998 (2d Cir. 1969)(upholding in part and striking down in part, federal statute, 18 U.S.C. § 1304 prohibiting broadcasts of information concerning lotteries).

THE POST-*VALENTINE* JEHOVAH'S WITNESS CASES: *JONES v. OPELIKA*, 316 U.S. 584 (1942), et al.

In a series of Jehovah's Witness cases decided within two months of the *Valentine* decision and involving evangelistic activities, the Supreme Court was forced to begin to define the scope of its newly formulated commercial speech doctrine of *Valentine*. The initial series of decisions involving door-to-door handbilling activities by the Jehovah's Witnesses saw the Supreme Court initially reject the arguments that these activities were protected by the First Amendment. After rehearing the following term, several justices changed their votes and reversed the disposition in those cases to recognize that the activities of the Jehovah's Witnesses were constitutionally protected. Local officials who attempted to halt the evangelistic activities of the Witnesses made frequent reference to the so-called commercial element in their solicitations of funds and in their sales of brochures and booklets through which the Witnesses financed their cause and disseminated their religious opinions.

Although the Court vacated the judgment on rehearing the following term in connection with its decision in *Murdock v. Pennsylvania*, 319 U.S. 105, 117

(1943), the Court's initial decision in *Jones v. City of Opelika*, 316 U.S. 584 (1942), which was handed down only two months after *Valentine v. Chrestensen*, involved the constitutionality of several city ordinances of Opelika, Alabama, which imposed license taxes on the sale of printed matter, including books. Rosco Jones, a member of the Jehovah's Witness sect and an ordained minister, was prosecuted under these ordinances for selling books without a license, for operating as a book agent without a license, and for operating as a transient agent, dealer, or distributor of books without a license. Opelika's license fee for book agents, except for those distributing Bibles, was $10.00 per annum and for transient agents, dealers, or distributors of books, $5.00 per annum. The Opelika City Commission retained the power to revoke such licenses without notice. Jones was convicted of violations of these provisions of the Opelika ordinances on evidence that without a license he had been displaying pamphlets in his upraised hand and walking on a city street selling them two for 5¢. The trial court had excluded evidence offered on Jones's behalf that his activities were in furtherance of his beliefs and the teachings of Jehovah's Witnesses. Several companion cases to *Jones* presented similar issues. The *Bowden* and *Sanders* cases, 316 U.S. 584 (1942), *vacated* 319 U.S. 103 (1943), involved the convictions of members of the Jehovah's Witness sect for violation of a Fort Smith, Arkansas, ordinance that required a license to peddle any "articles." The Fort Smith license fee ranged from $2.50 per day to $25.00 per month. Bowden and Sanders were arrested while they were going from house to house without a license, in the exercise of their religious beliefs, playing phonographic transcriptions of Bible lectures, and, in return for a contribution of 25¢, distributing books that set forth their views. Some recipients of the books who were unable to contribute were given free copies.

The *Jobin* case, 316 U.S. 584 (1942), *vacated* 319 U.S. 103 (1943), involved the constitutionality of a Casa Grande, Arizona, ordinance that made it unlawful for any person to carry on any occupation or business specified without a license. The Casa Grande fee was $25.00 per quarter. In particular, the ordinance required that licenses be purchased by any "transient merchant," defined as "any person who, not for or in connection with a business at a fixed place within the City of Casa Grande, solicits orders from house to house for the future delivery of goods, or who shall deliver goods previously solicited by a solicitor, at retail, or an order for future delivery." Jobin, a member of the Jehovah's Witness sect, was tried and convicted of violation of the ordinance in going from door to door with his wife offering for sale books and pamphlets of religious nature and offering to play a portable phonograph on the porch.

Inevitably, local authorities attempting to suppress the activities of the Witnesses tried to capitalize on the commercial speech exception recently announced in *Valentine*. The commercial element in these cases, however, was presented in a number of distinct ways. As part of their broader evangelistic efforts, the defendants in these cases solicited residents to purchase books and pamphlets. These "in-person solicitations" involved a mixture of speech and conduct because the Witnesses presented themselves on the doorsteps of private homes. The speech element was commercial only in the sense that its content often included the proposal of a commercial transaction, although the commercial transaction may have taken on religious significance to the buyer and may have been intended by the seller to achieve something more significant in religious terms—something more than a simple exchange of money for goods. A distinguishing aspect of the commercial element in these cases was the fact that, although the Witnesses' sales solicitation proposed a commercial transaction, the articles to be sold—books—were also materials that are protected by the First Amendment.

In addition, the facts of these cases suggest that the profit motive was not the only or even the primary purpose for collecting the price of the books from purchasers. Thus, in the *Bowden* and *Sanders* cases, the Court went out of its way to observe that the petitioners "contended that their enterprise was operated at a loss," 316 U.S. at 592. They distributed the pamphlets, and sometimes the books, gratis when the resident was unwilling or unable to pay for them, *id*. at 607. The literature that was sold was published for the express purpose of such distribution by a non-profit charitable corporation that the Jehovah's Witnesses had organized. The Jehovah's Witness sect used the funds collected for the support of their religious movement; no one realized a profit from the publication and distribution of the literature, *id*. at 607. The entire Court, however, did not share this view. Justice Jackson, in his dissenting opinion in the *Douglas*, *Murdock*, and *Martin* cases, 319 U.S. 157 (1943), wrote:

The assumption that [the Watch Tower Bible and Tract Society] is a "non-profit charitable" corporation may be true, but it is without support beyond mere assertion. In none of these cases has the assertion been supported by such evidence as a balance sheet or an income statement. What its manufacturing costs and revenues are, what salaries or expenses it pays, what contracts it has for supplies or services we simply do not know. The effort of counsel for Jeannette to obtain information, books and records of the local "companies" of Witnesses engaged in the Jeannette campaign in the trial was met by contradictory statements as to the methods and meaning of such meager accounts as were produced. . . . The full-time Witnesses acquire their literature from the Watch Tower Bible and Tract Society at a figure which enables them to distribute it at the prices printed thereon with a substantial differential. Some of the books they acquire for 5¢ and dispose of for a contribution of 25¢, on others the margin is less. Part-time ministers have a differential between the 20¢ which they remit to the Watch Tower Society and the 25¢ which is the contribution they ask for the books. Apart from the fact that this differential exists and that it enables the distributors to meet in whole or in part their living expenses, it has proven impossible in these cases to learn the exact results of the campaigns from a financial point of view. 319 U.S. at 169–170

Furthermore, although the trial court in the *Jones* case "excluded as irrelevant, testimony designed to show that the petitioner was an ordained minister, and that his activities were in furtherance of his beliefs and the teachings of Jehovah's

Witnesses," 316 U.S. at 587–588, the Supreme Court in *Bowden* and *Sanders* stated that petitioners had been convicted of engaging in the proscribed conduct "in the exercise of their beliefs concerning their duty to preach the gospel," 316 U.S. at 589, and the Chief Justice referred to a "stipulation or undisputed testimony" that the defendants were "engaged in spreading their religious doctrines in conformity to the teachings of St. Matthew, Matt. 10:11–14 and 24:14, by going from city to city, from village to village, and house to house, to proclaim them," *id.* at 606–607. The cases thus appear to provide an example of an effort to make speech pay, in whole or in part, for its own dissemination, in the exercise of a religious belief that the dissemination of such speech is, in itself, a good.

In these respects, the commercial element in the early Jehovah's Witness cases is to be sharply distinguished from the commercial element in the two-sided handbills distributed in *Valentine*. First, the prohibited speech was not itself being sold in *Valentine*; the handbills were given away. Second, the motive for distributing the one-sided handbills in *Valentine* was the profit motive. At least one of the motives for distributing the revised, two-sided handbill in *Valentine* was the profit motive. The content of one side proposed a commercial transaction. The content of the other contained a political message. Moreover, the purpose of the dissemination of handbills and the display of the submarine was not part of the exercise of any religious belief, for example, that the viewing of the submarine constituted a good in itself in a religious sense.

It is surprising that the Supreme Court initially upheld the convictions in the *Jones*, *Bowden*, *Sanders*, and *Jobin* cases. In its first opinion, which was later vacated, Justice Reed wrote for the Court that these restrictions were simply non-discriminatory "time, place and manner regulations" and that "the proponents of ideas cannot determine entirely for themselves the time and place and manner for the diffusion of knowledge or for their evangelism, any more than the civil authorities may hamper or suppress the public dissemination of facts and principles by the people," 316 U.S. at 594. The Court drew a distinction between "non-discriminatory regulation of operations which are incidental to the exercise of religion or the freedom of speech or the press and those which are imposed upon the religious rite itself or the unmixed dissemination of information," 316 U.S. at 596. The Court's opinion centered directly on the financial aspects of this type of dissemination of religious opinion and concluded that the fact that money is earned was sufficient to bring the case within the concept of *Valentine v. Chrestensen*:

When, as in these cases, the practitioners of these noble callings [teachers and preachers] choose to utilize the vending of their religious books and tracts as a source of funds, the financial aspects of their transactions need not be wholly disregarded. To subject any religious or didactic group to a reasonable fee for their money-making activities does not require a finding that the licensed acts are purely commercial. It is enough that money is earned by the sale of articles." *Id.*

In passing, the Court cited its decision in *Valentine*, pointing out that "commercial advertising cannot escape control by the simple expedient of printing matter of public interest on the same sheet or handbill," *Id.*, at 597. Although the Court commented on the fact that "money is earned by the sale of articles," the Court's central conclusion was also based on the use of "ordinary commercial methods." The Court failed to define with precision the commercial element. The Court did not intimate whether this expressive activity would have enjoyed full protection if the transactions had resulted in a commercial net loss. The Court also did not attempt to define the category of ordinary commercial methods which warranted this kind of disfavored treatment:

When proponents of religious or social theories use the ordinary commercial methods of sales of articles to raise propaganda funds, it is a natural and proper exercise of the power of the state to charge reasonable fees for the privilege of canvassing. . . . It is because we view these sales as partaking more of commercial than religious or educational transactions that we find the ordinances, as here presented, valid. 316 U.S. at 597

The Court recognized that the proceeds from the sale of the religious literature were not to be put to any commercial use and were not for the personal financial gain of any company or individual. On the contrary, as the Court acknowledged in its reference to "sales of articles to raise propaganda funds," the proceeds were to be devoted to financing of further First Amendment expressive activity. The initial majority opinion failed to recognize any significance in the fact that in these cases speech was merely being required to "pay its own way," as books, magazines, journals, and newspapers usually do.

The Court equated an exemption from the license fee for distribution of books with a governmental "subsidy" for their distribution, 316 U.S. at 599. The Court also rejected the argument in the *Jones* case that the ordinance failed to specify any criteria governing administrative discretion in granting or revoking such licenses. The conviction rested solely on sales without a license and, according to the Court, presented no issue pertaining to the constitutionality of the criteria (or the absence of criteria) that the local police might have applied had the petitioners made an application for licenses, or had the local officials revoked licenses previously granted.

In its initial opinion in these cases, the Court was sharply divided. Chief Justice Stone, as well as Justices Black, Douglas, and Murphy, dissented. Chief Justice Stone's opinion adverted to the holding in *Lovell v. Griffin* in which the Court had invalidated an ordinance requiring a license for the distribution of pamphlets because of the absence of precise criteria. It went further, however, to deal not only with the propriety of the licensing procedure but also with the restriction of the ordinance itself and with the significance of the commercial element in the conduct. The majority of the Court held, in effect, that the presence of the commercial element justified the intervention of the state, regardless of other motivations for the distribution and regardless of the religious subject matter of the books and pamphlets that Jones had sold. The majority treated the license requirement of the ordinances as a valid "time, place and manner" regulation, and in doing so apparently assumed that the speech involved in the door-to-door solicitation as well as the content of the pamphlets and books was constitutionally protected. In the view of the dissenters, the assessment of license fees completely undermined the claim that the ordinances were no more than "regulation." The license fee requirement invited comparison between these ordinances and the notorious taxes on knowledge, stamp taxes on newspapers and pamphlets, and similar devices that had been used in England and in the Colonies to suppress the dissemination of unpopular social, political, and religious ideas.

The majority did not rest its holding expressly on the doctrine that constitutionally protected activity which is a constituent element of an otherwise unlawful course of conduct does not defeat a law designed to make the course of conduct illegal. Chief Justice Stone's dissenting opinion, however, acknowledged this principle when he observed: "The immunity which press and religion enjoy may sometimes be lost when they are united with other activities not immune." The dissenting opinion cited as authority for this proposition was *Valentine v. Chrestensen, id.* at 608. The scope of the principle governing "speech brigaded with conduct" in the commercial speech area is considered in greater detail, *infra* at chapter 5. It suffices to note that the Supreme Court has held in many cases and in many different legal contexts that "[t]he most innocent and constitutionally protected of acts or omissions may be made a step in a criminal plot, and if it is a step in a plot, neither its innocence nor the Constitution is sufficient to prevent the punishment of the plot by law," *Aikens v. Wisconsin*, 195 U.S. 194, 206 (1904); *W.W. Montague & Co. v. Lowry*, 193 U.S. 38, 46 (1904); *Swift Co. v. U.S.*, 196 U.S. 375 (1905); *United States v. Reading Co.*, 226 U.S. 324, 357 (1912); *United States v. Patten*, 226 U.S. 525 (1913); *Binderup v. Pathe Exchange*, 263 U.S. 291 (1923). Chief Justice Stone made the important additional point, however, that in *Jones v. Opelika* "the only activities involved are the dissemination of ideas, educational and religious, and the collection of funds for the propagation of those ideas, which we have said is likewise the subject of constitutional protection," *id.* Thus, each constituent element of the course of conduct was constitutionally protected. In Chief Justice Stone's view, therefore, the principle that deprives otherwise protected activity of its immune status when such activity is united with other activities that are not immune was simply inapplicable. The majority did not attempt to answer Chief Justice Stone's observation.

Comparison of the majority opinion and Chief Justice Stone's dissenting opinion also illustrates a difference in sophistication of analytical approach. The initial majority opinion depended on the technique of breaking down into constituent elements a single course of conduct that included some commercial element. Having identified the commercial element, the majority overlooked the overall character and purpose of what the Jehovah's Witnesses were engaged in. By contrast, Chief Justice Stone and those who joined in his dissenting opinion kept the character of the overall course of conduct clearly in mind. The error of Justice Reed's analysis is the same error the Court has been quick to correct in other contexts, *see Continental Ore Co. v. Union Carbide & Carbon Corp.*, 370 U.S. 690, 699 (1962)("the character and effect of a conspiracy are not to be judged by dismembering it, but only by looking at it as a whole"); *United States v. Scophony Corp. of America*, 333 U.S. 795, 817 (1948) (emphasis on "the actual unity and continuity of the whole course of conduct" and disapproving of "atomizing it into minute parts or events").

Justice Murphy's separate dissenting opinion dealt briefly with the commercial aspect of the solicitation. He wrote: "It matters not that petitioners asked contributions for their literature. Freedom of speech and freedom of the press cannot and must not mean freedom only for those who can distribute their broadsides without charge. There may be others with messages more vital but purses less full, who must seek some reimbursement for their outlay or else forego passing on their ideas," *id.* at 619. He believed that "[p]etitioners were not engaged in a traffic for profit," *id.* Here, he also gave special emphasis to the question of the motives of the speakers: "The exercise, *without commercial motives*, of freedom of speech, freedom of the press, or freedom of worship are not proper sources of taxation for general revenue purposes," *id.* at 620 (emphasis added). Justices Black and Douglas took the opportunity in a brief dissenting opinion to state that although they had joined in the Court's opinion in *Minersville School District v. Gobitis*, 310 U.S. 586 (1940), in which the Court had held that children of Jehovah's Witnesses could constitutionally be compelled, contrary to their religious beliefs, to salute the flag of the United States in public schools, they believed the case had been "wrongly decided." *Minersville* was shortly thereafter overruled in *West Virginia v. Barnette*, 319 U.S. 624 (1943), with Justices Black and Douglas voting in accordance with their revised views.

Approximately a year after its decision in *Valentine*, the Court decided *Jamison v. Texas*, 318 U.S. 413 (1943). Jamison, a Jehovah's Witness, was convicted of violating a Dallas ordinance that prohibited distribution of handbills on the streets. Like the handbill in *Valentine*, the handbill Jamison was distributing had printing on both sides. One side contained an invitation to attend a religious gathering in Dallas. On the other side was a description of two books of a religious nature which were offered for sale "postage prepaid for your contribution of $.25." "While the books were not actually sold on the street, Jamison would have delivered them to the home of anyone who made the twenty-five cents contribution," *id.* at 414–415. Because of what might be characterized as a commercial solicitation on one side of the handbill, therefore, the Court was presented almost immediately after its decision in *Valentine* with the problem of defining the proper scope of the commercial speech doctrine. In an opinion by Justice Black, the Court unanimously reversed Jamison's conviction. The Court noted that "[t]he books would have cost [Jamison] more than twenty-five cents," *id.* at 415. The city of Dallas contended, nonetheless, that the prohibition was permissible "because the handbills, although they were distributed for the unquestioned purpose of furthering religious activity, contained an invitation to contribute to the support of that activity by purchasing books related to the work of the group," *id.* at 416. The Court held, however, that "[t]he mere presence of an advertisement of a religious work on a handbill of the sect distributed here may not subject the distribution of the handbill to prohibition," *id.* at 416. The Court commented that the handbills in the *Schneider* case, which bore a notice of a public gathering containing "a statement of an admission fee," nonetheless had been held to warrant the protection of the First Amendment. No admission fee was charged for the meeting which was advertised on the reverse side of Jamison's leaflet.

The Court distinguished *Valentine v. Chrestensen*, in unconvincing fashion, on the basis of the assumed motive for raising funds, noting that the Jehovah's Witnesses were attempting to raise funds "for religious purposes":

The state can prohibit the use of the street for the distribution of purely commercial leaflets even though such leaflets may have "a civil appeal or a moral platitude" appended. *Valentine v. Chrestensen*, 316 U.S. 52, 55. . . . They may not prohibit the distribution of handbills in the pursuit of a clearly religious activity merely because the handbills invite the purchase of books *for the improved understanding of the religion* or because the handbills seek in a lawful fashion to promote the raising of funds *for religious purposes.*" *Id.* at 417 (emphasis added)

In these cases, the Supreme Court drew a distinction between commercial content of the handbills and commercial motivation. The Court was inclined to give significance to the presence or absence of a commercial motive underlying the speech but was not prepared to give controlling weight to commercial content or to the presence of some isolated commercial aspect. Although the handbills in the *Schneider*, *Valentine*, and *Jamison* cases were all commercial in content in the sense that they proposed commercial transactions, *e.g.*, attendance at a meeting for which an entrance fee was charged or purchase of a book or pamphlet at a stated price, in the Court's view the handbills and solicitations were not commercially motivated. In these Jehovah's Witness cases the Court ultimately recognized that the purpose of the fund-raising was to finance the propagation of certain religious beliefs of the sect. It rested its holding on that conclusion. In initially upholding the license fee, in *Jones v. Opelika*, the Court had, by contrast, rested its holding on the conclusion that the proponents of the "religious or social theories" in that case had used "the ordinary commercial methods of sales of articles." Thus, in struggling to formulate suitable criteria to define more precisely the disfavored category of commercial speech, identified in *Valentine*, the Court initially relied on a standard that focused on a mixture of three factors: (1) commercial features of the content of the message, (2) commercial aspects of the motivation of the speaker, and (3) the commercial nature of the methods used.

The Court returned to these vexing issues in *Murdock v. Pennsylvania*, 319

U.S. 105 (1943), which was argued March 10 and 11, 1943, within two days of the Court's decision in *Jamison* and which was decided two months later. *Murdock* involved the constitutionality of an ordinance of the city of Jeannette, Pennsylvania, which required "all persons canvassing or soliciting orders for goods, paintings, pictures, wares, or merchandise of any kind or persons delivering such articles under orders so obtained" to obtain a license to transact that business and to pay the associated license fee, 319 U.S. at 106. At the time of their arrest, Murdock and other members of the Jehovah's Witness sect were going door-to-door in the city of Jeannette, without the required license, distributing literature, and soliciting people to purchase certain religious books and pamphlets published by the Watch Tower Bible and Tract Society, an entity alleged to be a non-profit charitable corporation. Two religious books, *Salvation* and *Creation*, were sold at 25¢ each. The price of the pamphlets was 5¢. As in *Cantwell*, the canvassers used a phonograph on which they played a record expounding certain of their religious views. All had made sales of the books. In making the solicitations, Murdock's practice was to request a "contribution" of 25¢ for each book and 5¢ for each pamphlet but to accept less or even to donate the volumes in case an interested person was without funds, *id.* at 107. Some donations of pamphlets were made when books were purchased.

Having by this time granted the petitions for rehearing in *Jones v. Opelika* and having heard argument in the *Murdock* case together with reargument in the *Jones* case, the Court reversed Murdock's conviction and set aside its earlier decision in *Jones v. Opelika*, in an opinion by Justice Douglas. The Court's characterization of the activities carried with it the disposition: "[Petitioners' activity] is more than preaching; it is more than distribution of religious literature. It is a combination of both. Its purpose is as evangelical as the revival meeting. This form of religious activity occupies the same high estate under the First Amendment as do worship in the churches and preaching from the pulpits," *id.* at 109. The Court was obliged to distinguish *Valentine v. Chrestensen*, because the city of Jeannette defended the ordinance precisely on the ground that "the religious literature is distributed with a solicitation of funds," *id.* at 110. The Court held, however, that this "solicitation" was "religious" in nature and was not "purely commercial." Quoting from its opinions in *Jamison* and *Valentine*, the Court acknowledged that "[s]ituations will arise where it will be difficult to determine whether a particular activity is religious or purely commercial. The distinction at times is vital," *id.* at 110. The Court rested its decision squarely on the religious nature of this activity. Thus, the Court explicitly distinguished between Murdock and others who went door-to-door selling books and pamphlets in the exercise of their religious beliefs, and the activity of going door-to-door selling books solely for economic gain. "The constitutional rights of those spreading their religious beliefs through the spoken and printed word are not to be gauged by standards governing retailers or wholesalers of books. The right to use the press for expressing one's views is not to be measured by the protection afforded commercial handbills," *id.* at 111.

The Court did not specify whether someone going door-to-door selling books relating to political, social, aesthetic, or philosophical matters or anti-religious books and pamphlets, either in an attempt to convert others to his views or solely for gain, would enjoy the same degree of protection. The Court intimated, however, that someone selling books or taking orders for books for gain might not enjoy such protection, in stating that "an itinerant evangelist however misguided or intolerant he may be, does not become *a mere book agent* by selling the Bible or religious tracts to help defray his expenses or to sustain him. Freedom of speech, freedom of the press, freedom of religion are available to all, not merely to those who can pay their own way," *id*. at 111 (emphasis added).

The Court offered no clear criteria for distinguishing between commercial and religious ventures. Although passing reference is made to Murdock's purpose to spread his religious beliefs, the Court formulated no clear legal standard— no legal test turning, for example, on the speaker's motive, the content of the speech, or the solicitation or method adopted. Nor did the Court explain the rationale for its suggestion that the activities of *"a mere book agent"* would enjoy less protection under the First Amendment. It is simply acknowledged that "the problem of drawing the line between a purely commercial activity and a religious one will at times be difficult," *id*. at 111. The Court, however, apparently entertained no doubt that Murdock and the others were engaged in a "religious venture" rather than a commercial one, *id*. at 111. The Court suggested that the distinction between Murdock and the "mere book agent" lay in the fact that there was no guarantee that the book agent did not simply sell books to the public, having no interest at all in persuading the public to believe the ideas taught in the books and having no personal belief in the truth of the books. But it may well be asked why these factors should make the former a crucially more valuable state of affairs than the mere dissemination of the books for gain. The Court offered no answer. In his dissenting opinion, Justice Reed properly seized on the weakness of the majority's distinction between the so-called mere book agent and the religious canvasser selling books.

Compounding the complexity of the distinction between selling for personal gain and selling literature for religious reasons were the facts that Murdock paid 3¢ each for the pamphlets, which he sold for 5¢, and paid 20¢ each for books for which he charged 25¢. Witnesses working full-time as canvassers purchased the books for 5¢ each and resold them for 25¢, keeping a profit of 20¢ each. The facts thus supported an inference that the full-time canvassers supported themselves on the profits derived from selling the books. This fact, which the Court did not emphasize, further clouds the distinction the Court sought to draw between mere book agents and religious canvassers.

On May 3, 1943, the same day the Supreme Court handed down its decision in *Murdock* and vacated its initial decision in *Jones*, the Court decided *Martin v. City of Struthers*, 319 U.S. 141 (1943). At issue in *Martin*, which had been argued the same day the *Murdock* case was argued, was the constitutionality of an ordinance of Struthers, Ohio, making it unlawful "for any person distributing handbills, circulars or other advertisements to ring the door bell, sound the door knocker, or otherwise summon'' the homeowner. There was no charge for the circular involved, and, according to the circular, admission to the convention was also free. The distribution thus involved no commercial element. It was, in essence, a free distribution of an invitation to religious services. Notwithstanding the absence of any commercial element in the facts of the case, the decision assumed importance in later decisions involving door-to-door solicitation of commercial magazine subscriptions. The Court invalidated this ordinance. Essentially, the Court faced "the necessity of weighing the conflicting interests of the appellant in the civil rights she claims, as well as the right of the individual householder to determine whether he is willing to receive her message, against the interest of the community which by this ordinance offers to protect the interests of all of its citizens, whether particular citizens want that protection or not,'' 319 U.S. at 143. The Court viewed the competing interests as involving not simply the rights of a speaker against the community members' interest in privacy, but also the rights of potential recipients of information, homeowners, who, if presented with the opportunity to hear about the canvassers' religious beliefs and evangelistic efforts, might choose to listen.

The insight that the potential recipients of information also have protected interests in the dissemination of information came to play a very important role in the theory of the later commercial speech cases. From this perspective, the Court judged it important, first, that the ordinance did not control anything but the distribution of literature and, second, that it substituted the judgment of the community for the judgment of the individual householder, 319 U.S. at 144. The Court's decision striking down the ordinance was based not only on the combined interests of canvassers and potential recipients, but on the overall importance the Court found in the practice of door-to-door canvassing for dissemination of religious doctrines, for recruiting members of labor groups, for selling government war bonds, for obtaining support for political causes, and for circulating political nominating papers. Arrayed against these strong interests, the interest in preventing annoyance to sleeping homeowners and the interest in preventing burglars from using the guise of circular distribution to identify homes whose occupants were away were insufficiently weighty and sufficiently capable of being advanced by traditional legal methods, including local trespass laws, that the Struthers ordinance simply could not be justified. The Court carefully preserved the power of municipalities to enact ordinances making it unlawful for any person to ring the bell of a householder who has appropriately indicated in advance that he is unwilling to be disturbed. Such ordinances cured the constitutional defect by transferring back to the homeowner the decision as to whether distributors of literature may lawfully call, 319 U.S. at 148.

The Jehovah's Witness door-to-door solicitation cases presented a number of difficulties for the emerging commercial speech doctrine: (1) When is speech commercial? (2) Does one feature of the speech act make speech commercial, or is it a combination of factors, such as the method, medium, the content, or the speaker's motive? (3) If it is some single factor, which is it? (4) If it is a complex balance of factors, what rule governs how the proper identification of commercial speech can be made? (5) Is the state's legitimate interest balanced against the value of protecting the speech, taking into account its commercial nature? (6) Is the breadth of the manner in which the state's interest is advanced to be considered in relation to the state interest involved and the value of the message?

These cases illustrate the Court's early efforts to answer some of these questions. The Court made the motive of the speaker a dominant determining factor. In the Jehovah's Witness cases, motive was inferred from the record by the Supreme Court as "constitutional fact," without formal findings of fact from the lower courts. There were no challenges to the sincerity of the beliefs held by the solicitors; their motive was the religious one of propagating a set of beliefs in accordance with the teachings of the Bible, as understood by adherents of the sects. While the sales transactions were, in part, commercial, they were also integral aspects of a nationwide religious movement. Although the sect derived revenue from the sale of books and pamphlets, that revenue was devoted to publishing and distributing more literature over an even broader area and to providing a livelihood for those who were engaged in the dissemination of those opinions and beliefs. Revenue was used to spread more protected speech. And the Court noted, in several cases, that the Watch Tower Bible and Tract Society was alleged to be non-profit charitable, even if the records in the cases contained no express finding to that effect, *see*, *Murdock v. Pennsylvania*, *supra*, 319 U.S. at 107, n.1; *Jones v. Opelika*, 316 U.S. at 607 (dissenting opinion of Chief Justice Stone). The Court also acknowledged the contention that the distribution process was not a moneymaking operation for the canvassers, *Jones v. Opelika*, 316 U.S. at 592. (In *Murdock*, however, it appeared that full-time solicitors bought the books for 5¢ and sold them for 25¢—allowing 20¢ profit on each book, 319 U.S. at 107, n.2.)

The Court began to struggle with the difficult issues involved in applying new constitutional doctrine to mixed commercial and non-commercial speech. The Court also began to grapple with the problems posed by forms of speech that were mixed with elements of action. In particular, the Court was dealing not with pure speech but with solicitation as a special category of the speech act. The Court discussed the conduct as solicitation in several of these cases, *see*, *Cantwell v. Connecticut*, 310 U.S. at 304, 305, 306. Solicitation of funds to propagate ideas was regarded by some of the justices simply as protected conduct. As Chief Justice Stone put it in his dissenting opinion in *Jones*, " . . . here the only activities involved are the dissemination of ideas, educational and religious, and the collection of funds for the propagation of those ideas which we have said is likewise the subject of constitutional protection," 316 U.S. at 608. These themes recur in later commercial speech cases.

BREARD v. ALEXANDRIA: DOOR-TO-DOOR
SOLICITATION OF NON-RELIGIOUS MAGAZINE
SUBSCRIPTIONS

The Court dealt with the "mere book agent" and clarified one aspect of the *Valentine v. Chrestensen* commercial speech exception in *Breard v. City of Alexandria*, 341 U.S. 622 (1951). In that decision, the Court affirmed the conviction of a salesman who had solicited magazine subscriptions door-to-door, in violation of a local ordinance that prohibited "the practice of going in and upon private residences in the City of Alexandria, Louisiana by solicitors, peddlers, hawkers, itinerant merchants or transient vendors of merchandise not having been requested or invited to do so by the owner or owners, occupant or occupants of said private residences for the purpose of soliciting orders for the sale of goods, wares and merchandise and/or disposing of and/or peddling or hawking the same," 341 U.S. at 624–625. Although the Court upheld the constitutionality of the Alexandria ordinance, it took pains to point out that "the fact that periodicals are sold does not put them beyond the protection of the First Amendment," 341 U.S. at 642. In other words, the magazines that Breard sold were themselves unquestionably protected by the First Amendment, even though they were sold or offered for sale. The Court noted, however, that "the selling . . . brings into the transaction a commercial feature," 341 U.S. at 642. The doorstep "transaction" involved an additional commercial element, separate from the fact that the magazines were sold for a profit.

The Court distinguished *Martin v. Struthers*, in which the Court had invalidated a local ordinance forbidding anyone from summoning occupants of residences to the door to receive free advertisements of religious meetings. In *Breard*, the Court noted (1) that the ordinance involved in *Martin v. Struthers* was not aimed "solely at commercial advertising," (2) that in that case "no element of the commercial entered into [the] free solicitation," and (3) that Martin was engaged in "free distribution of an invitation to religious services," 341 U.S. at 642–643. It may be doubted whether the Court's first distinction of *Martin* is sound. The Struthers ordinance was not limited on its face to commercial advertising. It was broad enough by its terms to encompass any advertising. The lower state courts in Ohio had, after all, interpreted the ordinance as applying to the religious advertising involved in the *Martin* case. The Court was correct, however, in its observation that no commercial element had been involved in the *Martin* case. In view of these distinctions, the Court said, *Martin v. Struthers* "is not necessarily inconsistent with the conclusion reached in this case," 341 U.S. at 643. Justice Black, dissenting, rejected the attempt to distinguish the *Martin* case but did not comment on "the element of the commercial" which the majority had identified as the distinguishing feature. To Justice Black and Justice Douglas, who joined in Justice Black's dissenting opinion, door-to-door solicitors of magazine subscriptions such as Breard are "agents of the press" in the dissemination of protected communications. Residents, but not local governments, had the right to prevent their presence on private property.

The *Breard* case, then, appears to hold that the profit motive in selling the magazines is sufficient to deprive the door-to-door solicitation of magazine subscriptions of the protection of the First Amendment. The Court did not, as it did in *Valentine*, use the commercial element as the basis for holding that the solicitation activity was completely outside the First Amendment's protection. Rather the Court identified the two competing interests: (1) "the publisher's right to distribute publications in the precise way that those soliciting for him think brings the best results" and (2) "some householders' desire for privacy." The Court stated that "the constitutionality of Alexandria's ordinance [turns] upon a balancing of the conveniences" between these rights or interests, 341 U.S. at 644.

The "balancing test" which the Court used in *Breard* thus reflects an approach different from the blanket exception for commercial speech which the Court created in *Valentine*. The "mere fact that the periodicals are sold" did not completely deprive them of First Amendment protection, but the "selling" of them brought into the transaction "a commercial feature" that justified a treatment different from that accorded to "free distribution" of religious literature in *Martin v. Struthers*. Although the Court founded its distinction on the selling, rather than on the means or method, *Breard* may be interpreted as focusing on the nature of the conduct associated with the dissemination of speech, rather than on the speech itself. Considered in this light, *Breard* might be viewed as an early recognition that commercial speech is analogous to "speech plus conduct." Such an analysis might make the combination expression plus conduct subject to governmental regulation under the balancing test articulated in cases such as the draft-card burning case, *United States v. O'Brien*. These strands of current First Amendment doctrine are addressed in chapter 5, *compare United States v. O'Brien*, 391 U.S. 367, 375–377 (1968), with *Central Hudson Gas & Electric Corp. v. Public Service Commission*, 447 U.S. 557, 561–566 (1980).

PAID EDITORIAL ADVERTISING: *NEW YORK TIMES CO. v. SULLIVAN*, 376 U.S. 254 (1964), AND THE "MEIKLEJOHN INTERPRETATION" OF THE FIRST AMENDMENT

The next major Supreme Court precedent to consider the issues raised by the *Valentine* ruling was the momentous decision in *New York Times Co. v. Sullivan* 376 U.S. 254 (1964), a libel action by the Commissioner of Public Affairs of the city of Montgomery, Alabama, against the *New York Times* and several individuals, which arose out of statements made in a full-page editorial advertisement in the *New York Times* issue of March 29, 1960, describing local police retaliation in the struggle for civil rights throughout the South generally and in

Montgomery, Alabama, in particular. The principal holding of the case was that the rule of libel law applied by the Alabama courts was constitutionally deficient because it failed to provide the safeguards for freedom of speech and of the press required by the First and Fourteenth Amendments in libel actions by public officials against critics of their official conduct. The Court held, moreover, that the Montgomery, Alabama, sheriff's evidence was insufficient under the constitutional standards for libel. Specifically, the Court held that factual error in this context provides an insufficient basis on which to support an award of damages against a newspaper and that "actual malice"—knowledge that statements are false, or publication that is made in reckless disregard of the truth—must be alleged and proved.

The Court was met at the outset, however, with Sullivan's contention that the constitutional guarantees of freedom of speech and of the press are totally inapplicable "at least so far as the Times is concerned," because the allegedly libelous statements were published as part of a paid, commercial advertisement. This argument was explicitly based on *Valentine v. Chrestensen*, and the Court rejected it. Justice Brennan distinguished *Valentine* by restating the Court's characterization of the advertising at issue in *Valentine*: The holding was based upon "the factual conclusions that the handbill was 'purely commercial advertising' and that the protest against official action had been added only to evade the ordinance," 376 U.S. at 266. The paid advertisement in *New York Times Co. v. Sullivan* was not a commercial advertisement in the sense in which the word was used in the *Valentine* case. It "communicated information, expressed opinion, recited grievances, protested claimed abuses, and sought financial support on behalf of a movement whose existence and objectives are matters of the highest public interest and concern," 376 U.S. at 266. The Court held that the fact "[t]hat the Times was paid for publishing the advertising is as immaterial in this connection as is the fact that newspapers and books are sold. *Smith v. California*, 361 U.S. 147, 150; *cf. Bantam Books, Inc. v. Sullivan*, 372 U.S. 58, 64 n.6," *id.*

The Court's opinion provides a fully rationalized argument for this conclusion. The Court was concerned in *New York Times* with the status of "editorial advertisements," *i.e.*, non-commercial, paid newspaper advertisements, and therefore with the rights of "persons who do not themselves have access to publishing facilities." The Court recognized that a holding that editorial advertisements are outside the First Amendment "would discourage newspapers from carrying" them. If newspapers were not to carry them, the rights of persons who wish to exercise their freedom of speech, even though they are not members of the press, would be indirectly limited by the newspapers' reluctance to carry them. Ultimately, the effect would be "to shackle the First Amendment in its attempt to secure 'the widest possible dissemination of information from diverse and antagonistic sources,'" 376 U.S. at 266. The Court did not base this conclusion explicitly on the rights of citizens to have access to the opinions and viewpoints contained in editorial advertisements. Rather, it held that editorial advertisements are protected because of the speech interests of the speakers who pay for them. Protection of the newspapers' action in publishing them is ancillary to protection of the speakers. But other passages of the Court's opinion in *New York Times v. Sullivan* articulate a far broader rationale for First Amendment protection. Thus, according to the Court's account, the First Amendment was adopted (1) to assure unfettered interchange of ideas for the bringing about of political and social changes desired by the people, *id*. at 269; (2) to permit the government to be responsive to the will of the people, *id*. at 269; (3) to assure stability of the government by guaranteeing an opportunity to bring about change by "lawful means," *id*. at 269; and (4) to foster "right conclusions," from "a multitude of tongues, than through any kind of authoritative selection," *id*. at 270. In a justly famous passage, Justice Brennan also wrote: "[W]e considered this case against the background of a profound national commitment to the principle that debate on public issues should be uninhibited, robust, and wide-open, and it may well include vehement, caustic, and sometimes unpleasantly sharp attacks on government and public officials," *id*. at 270. In this passage and in the fourth consideration listed above, the Court elaborated an important new source of First Amendment theory.

The *New York Times* case touches the commercial speech doctrine only tangentially. The speech involved was commercial only in the sense that the advertisement was paid for. The advertisements were not commercial in content, but were political protests. Nonetheless, the decision is important to commercial doctrine. It contains the germ of theory which the Court used to narrow the holding in *Valentine v. Chrestensen*. The modern commercial speech doctrine rests primarily not on the rights of the speaker, but on the rights of potential recipients of information and opinion. The *New York Times* case recognized this important source of constitutional protection.

New York Times v. Sullivan illustrates a number of the strands in the constitutional reasoning. The design envisioned by the framers of the Constitution and the Bill of Rights was a simple one. The speech and press clause of the First Amendment commands that "Congress shall make no law abridging the freedom of speech, or of the press." The fourteen words of this provision embody what the Supreme Court in *New York Times v. Sullivan* termed our "profound national commitment to the principle that debate on public issues should be uninhibited, robust and wide-open."[1] The speech and press clause is cast not in terms of protection of any particular, enumerated sources of speech, but in absolute terms as a restraint upon congressional power in this field. The speech and press clause protects the freedom of those activities of thought and communication by which we as citizens govern. It is concerned not with a private right but with a public power. In a broader fashion, the First Amendment protects and preserves what Thomas Emerson has called "the system of freedom of expression."[2]

James Madison, who probably drafted the First Amendment, explained it by pointing to "the essential difference between the British Government and the American Constitutions." In the United States, the people and not the government possess the absolute sovereignty. The legislative and executive branches are under limitations of power. A government which is "elective, limited and responsible" in its branches may well be supposed to require "a greater freedom of animadversion" than might be tolerated by one that is composed of an irresponsible hereditary king and upper house and an omnipotent legislature. It was one of the very objects of the Revolution to get rid of the English common law that restrained the liberty of speech and press.[3] Alexander Meiklejohn, an American political scientist, emphasized this point in an influential book, *Free Speech and Its Relation to Self-Government*.[4] Meiklejohn rejected the natural rights theory of freedom of speech in favor of a pragmatic approach. Instead, he deduced the necessity for open discussion from the fundamental program of self-government defined in other parts of the Constitution. Without free and open discussion of all viewpoints, the public's deliberation on public issues is skewed. Free speech is essential on this view to proper public decision making in a democratic system. This is the simple, pragmatic basis of that "profound national commitment to the principle that debate on public issues should be uninhibited, robust and wide-open" to which the Supreme Court referred in *New York Times v. Sullivan*. Justice William Brennan noted that Meiklejohn, at the age of ninety, greeted the decision in that case as "an occasion for dancing in the streets."[5]

Meiklejohn's conclusions were essentially consistent with Mill's position in chapter 2 of his classic, *On Liberty*.[6] Mill maintained that no viewpoint can properly be suppressed, whether it is believed true or false.[7] Mill also recognized a positive value in the circulation of false opinions: The "collision with error," as he put it, produces a "clearer perception and livelier impression of truth." Mill argued that suppression of false opinions is mistaken because the absence of the false opinion obscures the perception of that which is true in a true opinion.[8]

The ideas of Madison, Meiklejohn, and Mill form an important backdrop to any contemporary understanding of the scope of the First Amendment as applied to corporate, commercial or political speech. The "gradual process of judicial inclusion and exclusion"[9] which served so well to define other clauses in the federal Constitution through case-by-case clashes of antagonistic interests in concrete factual circumstances did little to clarify the speech and press clause of the First Amendment until this century. The First Amendment cases in this century are probably best seen as part of a process of discovery of older constitutional values, which were clearly perceived by the framers of the amendment but blurred by disuse. Even the fundamental question of the applicability of the First Amendment to the states was in doubt as late as 1920 by reason of the Court's decision in *Prudential Insurance Co. v. Cheek* 259 U.S. 530 (1922); and despite the famous dictum in 1925, in *Gitlow v. New York*, 268 U.S. 652, and the tacit assumption of applicability to the states in *Whitney v. California*, 274 U.S. 357, in 1927, this important question was not decided until *Fiske v. Kansas*, 274 U.S. 380 (1927), *Stromberg v. California*, 283 U.S. 359 (1931), and the famous "prior restraint" case decided in 1931, *Near v. Minnesota*, 283 U.S. 697. The attention to Meiklejohn's conception of the First Amendment is warranted by its importance for constitutional protection of corporate speech, particularly as demonstrated in *First National Bank of Boston v. Bellotti*, 435 U.S. 765 (1978), and in the commercial speech cases of the 1970s.

Acceptance of the notion mentioned in *New York Times v. Sullivan* that the First Amendment protects a "system of freedom of expression" and the idea that it protects a right of citizens to hear and to receive opinions, regardless of the source of the communication, is the development in the First Amendment theory which permitted judicial recognition of the constitutional dimension of corporate and commercial speech. Meiklejohn's deduction of the First Amendment from the program of self-government became the premise for all constitutional protection for corporate speech.

Until this development, corporations were said to be nothing but legal fictions. It was said that corporations are not natural persons yet enjoy the constitutional rights and guarantees to the same extent as natural persons. Corporations are denied the privileges and immunities of citizens of the United States and do not enjoy the Fifth Amendment privilege against self-incrimination. Corporations, in short, are creatures of state law and possess only those rights and privileges which the states choose to confer on them. In the quaint language of one court, "These artificial creatures are not citizens of the United States, and, so far as the franchise is concerned, must at all times be held subservient and subordinate to the government and the citizenship of which it is composed."[10] Until the Supreme Court recognized and articulated the broader purposes of the speech and press clause, proponents of prohibition or strict regulation of corporate speech distinguished corporations that are involved in a "First Amendment business"— *i.e.*, in the distribution and exhibition of films, magazines, and newspaper and magazine business—from all other corporations. The First Amendment specifically protects the former by explicit reference to "the freedom of the press." Although the press, whether in corporate form or otherwise, could properly invoke the protection of the First Amendment, other corporations could not, according to this view. The question was framed as whether corporations have First Amendment rights, rather than whether their speech is protected.

Rejection of this narrow conception of the First Amendment can be traced at least to *Red Lion Broadcasting Co. v. FCC*, 395 U.S. 367, decided in 1969, where the Court said that "the people as a whole retain their interest in free speech by radio and their collective right to have the medium function consistently with ends and purposes of the First Amendment. It is the right of the viewers and listeners, not the right of the broadcasters, which is paramount," 395 U.S. at 390. Quoting from *Garrison v. Louisiana*, 379 U.S. 64 (1964), the Court recognized that "speech concerning public affairs is more than self-expression" and said: "It is the essence of self-government. . . . It is the right of the public to receive suitable access to social, political, esthetic, moral and other ideas and experiences which is crucial here. The right may not constitutionally be abridged either by Congress or the F.C.C.," 395 U.S. at 390.

This same "First Amendment goal of producing an informed public capable of conducting its own affairs,'' 395 U.S. at 390, was important in the cases defining press access to prisoners for interviews. In *Saxbe v. Washington Post*, 417 U.S. 843, decided in 1974, Justice Powell expressed in his dissenting opinion the notion that the First Amendment

embodies our nation's commitment to popular self-determination and our abiding faith that the surest course for developing sound national policy lies in a free exchange of views on public issues, and public debate must not only be unfettered; it must also be informed. For that reason this court has repeatedly stated that *First Amendment concerns encompass the receipt of information and ideas as well as the right of free expression.* 417 U.S. at 862–863 (emphasis added)

NOTES

1. 376 U.S. 254, 270–271 (1964).
2. Emerson, *The System of Freedom of Expression* (1970).
3. See Madison, ''Report on the Virginia Resolutions,'' in Eliot's Debates 596–598 (2d ed., 1937).
4. Reprinted in Meiklejohn, *Political Freedom* (1965). Meiklejohn observed:

What, then, does the First Amendment forbid? Here . . . the town meeting suggests an answer. That meeting is called to discuss and, on the basis of such discussion, to decide matters of public policy. For example, shall there be a school? Where shall it be located? Who shall teach? What shall be taught? The community has agreed that such questions as these shall be freely discussed and that, when the discussion is ended, decision upon them will be made by vote of the citizens. Now, in that method of political self-government, the point of ultimate interest is not the words of the speakers, but the minds of the hearers. The final aim of the meeting is the voting of wise decisions. The voters, therefore, must be made as wise as possible. The welfare of the community requires that those who decide issues shall understand them. They must know what they are voting about. And this, in turn, requires that so far as time allows, all facts and interests relevant to the problem shall be fully and fairly presented to the meeting. Both facts and interests must be given in such a way that all the alternative lines of action can be wisely measured in relation to one another. As the self-governing community seeks, by the method of voting, to gain wisdom in action, it can find it only in the minds of its individual citizens. If they fail, it fails. That is why freedom of discussion for those minds may not be abridged. *Id.* at 25–26.

Meiklejohn also wrote (at 27):

Just so far as, at any point, the citizens who are to decide an issue are denied acquaintance with information or opinion or doubt or disbelief or criticism which is relevant to that issue, just so far the result must be ill-considered, ill-balanced planning for the general good. *It is that mutilation of the thinking process of the community against which the First Amendment to the Constitution is directed.* The principle of the freedom of speech springs from the necessities of the program of self-government. It is not a law of nature or of reason in the abstract. It is a deduction from the basic American agreement that public issues shall be decided by universal suffrage. (Emphasis in original.)

5. See Brennan, *The Supreme Court and the Meiklejohn Interpretation of the First Amendment*, 79 Harv. L. Rev. 17 (1965); Kalven, *The New York Times Case: A Note on the General Meaning of the First Amendment*, 1964 Supreme Court Review 191, 209.
6. World's Classics Edition (1974).
7. Mill argued that suppression of opinion is pragmatic error:

The peculiar evil of silencing the expression of an opinion is, that it is robbing the human race; posterity as well as the existing generation; those who dissent from the opinion, still more than those who hold it. If the opinion is right, they are deprived of the opportunity of exchanging error for truth: If wrong, they lose, what is almost as great a benefit, the clearer perception and livelier impression of truth, produced by its collision with error.

8. Mill cited the example of Cicero, who, as the greatest advocate of his day, made it his practice to study his adversary's case with the same diligence he devoted to his own case. Mill wrote:

What Cicero practised as the means of forensic success, requires to be imitated by all who study any subject in order to arrive at the truth. He who knows only his own side of the case, knows little of that. His reasons may be good, and no one may have been able to refute them. But if he is equally unable to refute the reasons on the opposite side; if he does not so much as know what they are, he has no ground for preferring either opinion.

9. Davidson v. New Orleans, 96 U.S. 97, 104 (1877)(Miller, J.).
10. United States v. U.S. Brewers Ass'n, 239 F. 163 (W.D.Pa. 1916).

2

The Rejection of the "Commercial Speech Exception" to the First Amendment: *Pittsburgh Press* to *Bigelow*

The recognition of "the right of the public to receive suitable access to social, political, esthetic, moral and other ideas and experiences" became a dominant theme in the cases that followed in the late 1970s, and it played a central role in the Court's rejection of the doctrine of *Valentine v. Chrestensen* that commercial speech is entitled to no protection under the First Amendment. The Court's almost offhand statement in *Valentine* that "we are . . . clear that the Constitution imposes no such restraint on governments as respects purely commercial advertising," 316 U.S. at 54 (1942), was drastically qualified. In a series of cases decided between 1973 and 1976—*Pittsburgh Press Co. v. Pittsburgh Commission on Human Relations*, 413 U.S. 376 (1973), *Bigelow v. Virginia*, 421 U.S. 809 (1975), and *Virginia State Board of Pharmacy v. Virginia Citizens Consumer Council*, 425 U.S. 748 (1976)—the Supreme Court rejected the commercial speech exception. Although the Court in *Pittsburgh Press* upheld an ordinance that prohibited sex-designated help-wanted advertisements in a newspaper, instead of relying on *Valentine* the Court emphasized that the commercial activity facilitated by such advertising—sex discrimination in employment—was unlawful.

In *Pittsburgh Press*, the Supreme Court upheld a decision and order of the Human Relations Commission of Pittsburgh, in a proceeding against a major daily newspaper of that city arising out of the newspaper's practice of separately grouping classified employment advertisements into "Male Help Wanted," "Female Help Wanted," and "Male-Female Help Wanted" and then organizing the captions "Jobs-Male Interest" and "Jobs-Female Interest," according to the expressed wishes of the advertiser. The commission found that advertisers requesting listing of their advertisements in this fashion were in violation of Pittsburgh's Human Relations ordinance and also issued a cease and desist order directly to the newspaper. On appeal to the Pennsylvania Commonwealth Court, the order was modified to permit the grouping of advertisements by gender to the extent permitted by the exemptions in the ordinance.

The Pittsburgh Press attacked the commission's cease and desist order in the Supreme Court on First Amendment grounds, and the Human Relations Commission placed its primary reliance on *Valentine v. Chrestensen, supra*. Although the Court adverted to the "brief opinion" in that case and to the Court's subsequent statements that speech is not rendered commercial by the mere fact that it relates to an advertisement, the Court identified as "[t]he critical feature of the advertisement in *Valentine v. Chrestensen*" the fact that the advertisement in that case "did no more than propose a commercial transaction, the sale of admission to a submarine," 413 U.S. at 385. As the Court conceived its task in *Pittsburgh Press*, the central problem was to determine whether the gender-based classified advertisements were more similar to the submarine-tour handbill in *Valentine* or to the advertisement concerning civil rights violence in the South involved in *New York Times v. Sullivan*. This inquiry was easily answered. The employment advertisements were "classic examples of commercial speech," 413 U.S. at 385.

Pittsburgh Press sought to avoid this result by arguing that the focus of the case must be on the exercise of editorial judgment by the newspaper with respect to the placement of the advertisement. The Court held, however, that "a commercial advertisement remains commercial in the hands of the media, at least under some circumstances," 413 U.S. at 387. That the newspaper retained— even if it did not exercise—a degree of editorial discretion over the location of advertisements in the newspapers did not add anything to the concededly commercial content of the advertisement to take the case out of the ambit of *Valentine v. Chrestensen*, and *Capital Broadcasting Co. v. Acting Attorney General*, 333 F.Supp.582 (D.C. Cir. 1971), *aff'd* 405 U.S. 1000 (1972)(cigarette advertising prohibition on electronic media), in which the Court had similarly dealt with a First Amendment challenge by the owner of the medium of communication.

Even if it were commercial speech, this package of advertisement and placement, Pittsburgh Press argued, was entitled to greater protection than that accorded commercial speech in *Valentine*. The Court, however, rejected this contention, pointing out that discrimination in employment "is not only commercial activity, it is illegal commercial activity under the Ordinance," 413 U.S. at 388. The Court continued:

We have no doubt that a newspaper constitutionally could be forbidden to publish a want ad proposing a sale of narcotics or soliciting prostitutes. Nor would the result be different if the nature of the transaction were indicated by placement under columns captioned "Narcotics for Sale" and "Prostitutes Wanted" rather than stated within the four corners of the advertisement.

Section 8(j) of the Pittsburgh Ordinance made it unlawful for "any person . . . to aid . . . in the doing of any act declared to be an unlawful employment practice by this ordinance." The Court upheld the determination of the Human Relations Commission that the newspaper's practice constituted a violation of this provision.

The American Newspaper Publishers Association, in an *amicus curiae* brief, also contended that the commission's cease and desist order constituted a "prior restraint" on protected speech within the doctrine of *Near v. Minnesota*, 283 U.S. 697 (1931). This argument is one of great potential interest, for the Court has not yet made it entirely clear whether the doctrine of prior restraint is applicable to commercial speech under the modified doctrine evolving from the Court's more recent decisions. The Court, however, did not answer this question directly. Instead, the Court said that the cease and desist order "does not endanger arguably protected speech." Because the case involved a "continuing course of repetitive conduct," the Court was not asked to speculate as to the effect of publication. The Court also emphasized the narrow and precise scope of the cease and desist order.

The Court had no occasion to address the continuing vitality of *Valentine v. Chrestensen* in *Pittsburgh Press*. The primary significance of *Pittsburgh Press* is the fact that it marked one of the clear limitations to constitutional protection which it continued to apply even in later decisions which recognized that commercial speech enjoys some constitutional protection. The Court's opinion leaves open the many difficult questions concerning the manner in which advertising may be "related to" unlawful conduct in a fashion such that the advertising loses the degree of protection to which later decisions of the Supreme Court were to find such speech entitled. Although these problems are somewhat less complicated where the party challenging the regulation is the advertiser and where the advertising may be viewed as an integral part of a broader, unlawful course of conduct, the difficulties increase where the actions of a "stranger" to the broader course of conduct are made subject to the same principle, as in *Pittsburgh Press*.

In *Bigelow v. Virginia*, 421 U.S. 809 (1975), the Court invalidated, as applied, a Virginia criminal statute that prohibited the advertising of abortion services. The Court emphasized that the commercial activity—abortion services—implicated the constitutional considerations articulated in the right-to-abortion cases, *Roe v. Wade*, 410 U.S. 113 (1973), and *Doe v. Bolton*, 410 U.S. 179 (1973). However, this important step in the near-total erosion of the commercial speech exception depended on a broader conception of the First Amendment. As Justice Blackmun wrote: "Here, Virginia is really asserting an interest in regulating what Virginians may *hear* or *read* about the New York services. It is, in effect, advancing an interest in shielding its citizens from information about activities outside Virginia's borders, activities that Virginia's police powers do not reach," 421 U.S. at 827–828. The details of the case warrant careful analysis.

Bigelow was a criminal prosecution of the managing editor of the *Virginia Weekly*, a local Charlottesville newspaper that billed itself as an "underground newspaper" and focused on the campus of the University of Virginia. The *Virginia Weekly* ran a paid advertisement by the Women's Pavillion of New

York City, announcing that abortions were legal in New York without residency requirements and offering to readers of the *Virginia Weekly* to "make all arrangements" for "immediate placement in accredited hospitals and clinics at low cost" of women seeking abortions, 421 U.S. at 812. The advertisement listed the name, address, and telephone numbers in New York of the advertiser's abortion referral and counseling service. In this respect the advertisement was clearly informative. Bigelow was charged and convicted of a violation of a Virginia statute making it a misdemeanor for "any person, by publication, lecture, advertisement, or by the sale or circulation of any publication . . . [to] encourage or prompt the procuring of abortion or miscarriage," 421 U.S. at 812–813. Bigelow's conviction was affirmed by the Virginia Supreme Court, which held that the advertisement went beyond the "purely informational" and "constituted an active offer to perform a service rather than a passive statement of fact," 213 Va. 191, 193, 191 S.E.2d 173, 174 (1972). The Virginia Supreme Court held that the advertisement was a "commercial advertisement" and, as such, could be constitutionally prohibited by the state. The Virginia Supreme Court also held that, notwithstanding his association with a newspaper, Bigelow, whose interest "was of a purely commercial nature," had no standing to rely upon the rights "of those in the non-commercial zone," *id.* at 198, 191 S.E.2d at 177–178. During the pendency of Bigelow's initial appeal to the Supreme Court, the Court decided the constitutionality of state statutes prohibiting abortions in *Roe v. Wade* and *Doe v. Bolton, supra.* The Supreme Court vacated Bigelow's conviction and remanded the case to the Virginia Supreme Court, which again affirmed his conviction, notwithstanding that abortions could not be constitutionally prohibited then in either New York or Virginia.

The United States Supreme Court's opinion in *Bigelow* dealt in turn with Bigelow's standing to raise the First Amendment issue, the constitutional status of paid commercial advertisements, and the balance to be struck between the importance of the commercial advertising and the importance of the state interests that allegedly supported the statute. The Supreme Court first rejected the Virginia Supreme Court's conclusion denying Bigelow standing to raise the question of the overbreadth of the Virginia statute where "pure speech" rather than conduct was involved and where the Virginia Supreme Court had failed to assess whether the alleged overbreadth was or was not "substantial." The Court held that the requirement of "specific present objective harm or a threat of specific future harm"—a general prerequisite for standing to sue—was satisfied by the fact that Bigelow had actually been convicted of violation of the statute. The Court declined, however, to rest its decision on overbreadth of the Virginia statute, because the statute in the interim had been amended to apply only with respect to advertising to an abortion illegal in Virginia. The overbreadth issue had, therefore, become moot for the future.

The Court rejected the Virginia Supreme Court's conclusion that, as a "paid commercial advertisement," the abortion referral advertisement was outside the First Amendment, 421 U.S. at 818–826. The Court held that the fact that the particular advertisement had commercial aspects or reflected the advertiser's commercial interests did not negate all First Amendment guarantees. Citing its decisions in *Murdock*, *New York Times*, and *Thomas v. Collins*, 323 U.S. 516 (1945), the Court held that Virginia was not free of the constitutional restraints of the First Amendment simply because the advertisement "involved sales or 'solicitations,' " or because Bigelow was "paid for printing it," or because Bigelow's motive or the advertiser's motive may have "involved financial gain," 421 U.S. at 818. The language of the advertisement did not constitute fighting words, obscenity, libel, or incitement and therefore did not fall within any of the other established categories of speech which do not enjoy the protection of the First Amendment.

The Court was confronted, however, with Virginia's reliance on the Court's decision in *Valentine v. Chrestensen* which Virginia argued had made it clear that purely commercial advertising, like fighting words, obscenity, libel, and incitement, is completely outside the ambit of First Amendment protection. The Court's treatment of the precedent of *Valentine v. Chrestensen* was cautious. Without overruling the decision, the Court observed that its own decision in *Valentine*, "in a brief opinion," was limited, 421 U.S. at 819. Taking note of the sweeping statement in *Valentine* that "[w]e are . . . clear that the Constitution imposes no restraint on government as respects purely commercial advertising," the Court emphasized that "the holding of *Valentine*"—as contrasted with the language in which that holding was couched—"is a distinctly limited one." And the holding of *Valentine*, according to the *Bigelow* court, was only that "the ordinance was upheld as a reasonable regulation of the manner in which commercial advertising could be distributed," 421 U.S. at 819.

In retrospect, the Court's treatment of *Valentine* as precedent in *Bigelow* is an illustration of one step of the classic gradual technique used by appellate courts of "killing off" a precedent. According to the *Bigelow* Court, *Chrestensen* was not "authority for the proposition that all statutes regulating commercial advertising are immune from constitutional challenge. The case obviously does not support any sweeping proposition that advertising is unprotected *per se*," 421 U.S. at 820. The Court took the opportunity in a footnote to intimate the imminence of the overruling of *Valentine v. Chrestensen*, by quoting Justice Douglas's statement in his concurring opinion in *Cammarano v. United States*, 358 U.S. 498, 514 (1959), that "[t]he ruling was casual, almost offhand. And it has not survived reflection." In a partial "nose count" of justices in the same footnote, the Court pointed out that four of the then current justices had joined in Justice Brennan's statement in this dissenting opinion in *Lehman v. City of Shaker Heights*, 418 U.S. 298 (1974), at 314 n.6, that "[t]here is some doubt concerning whether the 'commercial speech' distinction announced in *Valentine v. Chrestensen* . . . retains continuing validity." The Court also relied on the ground on which it had distinguished *Valentine v. Chrestensen* in the *New York Times* case, which had involved libel charges arising from a paid advertisement appearing in the *Times*. The *Times* Court had noted that the *Valentine* handbill advertisement "did no more than propose a purely commercial transaction," as the *Bigelow* Court characterized it. In *New York Times*, by contrast, the advertisement "communicated information, expressed opinion, recited grievances, protested abuses, and sought financial support on behalf of a movement whose existence and objectives are matters of the highest public interest and concern," 376 U.S. at 266.

Beyond characterizing the advertisement in *Valentine* as one that "did no more than propose a purely commercial transaction," the Court in *Bigelow* also commented on the nature of the advertising at issue in the *Pittsburgh Press* case. The Court's discussion of the nature of the advertising in these cases, and the distinctions it was prepared to draw, are important because the Court's remarks shed light on the difficult questions involved in defining precisely what commercial speech is, both in *Valentine* and in the post-*Bigelow* cases. The difficulty of defining commercial speech is a theme that persists even in the Court's recent pronouncements on the commercial speech doctrine. The Court noted that the opinion in *Pittsburgh Press* had referred to the gender-based help-wanted advertisements at issue as "classic examples of commercial speech" in that each was "no more than a proposal of possible employment." The significance of the characterization of commercial speech as speech that "did no more than propose a purely commercial transaction" or as speech that was "no more than a proposal of possible employment" is revealed by cases such as *Bigelow*, where the advertising in question did more than merely propose a commercial transaction—that is, contained information beyond the terms and conditions of the proposed transaction and the identity of the seller. The advertisement in *Bigelow*, for example, contained information concerning the legal status of abortions in New York. To this extent, the advertising was distinguishable on its facts from that involved in *Valentine*.

The Court's opinion in *Bigelow* relied on the dictum in *Pittsburgh Press* to the effect that had the commercial proposal in *Pittsburgh Press*, *i.e.*, gender-based employment, been a lawful practice, the advertising would not have been without protection of the First Amendment. The Court said that it had "indicated [in *Pittsburgh Press*] that the advertisements would have received some degree of First Amendment protection if the commercial proposal had been legal," 421 U.S. at 821. The illegality of the advertised activity had been stressed in *Pittsburgh Press*.

The *Bigelow* Court rested its decision squarely on the difference between the purely commercial nature of the advertising in *Valentine v. Chrestensen*, and the factual nature of clear "public interest" involved in *Bigelow*. Thus, the Court specifically singled out the statement in the advertisement: "Abortions are now legal in New York. There are no residency requirements." The advertisement contained information of interest not only to women seeking abortions, but to the general public. Indeed, the mere existence of the Women's Pavillion in New York was a matter of public interest. The Court also apparently gave weight to the fact that "the activity pertained to constitutional interests," a circumstance that was related to the Court's recent decisions involving the constitutionality of state legislation restricting or outlawing abortions.

The Court's opinion noted several additional factors of importance. The abortion placement service in New York was legal in New York. Virginia could not have regulated the advertiser's activity in New York and could not have proscribed that activity in New York. Virginia likewise could not prevent its citizens from traveling to New York for the purpose of availing themselves of these services in New York. The Court held that a state "may not, under the guise of exercising internal police powers, bar a citizen of another state from disseminating information about an activity that is legal in that state," 421 U.S. at 824–825. The Court rejected the Virginia Supreme Court's position that the advertising enjoyed no First Amendment protection, but expressly declined to decide "the precise extent to which the First Amendment permits regulation of advertising that is related to activities the state may legitimately regulate or even prohibit," *id*. The Court implicitly rejected the notion that a state can permissibly discourage lawful conduct by its citizens by keeping its citizens in ignorance. The Court said, "Virginia is really asserting an interest in regulating what Virginians may *hear* or *read* about the New York services," 421 U.S. at 827. The Court said: "It is, in effect, advancing an interest in shielding its citizens from information about activities outside Virginia's borders, activities that Virginia's police powers do not reach. This assertion . . . was entitled to little, if any, weight under the circumstances," 421 U.S. at 827–828. As the Court's later decision in *Central Hudson Gas & Electric Corp*. shows, this factor has very important implications.

Since the Court held that the advertising was not entirely without protection under the First Amendment, the Court in *Bigelow* was obliged to go further to determine whether the Virginia statute was unconstitutional. The Court listed what it regarded as important in making this determination:

To the extent that commercial activity is subject to regulation, the relationship of speech to that activity may be one factor, among others, to be considered in weighing the First Amendment interest against the governmental interest alleged. Advertising is not thereby stripped of all First Amendment protection. The relationship of speech to the marketplace of products or of services does not make it valueless in the marketplace of ideas. 421 U.S. at 826

The Court's opinion, as we have noted, suggested a definition of commercial speech, *e.g.*, speech that "[does] no more than propose a purely commercial transaction," 421 U.S. at 820–821. This definition would appear to focus exclusively on the content of the speech as determining its status as commercial or non-commercial. Elsewhere in its opinion in *Bigelow*, however, the Court left room for factors other than content as determining status of speech as commercial or non-commercial. The Court also appeared willing to recognize that speech that was commercial in nature could be more or less commercial—that is, the commercial–non-commercial distinction created a false dichotomy and, instead, a continuum existed across which particular examples could be plotted. "The diverse motives, means, and messages of advertising may make speech 'commercial' in widely varying degrees," 421 U.S. at 826.

The Court's reference to "motives, means and messages" echoes the Court's vacillation over the classification of speech in the post-*Valentine* Jehovah's Witness cases reviewed in chapter 1. The Court seemed to intimate in *Bigelow* that the degree of protection to which particular examples of speech were entitled was a function of their position on the commercial–non-commercial continuum.

The task of balancing the interests implicated would normally have been remanded to the Virginia courts, but the result was so clear that this was unnecessary. Virginia had no legitimate governmental interest because, as applied to *Bigelow*, the statute was directed at the publishing of informative material relating to services offered in New York and "was not directed at advertising by referral agency or a practitioner whose activity Virginia had authority or power to regulate."

The Court also felt obliged to dispel any suggestion that the advertisement appearing in Bigelow's paper was "deceptive or fraudulent." The Court also rejected any suggestion that the readers constituted a "captive audience," such as the transit car passengers protected by the ban on transit car political advertising in *Lehman v. City of Shaker Heights*.

Again, the Court was careful also to point out that its holding carried no implications for the result in a case where the advertising was related to or "promoted" or was part of a solicitation to engage in conduct that would have been illegal where it was contemplated to be carried out:

We are not required to decide here what the First Amendment consequences would be if the Virginia advertisement promoted an activity in New York which was then illegal in New York. An example would be an advertisement announcing the availability of narcotics in New York City when the possession and sale of narcotics was proscribed in the State of New York. 421 U.S. at 828 n.14

The Court intimated that Bigelow's First Amendment interests were even greater than those of the advertiser, presumably because of the advertiser's purely or largely financial interest—although the Court did not elaborate on any evidence of commercial interest or point to any evidence that Bigelow's financial interest, or that of his paper, was less vital than the interests of the advertiser.

The dissenters were inclined to see no difference between the advertisement and that in *Valentine v. Chrestensen*, since both had a degree of political or informational content. The dissenting opinion also quarreled with the "rigid territorial limitation" on the power of all the states which was implicit in the majority holding that Virginia could not regulate in the sphere affecting activities in New York.

Bigelow is the source of a number of insights which became critical components of the evolving commercial speech doctrine of later decisions. If the decision added little except to mention one among several formulas used to define commercial speech, it decisively limited *Valentine v. Chrestensen* to its facts and continued the criticism of *Valentine* that ultimately led to its modification. The Court for the first time also articulated the balancing process between First Amendment interests of publishers and advertisers, on one hand, and governmental interests in the regulation of advertising on the other. The decision also carefully identified the factors of (1) "deceptive or fraudulent" character of speech, and (2) tendency or purpose to promote conduct that is illegal, as factors which act to defeat or limit the degree of constitutional protection to which commercial advertising may be entitled. Finally, the Court laid down an important principle regarding standing to challenge restrictions on overbroad regulations which recognized the standing of a class of persons other than the advertiser: the publisher of the advertising. The Court qualified its holding, by pointing out that the advertisement at issue "did more than simply propose a commercial transaction" and that "[i]t contained factual material of clear 'public interest,' " *id.* at 822, and by advertising the fact that "the advertisement related to activity with which, at least in some respects, the state could not interfere," *id.* The qualification was carefully designed to indicate that the Court was not squarely presented with the question of the continuing vitality of the doctrine of *Valentine v. Chrestensen*, which by its terms, at least, if not by its holding, denied any constitutional protection to "purely commercial advertising." Indeed the Court's qualification of its holding supported the lingering notion that the commercial speech exception might still have retained some vitality. This "fragment of hope for the continuing validity of a 'commercial speech' exception" was dispelled by the Court during the following term in *Virginia Pharmacy Board*.

3

The Emergence of the Modern Commercial Speech Doctrine: *Virginia Board of Pharmacy* to *Schaumberg*

VIRGINIA BOARD OF PHARMACY

In *Virginia Board of Pharmacy v. Virginia Citizens Consumer Council*, 425 U.S. 748 (1976), the Court struck down a Virginia statute declaring it unprofessional for a pharmacist to advertise prices of prescription drugs. Because the plaintiffs in that case were prospective recipients of the forbidden advertising, the Court gave extended consideration of the First Amendment right of citizens to receive communications. The right to receive information was, again, the crucial premise for invalidating the statute.

The Court stated that speech does not lose its First Amendment protection because money is spent to project it, as in a paid advertisement, that speech is protected even though it is carried in a form that is sold for profit, and that speech is protected even though it may involve a solicitation to purchase or otherwise pay or contribute money. The central question before the Court, however, was whether speech which "does no more than propose a commercial transaction" is so removed from any exposition of ideas and from "truth, science, morality, and art in general, in its diffusion of liberal sentiments on the administration of government" that it lacks all protection. Responding to this question, the Court wrote, "Our answer is that it is not," 425 U.S. at 762.

Writing for the Court, Justice Blackmun said that "society also may have a strong interest in the free flow of commercial information," *id*. at 764. "Advertising," he said, "is nonetheless dissemination of information as to who is producing and selling what product, for what reason, and at what price"—information which, through its impact on "numerous private economic decisions," influences the allocation of resources in a predominantly free enterprise economy. The Court said: "It is a matter of public interest that those decisions, in the aggregate, be intelligent and well informed. To this end, the free flow of commercial information is indispensable," *id*. at 765. Finally, the Court's opinion expressly acknowledged, in a footnote, its debt to Alexander Meiklejohn, whom the Court cited in support of this statement:

[I]f it is indispensable to the proper allocation of resources in a free enterprise system, it is also indispensable to the formation of intelligent opinions as to how that system ought to be regulated or altered. Therefore, *even if the First Amendment were thought to be primarily an instrument to enlighten public decision making in a democracy we would not say that the free flow of information does not serve that goal.* 425 U.S. at 765

In *Virginia Board of Pharmacy*, two non-profit organizations, the Virginia Citizens Consumer Council and the Virginia State AFL-CIO, and a Virginia resident who suffered from diseases that required daily treatment with prescription drugs, brought suit in a Virginia federal district court challenging the constitutionality of § 54–524.35 of the Virginia Code, a component of Virginia's regulatory scheme for licensure of the professions that was administered by the Virginia State Board of Pharmacy. The Board was charged with the responsibility of enforcing the provisions of that law relating to "unprofessional conduct" by licensed pharmacists. Section 54–524.35 provided that a pharmacist licensed in Virginia is guilty of unprofessional conduct if he "(3) publishes, advertises or promotes, directly or indirectly, in any manner whatsoever, any amount, price, fee, premium discount, rebate or credit terms . . . for any drugs which may be dispensed only by prescription." Since only a licensed pharmacist could dispense prescription drugs in Virginia, advertising or other affirmative dissemination of prescription drug price information was effectively forbidden in Virginia. The three-judge district court declared the Virginia statute unconstitutional, and the Supreme Court affirmed the judgment.[1]

The drug price advertising issue in *Virginia Board of Pharmacy* was related to price advertising restrictions on other professions, including optometrists' services, eyeglass frames, and dentists' services. The Supreme Court had rejected due process challenges to these restrictions in earlier cases, *Head v. New Mexico Board*, 374 U.S. 424 (1963)(optometrists' prices); *Williamson v. Lee Optical of Oklahoma, Inc.*, 348 U.S. 483 (1955)(prices of eyeglass frames); *Semler v. Dental Examiners*, 294 U.S. 608 (1935)(dentists' prices). The First Amendment challenges succeeded.

As in *Bigelow* and *Pittsburgh Press*, in which the position was presented by publishers, the constitutional challenge in *Virginia Board of Pharmacy* was mounted by parties other than the pharmacists which were the potential advertisers. The plaintiffs in *Virginia Board of Pharmacy* rested their challenge to the ban on drug price advertising on their rights as consumers, and in the case of the associations, on behalf of consumers, to receive drug price advertising. Their primary reason for seeking such advertising was the economic or financial motive of saving money on prescription drug purchases by guaranteeing that they had information that would enable them to ascertain the lowest-priced source of such drugs. The Court's exegesis, quoted above, on the protection afforded to "the communication, to its source and to its recipients both,'' led to the Court's acceptance of the standing of the plaintiffs to raise the constitutional issues.[2]

Virginia based its defense of the ban on drug price advertising explicitly on the Court's holding in *Valentine v. Chrestensen*, and its progeny, including *Breard v. Virginia*, as well as the cases in which the Court had distinguished *Valentine* on the basis that non-commercial speech was involved, as in *New York Times v. Sullivan, supra*. The majority reviewed the checkered career of *Valentine v. Chrestensen*, adverting to the accumulating criticism of its holding as being "casual, almost offhand" and calling it a holding that "has not survived reflection," 425 U.S. at 759 n.16. The Court concluded with a gloss on its holding in *Bigelow* that "the notion of unprotected 'commercial speech' all but passed from the scene," *id*. The Court said:

Some fragment of hope for the continuing validity of a "commercial speech" exception originally might have persisted because of the subject matter of the advertisement in *Bigelow*. We noted that in announcing the availability of legal abortions in New York, the advertisement "did more than simply propose a commercial transaction. It contained factual material of clear "public interest." *Id*. at 822. And, of course, the advertisement related to activity with which, at least in some respects, the state could not interfere. *See*, *Roe v. Wade*, 410 U.S. 113 (1973); *Doe v. Bolton*, 410 U.S. 179 (1973). . . .

Here, in contrast, the question whether there is a First Amendment exception for "commercial speech" is squarely before us. 425 U.S. 760

The majority summarized the principles, drawn from prior decisions, which define a number of senses in which speech may be said to be commercial yet, in those prior decisions, had been held to be entitled to constitutional protection, 425 U.S. at 761:

It is clear, for example, that speech does not lose its First Amendment protection because money is spent to project it, as in a paid advertisement of one form or another. *Buckley v. Valeo*, 424 U.S. 1, 35–39 (1976); *Pittsburgh Press Co. v. Human Relations Commission*, 413 U.S. at 384; *New York Times Co. v. Sullivan*, 376 U.S. at 266. Speech likewise is protected even though it is carried in a form that is "sold" for profit, *Smith v. California*, 361 U.S. 147, 150 (1959)(books); *Joseph Burstyn, Inc. v. Wilson*, 343 U.S. 495, 501 (1952)(motion pictures); *Murdock v. Pennsylvania*, 319 U.S. at 111 (religious literature), and even though it may involve a solicitation to purchase or otherwise pay or contribute money. *New York Times Co. v. Sullivan, supra*; *NAACP v. Button*, 371 U.S. 415, 429 (1963); *Jamison v. Texas*, 318 U.S. at 417; *Cantwell v. Connecticut*, 310 U.S. 296, 306–307 (1940). 425 U.S. 701

Contrary to the implication of its statement in *Bigelow* that "[t]he diverse motives, means and messages of advertising may make speech 'commercial' in widely varying degrees," 421 U.S. at 826, the Court in *Virginia Board of Pharmacy* narrowed the focus to "the message" as the touchstone for classifying speech as commercial in the relevant sense. The Court said, "If there is a kind of commercial speech that lacks all First Amendment protection, therefore, it must be distinguished by its *content*," 425 U.S. at 761 (emphasis added).

The Court in *Virginia Board of Pharmacy* attempted to define with precision which of the many possible features of the content of a commercial message were relevant for determining that the message was either entitled to no protection at all, under the doctrine of *Valentine v. Chrestensen*, or might be entitled to less than full protection of the First Amendment if the Court decided to abolish the commercial speech exception and modify it by transforming the exception into a rule recognizing a limited degree of protection. The Court said:

[T]he speech whose content deprives it of protection cannot simply be speech on a commercial subject. No one would contend that our pharmacist may be prevented from being heard on the subject of whether, in general, pharmaceutical prices should be regulated, or their advertisement forbidden. Nor can it be dispositive that a commercial advertisement is noneditorial, and merely reports a fact. Purely factual matter of public interest may claim protection. *Bigelow v. Virginia*, 421 U.S. at 822; *Thornhill v. Alabama*, 310 U.S. 88, 102 (1940). 425 U.S. at 761–762

Having disposed of these features of the commercial content of the message as constitutionally determinative, the Court singled out one other possible feature of the content of commercial messages:

Our question is whether speech which does "no more than propose a commercial trans-action," *Pittsburgh Press Co. v. Human Relations Commission*, 413 U.S. at 385, is so removed from any "exposition of ideas," *Chaplinsky v. New Hampshire*, 315 U.S. 568, 572 (1942), and from "truth, science, morality, and arts in general, in its diffusion of liberal sentiments on the administration of Government," *Roth v. United States*, 354 U.S. 476, 484 (1957), that it lacks all protection. Our answer is that it is not. 425 U.S. at 762

This passage of the majority opinion in *Virginia Board of Pharmacy* may appear decisively to have defined commercial speech as speech that "does no more than propose a commercial transaction." Whether the Court's transition from several of the irrelevant senses in which the content of a message may be said to be commercial to that single commercial feature of its content exhausts all of the possible forms that commercial speech may take and still not enjoy full protection of the First Amendment under the Court's decisions in this field remains to be seen, particularly in view of discussions in both earlier and later decisions concerning the relevance of "motives, means and messages of adver-tising."[3] The Court in this passage also began the task of sketching out a rationale for non-protection of some types of speech—that is, the process of stating the reasons why certain categories of speech which might otherwise fall within the protection of the First Amendment nonetheless are not entitled to its protection. The Court's citation of those cases in which "fighting words" and "obscenity" were held to be outside the scope of speech protected by the First Amendment, and the rationale for classifying such speech in the non-protected category, was designed to provide the touchstone for determining whether speech which "does no more than propose a commercial transaction" belongs in the same unprotected category.

The Court's analysis proceeded by breaking down the "transaction," or speech act, in terms of the parties whose interests were implicated in the prohibition of drug price advertising: (1) the advertiser, (2) the consumer, and (3) society as a whole. Although the advertiser's interest may be a "purely economic one," that does not disqualify the advertisement from constitutional protection. As the Court pointed out, precedents in the labor relations field such as *NLRB v. Gissel Packing Co.*, 395 U.S. 575, 617–618 (1969); *NLRB v. Virginia Electric & Power Co.*, 314 U.S. 469, 477 (1941); *AFL v. Swing*, 312 U.S. 321, 325–326 (1941); and *Thornhill v. Alabama*, 310 U.S. at 102, all recognize constitutional protection for speech in labor disputes between unions, employees, and company management, notwithstanding the fact that the primary interests of all the parties to such disputes are purely economic. In these cases "speech of an entirely private and economic character enjoyed the protection of the First Amendment," 425 U.S. at 763 n.17. The consumer's interest in drug price advertising and "in the free flow of commercial information" may be keen. The poor, the sick, and the aged most particularly benefit from information concerning drug prices. Society also may have an interest:

Even an individual advertisement, though entirely "commercial," may be of general public interest. The facts of decided cases furnish illustrations [citing *Bigelow* and other cases]. . . . Obviously, not all commercial messages contain the same or even a great public interest element. There are few to which such an element, however, could not be added. Our pharmacist, for example, could cast himself as a commentator on store-to-store disparities in drug prices, giving his own and those of competitors as proof. We see little point in requiring him to do so, and little difference if he does not. 425 U.S. at 764–765

In *Virginia Board of Pharmacy*, the Court went further to suggest a rationale for protection of commercial speech, in the sense of speech that "does no more than propose a commercial transaction" when it logically derived the necessity for free flow of commercial information and, therefore, for the constitutional protection of speech containing commercial information of this type, directly from the internal structure and the preconditions of the efficient and precise operation of the "free enterprise economy" itself:

Advertising . . . is nonetheless dissemination of information as to who is producing and selling what product, for what reason, and at what price. So long as we preserve a predominantly free enterprise economy, the allocation of our resources in large measure will be made through numerous private economic decisions. It is a matter of public interest that those decisions, in the aggregate, be intelligent and well-informed. To this end, the free flow of commercial information is indispensable. [Citations omitted.] And if it is indispensable to the proper allocation of resources in a free enterprise system, it is also indispensable to the formation of intelligent opinions as to how that system ought to be regulated or altered. 425 U.S. at 765

As was noted above, this rationale for the protection of commercial speech is supported directly by reference to the views of Alexander Meiklejohn with regard to the importance to citizens of the guarantee of freedom of speech and press in the realm of political speech. In other words, potential recipients, as citizens in a democratic government who must make intelligent choices of their political leaders and knowing and intelligent choices concerning alternative public policies, must have full access to all sources of information, opinion, and viewpoint or risk that, through limited exposure to facts and opinion, the wrong public judgment will be made. Indeed in footnote 19 of the *Virginia Board of Pharmacy* decision the Court referred to Meiklejohn's book, *Free Speech and Its Relation to Self-Government* (1948).

The Court also examined the justification proposed by Virginia for the restriction, but found it insufficient. Virginia argued that drug price advertising would reduce pharmacists to little more than retailers and would discourage the degree of professionalism which it was Virginia's prerogative to attempt to promote. The Court observed, however, that the professionalism of pharmacists was adequately preserved by other portions of the law closely regulating the practice of pharmacists, 425 U.S. at 768. The state's interest was insufficiently advanced by the statute, because "[t]he state's protectiveness of its citizens rests in large measure on the advantages of their being kept in ignorance," 425 U.S. at 769:

The advertising ban does not directly affect professional standards one way or the other. *It affects them only through the reactions it is assumed people will have to the free flow of drug price information. . . .*

It appears to be feared that if the pharmacist who wishes to provide low cost, and assertedly low quality, services is permitted to advertise, he will be taken up on his offer by too many unwitting customers. They will choose the low-cost, low-quality service and drive the "professional" pharmacist out of business. They will respond only to costly and excessive advertising, and end up paying the price. . . . All this is not in their best interests, and all this can be avoided if they are not permitted to know who is charging what.

There is, of course, an alternative to this highly paternalistic approach. That alternative is to assume that this information is not in itself harmful, that people will perceive their own best interests if only they are well enough informed, and that the best means to that end is to open the channels of communication rather than to close them. . . . But the choice among these alternative approaches is not ours to make or the Virginia General Assembly's. It is precisely this kind of choice, between dangers of suppressing information, and the dangers of its misuse if it is freely available, that the First Amendment makes for us. Virginia is free to require whatever professional standards it wishes of its pharmacists, it may subsidize them or protect them from competition in other ways. *Cf. Parker v. Brown*, 317 U.S. 341 (1943). But it may not do so by keeping the public in ignorance of the entirely lawful terms that competing pharmacists are offering. In this sense, the justifications Virginia has offered for suppressing the flow of prescription drug price information, far from persuading us that the flow is not protected by the First Amendment, have reinforced our view that it is. We so hold. 425 U.S. at 769–770 (emphasis added)

The Court's attack in *Virginia Board of Pharmacy* on the "highly paternalistic," indirect means through which, by suppression of drug price advertising, Virginia sought to promote its otherwise legitimate interest in advancing the professionalism of pharmacists in Virginia and the health, safety, and welfare of Virginia residents centered primarily on (1) the nature or directness of the relationship between the governmental interest and the form of the legislation selected as the instrument to advance that interest, and (2) an evolving theory concerning the general impermissibility of certain paternalistic means of advancing governmental interests, in particular the means of advancing otherwise legitimate governmental interests by "keeping the public in ignorance of the entirely lawful terms" of a proposed commercial transaction. These are themes to which the Court returned in its landmark decision in *Central Hudson Gas & Electric Corp. v. Public Service Commission*, 447 U.S. 557 (1980), which is discussed later in this chapter.

Having held that commercial speech "is protected," the Court cautioned that a wide field nonetheless remained for state regulation of commercial speech: (1) regulation of the "time, place and manner" of commercial speech; (2) prohibition or regulation of "false and misleading" commercial speech; (3) prohibition of commercial speech in which "the transactions proposed in the forbidden advertisements are themselves illegal," and (4) regulation of commercial speech over the electronic media, which involves "special problems" that, in turn, need special rules.

Having held that commercial speech is entitled to constitutional protection, the *Virginia Board of Pharmacy* majority logically was forced to address the question of the degree of protection to which commercial speech was entitled— whether the same degree, or a lesser degree than for political speech—and, if less protection, the rationale for providing a lesser degree of protection. This the Court attempted to answer in the vitally important footnote 24 of its opinion as follows, in which the Court pointed to "*common sense differences* between speech that does 'no more than propose a commercial transaction' and other varieties":

In concluding that commercial speech enjoys First Amendment protection, we have not held that it is wholly undifferentiable from other forms. There are common sense differences between speech that does "no more than propose a commercial transaction," *Pittsburgh Press Co. v. Human Relations Commission*, 413 U.S., at 385, and other varieties. Even if the differences do not justify the conclusion that commercial speech is valueless, and thus subject to complete suppression by the State, they nonetheless suggest that a different degree of protection is necessary to insure that the flow of truthful and legitimate commercial information is unimpaired. The truth of commercial speech, for example, may be more easily verifiable by its disseminator than, let us say, news reporting or political commentary, in that ordinarily the advertiser seeks to disseminate information about a specific product or service that he himself provides and presumably knows more about than anyone else. Also, commercial speech may be more durable than other kinds. Since advertising is the sine qua non of commercial profits, there is little likelihood of its being chilled by proper regulation and foregone entirely.

Attributes such as these, the greater objectivity and hardiness of commercial speech, may make it less necessary to tolerate inaccurate statements for fear of silencing the speaker. *Compare New York Times Co. v. Sullivan*, 376 U.S. 254 (1964), with *Dun & Bradstreet, Inc. v. Grove*, 404 U.S. 898 (1971). They may also make it appropriate to require that a commercial message appear in such a form, or include such additional information, warnings, and disclaimers, as are necessary to prevent its being deceptive. *Compare Miami Herald Publishing Co. v. Tornillo*, 418 U.S. 241 (1974), with *Banzhaf v. FCC*, 132 U.S. App. D.C. 14, 405 F.2d 1082 (1968), *cert. denied* sub nom. *Tobacco Institute, Inc. v. FCC*, 396 U.S. 842 (1969). *Cf. United States v. 95 Barrels of Vinegar*, 265 U.S. 438, 443 (1924) ("It is not difficult to choose statements, designs and devices which will not deceive"). They may also make inapplicable the prohibition against prior restraints. *Compare New York Times Co. v. United States*, 403 U.S. 713 (1971), with *Donaldson v. Read Magazine*, 333 U.S. 178, 189–191 (1948); *FTC v. Standard Education Society*, 302 U.S. 112 (1937); *E.F. Drew & Co. v. FTC*, 235 F.2d 735, 739–740 (2d Cir. 1956), *cert. denied*, 352 U.S. 969 (1957). 425 U.S. at 771–772 n.24 (emphasis added)

Thus, the Court in this important footnote pointed to (1) ease of verification or "greater objectivity" and (2) the greater durability or hardiness of commercial speech, as reasons that "may" make it less necessary to tolerate inaccurate statements.

The Court's sweeping endorsement of the Meiklejohn conception of the First Amendment—taking the theory, which he applied only to political speech, to a point well beyond Meiklejohn's position—has many broad implications. The Court, in footnote 24, was careful, however, to preserve the jurisdiction of the Federal Trade Commission to regulate false and deceptive advertising, 425 U.S. at 771 n.24. The Court also reiterated the principle of *Pittsburgh Press* which preserves the state's power to prohibit advertising of illegal transactions, 425 U.S. at 772. This conception of the First Amendment as governed by the interests of potential recipients of speech, once accepted, however, is not easily contained. The point was forcefully made by Justice Rehnquist in *Bates v. State Bar of Arizona*, 433 U.S. 350 (1977). The principles laid down by *Virginia State Board of Pharmacy* were relied on by the Court in *Bates*, decided the following year, in striking down an Arizona Supreme Court disciplinary regulation prohibiting advertising by attorneys.

LINMARK ASSOCIATES v. WILLINGBORO

These evolving principles were applied again in *Linmark Associates, Inc. v. Willingboro*, 431 U.S. 85 (1977), which presented the question of the constitutionality of a Willingboro, New Jersey, ordinance prohibiting the posting of truthful ''For Sale'' or ''Sold'' signs on residential properties. The municipality claimed that it had enacted the ordinance to stem what it perceived as the flight of white homeowners from a racially integrated community, allegedly evidenced by ''panic selling'' by the white population. There was evidence that Willingboro is to a large extent a transient community, partly because of its proximity to the Army base at Fort Dix. The district court noted that there was no evidence that whites were leaving Willingboro *en masse* as ''For Sale'' signs appeared but merely an indication that its residents were concerned that there might be a large influx of minority groups moving into the town with the result being a reduction in property values.

The Supreme Court invalidated the ordinance on First Amendment grounds. Writing for a unanimous Court, Justice Marshall chose as his starting point the *Bigelow* and *Virginia Board of Pharmacy* decisions ''in which this Court has eroded the 'commercial speech' exception to the First Amendment.'' Justice Marshall extracted from *Bigelow* the emerging balancing test in ''assessing the First Amendment interest at stake and weighing it against the public interest allegedly served by the regulation,'' 431 U.S. at 91.

Willingboro defended its ordinance on several grounds, all ultimately unsuccessful. Characterizing the ordinance as a ''time, place and manner'' regulation, Willingboro argued that the ordinance restricted only one method of communicating, leaving many other alternatives open. Justice Marshall rejected this argument for two reasons. The ordinance was not a true regulation of the ''place'' of speech, because Willingboro did not prohibit use of other types of signs on residential property. The ordinance was tantamount to a direct governmental regulation of the content of signs. Additionally, the Court doubted that the ordinance could be justified as a valid ''time, place and manner'' regulation, because the alternatives to advertising by residential ''For Sale'' signs were arguably less effective, more costly, and less likely to reach persons not deliberately seeking sales information. The signs were not overly intrusive on the privacy of others. As in *Bigelow*, the regulation was directly aimed at the *content* of the message because of the state's desire to prevent a certain effect that might result from a free flow of information on the subject matter of the advertising: ''Willingboro has proscribed particular types of signs based on their content because it fears their 'primary' effect—that they will cause those receiving it to act upon it,'' 431 U.S. at 94.

The Court was willing to assume that Willingboro's purpose in enacting its ban on residential ''For Sale'' signs was to promote stable, racially integrated housing, but found *Virginia Board of Pharmacy* indistinguishable. In *Virginia Pharmacy Board*, too, the Court had acknowledged Virginia's legitimate interest in maintaining professionalism on the part of pharmacists but held that the law was not necessary to achieve that objective and that Virginia could not pursue that legitimate purpose by restricting the free flow of truthful information. The Willingboro ordinance suffered from the same defects. The evidence of need for the ordinance to assure that Willingboro remained an integrated community was weak. There was no substantial incidence of panic selling, and the Court therefore left it open whether an ordinance such as Willingboro's might be sustained under different circumstances, 431 U.S. at 95 n.9.

Linmark, like *Virginia Board of Pharmacy*, rests on the invalidity of the ordinance as a restriction on the right of residents to receive certain information, rather than on the right of the realty company, which challenged the ordinance. The Court rejected the "highly paternalistic approach" on which such restriction was based.

Justice Marshall expressly left open two related issues in his *Linmark* opinion. He wrote, "Laws dealing with false or misleading signs, and laws requiring such signs to 'appear in such form, or include such additional information as is necessary to prevent their being deceptive' . . . would raise very different constitutional questions," 431 U.S. at 97.

FIRST NATIONAL BANK OF BOSTON v. BELLOTTI: CORPORATE POLITICAL SPEECH AND MEIKLEJOHN REVISITED

First National Bank of Boston v. Bellotti, 435 U.S. 765 (1978), is the end of the beginning of development of a theory of First Amendment protection for corporate speech. In that case, a number of banks and corporations wished to spend corporate funds to publicize their views opposing a referendum proposal in a Massachusetts election to amend the Massachusetts Constitution to enact a graduated personal income tax. A Massachusetts criminal statute prohibited specified business corporations from making contributions or expenditures "for the purpose of . . . influencing or affecting the vote on any question submitted to the voters, other than those questions which materially affect any of the property, business or assets of the corporation." The statute also stated, "No question submitted to the voters solely concerning the taxation of the income, property, or transactions of individuals shall be deemed materially to affect the property, business or assets of the corporation." The corporations brought suit in Massachusetts state court seeking a declaration that the statute was unconstitutional. The Massachusetts Supreme Court framed the question in terms of the rights of corporations, *i.e.*, "whether business corporations, such as appellants, have First Amendment rights co-extensive with those of natural persons or associations of natural persons." Since the due process clause of the Fourteenth Amendment, through which the First Amendment is applicable to the states, speaks in terms of "protection of persons," the Massachusetts court looked to the limitation of the due process clause to protection of persons from deprivation of their property without due process of law. The court held that while property interests of corporations are protected by the due process clause, a corporation's "right of speech and expression" is protected "only when a general political issue materially affects a corporation's business property or assets.'' The Massachusetts court upheld the statute.

By April 1978, when *Bellotti* was decided by the Supreme Court, the result of the appeal was almost inevitable. The Supreme Court of the United States simply refused to address the question as framed by the Massachusetts Supreme Judicial Court, without considering the interests of citizens who might desire to receive the viewpoint of banks and corporations on the ballot issue. The Court said:

We believe that the [Massachusetts] Court posed the wrong question. The Constitution often protects interests broader than those of the party seeking their vindication. The First Amendment, in particular, serves significant societal interests. The proper question is not whether corporations ''have'' First Amendment rights and, if so, whether they are co-extensive with those of natural persons. Instead, the question must be whether Section 8 abridges expression that the First Amendment was meant to protect. 435 U.S. at 776

If, as Meiklejohn suggested, *New York Times v. Sullivan* was an ''occasion for dancing in the streets,'' *Bellotti* was an occasion for dancing not only in the streets but in the corporate boardrooms as well. As the logical application of the principles brought together in *Virginia Board of Pharmacy*, *Bellotti* represents the final and complete triumph for the modified Meiklejohnian conception of the First Amendment. In *Bellotti*, the Court derived constitutional protection for speech on governmental affairs directly from the nature of the speech itself and the interest of citizens in receiving the opinions and viewpoints. Since the speech at issue related to governmental affairs, no question of the contours of the commercial speech doctrine was presented. The Court rejected in resounding terms the argument that corporations, as creatures of state law, have only those rights granted them by the states, 435 U.S. at 778 n.14, and rejected, as well, the entire analysis presumed by that argument.

The Court's opinion focused on the nature of the speech itself, rather than on the source of the speech. Having found the proposed speech of a type which falls within the ''core concern'' of the First Amendment, the Court reiterated the various tests applicable to scrutiny of statutes affecting First Amendment rights:

1. They must be ''closely drawn to avoid unnecessary abridgement.''

2. The ''state may prevail only upon showing a subordinating interest which is compelling.''

3. The ''burden is on the government to show the existence of such an interest.''

The Massachusetts statute failed to pass muster under the exacting standards of normal First Amendment scrutiny. The statute was both overinclusive and underinclusive in terms of its purported purposes, and the governmental interest in purifying referenda from the dominant influence of corporations was not sufficiently compelling to override the needs of citizens to receive the corporate viewpoint. The decision provoked a dissenting opinion by Justice White, expressing the views of three justices. It is surprising to note that it was joined in by Justice Brennan—the author of one of the Court's key opinions on the Federal Election Campaign Act in *Pipefitters Local No. 562 v. United States*, 407 U.S. 385 (1972), and a dominant figure in the Warren Court's decisions in the First Amendment area—and by Justice Marshall, whose own contributions to the development of the First Amendment have been substantial and progressive.

Dealing as it does with corporate political speech, *Bellotti* is considered in greater detail in Part II. Its doctrinal underpinnings, however, are linked to those of the commercial speech cases because of the prominence that the rights of hearers play in the constitutional analysis in both areas of First Amendment jurisprudence.

THE ATTORNEY ADVERTISING AND CLIENT SOLICITATION CASES: *BATES, OHRALIK,* AND *PRIMUS*

Three cases involving commercial advertising and solicitation by lawyers, *Bates v. State Bar of Arizona*, 433 U.S. 350 (1977), *Ohralik v. Ohio State Bar Association*, 436 U.S. 447 (1978), and *In Re Primus*, 436 U.S. 412 (1978), led to further clarification of the scope of the commercial speech doctrine in 1977 and 1978.

In *Bates*, the appellants' attorneys, licensed to practice in Arizona, were charged in a disciplinary proceeding with advertising their services in violation of the Arizona Supreme Court's disciplinary rules for attorneys. Bates and others had placed a newspaper advertisement for their legal clinic, stating that they were offering "legal service at reasonable prices," and listed their fees. Bates defended his advertising on the ground that the state Supreme Court's disciplinary rule prohibiting advertising had the purpose and effect of eliminating price competition among lawyers, *i.e.*, was tantamount to government-sponsored price-fixing by lawyers. The appellants argued that the practice violated sections 1 and 2 of the Sherman Act, 15 U.S.C. §§1 and 2. The Court rejected this argument, holding that the rule was sufficiently the product of "state action," through the Arizona Supreme Court, and that the restraint was "compelled by direction of the State acting as a sovereign" and therefore was immune from the Federal antitrust laws under the Court's prior decision in *Parker v. Brown*, 317 U.S. 341 (1943). As a direct governmental restraint on commercial speech by lawyers, however, the Arizona Supreme Court's disciplinary rule violated the First Amendment, as the Court had interpreted it in *Virginia Board of Pharmacy*. The Court first reviewed several fundamental rules:

1. "[O]ur cases long have protected speech even though it is in the form of a paid advertisement, *Buckley v. Valeo*, 424 U.S. 1 (1976); *New York Times Co. v. Sullivan*, 376 U.S. 254 (1964)."

    (a) "in a form that is sold for profit, *Smith v. California*, 361 U.S. 147 (1959); *Murdock v. Pennsylvania*, 319 U.S. 105 (1943)."

(b) "or in the form of a solicitation to pay or contribute money, *New York Times Co. v. Sullivan, supra; Cantwell v. Connecticut*, 310 U.S. 296 (1940)."

If commercial speech is to be distinguished, the Court said, it "must be distinguished by its content," 433 U.S. at 363, *i.e.*, "because it proposed a mundane commercial transaction."

2. "Even though the speaker's interest is largely economic, the Court has protected such speech in certain contexts. *See, e.g.*, *NLRB v. Gissel Packing Co.*, 395 U.S. 575 (1969); *Thornhill v. Alabama*, 310 U.S. 88 (1940)." 433 U.S. 364

The Court appears once again to have relied primarily on the interest of potential recipients of the information. Having held in *Virginia Board of Pharmacy* that consumers had a legitimate and protectible interest in receiving price information concerning drugs, the Court was committed to holding that consumers' interest in receiving information concerning the prices of legal services also rose to constitutional dimension. "The listener's interest is substantial: The consumers' concern for the free flow of commercial speech often may be far keener than his concern for urgent political dialogue. Moreover, significant societal interests are served by such speech. Advertising, though entirely commercial, may often carry information of import to significant issues of the day, *see Bigelow v. Virginia*, 421 U.S. 809 (1975)."

Reviewing its decision in *Virginia Board of Pharmacy*, the Court also premised its holding on one of the fundamental precepts of the conservative "law and economics" movement in contemporary jurisprudence, the faith in the optimally allocative functions of the market system: "[C]ommercial speech seems to inform the public of the availability, nature, and prices of products and services, and thus, performs an indispensable role in the allocation of resources in a free enterprise system. *See FTC v. Proctor & Gamble Co.*, 386 U.S. 568, 603–604 (1967)(Harlan, J., concurring). In short, such speech serves individual and societal interests in assuring informed and reliable decision making," 425 U.S. at 761–765.

Having thus determined that attorney price advertising, like price advertising of drugs, enjoyed some constitutional protection as commercial speech, the Court proceeded to assess the significance of the competing Arizona public policy that the disciplinary rule allegedly was designed to serve, 433 U.S. 364. On this score, the Court agreed that encouraging professionalism of attorneys and maintaining the confidence of clients that attorneys are not motivated solely by their own commercial self-interest were legitimate concerns. The Court, however, found "the postulated connection between advertising and the erosion of true professionalism to be severely strained," 433 U.S. at 368.

The Court's analysis, then, focused initially on whether the speech was of a kind the First Amendment protected at all. Having held that it was, the Court examined the substantiality of the governmental interests that were advanced by Arizona to justify the restrictions. Granting that Arizona's interests were not insubstantial, the Court then focused attention on the question whether the specific form of regulation adopted by the disciplinary rule was well designed to advance the state's legitimate interest, *i.e.*, whether it was likely that the regulation actually did promote that interest to the degree that it could be expected to.

The court buttressed its conclusion that the regulation did not well serve the state's interest with the observation that the practice of refraining from advertising historically was no more than a tenet of correct "etiquette" among lawyers. The Court also dismissed the state's suggestion that professional advertising is inherently misleading because legal services are so individualized that they defy rational comparison in terms of price, that the consumer of legal services is unable to determine what legal services may be needed, or because attorneys would advertise irrelevant factors and would fail to show the relevant factor of skill, 433 U.S. at 372.

The Court rejected each of the proposed justifications of the regulation: (1) the alleged adverse effect on professionalism, (2) the inherently misleading nature of attorney advertising, (3) the alleged adverse effect on the administration of justice, (4) the undesirable economic effects of advertising, (5) the alleged adverse effect of advertising on the quality of legal services, and (6) the difficulties of enforcement.

The Court in *Bates* acknowledged its prior decisions applying the overbreadth doctrine, *i.e.*, the doctrine that permits a litigant to challenge an overly broad statute without the requirement that the litigant demonstrate that his specific conduct was protected. The Court held, however, that "the justification for the application of overbreadth analysis applies weakly, if at all, in the ordinary commercial context," 433 U.S. at 380. The Court wrote: "Since advertising is linked to commercial well-being, it seems unlikely that such speech is particularly susceptible to being crushed by overbroad regulation," *id*. Although that strong implication exists, the Court did not actually hold in *Bates* that overbreadth analysis could never be relevant in cases challenging regulation of commercial speech. The Court was content to "decline to apply it to professional advertising, a context where it is not necessary to further its intended objective," 433 U.S. at 381.

The Court rejected three contentions that the appellants' advertising was misleading and concluded by holding that the disciplinary rule was unconstitutional as applied and held that "advertising by attorneys may not be subjected to blanket suppression," *id*. at 383. In dictum, the Court was careful enough to limit its holding with several explicit provisos:

1. "Advertising that is false, deceptive or misleading . . . is subject to restraint."
2. "Restraints on in-person solicitation" might be justifiable, *id*. at 384.
3. "[T]here may be reasonable restrictions on the time, place and manner of advertising," *id*.

4. "Advertising concerning transactions that are themselves illegal obviously may be suppressed."

5. "[T]he special problem of advertising on the electronic broadcast media will warrant special consideration," *id*. 384.

The First Amendment issues in *Bates* sharply divided the Court in a 5 to 4 decision. Justice Blackmun, the author of the Court's *Virginia Board of Pharmacy* opinion, again wrote the opinion of the Court, in which Justices Brennan, White, Marshall, and Stevens joined. Justice Powell, who had concurred in *Virginia Board of Pharmacy*, distinguished legal services from drugs on the ground of "the vastly increased potential for deception and the enhanced difficulty of effective regulation in the public interest," *id*. at 391. Justice Powell rejected the assumption that any legal services could be fairly described as "routine" and therefore sufficiently discrete and identifiable to warrant advertising the set fees for such services.

In *Ohralik*, which was decided the next year, the Court dealt with the distinct but related question of in-person solicitation of potential clients by lawyers, as contrasted with the newspaper advertisement involved in *Bates*. The facts were aggravated, and the *Ohralik* case presented the perfect vehicle for drawing a sharp distinction between commercial in-person solicitation and published commercial advertising. Ohralik, an Ohio lawyer, paid an uninvited visit in the hospital to an 18–year-old, who had been involved in an automobile accident, and secured her signature on a written contingent fee agreement to represent her in making a claim against the driver of the other vehicle. Ohralik also entered into an oral contingent agreement with the driver's 18–year-old female passenger at her home on the day she was released from the hospital. Both accident victims later discharged him, but Ohralik succeeded in obtaining a share of the driver's insurance recovery in settlement of his lawsuit against her for breach of the contingent fee contract.

On the complaint of the two young women, the Disciplinary Board of the Ohio Supreme Court found that Ohralik had solicited the women in violation of certain disciplinary rules. Over Ohralik's First Amendment objection, the Ohio Supreme Court accepted the board's findings and indefinitely suspended Ohralik from the practice of law in Ohio.

Ohralik presented issues involving mixed speech and conduct. The question before the Court was the applicability of its prior decision in *Bates*, which had been handed down after the conclusion of the proceedings in the Ohio Supreme Court. The Court distinguished its holding in *Bates* and upheld the disciplinary action taken by the Ohio Supreme Court, 436 U.S. 454. The Court found that "[t]he entitlement of in-person solicitation of clients to the protection of the First Amendment differs from that of the kind of advertising approved in *Bates*, as does the strength of the State's countervailing interest in prohibition," 436 U.S. at 455.

The Court's decision in *Ohralik* is an important one because it clarified several new principles of the commercial speech doctrine and reaffirmed several principles that had been applied in earlier decisions. The Court reiterated that commercial speech is not "wholly indifferentiable from other forms" and that the "common sense" differences mentioned in footnote 24 of *Virginia Board of Pharmacy* could require results different from decisions regarding purely political speech, 436 U.S. at 455. To ignore these distinctions, the Court said, "could invite dilution simply by a leveling process, of the force of the Amendment's guarantee with respect to the latter kind of speech," *id*. The Court's announced solution was to afford "commercial speech a limited measure of protection, commensurate with its subordinate position in the scale of First Amendment values, while allowing modes of regulation that might be impermissible in the realm of non-commercial expression," *id*.

Second, and more important, the Court's decision in *Ohralik* began to develop rules for untangling speech and conduct for First Amendment purposes in the commercial speech field. Thus, relying on its decision in *Giboney v. Empire Storage & Ice Co.*, 336 U.S. 490, 502 (1949), the Court wrote:

[I]t has never been deemed an abridgement of freedom of speech or press to make a course of conduct illegal merely because the conduct was in part initiated, evidenced, or carried out by means of language, either spoken, written or printed. *Giboney v. Empire Storage & Ice Co.*, 336 U.S. 490 (1949). Numerous examples could be cited of communications that are regulated without offending the First Amendment, such as the exchange of information about securities, *SEC v. Texas Gulf Sulphur Co.*, 401 F.2d 833 (2nd Cir. 1968), *cert. denied*, 394 U.S. 976 (1969), corporate proxy statement, *Mills v. Electric Auto-Lite Co.*, 396 U.S. 375 (1970), the exchange of price and production information among competitors, *American Column & Lumber Co. v. United States*, 257 U.S. 377 (1921), and employers' threats of retaliation for the labor activities of employees, *NLRB v. Gissel Packing Co.*, 395 U.S. 575 (1969). See *Paris Adult Theatre I v. Slaton*, 413 U.S. 49, 61–62 (1973). Each of these examples illustrates that the State does not lose its power to regulate commercial activity deemed harmful to the public whenever speech is a component of that activity. Neither *Virginia Pharmacy Board* nor *Bates* purported to cast doubt on the permissibility of these kinds of commercial regulation. 436 U.S. at 456

Against this analytical backdrop, the Court concluded that "[i]n-person solicitation by a lawyer of remunerative employment is a business transaction in which speech is an essential but subordinate component," *id*. at 457. The significance of this analytical step, the Court said, is that "it lowers the level of appropriate judicial scrutiny," *id*.

Because of the central importance of the *Giboney* doctrine relating to the constitutional status of "a course of conduct" which is, in part, "initiated, evidenced or carried out by means of language either spoken, written or printed"— a topic to which a portion of chapter 5 is devoted—it is worthwhile to pay special attention to the Court's first efforts to analyze this problem in *Ohralik*. With the exception of *Paris Adult Theatre I*, the Court's citations in this passage are to older decisions which in some cases antedate the modern era in First Amendment jurisprudence. Commercial speech very often does not assume the simple form of paid newspaper advertising and part of what might be called a "course of conduct." For example, it may fairly be asked whether the door-to-door solicitation in the Jehovah's Witness cases involves speech which was only a constituent element of a "course of conduct" that in reality transcended the simple speech itself. Does door-to-door distribution of advertising material involve speech that is part of a "course of conduct"? In a sense, does not all "in-person solicitation" involve speech only as a part of a "course of conduct"? Since the classification of speech as being only a constituent element of a course of conduct presumably carries with it a significant reduction in the level of judicial scrutiny, the criteria for determining when it can appropriately be said that speech is part of a course of conduct and when the speech is, in a relevant sense, independent of some other contemporaneous course of conduct are important questions. Based on the First Amendment decisions to date, the concept of being a part of a course of conduct may need to be further elaborated and further defined by some neutral principles. A number of problems arise in attempting to formulate such principles in satisfactory fashion. Additionally, how is the "lower" level of judicial scrutiny, to which such intermixed speech is entitled, to be defined? Does the applicability of this doctrine of reduced judicial scrutiny depend on whether the speech element of the course of conduct is subordinate, and, if so, what criteria determine when the speech element is subordinate and when it is predominant? What relation, if any, is there between this doctrine and the standard of constitutional review which the Court devised in cases such as *United States v. O'Brien*, 391 U.S. 367 (1968), for determining the level of review or the degree of constitutional protection appropriate to "speech plus conduct"?

The Court in *Ohralik* identified several features of the in-person solicitation which distinguish it from attorney newspaper advertising which the Court addressed in *Bates*:

1. The immediacy of a particular communication and the imminence of harm are factors that have made certain communications less protected than others. Compare *Cohen v. California*, 403 U.S. 15 (1971), with *Chaplinsky v. New Hampshire*, 315 U.S. 568 (1942); see *Brandenberg v. Ohio*, 395 U.S. 444 (1969); *Schenck v. United States*, 249 U.S. 47 (1919). 436 U.S. at 457 n.13

2. Unlike a public advertisement, which simply provides information and leaves the recipient free to act upon it or not, in-person solicitation may exert pressure and often demands an immediate response, without providing an opportunity for comparison or reflection. 436 U.S. at 457

3. In-person solicitation is as likely as not to discourage persons needing counsel from engaging in a critical comparison of the "availability, nature and prices" of legal services, *cf. Bates*, 433 U.S. at 364, it actually may disserve the individual and societal interest, identified in *Bates*, in facilitating "informed and reliable decision making." 436 U.S. at 457–458

This passage warrants close scrutiny because of its broader implications in other commercial speech cases that involve some form of in-person solicitation. First, the Court placed great value on avoiding pressure by sales solicitors, presumably by the simple expediency of requesting the solicitor to leave. Moreover, pressure tactics may prove to be counterproductive simply because the recipient may be offended. If pressure from sales personnel is a harm, it is arguably a self-healing harm. Second, the Court exhibited little faith in the independence of the recipient in the exercise of commercial choice. Third, the Court's analysis elevates to the level of constitutional dimension the process of "critical comparison of availability, nature and prices" of consumer products and services. It is interesting to conjecture whether the case would have produced the same result if the parties solicited were not 18–year–olds or if the in-person sales solicitation was made, for example, to a seasoned buyer in the purchasing department of a major industrial corporation, *i.e.*, an individual largely impervious to the pressure of a sales solicitation.

Citing *NAACP v. Button*, 371 U.S. 415, 439–443 (1963), the Court held that a "lawyer's procurement of remunerative employment is a subject only marginally affected with First Amendment concerns." The Court said that this activity "[f]alls within the state's proper sphere of economic and professional regulation. While entitled to some constitutional protection, appellant's conduct is subject to regulation in furtherance of important state interests," 436 U.S. at 459. The Court did not go so far as to hold that Ohralik's conduct was entitled to no constitutional protection simply because it was intermixed with conduct elements that were not protected or because it was part of a course of conduct that produced anti-social consequences. The Court's opinion, however, failed to define what degree of constitutional protection Ohralik's conduct would enjoy. There is an important difference between saying that speech or expressive conduct loses its immunity when it is a constituent element of an otherwise unlawful course of conduct and saying that speech loses only some of its constitutional protection (or will be valued less highly for balancing purposes) when it is a constituent element of such a course of conduct. In the former case, any legitimate state interest, however insubstantial, would presumably be sufficient to justify its suppression. In the latter case, it is conceivable that on balance the value of the speech might still outweigh a relatively less substantial governmental purpose.

The second branch of the Court's analysis in *Ohralik* involved assessing the state's interest in regulating Ohralik's conduct and expression. The Court recognized the substantiality of the state's interest in regulating lawyers as officers of the court. Although the ban on in-person solicitation, like the ban on lawyer advertising, originated "as a rule of professional etiquette," the Court noted the state's asserted interest in reducing "the likelihood of overreaching and the exertion of undue influence on lay persons," in protecting "the privacy of individuals" and in avoiding "situations where the lawyer's exercise of judgment on behalf of the client will be clouded by his own pecuniary self-interest," *id* at 461. The Court assumed these interests were "legitimate" and "indeed 'compelling.' " Ohralik conceded this point. Whether the Court's decision required that the state's interest be compelling or only legitimate and substantial is unclear. The Court agreed "that protection of the public from these aspects of solicitation is a legitimate and important state interest" but did not elaborate on the asserted state interest supporting regulation of attorney in-person solicitation.

The Court touched on the applicability of the First Amendment overbreadth doctrine to commercial speech, a subject also mentioned in *Bates*. The Court rejected Ohralik's contention that the disciplinary rule, as "indiscriminately applied" to him, was unconstitutional because none of the evils of "fraud, undue influence, intimidation, overreaching or other forms of 'vexatious conduct' " were involved in his in-person solicitation. The Court pointed out that Ohralik's contention was simply that the disciplinary rule was unconstitutional as applied to him, not that the rule was overbroad. Had Ohralik framed his argument as an overbreadth challenge, he would have been confronted with the Court's statement in *Bates*, repeated in *Ohralik*, *id*. at 462 n.20, that "the justification for the application of overbreadth analysis *applies weakly, if at all, in the ordinary commercial context*," 433 U.S. at 380 (emphasis added). The *Ohralik* Court went on to explain that "[c]ommercial speech is not as likely to be deterred as non-commercial speech, and therefore does not require the added protection afforded by the overbreadth approach," *id*. at n.20. The question of the applicability of the overbreadth doctrine in commercial speech is dealt with in chapter 5.

The Court's analysis of the record evidence, which was necessitated by Ohralik's "as applied" challenge to the constitutionality of the disciplinary rule, perhaps points up another difference between an "as applied" challenge in commercial speech in contrast with the same kind of challenge in other First Amendment contexts. The Court held that evidence of "actual harm" to the solicited individual from overreaching or undue influence need not be presented and held that it was sufficient if the state could show that conduct such as Ohralik's *"more often than not will be injurious to the person solicited,"* *id*. at 466 (emphasis added). In other First Amendment contexts, legislative restrictions on expression ordinarily do not enjoy a presumption of constitutionality and must be narrowly drawn to meet the precise evil to be prevented, *Thomas v. Collins*, 323 U.S. 516, 530 (1945); *Thornhill v. Alabama*, 310 U.S. 88, 95 (1940); *Schneider v. State*, 308 U.S. 147, 161 (1939). The Court has said: "Broad prophylactic rules in the area of free expression are suspect. . . . Precision of regulation must be the touchstone," *NAACP v. Button*, 371 U.S. 415, 438 (1963); *United States v. Robel*, 389 U.S. 258, 265 (1967). In *Ohralik*, however, by contrast, the Court upheld restrictions on commercial speech in the form of disciplinary rules prohibiting in-person solicitation which the Court specifically described as *"prophylactic measures* whose objective is the prevention of harm before it occurs," 436 U.S. at 464 (emphasis added). Although broad prophylactic rules are clearly impermissible in political speech, *Ohralik* suggests that they will be tolerated in commercial speech.

In *Ohralik*, the Court also began to articulate its theory of why in-person solicitation deserves special treatment. True, there are special features of in-person solicitation by lawyers—the issue involved in *Ohralik*. Lawyers are "trained in the art of persuasion" and their "marketing" efforts present special dangers of "overreaching," *id*. at 465. Persons in need of legal services may be emotionally distressed about legal or personal problems and may therefore be "more vulnerable to influence." Laymen are almost by definition unsophisticated in legal matters and are not knowledgeable about what legal services they may require or for what contractual arrangements using lawyers may be advantageous or possible.

The Court, however, generalized its analysis of in-person solicitation with the observation that "[t]he detrimental aspects of face-to-face selling even of ordinary consumer products have been recognized and addressed by the Federal Trade Commission," *id*. at 464. The Federal Trade Commission has observed that "[t]he door-to-door selling technique strips from the consumer one of the fundamentals in his role as an informed purchaser, the decision as to when, where and how he will present himself to the marketplace," 37 Fed. Reg. 22934, 22929 n.4; 436 U.S. at 464 n.23. To this can be added the Court's observations about the emotional vulnerability of the solicited consumer, the intrusiveness of in-person solicitation, its inherent character as an invasion of privacy, the effects on the individual of the sales techniques of persons "trained in the art of persuasion," the individual's relative ignorance concerning the product or service, the increased vulnerability of the individual to fraud, and the inceased vulnerability to overreaching of the individual who is separated from friends or family and without the advantage, perhaps, of prior consultation with others more knowledgeable about the ways of commerce. These specific features of in-person solicitation might, to a greater or lesser degree, characterize every direct commercial transaction.

One further comment concerning *Ohralik* is appropriate. In several of the "captive audience" cases, the Court has examined the intrusive character and unavoidable nature of particular modes of expression as a factor of possible significance to constitutional analysis, *Cohen v. California*, 403 U.S. at 21 (1971)(offensive epithet critical of the draft on the back of a jacket worn in a courtroom); *Erznoznik v. Jacksonville*, 422 U.S. 205, 211 (1975)(visibility from public streets of sexually explicit scenes on drive-in theatre screen); *Lehman v. Shaker Heights*, 418 U.S. 298, 320 (1974)(transit car political advertising placards); *Consolidated Edison Co. v. Public Service Commission*, 447 U.S. 530, 541–543 (1980)(pro-nuclear power message included with bill in utility monthly billing envelope). In situations where a captive audience truly cannot avoid objectionable speech, the Court has occasionally suggested that legislative restriction may be justifiable, even though actual examples of this are rare and controversial, *see*, *Lehman v. Shaker Heights*, *supra*. Where, on the other hand, customers or potential recipients of information may "effectively avoid bombardment of their sensibilities simply by averting their eyes," the Court has

rejected this reason for restrictions on potentially intrusive, offensive, or unwanted speech, *Cohen v. California, supra; Consolidated Edison Co. v. Public
Service Commission, supra.* Particularly anxious to support its distinction between the in-person solicitation in *Ohralik* and the newspaper advertisement in
Bates, the Court, in *Ohralik*, drew a potentially important parallel between the
subject of an in-person commercial solicitation and the victim of offensive speech
in a truly captive audience situation (436 U.S. at 466 n.25):

> Unlike the reader of an advertisement, who can "effectively avoid further bombardment
> of [his] sensibilities simply by averting [his] eyes." . . . The target of the solicitation may
> have difficulty avoiding being importuned and distressed even if the lawyer seeking
> employment is entirely well meaning. *Cf. Breard v. Alexandria*, 341 U.S. 622 (1951).

Although the Court's comment was directed specifically to features of in-person
solicitation by lawyers, the Court's citation of *Breard, supra*, a case involving
door-to-door selling of magazine subscriptions, may have prophetic significance.
That is, in-person sales solicitation for commercial products and services generally may stand on different constitutional footing from newspaper advertisements of the same products and services and may be subjected to more pervasive
and more restrictive governmental control than advertising. The commercial
speech doctrine evolved relatively slowly from 1938 to 1973 when the Court
was primarily addressing the issue as it arose in cases involving door-to-door
canvassing and solicitation, but the doctrine developed rapidly in the cases in
the 1970s, which involved almost exclusively paid commercial advertising in
newspapers. Perhaps it was the unique features of in-person solicitation, rather
than the commercial content of the speech, that had bothered the Court from the
beginning and affected the development of constitutional doctrine in this area.

In re Primus, 436 U.S. 412 (1978), the companion case to *Ohralik*, presented
questions concerning attorney solicitation that were similar to those presented
in *Ohralik* but led to opposite results. At least since the turbulent period of civil
rights advocacy in the 1960s, exemplified in *NAACP v. Button*, 371 U.S. 415
(1963), the Supreme Court has been solicitous of the efforts of civil rights
advocates to clear away discriminatory and repressive state legislation through
constitutional litigation in the lower federal courts. The Court has endeavored
through its decisions in the First Amendment "right of association" cases to
discourage local governmental attempts to apply attorney disciplinary codes to
suppress meritorious litigation brought by dedicated civil rights lawyers, frequently serving the cause of racial justice for little or no pay.

Primus, a practicing attorney in South Carolina who was also a cooperating
lawyer with a branch of the American Civil Liberties Union (ACLU), was
disciplined by the South Carolina Supreme Court for writing a letter to a potential
client advising her that free legal service was available from the ACLU in
connection with a possible claim of deprivation of constitutional rights arising
out of her sterilization by the state of South Carolina, which attached the condition

of voluntary sterilization to the payment of public medical assistance benefits. Primus wrote the letter after a meeting held to advise women of their legal rights. The Court held that South Carolina's application of its Disciplinary Rule against solicitation to Primus violated the First and Fourteenth amendments. Primus was associated with the Carolina Community Law Firm, an expense-sharing arrangement among three attorneys, and was an officer of and cooperating lawyer with the Columbia, South Carolina, branch of the ACLU. Primus received no compensation for her work on behalf of the ACLU but was paid a retainer by the South Carolina Council on Human Relations, a non-profit organization in Columbia. A citizen who had learned of the state's sterilization program called the council and through its offices set up a meeting with Primus, whom he had not previously met, and with several women who had been sterilized or threatened with sterilization. Primus advised the women of their legal rights and thereafter wrote to one of them, on behalf of the ACLU, to inform her of the ACLU's offer of free legal services in connection with a damage suit, which the woman had indicated at the meeting she wished to institute.

The Supreme Court distinguished its holding in *Ohralik* on the ground that Primus's act of writing to a woman with whom she had met earlier to discuss the possibility of seeking legal redress "was not in-person solicitation for pecuniary gain," 436 U.S. at 422. As the Court's remark indicates, the Court seems to have relied not only on the fact that the solicitation was not in person, but also on the fact that it was not for pecuniary gain. (Indeed, the Court's focus on the non-economic motive for the solicitation suggests that not only the commercial content but also the commercial motive of speech, at least in some circumstances, may be relevant in determining the protected status of commercial speech.) The Court did not appear to approach the issue in *Primus* on the assumption that the speech was truly commercial at all. If a commercial transaction contemplates the exchange of money, or some pecuniary gain on the part of the seller, Primus's letter offering free legal services arguably would not qualify. The Court observed, "Appellant was communicating an offer of free assistance by attorneys associated with the ACLU, not an offer predicated on entitlement to a share of any monetary recovery. And her actions were undertaken to express her personal political beliefs and to advance the civil liberties objectives of the ACLU, rather than to derive financial gain," 436 U.S. at 422.

The First Amendment rights involved in Primus were the associational rights of the ACLU and the right of Primus to exercise her rights to express her personal political beliefs through litigation. There, as in *NAACP v. Button*, solicitation of non-members for the purpose of bringing suit came within "the 'right to engage in association for the advancement of beliefs and ideas,'" 436 U.S. at 424. The possibility that the ACLU might obtain an award of attorney's fees if successful in its litigation did not alter the constitutional status of its activities. Primus received no compensation for any of the activities in question and neither the ACLU nor any lawyer associated with it would have shared in any monetary recovery by the plaintiffs in the underlying litigation. The Court noted that at the time of the litigation in question attorney fee awards were limited to narrow circumstances, and even where a court in its discretion awarded attorney's fees to a successful plaintiff in a civil rights suit, the amounts awarded were generally much less than fees paid by clients in other litigation. Any fees recovered would have gone to the central fund of the ACLU and would not have been distributed to local chapters or to attorneys affiliated with the local chapter. The Court expressed no opinion whether its analysis would be different if such fees had been shared between ACLU state affiliates and cooperating attorneys, 436 U.S. at 430 n.24.

The Court's first step was, thus, to determine whether the regulated attorney activity was protected at all. Finding that it was, the Court next examined the asserted state interest served by the disciplinary rules and finally examined the relationship between the terms of the disciplinary rule and the state's interest, to determine whether the restriction was broader than necessary and whether the rule sufficiently advanced the state interest, 436 U.S. at 432–439. The First Amendment interests at issue in *Primus* were "core First Amendment rights." In order to overcome constitutional rights of this dimension, the Court held that South Carolina would be required to demonstrate (1) "a subordinating interest which is compelling," and (2) "that the means employed in furtherance of that interest are closely drawn to avoid unnecessary abridgment of associational freedoms," 436 U.S. at 432. The Court did not doubt the importance of South Carolina's interest in preventing "undue influence, overreaching, misrepresentation, invasion of privacy, conflict of interest, lay interference and other evils that are thought to inhere generally in solicitation by lawyers of prospective clients," 436 U.S. at 432. But the Court held that the disciplinary rules did not exhibit that narrow specificity required in areas touching on the exercise of core First Amendment associational rights. The breadth of the rules, their potential applicability to clearly protected activity, and their potential for abuse through "discretionary enforcement against unpopular causes" were held to be fundamentally at odds with the First Amendment. As in *Ohralik*, the Court examined the record evidence itself and found no evidence of undue influence, overreaching, misrepresentation, or invasion of privacy. Findings on these issues were not necessary in *Ohralik*, because prophylactic rules in the area of commercial speech were held to be tolerable. Indeed, in *Primus* the Court said:

Where political expression or association is at issue, this Court has not tolerated the degree of imprecision that often characterizes government regulation of the conduct of commercial affairs. The approach we adopt today in *Ohralik, post*, p. 447, that the State may proscribe in-person solicitation for pecuniary gain under circumstances *likely to result in adverse consequences*, cannot be applied to appellant's activities on behalf of the ACLU. Although a showing of *potential danger* may suffice in the former context, appellant may not be disciplined unless her activity, in fact, involved the type of misconduct at which South Carolina's broad prohibition is said to be directed. 436 U.S. at 434 (emphasis added)

The Court explicitly held that Primus's letter was not commercial speech. Although the state "may regulate in a prophylactic fashion all solicitation activities of lawyers," that approach is limited to speech "that simply 'propose[s] a commercial transaction.' *Pittsburgh Press Co. v. Human Relations Commission*, 413 U.S. 376, 385 (1973). In the context of political expression and association, however, a State must regulate with significantly greater precision," 436 U.S. at 437–438.

Viewed side by side, then, *Ohralik* and *Primus* illustrate several important respects in which commercial speech, although constitutionally protected, and political-associational speech will be afforded different constitutional protection. These cases did not explicitly establish whether a different test is applied to commercial speech that is a constituent element of a cause of conduct with socially undesirable consequences from that applied to political speech that is a constituent element of a similar course of conduct. But several generalizations can be drawn.

First, the rationale of the overbreadth doctrine, formulated in the cases involving political expression, applies weakly, if at all, in the ordinary commercial context. The state, therefore, need not adduce evidence of actual harm in the concrete instances of commercial speech. Prophylactic rules will suffice, if conduct of the type proscribed "more often than not will be injurious."

Second, in-person commercial solicitation occupies a constitutional status different from that occupied by commercial solicitation by newspaper or magazine, as in *Bates*, or by letter, as in *Primus*. The Court, however, did not rely exclusively on the fact that the communication in *Primus* was by letter. Instead, the Court chose to reach the broader issues presented in *Primus* that the communication was not commercial at all, *i.e.*, it did not "propose a commercial transaction."

Third, an in-person commercial solicitation possesses certain features in common with the "captive audience" line of cases in which the Court or some of its members have voted to uphold government restrictions on the ground that the person solicited cannot easily avoid the unwanted communication.[4]

TRADE NAMES: *FRIEDMAN v. ROGERS*, 440 U.S. 1 (1979)

The next major Supreme Court decision touching commercial speech, *Friedman v. Rogers*, 440 U.S. 1 (1979), involved the constitutionality of the Texas Optometry Act, which prohibited the practice of optometry in Texas under a trade name. Optometrists in Texas are informally divided between the commercial optometrists and the professional optometrists, and the resulting controversy reflected itself in a struggle concerning the form of professional regulation under Texas law, specifically the 1969 Texas Optometry Act in issue in *Friedman*. The professional optometrists had achieved a degree of political ascendancy over their rivals. The act set up a six-person state regulatory board, the Texas

Optometry Board, on which four members were required to belong to a private trade association known as the Texas Optometric Association (TOA), a local group affiliated with a national association known as the American Optometric Association (AOA). Eligibility for membership in the AOA and TOA required adherence to the AOA Code of Ethics. Eligibility for four of the six seats on the Texas board, therefore, required adherence to the AOA Code of Ethics. The board had the power to grant and revoke the optometry licenses required for lawful practice of optometry in Texas and to enforce the provision of the act prohibiting the practice of optometry under a trade name.

Rogers, a commercial optometrist who had chosen to do business under the trade name Texas State Optical, brought suit in Texas federal court challenging the constitutionality of (1) the eligibility requirements for four of the restricted seats on the board, and (2) the prohibition against practicing optometry under a trade name. The Texas Senior Citizens Association intervened on Rogers's behalf, arguing their entitlement to representation on the board and challenging the denial of access to commercial communications contained implicitly in trade names. The TOA intervened on behalf of Texas. The three-judge district court upheld the board membership eligibility requirement but struck down the prohibition against practicing optometry under a trade name. The Supreme Court of the United States upheld the eligibility provision but disagreed with the lower court, holding that Texas could lawfully prohibit the practice of optometry under a trade name.

The *Friedman* decision poses the central question whether, just as there are different kinds of speech generally, commercial and non-commercial, there are also different kinds of commercial speech and, if so, whether the different kinds of commercial speech are, in turn, entitled to different levels of constitutional protection. The Court in *Friedman* answered this question by holding that there are different kinds of commercial speech. In particular, the Court held that there is (1) commercial speech that has intrinsic meaning, and (2) commercial speech that has no intrinsic meaning. What constitutes "intrinsic meaning," as the Court uses the term, assumes special importance because the Court in *Friedman* held that commercial speech, such as a trade name, which lacks intrinsic meaning, may be treated differently and is to be accorded a lesser degree of protection under the First Amendment.

The Court's starting point was its consideration of what a trade name is: "It may seem to identify an optometrical practice and also to convey information about the type, price and quality of services offered for sale in that practice," 440 U.S. at 11. The Court acknowledged that "the tradename is used as part of a proposal of a commercial transaction," *id*. Although a form of commercial speech and nothing more, it is "a significantly different form of commercial speech." It is different from the advertising involved in other commercial speech cases decided up until that time because that advertising (1) "contained statements about the products or services offered and their prices," and (2) included statements that "were self-contained and self-explanatory." A trade name, by contrast (1) has "no intrinsic meaning," and (2) conveys "no information about the price and nature of the services offered . . . until it acquires a meaning over a period of time by associations formed in the minds of the public between the name and some standard price or quality."

The Court's distinction seems unconvincing and self-contradictory, for the Court recognized that a trade name can come to possess a meaning that makes it simply a short expression for a longer message concerning price and quality. For example, many firms advertise heavily to create these associations.

The Court held that the unique susceptibility of trade names to manipulation for the purpose of misleading the public warrants more extensive governmental regulation of trademarks than might be permissible in the case of narrative advertising that explicitly states the price and describes the relevant attributes of products or services. These "possibilities for deception" included continued use of the name after the identity of staff members had changed and the use of different names at shops owned and managed by the same individuals, thus giving a false impression of competition. The Court also noted that use of a trade name "facilitates the advertising essential to large-scale commercial practices—conduct the State rationally may wish to discourage while not prohibiting commercial optometrical practice altogether," 440 U.S. at 13.

These are curious conclusions. Ordinarily, it would not be grounds for a charge of deception if a service business changed its personnel. Nor is it uncommon for firms which are, in fact, wholly owned by the same parent to sell goods under different trade names in apparent—and actual—competition with each other. For example, liquor distillers selling under different trade names but actually sharing common ownership may hold themselves out to the public by implication as competitors when they are not, *see Kiefer-Stewart Co. v. Joseph E. Seagram & Sons*, 340 U.S. 211 (1951). It may also be questioned why and whether the state might legitimately cripple "large scale commercial practices" in specific industries, a proposition the Court appears to have assumed was self-evident without need for further justification. Even more suspect is the suppressed premise that the state may do so indirectly by depriving the public of information—an assumption that appears to conflict with the Court's later decisions in the commercial speech field, *see, e.g., Central Hudson Gas & Electric Corp. v. Public Service Commission*, 447 U.S. 557 (1980); *Linmark Associates, Inc. v. Willingboro, supra*. The fact that "large-scale commercialization" may "enhance the opportunity for misleading practices," if it does, would not seem to warrant such sweeping remedial prohibition.

The Court held that Texas had "done no more than require that commercial information about optometrical services 'appear in such a form . . . as [is] necessary to prevent its being deceptive.' *Virginia Board of Pharmacy*, 425 U.S. at 772 n.24," 440 U.S. at 16. This holding divided the Court. Justice Blackmun, the author of the Court's decisions in *Bates*, *Virginia Board of Pharmacy*, and *Bigelow*, dissented and was joined by Justice Marshall. The dissent emphasized the importance to consumers of trade names and the "distinctly public interest" that Rogers's trade name served. It rejected the asserted grounds for the sweeping regulation.

Did the Supreme Court in *Friedman* hold that a trade name alone is not commercial speech and therefore not entitled to any First Amendment protection? Or did it hold that trade names, although commercial speech and protected, nonetheless do not enjoy the full degree of constitutional protection which other forms, because of their relatively lower susceptibility to being used to deceive, enjoy? The Court quite clearly held that a trade name, because of secondary meaning, is commercial speech. The Court's decision still makes it possible to argue that particular forms of state legislation and regulatory law relating to trade names must still pass similar scrutiny.

SOLICITATION: *VILLAGE OF SCHAUMBURG v. CITIZENS FOR A BETTER ENVIRONMENT*

The subject of First Amendment protection for in-person solicitation—this time in the context of in-person solicitation of charitable contributions—arose in *Village of Schaumburg v. Citizens for a Better Environment*, 444 U.S. 620 (1980). At issue in this case was the constitutionality of a Schaumburg, Illinois, ordinance prohibiting door-to-door or on-street solicitation of contributions by charitable organizations that do not use at least 75 percent of their receipts for charitable purposes and requiring a solicitation permit, granted only to those in compliance with the ordinance. In *Schaumburg*, the Court took the occasion to trace the development of the Court's decisions in the area of door-to-door solicitation, and the Court's opinion includes a helpful summary of the door-to-door distribution cases from *Schneider v. State* up to that date.

The Court concluded its analysis with the observation that charitable appeals for funds "involve a variety of speech interests—communication of information, the dissemination and propagation of views and ideas, and the advocacy of causes—that are within the protection of the First Amendment."

The Court's comments on solicitation as a form of protected activity are pertinent:

Soliciting financial support is undoubtedly subject to reasonable regulation but the latter must be undertaken with due regard for the reality that solicitation is characteristically intertwined with informative and perhaps persuasive speech seeking support for particular causes or for particular views on economic, political, or social issues, and for the reality that without solicitation the flow of such information and advocacy would likely cease. Canvassers in such contexts are necessarily more than solicitors for money. Furthermore, because charitable solicitation does more than inform private economic decisions and is not primarily concerned with providing information about the characteristics and costs of goods and services, it has not been dealt with in our cases as a variety of purely commercial speech. 444 U.S. at 632

The Court's criteria for picking out fully protected solicitation from commercial solicitation included (1) whether or not the solicitation "does more than inform private economic decision," and (2) whether or not the solicitation "is primarily concerned with providing information about the characteristics and costs of goods and services." Thus, the Court relies on both an objective standard—what the actual content of the communication is—and a subjective standard—what the primary purpose of the communication is.

In footnote 7 of its decision, the Court took the opportunity specifically to overrule its prior decisions that commercial speech is excluded from First Amendment protections:

7. To the extent that any of the Court's past decisions discussed in Part II [including *Valentine*] hold or indicate that commercial speech is excluded from First Amendment protections, those decisions, to that extent, are no longer good law. *Virginia Pharmacy Board v. Virginia Citizens Consumer Council*, 425 U.S. 748, 758–759, 762 (1976). For the purposes of applying the overbreadth doctrine, however, see *infra*, at 834–835, it remains relevant to distinguish between commercial and non-commercial speech. *Bates v. State Bar of Arizona*, 433 U.S. 350, 381 (1977). 444 U.S. at 632 n.7

The issue before the Court was "whether the Village has exercised its power to regulate solicitation in such a manner as not unduly to intrude upon the rights of free speech," *id.*, at 633. The charitable solicitation was entitled to full protection, and the case raised a question whether the Schaumburg ordinance was overbroad. The Court had intimated on several occasions that the doctrine of overbreadth is inapplicable to commercial speech. Since the Court in *Schaumburg* held that charitable solicitation is non-commercial, however, the standard overbreadth analysis was applied.

One class of charitable organizations cannot comply with the 75 percent requirement. Organizations of this type use paid solicitors to collect money and also hire other employees to obtain and process information and to arrive at and announce the organizations' positions on the issues of interest to them. They are not organizations that are merely conduits of funds intended for the poor, the needy, or other objects of charity, but their purpose is to gather and disseminate information and opinion. They cannot comply with the 75 percent requirement of the Schaumburg ordinance, and the Schaumburg ordinance made no exception for such organizations. The Court therefore held the ordinance overbroad. It was a "direct and substantial limitation on protected activity" that could not be sustained unless it "served a sufficiently strong, subordinating interest that the Village is entitled to protect," *id.* at 636. Schaumburg's interest was substantial: "protecting the public from fraud, crime and undue annoyance," *id.* at 636. But the Court held that it was "only peripherally promoted by the 75 percent requirement and could be sufficiently served by measures less destructive of First Amendment interests." The Court held that the relationship between the ordinance and the promotion of the state's valid purpose was insufficiently direct and that the ordinance was more drastic in its effects than was necessary. The Schaumburg ordinance barred fraudulent and non-fraudulent organizations alike. Here, as in other full-protection contexts, the Court held that greater precision of regulation was required and broad prophylactic rules are inadequate. Fraudulent misrepresentations can always be dealt with directly by ordinance, and homeowners are free to exclude all charitable solicitors by notices prominently displayed on their property.

One interesting feature of *Schaumburg* is that it is one of the few modern decisions that involves both elements of solicitation—conduct that also occurs in the context of commercial solicitation—and fully protected First Amendment activity. *Schaumburg* thus invites a comparison between those decisions that involve restrictions on in-person commercial solicitation and the decisions involving restrictions on political or non-commercial in-person solicitation. *Schaumburg* may provide the basis for determining the extent to which the different treatment accorded to in-person commercial solicitation is attributable to the fact that it involves an in-person solicitation, and the extent to which that lesser level of protection derives from the fact that the solicitation was commercial in nature. *Schaumburg* would tend to support the view that it was the commercial or non-commercial nature of the communication that makes the difference, rather than whether the communication was in person or was not. *Schaumburg* also raises the question when, if ever, does speech that is at least in part commercially motivated, *i.e.*, motivated by a desire to collect money—even if the collection of money is not the final end of the communication—become commercial speech, that is, speech that is not entitled to the full protection of the First Amendment? As noted above, the Court employed criteria based both on the content of the communication and on the primary purpose of the speaker in answering this question. Essentially, this is the question of the constitutional status of mixed speech.

NOTES

1. By the time Virginia Board of Pharmacy reached the Supreme Court, three states by court decision had struck down their prohibitions on drug price advertising, Florida Board of Pharmacy v. Webb's City, Inc., 219 So.2d 681 (Fla. Ct. App. 1969); Maryland Board of Pharmacy v. Sav-A-Lot, Inc., 270 Md. 103, 311 A.2d 242 (1973); Pennsylvania State Board of Pharmacy v. Pastor, 441 Pa. 186, 272 A.2d 487 (1971).

2. The Court based its recognition of the First Amendment rights of recipients on prior holdings in Kleindienst v. Mandel, 408 U.S. 753, 762–763 (1972)(right to "receive information and ideas" as basis for reviewing denial of visa privilege); Procunier v. Martinez, 416 U.S. 396, 408–409 (1974)(censorship of prison inmates' mail); Red Lion Broadcasting Co. v. FCC, 395 U.S. 367, 390 (1969); Stanley v. Georgia, 394 U.S. 557, 564 (1969); Griswold v. Connecticut, 381 U.S. 479, 482 (1965); Marsh v. Alabama, 326 U.S. 501, 505 (1946); Thomas v. Collins, 323 U.S. 516, 534 (1945); and Martin v. Struthers, *supra*. The dissenting opinion attempted to distinguish these cases as involving a "right to receive" only in instances in which the potential recipient objecting

to the restriction could not obtain the information in another way. The majority, however, rejected this ground of distinction on the facts of those cases, 425 U.S. at 757 n.15.

3. *See*, Bigelow v. Virginia, 421 U.S. at 826; Central Hudson Gas & Electric Corp. v. Public Service Commission, 447 U.S. 557, 579 (1980)(concurring opinion of Justice Stevens); Bolger v. Youngs Drug Products Corp., 463 U.S. 60, 103 S. Ct. 2875, 2880, and 2888 (concurring opinion of Justice Stevens)(1983).

4. In *Zauderer v. Office of Disciplinary Counsel*, 53 U.S.L.W. 4587 (May 28, 1985), the Supreme Court held that the First Amendment extended to a newspaper advertisement by an attorney offering his services to potential products liability plaintiffs interested in filing personal injury suits arising out of use of Dalkon Shield Interuterine Devices.

4

Landmark Reformulation of the Commercial Speech Doctrine: *Central Hudson v. Public Service Commission* and Its Aftermath

CONSOLIDATED EDISON AND CENTRAL HUDSON

On June 20, 1980, the Supreme Court handed down decisions in *Consolidated Edison Co. of N.Y., Inc. v. Public Service Commission*, 447 U.S. 530 (1980), and *Central Hudson Gas & Electric Corp. v. Public Service Commission*, 447 U.S. 557 (1980), that represented a major advance toward defining the directions of the commercial speech doctrine and the constitutional protection to be accorded corporate speech on controversial issues of public policy. In the *Consolidated Edison* case, which involved a constitutional challenge by a regulated utility to a New York Public Service Commission order banning the use of printed inserts addressing public issues included in monthly billing envelopes that were mailed to utility customers, the Supreme Court elaborated on principles applicable to constitutional protection of corporate speech, so discussion of the *Consolidated Edison* decision is therefore postponed until Part II.

In *Central Hudson*, the Supreme Court struck down, as violative of the First and Fourteenth amendments, a New York Public Service Commission order which completely banned electric utilities from advertising to promote the use of electricity. The New York Public Service Commission's (PSC) order banning advertising by electric utilities was based on the commission's finding that "the interconnected utility system in New York State does not have sufficient fuel stocks or sources of supply to continue furnishing all customer demands for the 1973–1974 winter," 447 U.S. at 559. The PSC order divided utility advertising into the "promotional" and the "institutional and informational" and declared all promotional advertising contrary to the national policy of conserving energy. The basis of the PSC order appeared to be that the state had a legitimate interest in preventing new electric service from being connected and in preventing further consumption of electric energy. The PSC chose to advance these objects by means of a general ban on advertising, *i.e.*, by manipulating public demand for electric service. The Supreme Court struck down this restriction on commercial speech by public utilities.

Justice Powell began his opinion for the Court by noting that the only speech restricted by the PSC order was commercial speech. The Court's formula for defining commercial speech, however, appears to vary from the definition given in earlier decisions. The problem of definition posed by the commercial speech doctrine was recognized as early as *Pittsburgh Press Co. v. Human Relations Commission, supra*, where the Court referred to speech as advertising that does "no more than propose a commercial transaction," 413 U.S. at 385. In *Bigelow*, a transitional decision to the modern commercial speech doctrine, the Court held that the abortion referral service advertisement for which Bigelow was indicted "did more than simply propose a commercial transaction. It contained factual material of clear 'public interest,' " 421 U.S. at 822. The *Bigelow* Court was not yet prepared to define commercial speech and said only that "[t]he diverse motives, means, and messages of advertising may make speech 'commercial' in widely varying degrees," *id*. at 826. In *Virginia Pharmacy Board*, the Court spoke of the drug price advertising banned by the Virginia regulation as "speech which does 'no more than propose a commercial transaction,' " 425 U.S. at 762, following the formulation of *Pittsburgh Press Co.* In *Linmark*, in the course of invalidating the ordinance prohibiting residential "For Sale" signs, the Court failed to employ any particular verbal formula or definition of the commercial category. In *Bates*, the Court spoke of speech that "proposed a mundane commercial transaction," 433 U.S. at 364. In *Ohralik*, which involved a ban on in-person solicitation on attorneys, the Court referred vaguely to "[e]xpressions concerning purely commercial transactions," 436 U.S. at 455.

The problems inherent in the definition of commercial speech are discussed in greater detail in chapter 5. For now, it suffices to note that the Supreme Court in *Central Hudson* spoke definitely of "expression related solely to the economic interests of the speaker and its audience," 447 U.S. at 561. Although formulations appearing in earlier decisions centered quite explicitly on the content of speech as the feature enabling commercial speech and non-commercial speech to be distinguished, the Court in *Central Hudson* speaks in terms of the "interests of the speaker and its audience," suggesting that speech is commercial only if it relates solely to the "economic interests" of "the speaker and its audience." Putting to one side the precise definition of commercial speech, a topic addressed in greater detail in chapter 5, the Court held that utility promotional advertising of the type involved in *Central Hudson* was commercial advertising and was therefore entitled to some degree of constitutional protection.

The Court undertook a full-scale restatement in *Central Hudson* of the rationale for the commercial speech doctrine (447 U.S. at 562–563):

1. Commercial speech not only serves the economic interest of the speaker, but also assists consumers and furthers the societal interest in the fullest possible dissemination of information. (562)

2. In applying the First Amendment to this area, we have rejected the "highly paternalistic" view that government has complete power to suppress or regulate commercial speech. (562)

3. [P]eople will perceive their own best interests if only they are well enough informed, and . . . the best means to that end is to open the channels of communication, rather than close them. (562)

4. Even when advertising communicates only an incomplete version of the relevant facts, the First Amendment presumes that some accurate information is better than no information at all. (562)

5. The First Amendment's concern for commercial speech is based on the informational function of advertising. (563)

Justice Powell also restated the fundamental principle of lesser protection and its rationale, and the Court's holdings can be schematized as follows:

1. *Principle of Lesser Protection*: The Constitution . . . accords a lesser protection to commercial speech than to other constitutionally guaranteed expression. (563)

2. *Rationale*: [O]ur decisions have recognized the "common sense" distinction between speech proposing a commercial transaction, which occurs in an area traditionally subject to government regulation, and other varieties of speech. (562)

3. *Rationale*: Two features of commercial speech permit regulation of its content. First, commercial speakers have extensive knowledge of both the market and their products. Thus, they are well situated to evaluate the accuracy of their messages and the lawfulness of the underlying activity. *Bates v. State Bar of Arizona*, 433 U.S. 350, 381 (1977). In addition, commercial speech, the offspring of economic self-interest, is a hardy breed of expression that is not "particularly susceptible to being crushed by overbroad regulation." *Ibid.* (564 at n.6)

Justice Powell emphasized the importance of drawing a clear distinction between commercial and non-commercial speech, particularly in areas involving mixed commercial and non-commercial speech, 447 U.S. at 562, n.5, an important issue which is dealt with in chapter 5.

The Court reviewed the exceptions to the commercial speech doctrine—namely, the inapplicability of the First Amendment to (1) untruthful commercial speech, and (2) commercial speech "related to" unlawful activities, *i.e.*, commercial speech soliciting or facilitating an unlawful course of conduct, or speech that is in some relevant sense a primary constituent element of an unlawful course of conduct:

[T]here can be no constitutional objection to the suppression of commercial messages that do not accurately inform the public about lawful activity. The government may ban forms of communication more likely to deceive the public than to inform it, . . . or commercial speech related to illegal activity. (564)

Against this doctrinal backdrop, the Supreme Court laid down the following fundamental and comprehensive standard of review for governmental regulation of commercial speech:

If the communication is neither misleading or related to unlawful activity, the government's power is . . . circumscribed. The State must assert a substantial interest to be achieved by restrictions on commercial speech. Moreover, the regulatory technique must be in proportion to that interest. The limitation on expression must be designed carefully to achieve the State's goal. Compliance with this requirement may be measured by two criteria. First, the restriction must directly advance the state interest involved; the regulation may not be sustained if it provides only ineffective or remote support for the government's purpose. Second, if the governmental interest could be served as well by a more limited restriction on commercial speech, the excessive restrictions cannot survive. (564)

On the basis of this explicit statement of the commercial speech doctrine, the Court set forth a four-part analysis to be applied by the lower courts in resolving issues concerning governmental regulation in this field (447 U.S. at 566):

At the outset, we, must determine (1) whether the expression is protected by the First Amendment. For commercial speech to come within that provision, it at least must (1A) concern lawful activity and (1B) not be misleading. Next, we ask (2) whether the asserted governmental interest is substantial. If both inquiries yield positive answers, we must determine (3) whether the regulation directly advances the governmental interest asserted, and (4) whether it is not more extensive than is necessary to serve that interest.

The Court applied this four-part test and invalidated the New York PSC order. Since the PSC did not claim that the advertising was inaccurate or that it "relate[d] to" unlawful activity, the Supreme Court concluded that the advertising was entitled to some degree of constitutional protection. The Court rejected the commission's argument that the status of the utility as a regulated monopoly altered the constitutional status of its expression, noting the existence of interfuel competition and acknowledging the value of the advertising to consumers faced with a choice of gas, electricity, or oil as alternative fuels. Under its four-part test, the Court therefore turned to an examination of the nature, legitimacy, and weight of the asserted interests of New York in regulating the utility's advertising—primarily, the claims that the PSC order served the state's interest in energy conservation, an interest the Court found plainly "substantial," 447 U.S. at 568. The Court also examined, and found to be "clear and substantial," New York's asserted interest in insuring that electric utility rates be fair and efficient—an interest New York claimed was implicated in the ban because promotional advertising, in its submission, would aggravate already existing inequities in the rate structure that were caused by Central Hudson's failure to base its rates for service on its marginal cost for the service.

Appraising the evidence on the third controlling factor, *i.e.*, the relationship between the state's interests and the advertising ban, the Court concluded that there was a "direct link between the state interest in conservation and the Commission's order," but concluded that the link between the advertising prohibition and Central Hudson's rate structure was "tenuous" and that the impact of promotional advertising on the equity of its rates was "highly speculative." The Court found an "immediate connection" between advertising and demand for electricity and noted that Central Hudson's very opposition to the ban was premised on the belief that the promotion would increase its sales.

The fourth factor—whether the commission's ban was "more extensive than necessary to further the State's interest in energy conservation"—proved to be the decisive factor supporting the Court's ruling that the state's ban was unconstitutional. It is noteworthy that in its analysis of this factor, the Court appeared to place the burden of proof on the state. Rather than requiring Central Hudson to identify the less extensive regulatory measures which might have served the state's interest, the Court appeared to require affirmative proof or a demonstration from the state "that a more limited restriction on the content of promotional advertising would not serve adequately the state's interests," 447 U.S. at 570. Critical to the Court's conclusion was the absence of any findings by the commission in the proceedings before it on the comparative efficiency of electric energy, when combined with use of the heat pump and the use of electric heat, as a backup to solar or other heat sources. The Court therefore felt itself bound to credit the utility's claim that electric heat can be an efficient alternative, at least under some circumstances.

The Court ruled, therefore, that "to the extent that the Commission's order suppresses speech that in no way impairs the State's interest in energy conservation, the Commission's order violates the First and Fourteenth Amendments and must be invalidated," 447 U.S. at 570. The Court also held that the commission had failed to show that its legitimate interest in energy conservation could not be protected adequately by more limited regulation of commercial expression. In this context, the Court itself suggested several less restrictive measures which the commission might have considered and adopted but which the commission's findings provided no basis to reject on the ground of ineffectuality. The Court referred to possible restrictions on the format and content of advertising that would require that the advertising include information about the relative efficiency and expense of the offered service, both under current conditions and in the foreseeable future. The Court concluded that "[i]n the absence of a showing that more limited speech regulation would be ineffective, we cannot approve the complete suppression of Central Hudson's advertising," 447 U.S. at 571.

Several of the concurring opinions in *Central Hudson* warrant examination because they contain the seeds of further development of the constitutional doctrines governing commercial speech. A number of the concurring opinions emphasized the peculiar premise of the New York regulation—namely, that the commission's suppression of commercial speech might be justified as a means of influencing public conduct by manipulating the availability of information. This highly paternalistic and anti-democratic approach to regulation provoked specific condemnation from Justices Brennan, 447 U.S. at 572, and Blackmun, 447 U.S. at 578. At oral argument, Justice Marshall also called attention to this feature of the New York regulation. The gist of this objection is stated in Justice Blackmun's concurring opinion. Although Justice Blackmun agreed that the level of "intermediate scrutiny" embodied in the Court's four-part analysis was the appropriate standard to be applied in appraising (1) a restraint on commercial speech that is "designed to protect consumers from misleading or coercive speech," or (2) a regulation related to the "time, place or manner of commercial speech," he expressed the view that the four-part test could not be appropriate to apply where, as in the case of the New York PSC's flat ban on promotional advertising, the state sought to suppress information about a product "in order to manipulate a private economic decision that the State cannot or has not regulated or outlawed directly," 447 U.S. at 573. On Justice Blackmun's analysis, the basis of the Court's ruling was too narrow and left open the unacceptable possibility of regulation of the demand for electricity by the paternalistic step of suppressing advertising of electricity. Suppression of information to manipulate conduct, in his view, could never constitute a legitimate means of achieving valid legislative objectives in such a context. Justice Blackmun's concurring opinion thus contains a further contribution to the constitutional theory concerning the use of regulation of speech as a means of regulation concerning legitimate state interest. He observed (447 U.S. at 574):

The Court recognizes that we have never held that commercial speech may be suppressed in order to further the State's interest in discouraging purchases of the underlying product that is advertised. . . . Permissible restraints on commercial speech have been limited to measures designed to protect consumers from fraudulent, misleading, or coercive sales techniques. *Those designed to deprive consumers of information about products or services that are legally offered for sale consistently have been invalidated.*

. . .

If the First Amendment means anything, it means that, absent clear and present danger, *government has no power to restrict expression because of the effect its message is likely to have on the public.* (emphasis added)

In support of this observation, Justice Blackmun pointed to the holding in *Virginia Pharmacy Board* that Virginia could not pursue its goal of encouraging patronage of professional pharmacists by keeping the public in the dark concerning drug prices offered by competing pharmacists. The same principle lay at the heart of the ruling in *Linmark*, striking down a prohibition of residential "For Sale" signs, enacted to promote stable, racially integrated housing—a restriction which was intended to achieve its goal by keeping the public ignorant of the availability of such housing. As Justice Blackmun pointed out (447 U.S. at 577): "The Court in *Linmark* resolved beyond all doubt that a *strict standard* of review applies to suppression of commercial information, where the purpose of the restraint is to influence behavior by depriving citizens of information,'' (emphasis added). The dispute over whether the strict standard or *Central Hudson's* four-part test of intermediate scrutiny was the applicable standard by which the New York PSC ban on promotional advertising was to be invalidated should not obscure the broad basis of agreement among the justices on the correct resolution of the case. Indeed, only Justice Rehnquist believed that the New York PSC order could be sustained.

Justice Stevens's concurring opinion touched on the critical issue of defining commercial speech. Justice Stevens wrote that ''because 'commercial speech' is afforded less constitutional protection than other forms of speech, it is important that the commercial speech concept not be defined too broadly lest speech deserving of greater constitutional protection be inadvertently suppressed,'' 447 U.S. at 579. The great value of Justice Stevens's concurring opinion in *Central Hudson* lies in its careful exegesis of the precise terminology used in Justice Powell's opinion for the Court. By isolating two formulas used by the Court to define the category of commercial speech, Justice Stevens showed the serious confusion that still exists in the Court's attempt to define the notion of commercial speech and pointed out the serious dangers of that confusion. Justice Stevens wrote (447 U.S. at 579):

[O]ne of the two definitions the Court uses in addressing that issue is too broad and the other may be somewhat too narrow. The Court first describes commercial speech as ''expression related solely to the economic interests of the speaker and its audience.'' *Ante*, at 2349. Although it is not entirely clear whether this definition uses the subject matter of the speech or the motivation of the speaker as the limiting factor, it seems clear to me that it encompasses speech that is entitled to the maximum protection afforded by the First Amendment. Neither a labor leader's exhortation to strike, nor an economist's dissertation on the money supply, should receive any lesser protection because the subject matter concerns only the economic interests of the audience. Nor should the economic motivation of a speaker qualify his constitutional protection; even Shakespeare may have been motivated by the prospect of pecuniary reward. Thus, the Court's definition of commercial speech is unquestionably too broad.

Justice Stevens also criticized as too narrow the Court's more frequently used definitional formula for commercial speech—''speech proposing a commercial transaction'' (447 U.S., at 580):

The Court's second definition refers to ''speech proposing a commercial transaction.'' *Ante*, at 562. A salesman's solicitation, a broker's offer, and a manufacturer's publication of a price list or the terms of his standard warranty would unquestionably fit within this concept. Presumably, the definition is intended to encompass advertising that advises possible buyers of the availability of specific products at specific prices and describes the advantages of purchasing such items. Perhaps it also extends to other communications that do little more than make the name of a product or a service more familiar to the general public. Whatever the precise contours of the concept, and perhaps it is too early to enunciate an exact formulation, I am persuaded that it should not include the entire range of communication that is embraced within the term "promotional advertising."

On this basis, Justice Stevens concurred in the Court's decision to strike down the New York ban on promotional advertising, not because he was satisfied with the Court's four-part test, but rather because the case, in his view, was not a commercial speech case at all. It was a case involving a flat prohibition of speech that should be entitled to maximum First Amendment protection under the Court's already well-developed doctrines for political speech.

Doctrinal development in the commercial speech area continued with the Court's decisions in 1981 in *Metromedia, Inc. v. City of San Diego*, 453 U.S. 490 (1981), involving outdoor display advertising and local governmental control of billboards and *In the Matter of R.M.J.*, 455 U.S. 191 (1982), involving further refinements of the commercial speech doctrine in the context of advertising by lawyers.

Metromedia involved the validity of San Diego Ordinance No. 10795 (New Series), imposing prohibitions on the erection of outdoor "advertising display signs" within the city, in the interest of traffic safety and aesthetic concerns. The ordinance prohibited

1. Any sign identifying a use, facility or service which is not located on the premises, 2. Any sign identifying a product which is not produced, sold, or manufactured on the premises, 3. Any sign which advertises or otherwise directs attention to a product, service or activity, event, person, institution or business which may or may not be identified by a brand name and which occurs or is generally conducted, sold, manufactured, produced or offered elsewhere than on the premises where such sign is located.

The California Supreme Court adopted a narrowing definition of the term "advertising display sign" to mean one "constituting, or used for the display of, a commercial or other advertisement to the public," *Metromedia v. San Diego*, 26 Cal. 3d 848, 164 Cal. Rptr. 510, 513, n.2, 610 P.2d 407, 410 (1980). On-site signs and twelve specific types of signs—including government, religious, historical, for-sale and for-lease signs, time-temperature-and-news signs, vehicular signs, and temporary political campaign signs—were explicitly excluded from this blanket prohibition. Metromedia, Inc., and several other companies in the business of owning and leasing space on outdoor, off-site commercial advertising billboards brought suit in California state courts seeking a declaration that the San Diego sign ban was unconstitutional. The parties stipulated that the ordinance would eliminate the outdoor advertising business in San Diego.

Metromedia produced no definitive opinion of the Court when it reached the Supreme Court but only a plurality result. The Court's judgment reversed the California Supreme Court's holding that the ordinance was constitutionally valid under the First Amendment, but did so in two opinions, neither of which commanded the votes of more than four of the nine justices participating in the decision. Justice Stevens, Chief Justice Burger, and Justice Rehnquist all dissented and filed separate opinions. Although the precise precedential import of the decision can be gleaned only from a careful examination of the separate opinions, the lengthy opinions provide some additional doctrinal clarification of commercial speech law.

The two principal opinions in the case were written by Justice White (concurred in by Justices Stewart, Marshall, and Powell) and by Justice Brennan (joined by Justice Blackmun). Justice White's opinion analyzed the constitutionality of the ordinance in two respects: first, insofar as the ordinance applied to commercial advertisements and, second, insofar as it applied to billboards containing non-commercial messages. Justice White began with an illuminating general restatement of the modern development of the law of commercial speech from *Valentine* to *Central Hudson*. In the course of this account, it is interesting to note, Justice White included in footnote 11 a significant comment concerning the standing of the appellants, the owners and lessors of the billboards, to raise the First Amendment interests of their customers, individuals who desired to lease space on billboards from the appellants. Justice White's footnote contrasted the evolving doctrines of standing in these commercial speech cases with the established overbreadth doctrine in the First Amendment context, 101 S. Ct. at 2890 n.11. Justice White adverted to the settled holding of *Bates v. State Bar of Arizona*, *supra*, 433 U.S. 350, 381, that "the overbreadth doctrine under which a party whose own activities are unprotected may challenge a statute by showing that it substantially abridges the First Amendment rights of parties not before court, will not be applied in cases involving 'commercial speech.' " He noted, nonetheless, that the Court had never held that one with a commercial interest in speech also cannot challenge the facial invalidity of a statute on the grounds of its substantial infringement of the First Amendment interests of others.

Thus, although the outdoor advertising companies primarily leased signs carrying commercial advertisements, their ownership of billboards which carried non-commercial advertising entitled them to argue not only that San Diego could not bar off-site commercial billboards, but also that San Diego could not constitutionally ban all non-commercial advertisement. Justice White drew a sharp distinction between the category of commercial speech and the category of individuals who have a "commercial interest" in protected speech. Individuals, such as the outdoor advertising companies, who have a commercial interest in non-commercial billboard advertisements are not without standing to raise the speech interests of their non-commercial advertising customers in a challenge to the facial invalidity of legislation, even though the overbreadth doctrine does not apply in the commercial speech context, *i.e.*, where the content of the speech is commercial.

In assessing the validity of the San Diego ordinance as a restriction on commercial speech under the four-part test of *Central Hudson*, Justice White and the plurality of the Court had no difficulty concluding that the commercial speech could be assumed to be truthful, "unrelated to" unlawful activity, and therefore protected by the First Amendment to some degree. Similarly, both traffic safety and aesthetics were proper governmental purposes, and the ordinance was no broader than necessary to advance those valid purposes.

The more serious question centered on the third *Central Hudson* factor, *i.e.*, whether the ordinance directly advanced the governmental interests in traffic safety and in the appearance of the city. Justice White noted the parties' dispute concerning the sufficiency of evidence in the record on this point, but the difference in approach on the allocation of burden of proof on this issue between the *Central Hudson* opinion and Justice White's approach in *Metromedia* merits comment. In *Central Hudson*, the Court appears to have rested its conclusion with respect to the issue of the adequacy of less restrictive means on the insufficiency of the state's evidence. In *Metromedia*, in dealing with the distinct issue of direct advancement of the state's interest, Justice White was content to allocate the burden of proof on this factor to the party challenging the ordinance, *i.e.*, the billboard owners. Indeed, there is some question whether Justice White's opinion treats this issue of direct advancement as an issue of fact at all, although the opinion notes the appellants' assertion that "the *record* is inadequate to show any connection between billboards and traffic safety," 101 S. Ct. at 2893 (emphasis added). The California Supreme Court had held "as a matter of law" that the ordinance relates to traffic safety. The Supreme Court couched its approval of this approach in slightly different terms when it said that "the California Supreme Court agreed with many other courts that a legislative judgment that billboards are traffic hazards is not manifestly unreasonable," *id*. Justice White's opinion regarded it as dispositive that "[t]here is nothing here to suggest that these judgments are unreasonable," *id*.

This passage highlights several areas of lingering uncertainty in the application of the four-part *Central Hudson* test. Which of the factors involve determinations of fact and which involve determinations of law? Who has the burden of proof on the issues of fact, the state as in *Central Hudson*, or the parties challenging the ordinance? Justice White's opinion also touches on a jumble of other approaches as well, adverting to the fact that "there is no claim in this case that San Diego has an ulterior motive in the suppression of speech" (suggesting that another standard might apply, or a different burden of proof would arise, if there were such a claim), and to the fact that "the judgment involved here is not so unusual as to raise suspicions in itself," id. at 2894. Justice White's opinion rejected the underinclusive nature of the ordinance (insofar as it did not ban on-site as well as off-site advertising) as a ground for invalidating the ordinance.

Although constitutional in its application to commercial billboards, on Justice White's analysis, the ordinance as a ban on billboard advertising of non-exempted non-commercial expression was unconstitutional. The plurality held that the distinctions which the ordinance drew on the basis of content of the advertising between the exempt and the non-exempt forms of non-commercial billboard advertising were inconsistent with the Court's prior decisions. The plurality also rejected San Diego's argument that the prohibition of outdoor off-site billboards was a valid "time, place and manner" restriction. Thus, the ordinance did not generally ban billboards. It was not a genuine "place" restriction, because the billboards that it banned were banned everywhere. Moreover, the ordinance did not leave open "alternative channels" of expression, as every valid "time, place and manner" regulation must do. Instead, according to the parties' own stipulation, the ordinance relegated potential users of billboards to other forms of advertising that were insufficient, inappropriate, and prohibitively expensive. Nor was the San Diego ordinance content-neutral—a further requirement for validity of any "time, place and manner" regulation; the distinctions between the exempt and non-exempt non-commercial billboards were based explicitly on their content.

Justice Brennan, joined by Justice Blackmun, concurred in the result but on the entirely different ground that the San Diego ordinance, in effect, constituted a total ban to be tested not under the four-part test of *Central Hudson* but instead under the more exacting standard of constitutionality laid down in *Schad v. Borough of Mt. Ephraim*, 452 U.S. 61 (1981), a case which simply synthesized the analysis set forth in earlier total ban cases such as *Schneider v. State, supra*; *Martin v. Struthers, supra*; and *Jamison v. Texas, supra*. Thus, a total ban could be sustained if the state could show the law promoted a "sufficiently substantial" governmental interest. Justice Brennan's analysis of the sign ban in *Metromedia* not only adopts a somewhat more exacting standard but, unlike the plurality opinion, places the burden of proof squarely on the state. The ordinance contained no exemption for signs not visible from the street but nevertheless visible from the boundary of the premises and, therefore, on Justice Brennan's view, violated the requirement that legislation affecting speech be narrowly drawn to accomplish the legislative objectives—in this case, the traffic safety goal. Justice Brennan also questioned the substantiality of the aesthetic factor as a ground of governmental action, at least with respect to the commercial and industrial areas of San Diego, where the absence of any "comprehensive coordinated effort in its commercial and industrial areas" to address aesthetic blight simply reinforced the view that the city lacked genuine commitment to improving its physical environment.

More important, Justice Brennan suggested that no ordinance which gives local officials unfettered discretion to determine whether a message is commercial or non-commercial would survive constitutional scrutiny and adhered to his view previously stated in *Lehman v. City of Shaker Heights*, 418 U.S. 298, 319 (1974)(Brennan, J., dissenting) that the line between ideological and non-ideological speech is impossible to draw with accuracy. In this respect, the implication of the plurality opinions, that local officials might be constitutionally empowered to draw distinctions, is squarely opposed to the views of Justices Brennan and Blackmun. Justice Brennan's comments on this score are a logical outgrowth of the views he expressed in *Lehman* and of the holdings of the Jehovah's Witness cases which turned on the constitutional infirmities with ordinances conferring unbridled discretion on local officials in the administration of restrictions. The plurality did not reach this point, but Justice Brennan's analysis introduces an important innovation in this area which may well become a subject of future litigation.

The plurality carefully preserved several issues that were not decided, including the constitutionality of the federal Highway Beautification Act of 1965, 23 U.S.C. § 131, and the question discussed in Justice Brennan's opinion whether a total prohibition of outdoor advertising would be constitutional. The plurality did intimate, in a footnote, that a total prohibition of billboards might offend principles discussed in *Schad v. Borough of Mt. Ephraim*, *supra*, in which the Court invalidated a borough zoning ordinance which erected a complete ban on the exhibition of live dancing. Justice Brennan, as noted above, reached this issue and resolved it against the city.

Because of the absence of a majority opinion, the full implications of the *Metromedia* decision remain unclear. In any event, the Court took considerable pains to narrow those implications to the area of outdoor advertising billboards, which, the Court emphasized, is a medium of expression that has engendered a law unto itself, because of its unique features.

Heffron v. International Society for Krishna Consciousness, Inc., 452 U.S. 640 (1981), marked the culmination of the federal courts' struggle with the constitutionality of local efforts to regulate the intrusive features of a new form of aggressive quasi-commercial, in-person solicitation by members of a nationwide group presenting itself as a non-profit religious organization at state fairs, airports, and other public and semi-public places. The issue in *Heffron* was the validity of Minnesota State Fair Rule 6.05, providing that "[s]ale or distribution of any merchandise, including printed or written material except under license issued [by] the society and/or from a duly-licensed location shall be a misdemeanor." This was attacked as a "time, place and manner" regulation that effectively prohibited a religious organization from distributing and selling religious literature and soliciting donations at other than assigned locations on a state fairground. The Court upheld the validity of this restriction as a permissible restriction on the place and manner of communicating the views of the Krishna religion. In the view the majority took of this case, the commercial speech doctrine was not involved at all, although one of the three activities involved was the sale of literature. In this respect, the case bears some similarities to the Jehovah's Witness cases which also involved the sale of literature. The regulation, however, applied equally to commercial and non-commercial activities, and the Court therefore found no occasion to make a determination whether the activities of this group were commercial or non-commercial. Indeed, by its citation of Jehovah's Witness cases such as *Schneider*, *Lovell*, and *Murdock*, the Court equated the constitutional status of Krishna activities to that of the door-to-door distribution and solicitation activities of the Jehovah's Witnesses.

The Court revisited the field of attorney advertising in *In the Matter of R.M.J.*, 455 U.S. 191 (1982), which arose from a Missouri Supreme Court disbarment proceeding under a rule prohibiting (1) deviations in advertising as announcements from the precise listing of areas of legal practice that was included in an addendum to the bar rules, (2) mention of the jurisdictions in which an attorney is licensed to practice, and (3) the mailing of cards announcing the opening of an office to persons other than "lawyers, clients, former clients, personal friends and relatives." The Supreme Court invalidated the Missouri rules relating to these forms of attorney advertising because of the absence of any showing that the advertising was misleading or that the mailings and handbills would be more difficult to supervise.

In its opinion in *In Re: R.M.J.*, the Supreme Court included a helpful and concise summary of "[c]ommercial speech doctrine, in the context of advertising for professional services" (455 U.S. 191):

Truthful advertising related to lawful activities is entitled to the protections of the First Amendment. But when the particular content or method of the advertising suggests that it is inherently misleading or when experience has proven that in fact such advertising is subject to abuse, the states may impose appropriate restrictions. Misleading advertising may be prohibited entirely. But the states may not place an absolute prohibition on certain types of potentially misleading information, *e.g.*, a listing of areas of practice, if the information also may be presented in a way that is not deceptive. Thus, the Court in *Bates* suggested that the remedy in the first instance is not necessarily a prohibition but preferably a requirement of disclaimers or explanation. 433 U.S. at 375, 97 S. Ct., at 2704. Although the potential for deception and confusion is particularly strong in the context of advertising professional services, restrictions upon such advertising may be no broader than reasonably necessary to prevent the deception. Even when a communication is not misleading, the state retains some authority to regulate. But the state must assert a substantial interest and the interference with speech must be in proportion to the interest served. *Central Hudson Gas Corp. v. Public Service Commission*, 447 U.S. at 563–564, 100 S. Ct. at 2350. Restrictions must be narrowly drawn, and the state lawfully may regulate only to the extent regulation furthers the state's substantial interest. Thus, in *Bates*, the Court found that the potentially adverse effect of advertising on professionalism and the quality of legal services was not sufficiently related to a substantial state interest to justify so great an interference with speech. *Id.*, 433 U.S. at 368–372, 375–377, 97 S. Ct. at 2704–2705.

These principles, when combined with the four-part test of *Central Hudson* which they restate, concisely summarize constitutional doctrine governing professional advertising.

Applying these principles to the specific prohibitions of the Missouri rule, the Court had no difficulty in determining that the advertising in question had not been found to be misleading and that it was not inherently misleading. The Court also held that the state had made no showing of the substantiality of its interests in limiting the listing of areas of legal specialization or in prohibiting the listing of jurisdictions in which a lawyer is licensed to practice. Turning to the petitioner's mailing of business announcements, which was more extensive than that permitted by the Missouri rules, the Court noted that the record was silent on the issue of the comparative difficulties of supervising mailings and handbills, as opposed to supervising newspaper advertising of the type involved in previous decisions such as *Bates*. The state had likewise failed to show that "absolute prohibition is the only solution." The Court found "no indication in the record of a failed effort to proceed along such a less restrictive path" as pre-mailing review, *id.* at 206.

Here, as in a number of the earlier decisions, including *Central Hudson* itself, the Court implicitly allocated to the states the specific burden of proof on critical components of the four-part test of *Central Hudson*—specifically in *R.M.J.* the burden of proof with respect to the *Central Hudson* component which requires the enactment to be no broader or more extensive than is necessary to advance the legitimate interests of the state.

In *Village of Hoffman Estates v. The Flipside*, 455 U.S. 489 (1982), the Supreme Court had occasion to clarify the principles governing constitutional protection of commercial speech where the commercial speech was related to illegal conduct, a factor that is part of the first *Central Hudson* criterion and which helps determine whether the advertising is entitled to constitutional expression at all. This case was a pre-enforcement facial challenge to a drug paraphernalia ordinance on the grounds of unconstitutional overbreadth and vagueness. The challenged local ordinance required businesses to obtain a license to sell any items that are "designed or marketed for use with illegal cannabis or drugs." The Supreme Court reversed the Seventh Circuit's determination that the ordinance was unconstitutionally vague on its face and upheld the legislation. The Court held that the ordinance did not directly infringe on non-commercial speech of businesses selling drug paraphernalia or interfere with the sale of drug-related or drug-oriented literature in "head shops." The Court held, with respect to commercial, drug-related expression incident to the operation of drug paraphernalia stores, that the only speech interest implicated was the "attenuated interest in displaying and marketing merchandise in the manner that the retailer desires," 455 U.S. at 496. The Court observed, however, that the ordinance was expressly directed at "commercial activity promoting or encouraging illegal drug use" and stated that "[i]f that activity is deemed 'speech,' then it is speech proposing an illegal transaction, which a government may regulate or ban entirely," *id.* In this discussion, the Court reiterated its holding that "the overbreadth doctrine does not apply to commercial speech," 455 U.S. at 497.

In 1983, in *Bolger v. Youngs Drug Products Corp.*, 463 U.S. 60, 103 S. Ct. 2875 (1983), the Court addressed the constitutionality of 39 U.S.C. § 3001(e)(2), which prohibits the mailing of unsolicited advertisements for contraceptives and found the statute to be an unconstitutional restriction on commercial speech. The Court affirmed a district court determination holding the statute unconstitutional as applied to three types of direct commercial mailings: (1)"multi-page, multi-item flyers promoting a large variety of products available at a drug store, including prophylactics"; (2) "flyers exclusively or substantially devoted to promoting prophylactics"; and (3) "informational pamphlets discussing the de-

sirability and availability of prophylactics or Youngs' products in particular,''
103 S. Ct. at 2878.

The Court first determined the proper classification, as commercial or non-commercial speech, of each of the three mailings, concluding that types (1) and (2) fell ''within the core notion of commercial speech—'speech which does no more than propose a commercial transaction,' '' 103 S. Ct. at 2880. The Court found the status of the informational pamphlets—which were a mixture of direct solicitation of a particular commercial transaction and speech of a more clearly informational variety—to be more problematic. The issue of mixed commercial and non-commercial advertising is an issue to which we return in chapter 5.

The Court's decision, however, began the work of laying down the guidelines for decision in mixed speech cases. The Court said that ''[t]he mere fact that these pamphlets are conceded to be advertisements clearly does not compel the conclusion that they are commercial speech,'' *id*. The Court also held that ''the reference to a specific product does not by itself render the pamphlets commercial speech,'' *id*. Likewise, the fact that Youngs had an economic motivation for mailing the pamphlet was not dispositive by itself with respect to the classification of the pamphlets as commercial or non-commercial. The Court, however, was willing to cumulate these evidentiary factors to support the determination that the pamphlets were commercial. The Court appears to have been content to treat this issue as one of law for the courts to determine, rather than as a question of fact. The Court, therefore, took an important step in its ruling that the mailings constituted commercial speech ''notwithstanding that they contain discussion of important public issues such as venereal disease and family planning,'' *id*. at 2881. Quoting from its opinion in *Central Hudson*, which grappled with a similar issue of mixed speech, the Court said, ''We have made clear that advertising which 'links a product to a current public debate' is not thereby entitled to the constitutional protection afforded non-commercial speech,'' *id*. at 2881.

The Court's treatment of this difficult and important issue of mixed speech does not seem fully articulated. The Court failed to specify any general features of mixed speech which might provide guidance toward its proper classification in a particular case, beyond the implicit criteria to be gleaned from the fact that the informational pamphlets in question (1) were admittedly advertisements, (2) contained references to specific products, and (3) were disseminated by the publisher from an ''economic motive.'' Significantly, the Court did intimate that where the item advertised is itself protected speech, *e.g.*, a book, magazine, or pamphlet, the standard for judging the propriety of legislation restricting advertising of it is entirely different. The problem of mixed speech, of course, was the central problem of *Valentine* itself, where the double-sided handbill contained both a non-commercial political message and an advertisement.

The forty-year-old controversy on this point was reopened in Justice Stevens's concurring opinion in *Bolger*, which recognized that ''advertisements may be complex mixtures of commercial and non-commercial elements: the non-com-

mercial message does not obviate the need for appropriate commercial regulation
. . . ; conversely, the commercial element does not necessarily provide a valid
basis for non-commercial censorship,'' *id*. at 2888. Justice Stevens took note
of the ''significant non-commercial component'' of the third type of mailing.
Here, again, however, the concurring opinion failed to articulate any clear criteria
for making the classification. Justice Stevens eschewed the tyranny of labels,
pointing out that ''significant speech so often comprises both commercial and
non-commercial elements.'' But once the degree of First Amendment protection
to speech is made to hinge on whether speech is commercial or non-commercial,
the tricky process of labeling and classification is inescapable.

The case highlights the uneasiness of some members of the present Court—
Justice Brennan and Justice Stevens, in particular—with the whole distinction
between commercial and non-commercial speech. Here, as in earlier cases, some
members of the Court appear caught in a seemingly unresolvable quandary
between the unacceptability of recognizing full constitutional protection for commercial speech—whether true, false, or misleading and whether or not ''related
to'' unlawful conduct (entailing the abolition of government control of fraud and
deceit in the commercial arena)—and the practical impossibility of drawing the
necessary line between commercial and non-commercial speech.

After determining that all three types of mailings were commercial speech,
the Court applied the fourth criterion of *Central Hudson*, deciding that the
mailings were neither false, deceptive, or misleading, nor ''related to'' illegal
behavior; consequently, they were all entitled to that lesser degree of constitutional protection accorded to commercial speech.

The Court's assessment of the asserted governmental interest in *Bolger* included recognition that the government had chosen not to rely on the moralistic
motivations that underlaid the original enactment of the Comstock Act, the
predecessor statutory provision to 39 U.S.C. § 3001, and focused instead on the
government's more modern set of justifications for this enactment: (1) protection
of recipients of mail from ''offensive'' matter, and (2) assistance to parents in
their efforts to control the manner in which their children become informed about
sensitive and important subjects such as birth control. The Court rejected the
government's first proposed rationale, based on the offensiveness–captive audience justification—a justification which the Court had rejected twice before,
in *Carey v. Population Services*, 431 U.S. 678 (1977) and in *Consolidated
Edison*. At the same time the Court acknowledged the substantial nature of the
government's second proposed rationale.

The crux of the Court's ruling, however, was the *Central Hudson* criterion
requiring that the restriction on commercial speech be no more extensive than
necessary, for the Court held that parents already enjoy practical control over
the mailbox and can also invoke the procedures of 39 U.S.C. § 3008 to ensure
that sexually oriented, ''offensive'' material is not mailed. (The Court upheld
the constitutionality of the ''stop-mail'' procedure of this section in *Rowan v.
Postmaster*, 397 U.S. 728 (1970).) Against this background, the Court regarded

any incremental benefit afforded by the ban on mailing as too marginal to justify the sweeping restriction. In the Court's view, section 3001(e)(2)'s blanket prohibition on mailing also "denies to parents truthful information bearing on their ability to discuss birth control and to make informed decisions in this area," 103 S. Ct. at 2884.

Two decisions during the Court's 1984 term continued the doctrinal developments in the commercial speech field. In *Zauderer v. Office of Disciplinary Counsel*, 53 U.S.L.W. 4587 (May 28, 1985), the Court held that the First Amendment extended to a lawyer's newspaper advertisement offering his services to potential products liability plaintiffs who might have sustained injury in the use of a particular product. The separate opinions in *Dun & Bradstreet, Inc. v. Greenmoss Builders, Inc.*, 53 U.S.L.W. 4866 (June 28, 1985), a libel action arising out of publication of a credit report, illustrate the continuing division among members of the Court concerning the proper definition of "commercial speech." Justice Powell's opinion, expressing the views of only three justices, contains the sweeping suggestion that *all* speech that does not address "a matter of public concern" and that is "speech solely in the individual interest of the speaker and its specific business audience" (53 U.S.L.W. at 4869)—whether or not "commercial" in the narrower sense of doing no more than proposing a commercial transaction—is entitled to less than full First Amendment protection. Justice Powell pointed to the "hardiness" of such speech, the profit motive behind its dissemination and the nature of the individual interest of "its specific business audience," stating that "[w]hether . . . speech addresses a matter of public concern must be determined by the expression's content, form, and context . . . as revealed by the whole record," 53 U.S.L.W. at 4869. This view would appear to result in a vast enlargement of the category of speech entitled to less than full protection beyond what is currently regarded as "commercial speech."

The foregoing review of the principal Supreme Court precedents between 1938 and 1985 concerning commercial speech traces (1) the emergence of a commercial speech exception to the First Amendment in the Jehovah's Witness cases, (2) the first statement of the exception in *Valentine v. Chrestensen*, (3) the Supreme Court's attempts to fashion limitations to the *Valentine* rule in the post-*Valentine* Jehovah's Witness cases, (4) the gradual erosion of the commercial speech exception from *Pittsburgh Press* through *Virginia Pharmacy Board*, and finally (5) the emergence of the modern doctrine of limited constitutional protection for commercial speech which the Supreme Court distilled and stated in the *Central Hudson* decision.

Making use of the Supreme Court's work in this field of constitutional law, as surveyed in the foregoing account, at this point we propose to describe the essential structural components of any complete doctrine regarding the constitutional status of commercial speech and, against that analysis, to summarize current constitutional doctrine. To this task the following chapter is devoted.

5

A Summary of Current Commercial Speech Doctrine

This chapter summarizes the current status of the commercial speech doctrine. For this purpose, the doctrine is broken down into its basic components, and the judicial decisions are organized in terms of these components. Of course, the doctrine can only be properly understood as a whole, and the following summary is based on a somewhat arbitrary analysis that recommends itself as one convenient way of grouping principles around the main questions that seem to be addressed so far in the decisions. Although, for the purpose of analysis, the main structural components of the Supreme Court's theory may be separated, these issues are in many instances highly interrelated. To take only one example, the rationale for protecting commercial speech at all will have important implications in devising a definition of commercial speech as well as for formulating the degree of protection such speech will enjoy.

The following main components of the doctrine will serve as the outline for the summary:

1. *Definition.* Commercial speech is defined.

2. *Protective Principle and the Rationale of Protection.* The principles that establish that commercial speech is entitled to some constitutional protection, and the reasons given for affording any degree of protection to commercial speech.

3. *Principles of Judicial Review of Regulation of Commercial Speech.* Principles that integrate the commercial speech doctrine into the existing law of judicial review of legislation. The existing doctrines of judicial review of legislation derive from other amendments, principally the due process and equal protection clauses of the Fourteenth Amendment and the due process clause of the Fifth Amendment and the equal protection component of the Fifth Amendment. These doctrines include principles (i) defining which governmental interests are legitimate ones, (ii) specifying what relationships must hold between the governmental interest served by the legislative measure and the particular form that legislation takes, and (iii) ranking the importance of the

legitimate governmental interests to be served by regulation. These principles include the contextual analogues to the ordinary principles that control the balancing of interests, including the selection of the companion levels of scrutiny and degree of permissible invasion of the interest: (i) absolute protection—"strict scrutiny," (ii) serious intrusion into the freedom—"intermediate or rational basis," or (iii) substantial burden. They also include principles that identify and prohibit the use of certain illegitimate means of achieving otherwise legitimate governmental interests, *e.g.*, advancing legitimate interests by keeping the public ignorant as in *Central Hudson* or *Virginia Pharmacy Board*, an impermissible means. Applying the general theory of judicial review in other contexts, the Supreme Court has had occasion to distinguish among (i) illegitimate governmental interests, (ii) legitimate governmental interests of only average importance, (iii) substantial governmental interests, and (iv) compelling governmental interests. Principles explaining the rationale for protecting commercial speech, thus, help to establish the weight of the interest in a particular case and help to define what counts as commercial speech. This includes the rationale for differential treatment of commercial speech as opposed to non-commercial speech.

4. *Principles Governing a Mixture of Protected Commercial Speech in an Unlawful Course of Conduct*. Principles are required to deal with cases in which the protected commercial speech is merely a constituent element of a course of conduct that is otherwise unlawful. These situations include commercial speech in which an illegal transaction is proposed.

5. *The Application of Ancillary Procedural and Protective Principles of the First Amendment to Commercial Speech*. A comprehensive theory would seem to require certain ancillary principles governing the manner in which the other principles shall be applied. Examples of this type of principle include: (i) principles of standing to sue, or standing to challenge certain types of restrictions for the public at large, for speakers, for listeners, for distributors of speech, and for instumentalities of speech, (ii) principles for allocating the burden of proof or persuasion on particular issues, (iii) principles defining the applicable presumptions, (iv) principles defining the status of prior restraints on commercial speech, (v) principles of construction of other rules, strict construction, strict or close scrutiny versus liberal application, (vi) principles for resolution of close cases, "doubt resolving" or allocation of the "burden of uncertainty," and (vii) principles recognizing or rejecting the need for *per se* rules, brightline distinctions, rules of thumb, and presumptions.

THE DEFINITION OF COMMERCIAL SPEECH

The Importance of Defining Commercial Speech

The problem of defining what speech is commercial is critically important. It is of fundamental importance primarily because the failure to develop a clear definition of commercial speech, which receives less than full constitutional protection, jeopardizes non-commercial speech, which is entitled to full protection. As an institutional matter, the failure to draw a clear line of demarcation increases the likelihood of misclassification of non-commercial speech as commercial speech, and thus increases the likelihood that non-commercial speech, which is entitled to full protection under the First Amendment, will be unconstitutionally restricted. As Justice Stevens has pointed out, it is important "that the commercial speech concept not be defined too broadly lest speech deserving of greater constitutional protection be inadvertently suppressed," *Central Hudson Gas & Electric Corp. v. Public Service Commission, supra,* 447 U.S. at 579 (concurring opinion of Justice Stevens).

Some members of the Supreme Court have continued to express uneasiness with an anomalous distinction on the basis of content between commercial and non-commercial speech. They have also raised the question whether, given the practical impossibility of drawing a sharp distinction, legislation in this area that delegates to local authorities the power of drawing that distinction is consistent with the Constitution. The Court's continued acceptance of the principle that the content of otherwise protected speech may be such that it warrants a lesser degree of protection has already produced aberrations. The problem arose, for example, in *Young v. American Mini-Theatres, Inc.,* 427 U.S. 50, 68 (1976), which involved the constitutionality of a local zoning ordinance that distinguished between motion picture theatres which exhibit sexually explicit, but non-obscene movies, and those that do not. Part III of Justice Stevens's opinion (joined only by the Chief Justice and Justices White and Rehnquist) relied on the content of expression as a basis for determining differential constitutional protection in the commercial speech area as a basis for extending the use of content to create other, less favored categories of expression as applied to sexually explicit but non-obscene communications. By contrast, Justice Powell declined to reach the question whether "non-obscene, erotic materials may be treated differently under First Amendment principles from other forms of protected expression," 427 U.S. at 73 n.1.

In his dissenting opinion in *Lehman v. City of Shaker Heights,* which addressed the constitutionality of a ban on political advertising placards in public transit vehicles, Justice Brennan pointed out that "[t]he line between ideological and non-ideological speech is impossible to draw," 418 U.S. at 319. This theme was also developed in *Virginia Pharmacy Board,* where, after noting that "not all commercial messages contain . . . a very great public interest element," the Court suggested that "[t]here are few to which such an element, however, could not be added," 425 U.S. at 764. The Court went on: "Our pharmacist [who was forbidden from directly advertising the prices of drugs], for example, could cast himself as a commentator on store-to-store disparities in drug prices, giving his own and those of a competitor as proof. We see little point in requiring him to do so, and little difference if he does not," *id.*

In *Metromedia,* Justice Brennan gave other examples which point up the apparent ease of evading any legal standard (*cf. Valentine v. Chrestensen*) that depends on the distinction between commercial and non-commercial speech. They also underscore the undesirability of having local officials regularly drawing the distinction and permitting the leveling effect on protected speech to occur by reason of the "ideological–non-ideological speech" distinction (191 S. Ct. at 2908):

It is one thing for a court to classify in specific cases whether commercial or non-commercial speech is involved, but quite another—and for me dispositively so—for a city to do so regularly for the purpose of deciding what messages may be communicated by way of billboards. Cities are equipped to make traditional police decisions, *see Saia v. New York, supra,* 334 U.S. at 564–565 (Frankfurter, J., dissenting), not decisions based on the content of speech. I would be unhappy to see city officials dealing with the following series of billboards and deciding which ones to permit: The first billboard contains the message "Visit Joe's Ice Cream Shoppe"; the second, "Joe's Ice Cream Shoppe uses only the highest quality dairy products"; the third, "Because Joe thinks that dairy products are good for you, please shop at Joe's Shoppe"; and the fourth, "Joe says to support dairy price supports; they mean lower prices for you at his Shoppe." Or how about some San Diego Padres baseball fans—with no connection to the team—who together rent a billboard and communicate the message "Support the San Diego Padres, a great baseball team." May the city decide that a United Automobile Workers billboard with the message "Be a patriot—do not buy Japanese-manufactured cars" is "commercial" and therefore forbid it? What if the same sign is placed by Chrysler?

I do not read our recent line of commercial cases as authorizing this sort of regular and immediate line-drawing by governmental entities. If anything, our cases recognize the difficulty in making a determination that speech is either "commercial" or "non-commercial."

The Court's attempts to define commercial speech have been fraught with difficulties and inconsistencies.

Overview and Current Status

The Supreme Court decisions on commercial speech reviewed in the preceding chapters show just how uncertain the boundaries of the commercial speech concept have been. In *Schneider v. Irvington, supra,* the Court drew a distinction between "commercial soliciting and canvassing," and in its reference to "those who canvass for private profit" (308 U.S. at 163) suggested that the speaker's motivation for the expression is a factor relevant to its classification. The Court also suggested, by implication, that speaker motivation would also be a factor relevant to determining the degree of constitutional protection to which it may be entitled.

The two-sided handbill in *Valentine v. Chrestensen, supra,* which protested New York's allocation of docking privileges and contained an invitation to buy an admission to the submarine tour, implicated two different kinds of commercial elements. The political protest against New York's docking regulations was motivated ultimately by the fact that the regulations frustrated Chrestensen's successful conduct of his business and impaired his ability to make a profit, or at least his ability to make as much profit as he believed he should have made. The Court was satisfied in *Valentine* simply to identify the "purely commercial advertising" side of Chrestensen's handbill and dismissed the protest of the docking policies on the basis that Chrestensen's affixing of the protest was done "with the intent and for the purpose of evading the prohibition of the ordinance," 316 U.S. at 55. The Court did not otherwise comment on Chrestensen's motivation but appeared to give controlling weight to the content of the advertising.

In some of the Jehovah's Witness cases, the Court touched on a number of commercial elements—the motivation and economic results of the activity, the commercial methods used, and the content of the commercial solicitations involved in the doorstep transactions at issue. In the final analysis, however, the Supreme Court's disposition in those cases did not actually turn upon the commercial nature of the transactions. Nonetheless, the Court took notice in the *Bowden* and *Sanders* cases that the petitioners contended that "their enterprise was operated at a loss," 316 U.S. at 592, and Justice Jackson in dissent in the *Douglas*, *Murdock*, and *Martin* cases saw fit to question that factual assumption, 319 U.S. at 169–170. Whether the Watch Tower Bible and Tract Society made a profit overall, and whether the full-time and part-time canvassers made a profit overall seem to have been given some weight, and the economic results of this work may also have been given significance insofar as it may have been relevant to show the motivation of the Society or of its members. When the Court initially upheld the convictions in the *Jones*, *Bowden*, *Sanders*, and *Jobin* cases, before granting reargument and reversing the convictions, the majority did so because it viewed the door-to-door sale of religious literature "as partaking more of the commercial than religious or educational transactions" and referred to the use of "ordinary commercial *methods* of sales of articles," 316 U.S. at 597. The dissenters also placed emphasis on motive but disagreed over the inferences of motive to be drawn from the evidence, 316 U.S. at 620.

In the earlier commercial speech cases, the Supreme Court was unable to fashion a definition of commercial speech. The Court made reference to (1) the content of the communication, (2) the motive of the speaker, and (3) the commercial methods used in the dissemination of ideas, suggesting that the definition of commercial speech was to be found in a consideration of these three factors.

Pittsburgh Press, which dealt with government restrictions on gender-based help-wanted advertising, referred to advertising that does "no more than propose a commercial transaction," 413 U.S. at 385. In *Bigelow*, the Court distinguished abortion referral advertising from commercial speech on the ground that it "did more than simply propose a commercial transaction," because it "contained factual material of clear 'public interest,' " 421 U.S. at 822. But the Court did not restrict itself to the single criterion of content of the message in classifying commercial speech. The Court noted that "[t]he diverse motives, means, and messages of advertising may make speech 'commercial' in widely varying degrees," 421 U.S. at 826.

Although in these transitional cases that heralded the modern commercial speech doctrine, the Court did not abandon reliance on (1) motive, (2) means, and (3) content, the need to refine the definition of commercial speech became increasingly apparent. In *Bates v. State Bar of Arizona, supra*, decided in 1977, the Court dismissed as irrelevant several of the criteria mentioned in earlier decisions. Thus, the Court said that speech is fully protected "even though it is in the form of a paid advertisement." As in *New York Times v. Sullivan*, the fact that expression "is in the form of a solicitation to pay or contribute money," the Court noted, likewise is not necessarily a distinguishing feature of commercial speech, at least where the solicitation is for the purchase of literature protected by the First Amendment. Moreover, the Court suggested that the speaker's motivation is not necessarily determinative, pointing out that "[e]ven though the speaker's interest is largely economic, the Court has protected such speech in certain contexts," *Bates v. State Bar of Arizona*, 433 U.S. 350. In *Bates*, the Court also declared that if commercial speech is to be distinguished from non-commercial speech, it "must be distinguished by its content," 433 U.S. at 363; *see also, Virginia Pharmacy Board v. Virginia Consumer Council*, 425 U.S. at 761. Thus, in *Bates*, the Court again spoke of communications that "proposed a mundane commercial transaction," 433 US. at 363.

In some subsequent decisions the Court appears to have adhered to content as the sole determining factor in the classification of speech as commercial. Thus, in *Friedman v. Rogers*, which involved governmental regulation of the use of trade names by optometrists, the Court referred to commercial advertising that "contained statements about the products or services offered and their prices," 440 U.S. 1. In *Village of Schaumberg v. Citizens for a Better Environment*, the Court's criteria for identifying a "commercial solicitation" for funds were whether the solicitation "does more than inform private economic decision," 444 U.S. at 632, and whether the solicitation "is primarily concerned with providing information about the characteristics and costs of goods and services," 444 U.S. at 632. In *Virginia Pharmacy Board*, the Court classified drug price advertising as commercial speech because it was "speech which does 'no more than propose a commercial transaction,'" 425 U.S. at 762, following the formulation in *Pittsburgh Press*. In its discussion of the *Valentine v. Chrestensen* commercial speech exception, the *Virginia Pharmacy Board* Court again emphasized content when it repeated the idea that "[i]f there is a kind of commercial speech that lacks all First Amendment protection . . . , it must be distinguished by its *content*," 425 U.S., at 761 (emphasis added).

In *Linmark*, the Court made no reference to any formula defining commercial speech, but the residential "For Sale" signs in that case were clearly within the category of "speech which does no more than propose a commercial transaction." *Ohralik*, which involved in-person solicitation of clients by attorneys, referred to "[e]xpressions concerning purely commercial transactions," 436 U.S. at 455. In *Primus*, the Court suggested that the state's regulatory powers were limited to speech "that simply propose[s] a commercial transaction," relying once again on the formulation of *Pittsburgh Press*. *Primus* involved a written solicitation of clients for free legal services by a lawyer affiliated with the American Civil Liberties Union, and the Court's holding appears to be based, at least in part, on the fact that the legal services being offered were free. The Court characterized Primus's communication as one that was not "for pecuniary gain," 436 U.S. at 422.

The Court's reference to the fact that communication in *Primus* was not for pecuniary gain appears to support the view that the motivation of the speaker remains a relevant factor in classifying speech as commercial. Even speech that is purely commercial in content, in the sense that it does no more than propose a commercial transaction, nonetheless may not qualify as commercial speech if the speaker's motivation is not for pecuniary gain. Such speech is therefore arguably entitled to full First Amendment protection. Thus, although the modern commercial speech cases of the 1970s began by explicitly rejecting speaker motivation as a factor relevant to the classification of commercial speech, and even suggested that the scope of the commercial speech doctrine would be relatively narrow, the Court's decisions continued to exhibit some confusion on the question whether speaker motivation is a relevant factor.

In *Central Hudson*, where the Court attempted a full restatement of the commercial speech doctrine, the Court's decision made reference to "expression related solely to the economic interests of the speaker and its audience," 447 U.S. at 561. That broad formulation appears not only to reimport the notion of speaker's economic interests or motivation, but also to affirm the notion that the interests or motivations of the actual or potential audience may be relevant. Is speech rendered commercial when the listeners or readers to whom it is addressed are interested in it solely as a means of advancing their own economic interests— say, a manual on how to run a business in a more profitable manner?

The diverse opinions in *Metromedia* suggest even further complications that must be taken into account in defining commercial speech. Like the Court's reference to "economic interests of the speaker and its audience" in *Central Hudson*, Justice White's opinion in *Metromedia* adopted the terminology of interests in pointing out that the interests of a third category of persons involved in the dissemination of speech were implicated in restrictions on speech—in that case the outdoor advertising companies who owned billboards and rented space on them for a profit. The position of the billboard companies is, thus, somewhat analogous to the standing of the publishers in *Pittsburgh Press* and *Bigelow*. In *Metromedia*, some of the regulated billboard advertising was non-commercial in content, but the outdoor advertising companies challenging the ordinance had a purely commercial or economic interest in defeating the ordinance, *i.e.*, pecuniary gain to be realized from the rental of billboard space. Justice White was prepared to uphold the standing of those who had purely commercial motives to challenge restrictions on non-commercial speech and to apply the more stringent standards of full constitutional protection to their claims relating to speech of non-commercial content.

In *Bolger v. Youngs Drug Products Co.*, *supra*, the definitional problems were presented by the third of the three categories of unsolicited direct mailings relating to contraceptive products. Like some of the informational advertising discussed in *Central Hudson* and the informative portions of the advertising in *Bigelow*, these informational pamphlets were a mixture of direct solicitation of a particular commercial transaction and speech of a more clearly informational variety. The Court appears to have departed from rigid adherence to the formulaic definition of commercial speech as speech that "does no more than propose a commercial transaction." In so doing, the Court also abandoned the idea, appearing explicitly in some earlier decisions, that if commercial speech is to be distinguished from non-commercial speech, it is to be distinguished solely on the basis of its content. Rather, in *Bolger* the Court was willing to consider (1) the fact that the pamphlets were advertisements, (2) the reference therein to a specific product, and (3) "the fact that Youngs has an economic motivation" for mailing the pamphlets. The Court stated that the presence of any one of the criteria by itself would not require or even permit the conclusion that the pamphlets were commercial speech, 103 S. Ct. at 2880. The Court's emphasis in *Bolger* on the "reference to a specific product" cannot be read as a definitive requirement that speech to constitute commercial speech must contain a "reference to a specific product." Indeed, in a footnote, the Court observed: "That a product is referred to generically does not, however, remove it from the realm of commercial speech," 103 S. Ct. at 2880 n.13. The Court gave two specific examples:

[A] company with sufficient control of the market for a product may be able to promote the product without reference to its own brand names. Or, a trade association may make statements about a product without reference to specific brand names. *See, e.g., National Commission on Egg Nutrition v. FTC*, 570 F.2d 157 (7th Cir. App. 1977).

These examples are important because, in providing them, the Court might appear to have laid down a rule requiring either (1) reference to a specific product as a commercial speech, or (2) generic reference to a product, accompanied by proof that the advertiser's market share was sufficient to guarantee the likelihood of the recipient's connecting the generic reference to the advertiser's product. In fact, the Court was careful in *Bolger* to include the fact that Youngs described itself as "the leader in the manufacture and sale" of contraceptives, 103 S. Ct. at 2880 n.13. On the basis of this statement, drawn from Youngs's brief, and a single reference to Youngs's product at the very bottom of the last page of the brochure, where appellee is identified as the distributor of Trojan-brand prophylactics, the Court was able to conclude that the pamphlet contained the requisite reference to a specific product. *Bolger*, however, left these questions open, for the Court said: "Nor do we mean to suggest that each of the characteristics present in this case must necessarily be present in order for speech to be commercial," *id.* at 2881 n.14.

The Court, in effect, revolutionized the definition of commercial speech by adopting the entirely new technique of cumulating commercial aspects of format, content, and motivation, rather than concentrating exclusively on content. The Court's holding concerning the definitional problem may herald a test that relies on a subjective balancing of these three factors. In dictum in a footnote, the Court also suggested that the nature of the product could be a relevant and dispositive factor—even where the three factors of format, content, and motivation all have commercial aspects. Cf. *Dun & Bradstreet, Inc. v. Greenmoss Builders, Inc. supra.* Citing its 1943 decision in *Murdock v. Pennsylvania,* discussed above, the Court intimated that where the product advertised is "an activity itself protected by the First Amendment," the advertisement may nonetheless be non-commercial speech entitled to the full protection of the First Amendment: "Of course, a different conclusion may be appropriate where the pamphlet advertises an activity itself protected by the First Amendment. *See Murdock v. Pennsylvania,* 319 U.S. 105 (1943) (advertisement for religious book cannot be regulated as commercial speech)," *id.* at 2880, n.14.

The Court's footnote seems to raise a question whether the "mere book agent" of *Breard v. Alexandria* or those selling magazine subscriptions door to door enjoy the same status as Murdock, who sold religious literature using the same methods, and doubts concerning the continuing vitality of *Breard.* Certainly the activity advertised in book advertisements is constitutionally protected. The close questions in this area will probably occur in cases involving mail solicitation of erotically oriented but non-obscene books and magazines.

The Status of "Image" or "Institutional" Advertising as Commercial Speech

After *Bolger,* the question arises as to whether "image" or "institutional" advertising is commercial speech.

Corporate image advertising is published not for the direct and immediate purpose of selling goods and services but for the purpose of selling ideas. Two distinct types of ideas are sold in such advertising: (1) the advertising corporation or institution as an abstract reality, and (2) the advertising corporation's or other institution's position on certain public issues. The latter is sometimes referred to as "issue advocacy advertising." The status of corporate image advertising and the power of the federal agencies to regulate image advertising has sparked a lively controversy.[1]

The Court has not definitively answered the question whether corporate image advertising is commercial speech, even though it may contain no reference to a specific product. In a footnote in *Bolger,* the Court in fact expressly left that issue open: "For example, we express no opinion as to whether reference to any particular product or service is a necessary element" of commercial speech.[2]

Is a Specific Product Reference Required?

The Court's intimation in *Bolger* that speech need not refer to a particular product or service to qualify as commercial speech does not seem entirely consistent with the Court's statements in earlier cases. For example, in *Friedman v. Rogers*, the entire rationale of differential treatment of commercial speech is made to hinge on the fact that commercial speech is about a "particular product or service":

Because it relates to a particular product or service, commercial speech is more objective, hence more verifiable, than other varieties of speech. Commercial speech, because of its importance to business profits, and because it is carefully calculated, is also less likely than other forms of speech to be inhibited by proper regulation. 440 U.S. at 10 (emphasis added)

The reference to a specific product did not by itself render the pamphlets to be commercial speech. The commercial motive of the drug company in mailing them was not by itself dispositive. The Court, however, cumulated these factors relating to format, content, and motivation to determine that the mailings were commercial speech, "notwithstanding that they contain[ed] discussion of important public issues." The Court reaffirmed the principle that "advertising which links a product to a current public debate is not thereby entitled to the constitutional protection afforded non-commercial speech," 103 S. Ct. at 2881. The *Bolger* Court did refer to "speech which does no more than propose a commercial transaction" as speech that falls within "the core notion of commercial speech," 103 S. Ct. at 2880. But the Court suggested that speech that does not fit within the core notion of commercial speech may still fall within the scope of commercial speech.

Summary

To date, the Supreme Court has failed to formulate a precise definition of commercial speech. After a period during which the Court seemed willing to recognize only speech that "proposes a commercial transaction" as commercial speech—a formula that identified only the content of speech as relevant to its classification—the Court began to expand its consideration of factors relevant to classification to include the speaker's economic motivation or lack thereof, in certain circumstances. Recent opinions suggest that the Court has rejected that simplistic and narrow version of the doctrine and now mentions not only the speaker's economic interests but also the economic interests of the speaker's audience and of persons other than the speaker who are involved in the dissemination of the speech. The Court's recognition of the complex matrix of economic and non-economic interests of speakers, audiences, and persons associated with the medium, and of the almost limitless variations in content, would seem to suggest that the Court is only now beginning the task of defining the concept of commercial speech.

In the senses in which the Supreme Court has discussed commercial speech, speech may be said to be commercial because (1) the speaker (or the publisher or the distributor) paid money to project it or disseminate it; (2) the speech itself is being sold, as in the case of many books and magazines; (3) the speech is commercial in content, *i.e.*, the subject matter relates exclusively to the characteristics of products or services, their prices, their suppliers and their customers, the means of production and distribution, and the like; (4) the speech is authored, published, or distributed for the purpose of advancing the commercial or economic interests of the speaker, publisher, or distributor (collectively, "the source"); (5) the speech has a tendency, or is intended by the source or perceived by the audience, to advance the economic interests of its audience, or part of its audience. The Court has noted, however, that some of these senses are not relevant or at least are not relevant standing alone.

Developing this conceptual scheme further, let us hypothesize that the following interests may be implicated in what might be called a communications transaction:

1. The interests or motivations of the author or speaker
2. The interests or motivations of the publisher
3. The interests or motivations of the distributor (other than the publisher)
4. The interests or motivations of the audience or potential audience

These interests may be commercial or non-commercial in the sense that the communications transaction in question may be regarded, in whole or in part, by one or more of these interested persons as a means to a financial or economic objective.

In addition, the speech may be characterized as commercial or non-commercial depending on some feature of its content or the method by which or context in which it is published or broadcast: (1) the character of the object or state of affairs described or depicted, (2) the nature of performance accomplished by the speech,[3] and (3) the medium through which the speech is communicated.

There are also (1) the consequences of the specific act of communication; (2) the consequences of all acts of communication of that kind (generalization); and (3) the consequence of the set of rules designed to govern the system of communication.

Only a moment's reflection on these factors is needed to realize that over two dozen permutations are possible. Most of them have not yet been represented by Supreme Court decisions.

THE PROTECTIVE PRINCIPLE AND THE RATIONALE OF PROTECTION OF COMMERCIAL SPEECH

The constitutional principle extending First Amendment protection to commercial speech is, of course, the core of the modern commercial speech doctrine. Between the date of the decision in *Bigelow* and the date of its decision in *Central*

Hudson, the Supreme Court overruled its holding in *Valentine v. Chrestensen* that commercial speech is entitled to no protection under the First Amendment against governmental interference. The Court has substituted for the sweeping rule announced in *Valentine* the narrower principle that commercial speech enjoys a degree of constitutional protection: *Bolger v. Youngs Drug Products Corp.*, 463 U.S. 60, 103 S. Ct. 2875, 2879 (1983); *Central Hudson Gas & Electric Corp. v. Public Service Commission*, 447 U.S. 557, 561 (1980) ("The First Amendment protects commercial speech from unwarranted governmental intrusion."); *Linmark Associates, Inc. v. Willingboro*, 431 U.S. 85 (1977); *Virginia Pharmacy Board v. Virginia Citizens Consumer Council*, 425 U.S. 748, 769– 770 (1976); *Bigelow v. Virginia*, 421 U.S. 809 (1975). For commercial speech to enjoy some measure of constitutional protection, "it at least must concern lawful activity and not be misleading," *Bolger v. Youngs Drug Products Corp.*, *supra*, 463 U.S. 60, 103 S. Ct. at 2881; *Metromedia, Inc. v. City of San Diego*, *supra*, 101 S. Ct. at 2892; *Central Hudson Gas & Electric Corp. v. Public Service Commission*, *supra*, 447 U.S. at 566. We refer to this rule as the fundamental principle of protection.

Since the rationale for protecting commercial speech at all can be relevant to determining the degree of protection, as well as the applicability of the basic principle to specific instances, it is important to clarify the Court's underlying rationale for protecting commercial speech. The Supreme Court has approached the rationale for constitutional protection of commercial speech from two different perspectives. First, the Court has delineated the positive factors that require that commercial speech enjoy some degree of protection. Second, the Court has compared and contrasted commercial speech with other categories of speech which do not enjoy constitutional protection.

Generally, commercial speech is protected for four main reasons which combined elevate to constitutional status the economic interests of speakers or advertisers, the personal welfare and personal interests of consumers or recipients of advertising, the general interest and curiosity of society as a whole, and the fundamental societal interest in political economy and the market system.

First, commercial speech is of economic importance to speakers, and, in that respect, the speaker's economic interests cannot be distinguished from the economic interests of speakers in other contexts, such as those involving speech by labor and management representatives in labor disputes (picketing speeches by management to employees in the course of union organization drives), in which it is already well established that the communications of disputants are constitutionally protected even though the subject matter of the communications is commerce, and the only interest of the speaker is the speaker's own economic gain, *Linmark Associates, Inc. v. Willingboro*, *supra*, 431 U.S. at 92; *Virginia Pharmacy Board*, *supra*, 425 U.S. at 762.

Second, commercial speech is protected because it is of interest and of utility to individual consumers who desire to receive it or hear it. Commercial speech can provide the means for securing "the alleviation of physical pain or the enjoyment of basic necessities," *Virginia Pharmacy Board, supra,* at 764; *see also, Linmark Associates, Inc. supra.* Commercial free speech can be defended on utilitarian grounds. Rules protecting freedom of commercial speech maximize pleasure over pain, or permit maximization of good over bad or the minimization of what is bad.

Third, as the Court has pointed out, "Society . . . may have a strong subjective interest in the free flow of commercial information," *Virginia Pharmacy Board, supra,* 425 U.S. 748; *Linmark Associates, Inc., supra.*

Fourth, and finally, the free flow of commercial information is indispensable to the proper operation of the free enterprise economy, which "through numerous private economic decisions" allocates resources, *Virginia Pharmacy Board, supra,* at 765; *Linmark Associates, Inc., supra.*

Put another way, "[c]ommercial expression not only serves the economic interest of the speaker, but also assists consumers and furthers the societal interest in the fullest possible dissemination of information," and protection of such expression is simply a rejection of the "highly paternalistic" view that government has complete power to suppress or regulate commercial speech, *Central Hudson Gas & Electric Corp., supra,* 447 U.S. at 561–562. The Supreme Court has not developed further the rationale for protecting commercial speech. As noted above, however, in earlier cases involving categories of speech which receive no constitutional protection, there do appear the beginnings of a rationale to cover the well-known exceptions to the First Amendment, of libel and slander, obscenity, incitement, and fighting words. The Court articulated this second, "negative" approach in *Virginia Pharmacy Board,* 425 U.S. at 762, where it is said:

Our question is whether speech which does "no more than propose a commercial transaction," *Pittsburgh Press Co. v. Human Relations Commission,* 413 U.S. at 385, is so removed from any "exposition of ideas," *Chaplinsky v. New Hampshire,* 315 U.S. 568, 572 (1942), and from "truth, science, morality, and arts in general, in its diffusion of liberal sentiments on the administration of Government," *Roth v. United States,* 354 U.S. 476, 484 (1957), that it lacks all protection.

In *Chaplinsky,* the Court affirmed the petitioner's conviction under a New Hampshire statute prohibiting the addressing of any "offensive, derisive or annoying word to any other person who is lawfully in any street or other public place." Chaplinsky, a member of the Jehovah's Witness sect, was accused of addressing the city marshal saying, "You are a God damned racketeer" and "a damned Fascist and the whole government of Rochester are Fascists or agents of Fascists." The spoken, not the written word, was involved in the case. The Court explained that "[t]here are certain well-defined and narrowly limited classes of speech, the prevention and punishment of which has never been thought to raise any Constitutional problem. These include the lewd and obscene, the profane, the libelous, and the insulting or 'fighting' words—those which by their very utterance inflict injury or tend to incite an immediate breach of the peace,'' 315 U.S. at 571–572. As the Court pointed out, these categories of completely unprotected speech are characterized by the common feature that ''their very utterance inflict[s] injury or tend[s] to incite an immediate breach of the peace,'' and continued by pointing to other differences between them and the broad category of protected speech:

It has been well observed that such utterances are no essential part of any exposition of ideas, and are of such slight social value as a step to truth that any benefit that may be derived from them is clearly outweighed by the social interests in order and morality. 315 U.S. at 572

The Court also referred to its statement in *Cantwell v. Connecticut, supra,* 310 U.S. at 309, that ''[r]esort to epithets or personal abuse is not in any proper sense communication of information or opinion safeguarded by the Constitution.'' The Court acknowledged its debt to Zechariah Chafee's description of the normal criminal law of words, in his book *Free Speech in the United States,* at 149–150. In that book, Chafee, whose specific subject was punishment under sedition acts, had written:

To restate the matter in accordance with the reasoning in the first chapter, the normal criminal law is interested in preventing crimes and certain non-criminal interferences with governmental functions like refusals to enlist or to subscribe to bonds. *It is directed primarily against actual injuries. Such injuries are usually committed by acts, but the law also punishes a few classes of words like obscenity, profanity, and gross libels upon individuals, because the very utterance of such words is considered to inflict a present injury upon listeners, readers, or those defamed,* or *else to render highly probable an immediate breach of the peace.* This is a very different matter from punishing words because they express ideas which are thought to cause a future danger to the State.

. . .

The existence of a verbal crime at common law shows the presence of a social interest which must be weighed in the balance, but the free speech guaranties, as I have argued at length, enact a countervailing social interest in the attainment and dissemination of truth, which was insufficiently recognized by the common law. Nor do I base my conclusion on the historical fact that the framers of the constitutions wanted to safeguard political discussion, because their own statements of freedom of speech in the address to the people of Quebec, the Virginia Toleration Statute, and the opening clause of the First Amendment itself, prove that they also wanted to safeguard scientific and religious freedom, both of which would be greatly restricted by a sweeping application of the common law of obscenity and blasphemy. *The true explanation is that profanity and indecent talk and pictures, which do not form an essential part of any exposition of ideas, have a very slight social value as a step toward truth, which is clearly outweighed by the social interests in order, morality, the training of the young, and the peace of mind of those who hear and see. Words of this type offer little opportunity for the usual process of counter-argument. The harm is done as soon as they are communicated, or is liable to follow almost immediately in the form of retaliatory violence.* The only sound explanation of the punishment of obscenity and profanity is that *the words are criminal, not because of the ideas they communicate, but like acts because of their immediate consequences to the five senses.* The man who swears in a street car is as much of a nuisance as the man who smokes there. Insults are punished like a threatening gesture, since they are liable to provoke a fight. Adulterated candy is no more poisonous to children than some books. Grossly unpatriotic language may be punished for the same reasons. The man who talks scurrilously about the flag commits a crime, not because the implications of his ideas tend to weaken the Federal Government, but because the effect resembles that of an injurious act such as trampling on the flag, which would be a public nuisance and a breach of the peace. This is a state but not a federal crime, for the United States has no criminal jurisdiction over offenses against order and good manners, although Congress may possibly have power to regulate the use of the national emblem. It is altogether different from sedition.

The absurd and unjust holdings in some of these prosecutions for the use of indecent or otherwise objectionable language furnish a sharp warning against any creation of new verbal crimes. Thus, the test of obscenity is very vague, and many decisions have utterly failed to distinguish nasty talk or the sale of unsuitable books to the young from the serious discussion of topics of great social significance.

. . .

[T]he authorities should be very reluctant to punish the contrary-minded, even though the prosecution be rested on some non-religious ground like the offensiveness of the defendant's irreligious language or the tendency of blasphemy to produce a breach of the peace.

This breach of the peace theory is peculiarly liable to abuse when applied against unpopular expressions and practices. It makes a man a criminal simply because his neighbors have no self-control and cannot refrain from violence. The *reductio ad absurdum* of this theory was the imprisonment of Joseph Palmer, one of Bronson Alcott's fellow-settlers at "Fruitlands," not because he was a communist, but because he persisted in wearing such a long beard that people kept mobbing him, until law and order were maintained by shutting him up. A man does not become a criminal because some one else assaults him, unless his own conduct is in itself illegal or may be reasonably considered a direct provocation to violence.

Thus all these crimes of injurious words must be kept within very narrow limits if they are not to give excessive opportunities for outlawing heterodox ideas. (footnotes omitted, emphasis added)

Chaffee also touched on the category of speech which is punished as "an attempt or solicitation, although it falls short of actual injury":

Besides these special classes of words which cause present injury, the normal law punished speech as an attempt or solicitation, although it falls short of actual injury; but the first chapter has shown that this is only when the words come somewhere near success and render the commission of actual crime or other tangible obstruction of state activities probable unless the state steps in at once and penalizes the conduct before it ripens into injury. The law of attempts and solicitation is directed not against the words but against acts, and the words are punished only because that is the necessary way to avoid harmful acts. When A urges B to kill C and tells him how he can do it, this has nothing to do with the attainment and dissemination of truth, and besides there is genuine danger that the murder will take place long before discussion will prove it to be a mistaken scheme.

In *Roth*, one of the early obscenity decisions, the Court upheld the constitutionality of the federal statute prohibiting the mailing of obscene publications and, in the course of doing so, expanded on the rationale for excluding obscene literature from the scope of the First Amendment. Justice Brennan's opinion for the Court, besides containing a historical review of state obscenity laws at the time of the adoption of the First Amendment, also set forth some of the rationale behind the adoption of the First Amendment (354 U.S. at 484):

The protection given speech and press was fashioned to assure unfettered interchange of ideas for the bringing about of political and social changes desired by the people. This objective was made explicit as early as 1774 in a letter of the Continental Congress to the inhabitants of Quebec: "The last right we shall mention, regards the freedom of the press. The importance of this consists, besides the advancement of truth, science, morality, and arts in general, in its diffusion of liberal sentiments on the administration of Government, its ready communication of thoughts between subjects, and its consequential promotion of union among them, whereby oppressive officers are shamed or intimidated, into more honourable and just modes of conducting affairs." 1 Journals of the Continental Congress 108 (1774). All ideas having even the slightest redeeming social importance—unorthodox ideas, controversial ideas, even ideas hateful to the prevailing climate of opinion—have the full protection of the guaranties, unless excludable because they encroach upon the limited area of more important interests.

Measured in terms of the rationales developed in the *Chaplinsky* and *Roth* decisions, commercial speech can be seen to be sharply distinguishable. Commercial speech does not share with other forms of unprotected speech the attribute that its very utterance "is considered to inflict a present injury upon listeners, readers, or those defamed, or else render highly probable an immediate breach of the peace," as Chaffee had described in that category. Nor does commercial speech fit neatly in the category of speech that has not even "the slightest redeeming social importance"—the formula the Court used in *Roth* to define obscenity and to distinguish obscenity from other speech on sexual subjects.

In developing a rationale for protection of commercial speech, therefore, the Court merely recognized the ways in which commercial speech does possess "redeeming social importance," and it rejected any notion that commercial speech, like libel and slander or fighting words, inflicts by its very utterance any kind of present injury on hearers. Its inherent value, in short, was not outweighed by other interests of social importance.

The Court in *Virginia Pharmacy Board* brought commercial speech into the mainstream of the constitutional rationale for protection of speech.

The Court's statement of a rationale for protecting commercial speech would lead to the conclusion that it should enjoy full protection, unless the Court develops, in addition, a rationale for differential protection. The Court began this task in footnote 24 of *Virginia Pharmacy Board* and continued it in *Central Hudson*, where it noted that ''[t]wo features of commercial speech permit regulation of its content'':

First, commercial speakers have extensive knowledge of both the market and their products. Thus, they are well situated to evaluate the accuracy of their messages and the lawfulness of the underlying activity. *Bates v. State Bar of Arizona*, 433 U.S. 350, 381 (1977). In addition, commercial speech, the offspring of economic self-interest, is a hardy breed of expression that is not ''particularly susceptible to being crushed by overbroad regulation.'' *Ibid*. 447 U.S. at 564, n.6

The Court repeated these two factors warranting lesser protection for commercial speech in *Friedman v. Rogers*, where it pointed out:

Because it relates to a particular product or service, commercial speech is *more objective, hence more verifiable*, than other varieties of speech. Commercial speech, because of its importance to business profits, and because it is carefully calculated, is also *less likely than other forms of speech to be inhibited by proper regulation*. 440 U.S. at 10 (emphasis added)

In particular cases, of course, these two generalizations may be doubted. Many businesses do not have the luxury to engage in extensive advertising, particularly if to do so requires costly legal review of advertising or opposition to overly extensive regulation. Moreover, the truth concerning the attributes of many products may be very expensive to ascertain with the degree of certainty required for advertising substantiation, if it can be ascertained at all. Conversely, the same may be said for certain types of non-commercial speech which is the ''offspring of economic self-interest,'' yet such speech enjoys full protection. Speech by labor and management in labor disputes is certainly the offspring of economic self-interest and can reasonably be expected to be every bit as hardy as commercial advertising. Some clearly political speech may also be easily verifiable. Putting these issues to one side, the question arises whether in an appropriate case where these attributes of commercial speech can be shown to exist the courts may acknowledge that fact and, in view of the lack of any rationale justifying differential treatment, grant such commercial speech full protection under the First Amendment.

What the Court has not emphasized concerning the rationale for differential protection of commercial speech is also significant. It has not placed too much emphasis on the fact that commercial speech possesses—either generally or in some instances—less ''redeeming social importance,'' to use the language of *Roth*, than non-commercial speech, although some comments along these lines are to be found in the Court's opinions on commercial speech. Indeed, the Court in *Virginia Pharmacy Board* even acknowledged that particular commercial communications can be of greater interest to citizens and of greater impact for the public health, safety, and welfare than relatively unimportant speech of a non-commercial nature. In *Virginia Pharmacy Board*, the Court observed that the consumer's interest in the free flow of commercial information "may be as keen, if not keener by far, than his interest in the day's most urgent political debate," 425 U.S. at 763.

It is true that in *Friedman v. Rogers*, the Court mentioned one rationale for differential treatment of commercial speech when it referred to its evolving commercial speech doctrine as "a substantial extension of traditional free-speech doctrine which poses special problems not presented by other forms of protected speech," 440 U.S. at 10 n.9. It is also true that in *Ohralik* the Court did refer to the "subordinate position in the scale of First Amendment values" occupied by commercial speech, 436 U.S. at 456. This comment, however, falls somewhat short of a fully reasoned analysis of the reasons requiring differential treatment. Besides identifying certain problems associated with commercial speech which arguably exist with respect to non-commercial speech as well, the Court has not to date fully explained the rationale that requires *differential* treatment of commercial speech. Cf. Dun & Bradstreet, Inc. v. Greenmoss Builders, Inc., _____ U.S. _____, 53 U.S.L.W. 4866 (1985) (Powell, J.).

PRINCIPLES OF JUDICIAL REVIEW OF REGULATION OF COMMERCIAL SPEECH

Having held that commercial speech is entitled to some degree of protection under the First Amendment, the Court was required to specify how much, the circumstances in which and the procedures by which such speech will be protected by the courts, and the standard of review for determining the validity of legislation that interferes with or prohibits commercial speech.

The general approach which the Court adopted requires a balancing test, which already assumes that the commercial speech in question is truthful and does not propose an illegal transaction. In order to specify further the nature of the balancing which lower courts are to conduct to determine the constitutional validity of these statutes, the Court has been obliged to develop some principles concerning the governmental interests that are sufficiently important to be considered as possibly outweighing the value of commercial speech. Second, the Court has had to develop a standard for review, *i.e.*, a principle for weighing the substantiality of the governmental interests. Finally, the Court has had to begin to develop a body of law defining certain means of regulation that are illegitimate, notwithstanding that the governmental interests advanced by particular legislation may be legitimate ones.

Basic Standard of Judicial Review

The current standard of judicial review of legislation of governmental action restricting commercial speech is the standard defined in *Central Hudson*, which requires an underlying "substantial interest" and requires that the regulation efficiently promote that interest and be no more restrictive of commercial speech than is necessary:

> If the communication is neither misleading nor related to unlawful activity, the government's power is more circumscribed. *The State must assert a substantial interest to be achieved by restrictions on commercial speech.* Moreover, the regulatory technique must be in proportion to that interest. The limitation on expression *must be designed carefully* to achieve the State's goal. Compliance with this requirement may be measured by two criteria. First, *the restriction must directly advance the state interest involved*; the regulation may not be sustained if it provides only ineffective or remote support for the government's purpose. Second, *if the governmental interest could be served as well by a more limited restriction on commercial speech, the excessive restrictions cannot survive.* 447 U.S. at 564 (Emphasis added)

The two stated preconditions for commercial speech to enjoy any protection—(1) that the speech not be "misleading" and (2) that the speech not be "related to unlawful activity"—are analyzed in succeeding portions of this chapter. The core of the *Central Hudson* standard, however, is the requirement that the state assert a "substantial interest" to be achieved by restrictions on commercial speech. What kind of interest will constitute a substantial interest within the meaning of this standard?

In fashioning a standard of judicial review for commercial speech, the Supreme Court did not start afresh with an untried doctrinal system. Instead, the Court made use of the existing law concerning judicial review of legislation. In order to comprehend the *Central Hudson* standard, therefore, it is necessary to set forth briefly the current law on standard of review of legislation under the due process and equal protection clauses of the Fourteenth Amendment and to relate this body of law to the standard of review embodied in the commercial speech doctrine. Since the end of the *Lochner*[4] era, the Supreme Court's standards for judicial review of legislation under the due process clauses (of the Fourteenth and Fifth amendments) and under the equal protection clause of the Fourteenth Amendment require only that the state demonstrate a "rational relationship" between a piece of legislation and a legitimate governmental interest or, in the case of legislation that makes a classification of individuals for the purpose of differential treatment of them, that the classification is rationally related to a legitimate governmental interest. The rational relationship test is the normal standard applied by the courts in determining the constitutionality of state or federal legislation.

Where, however, legislation infringes on the exercise of fundamental rights, or where legislation creates a classification of persons which is suspect (*e.g.*, alienage, race, national origin), the courts will not subject such legislation to less exacting normal scrutiny under the rational relationship standard, but instead will subject such legislation to strict scrutiny. Legislation affecting fundamental rights or depending on a suspect classification will survive strict scrutiny only if the legislation is supported by a compelling or very substantial governmental interest. The courts also may require a more direct relationship between legislative means selected by the state or federal legislation and the governmental interest and may examine more carefully the precision employed by the drafters in reaching the proper object of the legislation.

The current contours of judicial review under the equal protection clause are summarized in three related standards:

1. *Rational Relationship Test.* Under the rational relationship test, explained above, the Court has upheld classifications based on "a state of facts that reasonably can be conceived to constitute a distinction, or difference in state policy," *Allied Stores v. Bowers*, 358 U.S. 522, 530 (1959). If the legislation is arguably related to a legitimate governmental purpose, the courts will sustain the legislation. The Supreme Court has formulated this standard in *Parham v. Hughes*, 441 U.S. 347, 352 (1979), as follows:

Legislatures have wide discretion in passing laws that have the inevitable effect of treating some people differently from others, and legislative classifications are valid unless they bear no rational relationship to a permissible state objective. . . . [A legislative classification] will be upheld "unless the varying treatment of different groups or persons is so unrelated to the achievement of any combination of legislative purposes that we can only conclude that the legislature's actions were irrational."

This is a relatively relaxed and indulgent standard of judicial review.

2. *Strict Scrutiny.* As stated above, the strict scrutiny standard requires a compelling or overriding governmental purpose, not simply a legitimate one. Moreover, the strict scrutiny standard does not tolerate the same looseness of connection between legislative means and governmental ends which is tolerated under the rational relationship standard. The legislative means must be necessary to promote the compelling or overriding governmental purpose. Under modern equal protection, "it is a presumptive violation of equal protection for government to impose a disadvantage on persons classified on the basis of their exercise of a constitutional right."[5] The absence of precision, in narrowly tailoring the statutory language to eliminate the vice, can also be fatal.

3. *Intermediate Scrutiny.* The Court has applied a third standard of judicial review in certain cases, such as legislative classifications on the basis of gender. In such cases, the courts will sustain a law if it is substantially related to an important governmental objective, *see, Califano v. Goldfarb*, 430 U.S. 199, 210–211 (1977).

In *Central Hudson*, the Supreme Court appears to have applied neither the strict scrutiny standard of judicial review of the Public Service Commission's order, nor the rational relationship standard. Thus, the Court required only a substantial, not a compelling, governmental interest to justify governmental regulation of commercial speech. The Court's requirement of connection between governmental means and ends does not speak in terms of necessity of the restrictive measure to promote the governmental purpose. The *Central Hudson* test requires that the restrictive measure "directly advance the state interest involved," 447 U.S. at 564. It will not be upheld if it "provides only ineffective or remote support for the government's purpose." The "directly advance/ineffective or remote support" dichotomy certainly requires a relationship of means to end far less loose than that tolerated under the rational relationship standard. The degree of precision, however, is tightened by what amounts, in other words, to a least restrictive means standard, which is common in First Amendment contexts involving political speech. The Court said, "If the governmental interest could be served as well by a more limited restriction on commercial speech, the excessive restrictions cannot survive," 447 U.S. at 564. The *Central Hudson* standard thus appears to be a hybrid between the rational relationship standard and the strict scrunity standard, with the least restrictive means requirement added on.

Prior to *Central Hudson* the Court had already uniformly applied a principle requiring a direct connection between means and ends. In *Bates* and *Virginia Pharmacy Board*, the Court had concluded that a commercial advertising ban could not be imposed to protect the ethical or performance standards of a profession. The advertising ban in *Virginia Pharmacy Board* did not "directly affect professional standards one way or the other," 425 U.S. at 769. Similarly, in *Bates*, the Court said that "[r]estraints on advertising . . . are an ineffective way of deterring shoddy work," 433 U.S. at 378. The *Central Hudson* requirement merely codified these holdings in a somewhat clearer formulation. The Court explicitly adopted the least restrictive alternative part of the standard from cases dealing with both commercial and non-commercial speech, citing *First National Bank of Boston v. Bellotti, supra*, and *Primus*. The requirement that legislation in the First Amendment area be "narrowly drawn" was already a settled principle of judicial review in the area of non-commercial speech, *see, Cantwell v. Connecticut*, 310 U.S. 296 (1940); *Thornhill v. Alabama*, 310 U.S. 88 (1940); *Schneider v. State*, 308 U.S. 147 (1939); *DeJonge v. Oregon*, 299 U.S. 353 (1937).

It will be seen that the *Central Hudson* standard for commercial speech is similar in some respects to the standard applicable to cases where the expression involves elements of conduct. In *United States v. O'Brien*, 391 U.S. 367, 377 (1968), a case involving "expressive conduct," the burning of a Selective Service System draft registration card, the Court adopted a similar four-part test. Under that test, a governmental regulation is sufficiently justified, despite its incidental impact upon First Amendment interests, if it is within the constitutional power of the government; if it furthers an important or substantial governmental interest; if the governmental interest is unrelated to the suppression of free expression; and if the incidental restriction on First Amendment freedoms is no greater than is essential to the furtherance of that interest.

It is interesting to note that Justice Powell, in *Central Hudson*, concurred in the judgment in *Young v. American Mini-Theatres*, 427 U.S. 50, 73–84 (1976), in which the Court upheld a Detroit zoning ordinance prohibiting operations of adult bookstores within a thousand feet of any other such establishment, or within five hundred feet of a residential area. In his concurrence in that case dealing with sale of erotically oriented, non-obscene materials, Justice Powell expressed the view that the *O'Brien* standard of judicial review should apply. Justice Powell acknowledged that ''[t]he factual distinctions between a prosecution for destruction of a Selective Service registration certificate, as in *O'Brien*, and this case are substantial, *but the essential weighing and balancing of competing interests are the same*,'' 427 U.S. at 80 (emphasis added). This similarity touches on the same considerations which the Court mentioned in *Ohralik* when it pointed out that ''[i]n-person solicitation by a lawyer of remunerative employment is a business transaction in which speech is an essential but subordinate component,'' *id.* at 457. The Court went on to point out that this recognition ''lowers the level of appropriate judicial scrutiny,'' *id.*

The relationship between the *O'Brien* standard, mentioned in *Ohralik*, and the standard of judicial review that was eventually set down in *Central Hudson* was nearly made explicit in footnote 9 in *Friedman v. Rogers, supra*, in which the Court said:

The application of First Amendment protection to speech that does ''no more than propose a commercial transaction,'' *Pittsburgh Press Co. v. Human Relations Commission*, 413 U.S. 376, 385 (1973), had been recognized generally as a substantial extension of traditional free-speech doctrine which poses special problems not presented by other forms of protected speech. . . . By definition, commercial speech is linked inextricably to commercial activity, and while the First Amendment affords such speech ''limited measure of protection,'' it is also true that ''the State does not lose its power to regulate commercial activity deemed harmful to the public whenever speech is a component of that activity.'' *Ohralik v. Ohio State Bar Assn.*, 436 U.S. 447, 456 (1978)

The question remains, then, what governmental interests are vital enough to protect.

Legitimate Governmental Interests in Regulating Commercial Speech

The *Central Hudson* standard raises the question what governmental interests may be deemed substantial for purposes of justifying restrictions on commercial speech. Generalizations in this area might seem premature. It would appear nonetheless that any governmental purpose which has been classified as a compelling or overriding governmental interest for the purpose of the strict scrutiny standard would *a fortiori* qualify as sufficiently important to be substantial for the purpose of the hybrid intermediate level of scrutiny mandated by *Central Hudson*. Beyond this, the decisions to date offer little guidance, because practically all of the state restrictions on commercial speech which the Supreme Court has invalidated have been voided not on the ground that the state interest was insufficiently important or substantial but because the means selected to advance that interest was not directly related to the governmental interest, even if it were assumed that the state interest had qualified as a substantial one. This was certainly the case in *Bigelow*, *Bates*, *Linmark*, *Virginia Pharmacy Board*, and *Central Hudson*.

The following is a catalog of the governmental interests dealt with in the leading commercial speech decisions:

1. *Valentine v. Chrestensen*—The city's interest in preventing litter from accumulating on streets and sidewalks.

2. *Breard v. Virginia*—The privacy of residents and the prevention of crime.

3. *Bigelow v. Virginia*—State's questionable interest in preventing abortions in violation of Virginia law from occurring in New York.

4. *Virginia Pharmacy Board*—The state's interest in promoting professionalism and high quality of services rendered by licensed dispensing pharmacists.

5. *Linmark v. Willingboro*—The township's interest in promoting stable, racially integrated housing and suppressing panic selling because of accelerating integration of residential neighborhoods.

6. *Friedman v. Rogers*—The state's interest in preventing optometrists from using trade names to mislead the public as to the price or quality of optometry services.

7. *Bates, Ohralik, Primus*—The state's interest in promoting professionalism and high-quality services in the legal profession; the state's interest in reducing "the likelihood of overreaching and the exertion of undue influence [from in-person solicitation] on lay persons," in protecting the privacy of persons and in avoiding "situations where the lawyer's exercise of judgment on behalf of the client will be clouded by his own pecuniary self-interest" (assumed to be "legitimate . . . even compelling" state interests).

8. *Central Hudson*—State's interest in protecting fuel stocks during a time of oil shortage and in encouraging use of most efficient fuels for residential heating.

9. *Metromedia*—State interest in traffic safety and aesthetics.

10. *Bolger*—Government's interest in protecting recipients of mail from receiving offensive mail and in assisting parents in their efforts to control the manner in which their children become informed about sensitive and important subjects such as birth control.

Illegitimate Means of Governmental Regulation of Commercial Speech for Non-Speech Related Purposes

Regardless of the legitimacy of the state or governmental purpose offered to justify a restriction on commercial speech, the means selected to advance that governmental purpose may run afoul of the First Amendment. What kinds of means are inherently impermissible to advance otherwise legitimate state goals regarding commercial speech? The issue should not be confused with the separate and distinct issue of the required relation between means and ends. As noted above, that set of issues arises from the explicit terms of the *Central Hudson* standard, which requires a certain directness of connection between means and ends—that is, between the particular form the restriction takes and the governmental objective it is intended to serve or promote. The Supreme Court has already begun to develop a body of law to answer the question and in several cases has invalidated state regulation of commercial speech on this ground. The issue is illustrated in cases such as *Virginia Pharmacy Board*, *Linmark Associates*, and *Central Hudson*, although in *Central Hudson* the Court bypassed the question of the inherently impermissible nature of the means and instead rested its decision on the state's failure to demonstrate that no alternative less restrictive of protected commercial speech would suffice.

In all three of these cases, the Court dealt with forms of regulation that in their intended operation depended on the state's keeping the public ignorant of certain facts as a means to achieving the objective of the statute. The Court's quarrel with these provisions was not only that the connection between the means and ends was remote, speculative, and indirect, but also that even if the measure were effective in achieving its objective indirectly, it would do so only by depriving members of the public of certain information, the possession of which would probably motivate them to make certain choices and take certain actions that they would not otherwise know enough to do, or at least would not do in such frequency or in such numbers if they remained ignorant.

The Supreme Court termed this interposition of the state between the advertiser and the public to manipulate and skew public choice as a "highly paternalistic" form of legislation, which it undoubtedly is. It invariably involves the use of restrictions on commercial speech to achieve non-speech objectives. In each case in which the Supreme Court has detected the use of this kind of means to achieve non-speech objectives, the Court has invalidated the restrictions, although, as noted above, in *Central Hudson* without mentioning that feature of the regulation. For example, in *Virginia Pharmacy Board, supra*, the Court described the state's contentions regarding the impact on professionalism among pharmacists that the state believed price advertising would have, specifically, noting the following:

Price advertising, it is argued, will place in jeopardy the pharmacist's expertise and, with it, the customer's health. It is claimed that the aggressive price competition that will result from unlimited advertising will make it impossible for the pharmacists to supply professional services in the compounding, handling, and dispensing of prescription drugs. Such services are time consuming and expensive; if competitors who economize by eliminating them are permitted to advertise their resulting lower prices, the more painstaking and conscientious pharmacist will be forced either to follow suit or to go out of business. It is also claimed that prices might not necessarily fall as a result of advertising. If one pharmacist advertises, others must, and the resulting expense will inflate the cost of drugs. It is further claimed that advertising will lead people to shop for their prescription drugs among the various pharmacists who offer the lowest prices, and the loss of stable pharmacist-customer relationships will make individual attention—and certainly the practice of monitoring—impossible. Finally, it is argued that damage will be done to the professional image of the pharmacist. This image, that of a skilled and specialized craftsman, attracts to the profession and reinforces the better habits of those who are in it. Price advertising, it is said, will reduce the pharmacist's status to that of a mere retailer. 425 U.S. at 767–768

The Court perceived that the whole premise of this means of achieving the state's objective of professionalism of pharmacists—a non-speech objective—involved directly depriving the public of otherwise valuable information and only indirectly influencing the degree of pharmacists by altering the behavior of otherwise uninformed consumers:

The challenge now made, however, is based on the First Amendment. This casts the Board's justifications in a different light, for on close inspection it is seen that the State's protectiveness of its citizens rests in large measure on the advantages of their being kept in ignorance. The advertising ban does not directly affect professional standards one way or the other. It affects them only through the reactions it is assumed people will have to the free flow of drug price information.

. . .

It appears to be feared that if the pharmacist who wishes to provide low cost, and assertedly low quality, services is permitted to advertise, he will be taken up on his offer by too many unwitting customers. They will choose the low-cost, low quality service and drive the "professional" pharmacist out of business. They will respond only to costly and excessive advertising, and end up paying the price. They will go from one pharmacist to another, following the discount, and destroy the pharmacist-customer relationship. They will lose respect for the profession because it advertises. All this is not in their best interests, and all this can be avoided if they are not permitted to know who is charging what.

There is, of course, an alternative to this highly paternalistic approach. That alternative is to assume that this information is not in itself harmful, that people will perceive their own best interests if only they are well enough informed and that the best means to that end is to open the channels of communication rather than to close them.

. . .

Virginia is free to require whatever professional standards it wishes of its pharmacists; it may subsidize them or protect them from competition in other ways. *Cf. Parker v. Brown*, 317 U.S. 341 (1943). But it may not do so by keeping the public in ignorance of the entirely lawful terms that competing pharmacists are offering. *Id.* at 769–770

The Court's hostility to this form of paternalistic regulation raises some interesting issues. What is really at work in this example is a form of Adam Smith's "invisible hand" explanation of the market system.[6] Although invisible hand systems may result in good consequences, the fact that a state of affairs results automatically from the aggregation of a number of individual economic decisions does not in itself guarantee good or fair consequences. An invisible hand mechanism may in fact produce undesirable consequences. Virginia argued in *Virginia Pharmacy Board* that the general availability of more information would result in certain aggregate consequences. Not all of these consequences are necessarily good; therefore, the state should be able to alter the initial structure of the information system which fuels the individual economic decisions. If an invisible hand mechanism produces undesirable consequences, why should the state lack the power to interfere with it? The Supreme Court, however, has expressed hostility to state regulation that deals indirectly with the bad consequences of an invisible hand mechanism, by impeding its operation, rather than by dealing in other more direct, but perhaps less effective, ways. The Supreme Court has, in effect, suggested that the government does not have the power to manipulate citizens' conduct by depriving them of truthful information even if depriving them of information is the most efficient and least costly form of regulation.

In *Virginia Pharmacy Board*, the Court appears to have rested its decision largely on this ground, together with the consideration that the state had failed to demonstrate that it did not have at its disposal regulatory alternatives that were less restrictive of protected commercial speech than the technique embodied in the restriction against drug price advertising. In fact, the Court pointed out that the existing regulatory scheme already gave the board ample power to achieve its objectives in a direct manner, and that other plausible alternatives such as state-mandated price maintenance of the type involved in *Parker v. Brown* had not even been attempted before resort was made to techniques of regulation that involved restrictions on the information provided to the public.

In *Linmark*, the Court again referred to Willingboro's paternalistic approach as one of the grounds for invalidating a local ordinance forbidding residential "For Sale" signs, which the township believed might touch off panic selling and threaten its objective of promoting stable, racially integrated neighborhoods. The Court conceded the substantiality of that governmental purpose but chose to invalidate one of the speech-restrictive methods which the township had selected to achieve its non-speech objective. The Court was confronted again with a classic invisible hand phenomenon. (Indeed, Thomas Schelling has demonstrated through game-theoretic analysis how persons desiring to live in an evenly integrated neighborhood, by unilateral action in pursuit of that goal, will instead be led to a quite different result.)[7] The Court singled out the paternalistic feature of the Willingboro ordinance:

The constitutional defect in this ordinance, however, is far more basic. The Township Council here, like the Virginia Assembly in *Virginia Pharmacy Board* acted to prevent is residents from obtaining certain information. That information, which pertains to sales activity in Willingboro, is of vital interest to Willingboro residents, since it may bear on one of the most important decisions they have a right to make: where to live and raise their families. The Council has sought to restrict the free flow of these data because it fears that otherwise homeowners will make decisions inimical to what the Council views as the homeowners' self-interest and the corporate interest of the township: they will choose to leave town. The Council's concern, then, was not with any commercial aspect of "For Sale" signs—with offerors communicating offers to offerees—but with the substance of the information communicated to Willingboro citizens. *If dissemination of this information can be restricted, then every locality in the country can suppress any facts that reflect poorly on the locality,* so long as a plausible claim can be made that disclosure would cause the recipients of the information to act "irrationally." *Virginia Pharmacy Board* denies government such sweeping powers. As we said there in rejecting Virginia's claim that the only way it could enable its citizens to find their self-interest was to deny them information that is neither false nor misleading. 431 U.S. at 96–97 (emphasis added)

It is perhaps significant, given this background, that in *Central Hudson* the Court did not employ a similar rationale to invalidate the regulation but instead selected a narrower ground. In *Central Hudson*, the Court was confronted with a New York Public Service Commission order prohibiting promotional advertising of electric utility service by private, investor-owned utilities in New York. The New York Public Service Commission attempted to justify the restriction on the basis of its conviction that electric-utility service is a less efficient energy alternative and that in a time of oil shortages, restrictions on less efficient energy alternatives were appropriate and use of electric-utility service should be discouraged. The means selected by the commission of achieving that non-speech objective was flat prohibition of promotional advertising of electric service—a measure which the commission believed would lessen demand for that kind of service and therefore lead to either less usage or a lesser increase in usage of electric-utility service.

This scenario presented precisely the same fact pattern as *Virginia Pharmacy Board* and *Linmark* in that, once again, the state chose a means of achieving its non-speech objective which involved the suppression of truthful information relating to lawful activity. The case was accordingly ripe for application of the "illegitimate paternalistic means" test of *Virginia Pharmacy Board* and *Linmark*, but the Court's decision was predicated instead on a far narrower ground—the state's failure to exclude as feasible alternatives to suppression of speech techniques of regulation that were less restrictive of protected commercial speech. Whether the Court's decision in *Central Hudson* signals a retreat from previous attack on illegitimate paternalistic means is an open question. On the other hand, in *Central Hudson*, the Court adverted to this doctrine and added an additional justification for it when it said that it will "review with special care regulations that entirely suppress commercial speech in order to pursue a nonspeech-related policy," 447 U.S. at 566 n.9. The Court justified this special care standard of judicial review not on the ground of the paternalistic form of the regulation, but on a different ground:

In those circumstances, a ban on speech could screen from public view the underlying governmental policy. See *Virginia Pharmacy Board*, 425 U.S. at 780 n.8. (Stewart, J., concurring). Indeed, in recent years this Court has not approved a blanket ban on commercial speech unless the expression itself was flawed in some way, either because it was deceptive or related to unlawful activity. 447 U.S. at 566 n.9.

Although the Court did not specifically mention the earlier instances of paternalistic encroachment, it generalized from its prior discussions in referring to those cases as typically involving ''a nonspeech-related policy.'' The implication of the decisions seems to be that only speech-related policies will be held to justify restrictions on commercial speech and, even then, under *Central Hudson*, only substantial ones.

Weighing Principles for Balancing Commercial Speech against Governmental Interests

As we have noticed, under contemporary substantive due process standards of judicial review of legislation, the courts will recognize (1) legitimate governmental interests, (2) substantial governmental interests, and (3) compelling or overriding governmental interests. Depending on the activity being regulated (*e.g.*, whether it touches the exercise of ''fundamental right'') or, under equal protection analysis, the classification on which differential governmental conduct is predicated (*e.g.*, suspect classifications versus nonsuspect classifications), a governmental interest of greater or lesser substantiality will be required to warrant governmental interference. To restrict or prohibit commercial speech, the Supreme Court held in *Central Hudson*, requires a substantial governmental purpose, and it may be that it requires a substantial speech-related governmental interest. If the governmental interest promoted is found to be substantial, a question then arises as to whether the balancing ends and the legislation or governmental action is upheld, or whether the court's balancing of First Amendment interests and governmental interest has just begun. The question in other words is whether judicial balancing of interests in these cases is to be performed on the basis of classes of speech versus classes of governmental interests, or on the basis of a particular class of commercial speech versus a particular class of governmental interests, or on the basis of individual instances of commercial speech versus the strength of the particular governmental interest implicated in the context of the case. If either of the two latter procedures is the correct one, the need arises to fashion principles that define the relative strength of commercial speech interests and governmental interests that might be implicated in particular regulations of commercial speech.

An examination of the Supreme Court's decisions provides no definitive answer to this question. The Court's decision procedure in a number of the cases provides some support for the view that case-by-case balancing is appropriate—at least a balancing that is based on all commercial expression of a particular class, *e.g.*, all uses of residential ''For Sale'' signs or all instances of attorney in-person solicitation. In *Linmark*, for example, the Court did not doubt that Willingboro had a valid interest in preventing panic selling and in fostering stable, racially integrated neighborhoods. But the Court turned to the record evidence to determine the strength of Willingboro's interest. Thus, the Court specifically noted the district court's statements that there was '' 'no evidence' that whites were leaving Willingboro *en masse* as 'For Sale' signs appeared, but 'merely an indication that its residents are concerned that there may be a large influx of minority groups moving into the town with the resultant effect being a reduction in property values,' " 431 U.S. at 90. The Court said "[t]he record here demonstrates that respondents [Willingboro] failed to establish that this ordinance is needed to assure that Willingboro remains an integrated community," *id.* at 95. True, the Court went on to find a "far more basic" constitutional defect in the Willingboro ordinance, and it is unclear whether the lack of factual demonstration that the ordinance was necessary was merely dictum or alternative holding or something else. It provides some reason, however, to believe that the strength of the governmental interest is to be weighed on a case-by-case basis against the particular commercial speech involved.

In *Ohralik*, the Court also appears to have engaged in particularized balancing of the state's interest in that case against the commercial speech interests implicated by in-person attorney solicitation of remunerative legal work. Certainly, if the *Ohralik* standard was modeled on the *United States v. O'Brien* standard, governing "speech-plus-conduct," the applicable balancing process would require assessment of the individual interests. That is, inquiry into the constitutional validity involved in that case of a restriction on commercial speech does not stop as soon as a substantial governmental interest has been identified, and the directness of the relationship between statutory means and governmental objective is approved. A court must still determine whether the particular substantial governmental interest implicated is sufficient to overcome the constitutional values implicit in the particular commercial speech that may be involved. In *Bolger v. Youngs Drug Products*, the Court also appears to have engaged in detailed balancing of the contraceptive advertising and the governmental interests, 463 U.S. 60, 103 S. Ct. at 2881–2884.

In this connection, the Court has already acknowledged in several cases that the value in terms of public interest of particular specimens of commercial speech will vary widely. For example, in *Virginia Pharmacy Board*, the Court observed that "[o]bviously, not all commercial messages contain the same or even a great public interest element," 425 U.S. at 764. This being the case, a balancing of the same governmental interest against different specimens of commercial speech may well result in different determinations as to whether particular forms of restriction on commercial speech are unconstitutional as applied, even if substantial governmental interests are involved.

If commercial speech is to be weighed, the Court requires principles by which this can be done. For example, is commercial speech more or less valuable depending on the greater or lesser degree of public interest in it? If so, is greater public interest to be determined by the greater number of members of the public interested in it, or by the intensity of interest or by greater inherent interest, regardless of the number interested, or by a combination of both factors? Will the value of a particular specimen of commercial speech depend on the magnitude of the economic interest of the speaker? What factors will determine the value of a particular specimen of commercial speech in facilitating the allocative role of free market systems (*e.g.*, the number of terms or conditions of sales stated in the advertisement, the amount of descriptive information about the product or service, whether the product itself is of greater or lesser importance, *e.g.*, conducive to "the enjoyment of basic necessities" or instrumental to "the alleviation of physical pain" as in *Virginia Pharmacy Board*, or an inessential luxury)?

The Court's opinions do not yet provide clear answers to all the problems inherent in the balancing test formulated in *Central Hudson*.

PRINCIPLES GOVERNING A MIXTURE OF COMMERCIAL SPEECH WITH NON-COMMERCIAL SPEECH, WITH UNPROTECTED SPEECH, AND COMMERCIAL SPEECH THAT IS "BRIGADED" WITH CONDUCT

In the principal Supreme Court commercial speech decisions to date, the examples of commercial speech under consideration have either been presented alone or as part of a purely commercial communication. The exceptions to this were *Valentine v. Chrestensen* itself, in which the Court considered a mixture of commercial advertising and non-commercial, political speech on Chrestensen's two-sided handbill, and *Bolger v. Youngs Drug Products*, in which the Court was confronted with an informational pamphlet concerning contraceptive products that was virtually devoid of any commercial advertising content except in the last line the identification of the advertiser's product and trade name appeared. Until *Bolger*, the Court had not yet had an opportunity to consider mixed communications that combine commercial speech with other types of speech: (1) commercial speech with protected non-commercial speech, (2) commercial speech with unprotected speech (libel and slander, obscenity, incitement), and (3) commercial speech and conduct. Certain generalizations can be suggested with respect to these issues.

The Mixture of Commercial and Protected Non-Commercial Speech

It will be recalled that Judge Clark's opinion for the Second Circuit in *Valentine v. Chrestensen*, *supra*, discussed in chapter 1, grappled with the problem presented by Chrestensen's two-sided handbill and specifically rejected any test to determine constitutional protection for a mixture of commercial and non-commercial speech that depends on determining the dominant or primary motive of the advertising, 122 F.2d at 516. Despite the political protest on the reverse side of Chrestensen's handbill, the Supreme Court was content to treat the handbill as "purely commercial advertising," which it held was entitled to no constitutional protection.

The Supreme Court's more recent dicta and holdings appear finally to have resolved the question of treatment of communications that contain both commercial and non-commercial speech. The Court ruled in *Consolidated Edison Co. v. Public Service Commission*, 447 U.S. 530 (1980), the companion case to *Central Hudson*, that a privately owned utility's dissemination of its opinions on controversial issues of public policy enjoyed First Amendment protection. Although the flyers in its billing envelopes mailed to customers enjoyed the full protection of the First Amendment, this ruling paved the way for the Court's ultimate conclusion that mixed commercial and protected non-commercial speech is not entitled to the full protection of the First Amendment. Starting from its holding in *Consolidated Edison Co.*, and its earlier holding to the same effect in *First National Bank of Boston v. Bellotti, supra*, that corporate political speech enjoys First Amendment protection, the Court held that corporations can reasonably be required to separate their commercial messages from their non-commercial messages. Therefore, adding a protected non-commercial message to a commercial message will not immunize the mixed expression from full governmental regulation of the mixed communication under the diluted standard of judicial review applicable to commercial speech defined in *Central Hudson*. Before the Court had a specific occasion to address this problem in *Bolger v. Youngs Drug Products, supra*, the Court had intimated in *Central Hudson* that corporations could not gain full constitutional protection for their advertising by the simple expedient of including some pure political or non-commercial speech. Countering criticisms in Justice Stevens's concurring opinion, in *Central Hudson*, the Court had written:

[T]he concurring opinion of Mr. Justice Stevens views the Commission's order as suppressing more than commercial speech because it would outlaw, for example, advertising that promoted electricity consumption by touting the environmental benefits of such uses. *See post*, at 581. Apparently, the opinion would accord full First Amendment protection to all promotional advertising that includes claims "relating to . . . questions frequently discussed and debated by our political leaders." 447 U.S. at 562–563 n.5

Assuming contrary to its holding that Central Hudson's advertising was not entirely commercial speech, but a mixture of commercial and protected, non-commercial speech, the majority of the *Central Hudson* Court responded to this suggestion:

Although this approach responds to the serious issues surrounding our national energy policy as raised in this case, we think it would blur further the line the Court has sought to draw in commercial speech cases. *It would grant broad constitutional protection to any advertising that links a product to current public debate.* But many, if not most, products may be tied to public concerns with the environment, energy, economic policy, or individual health and safety. We rule today in *Consolidated Edison Co. v. Public Service Commission, ante*, p. 530, that utilities enjoy the full panoply of First Amendment protections for their direct comments on public issues. *There is no reason for providing similar constitutional protection when such statements are made only in the context of commercial transactions.* . . . This Court's decisions on commercial expression have rested on the premise that such [commercial] speech, although meriting some protection, is of less constitutional moment than other forms of speech. As we stated in *Ohralik*, the failure to distinguish betwen commercial and non-commercial speech "could invite dilution, simply by a leveling process, of the force of the [First] Amendment's guarantee with respect to the latter kind of speech." 436 U.S. at 456; 447 U.S. at 563 (emphasis added)

The Court had occasion to make this principle a holding in *Bolger*, where the Court considered a mixed commercial and non-commercial communication, 463 U.S. 60, 103 S. Ct. at 2881:

We have made clear that advertising which "links a product to a current public debate" is not thereby entitled to the constitutional protection afforded non-commercial speech. *Central Hudson Gas & Electric Corp. v. Public Service Commission*, 447 U.S. at 563 n.5. *A company has the full panoply of protections available to its direct comments on public issues, so there is no reason for providing similar constitutional protection when such statements are made in the context of commercial transactions.* See *Ibid*. Advertisers should not be permitted to immunize false or misleading product information for government regulation simply by including reference to public issues. *Cf. Metromedia, Inc. v. City of San Diego*, 453 U.S 490, 540 (1981) (Brennan, J., concurring).

It would seem, therefore, that mixed commercial and non-commercial speech will be entitled to no greater protection than the commercial advertising that makes up one of its components. The Court, therefore, has finally reaffirmed this aspect of its original holding in *Valentine v. Chrestensen*, although it has rewritten that aspect of the holding in *Valentine* which declared that commercial speech was entitled to no constitutional protection whatsoever.

Commercial Speech Mixed with Forms of Unprotected Speech

The question next arises whether otherwise unprotected speech can be immunized by inclusion with protected commercial speech. The Court has not yet had occasion to rule directly on the effect of mixing protected commercial speech with unprotected speech. The question of the appropriate standard of judicial review to apply to such communications might conceivably arise in the context of (1) obscene commercial advertising, or (2) slanderous or libelous commercial advertising, as for example in commercial comparative advertising that contains a trade libel or false assertion concerning the attributes of a competitive product or service, or (3) fighting words, such as group libel in commercial advertising.

The Court has held, as noted above, that corporations cannot immunize false statements in commercial advertising by combining commercial messages with fully protected non-commercial messages. It would seem to follow, by parity of reasoning, that a corporation should not be able to immunize otherwise unprotected speech that is subject to governmental restraint or prohibition by combining it with commercial speech which could otherwise be separately published and enjoy in such form the intermediate degree of protection to which commercial speech is entitled under the evolving commercial speech standard. Just as the corporation can be required to separate its commercial speech from its protected non-commercial speech, it might be suggested, the corporation can be required to separate its commercial speech from its unprotected speech. The unprotected portion of the message may indeed even be made unlawful since it is not entitled to First Amendment protection. If it is made unlawful, the commercial speech which is annexed to it may be "brigaded with" unlawful conduct or in some fashion "related" to it in a way that, under the *Central Hudson* standard, the combination of the two components deprives the commercial speech of the protection to which it might otherwise be entitled.

However, if the unprotected speech has not been made unlawful, a more difficult question is presented. Thus, libelous speech may not be unlawful in the sense in which *Central Hudson* uses the term, yet the constitutional status of the mixed commercial and unprotected speech may be relevant in a civil libel context or a civil trade libel context to determine liability. Alternatively, the notion of commercial speech that is related to unlawful conduct might be expanded to include not only unlawful conduct, but also conduct which, while not unlawful, may serve as the ground for civil liability and is thus, in some sense, part of a civil "wrong."

Two lower courts have addressed the constitutional problems associated with offensive commercial speech that is near the boundary of fighting words as defined in *Chaplinsky* or group libel in the doctrinal vicinity of such cases as *Beauharnais v. Illinois*, 343 U.S. 250 (1952), and *Collin v. Smith*, 578 F.2d 1197 (7th Cir.) *cert. denied*, 439 U.S. 916 (1978). The *Sambo's Restaurant* litigation illustrates the current approach to these issues. The original Sambo's Restaurant, opened in 1957 as a pancake house, was named for the association between the name of the restaurant and pancakes. The association derives from *The Story of Little Black Sambo*, written in 1899 by Helen Bannerman, as described in the Sixth Circuit's opinion, 663 F.2d at 687 n.1:

A childhood narrative, it is the tale of a small boy, Little Black Sambo, who loses his red coat, blue trousers, purple shoes and green umbrella to marauding tigers. In fighting among themselves, the tigers chase each other in a ring around a tree, running so fast that they melt away leaving nothing but a big pool of butter. Little Black Sambo and his parents then use that butter in preparing a delicious pancake supper.

The owners of the Sambo's trade name in the ensuing years invested substantial sums for advertising the trade name Sambo's and registered it with the United States Patent and Trademark Office. As additional restaurants were opened, the Sambo's franchise faced challenges supported by the NAACP to the continued use of the name on the grounds of its offensiveness. Typically, city officials denied building permits if the company insisted on using the name for new facilities. In *Sambo's of Ohio, Inc. v. City Council of the City of Toledo*, 466 F.Supp. 177 (N.D. Ohio 1979), for example, the district court upheld the company's right to use the trade name, stating that "[i]t is clear that the defendants' actions in undertaking to prevent the plaintiffs from the use of their trade name 'Sambo's' is an unconstitutional deprivation of the First Amendment right of free speech." The court adverted to the trademark cancellation procedure of 15 U.S.C. §§ 1051, 1064, which permits cancellation of trade names which "may disparage . . . institutions, beliefs or national symbols or bring them into contempt or disrepute." (The court did not comment on the constitutionality of this provision, but its constitutionality is not free from doubt.)

The Sixth Circuit reached the same conclusion in litigation arising out of Sambo's franchises in Ann Arbor, Michigan. In *Sambo's Restaurants, Inc. v. City of Ann Arbor*, 663 F.2d 686 (6th Cir. 1981), it appeared that Sambo's had originally adopted the trade name "Jolly Tiger" to assuage local officials who balked at issuing requisite building permits for construction and operation under the Sambo's trade name. In the Ann Arbor case, the court rejected the suggestion that Sambo's had waived its First Amendment rights and held that the name Sambo's was protected by the First Amendment, 663 F.2d at 693–695. In the Ann Arbor litigation, the city contended that the name "Sambo" "conveys to some citizens a pernicious racial stereotype of blacks as inferior," and that "Sambo's" is "no more than a form of latent vilification." Citing *Chaplinsky*, Ann Arbor labelled Sambo's a "racist trade name" and contended that the use of the words which, by their very utterance, inflict injury, are not protected by the First Amendment. The Sixth Circuit rejected this argument, pointing out that in *Gooding v. Wilson*, 405 U.S. 518, 524–527 (1972), and *Lewis v. City of New Orleans*, 415 U.S. 130 (1974), the Supreme Court had subsequently refined its holding in *Chaplinsky*, so that "suppression of speech which in no way tends to incite an immediate breach of the peace cannot be justified under *Chaplinsky*'s 'fighting words' doctrine."

The city did argue that Sambo's constituted a group libel within the teaching of *Beauharnais v. Illinois*, 343 U.S. 250 (1952) (affirming conviction under state statute that proscribed public dissemination of any lithograph that vilified identifiable racial, ethnic, or religious groups). Nonetheless, the Sixth Circuit observed that "[a]lthough *Beauharnais* has never been overruled, its continuing vitality has been questioned," pointing to the decisions in *Garrison v. Louisiana*, 379 U.S. 64, 82 (1964) (Douglas, J., concurring); *Collin v. Smith*, 578 F.2d 1197, 1205 (7th Cir.) *cert. denied*, 439 U.S. 916 (1978); *Tollett v. United States*, 485 F.2d 1087, 1094 n.14 (8th Cir. 1973); *Anti-Defamation League of B'nai B'rith v. FCC*, 403 F.2d 169, 174 n.5 (D.C. Cir. 1968), *cert denied*, 394 U.S. 390 (1969) (Wright, J., concurring). But, *see* Note, "Group Vilification Reconsidered," 89 Yale L.J. 308, 1450 (1979).

Ann Arbor also argued that otherwise protected commercial speech is stripped of that protection because of its ancillary offensiveness. However, the Court referred to the Supreme Court's acknowledgment that much commercial speech may be "tasteless and excessive," *Virginia Pharmacy Board*, 425 U.S. at 765, and its statement in *Carey v. Population Services International*, 431 U.S. 678, 701 (1977), rejecting suppression of advertisements of contraceptive products on the ground they would be "offensive and embarrassing to those exposed to them," on the ground that "these are classically not justifications validating the suppression of expression protected by the First Amendment," *id.* at 701.

Ann Arbor cited no factual support for its contention that the use of the name Sambo's to advertise a restaurant frustrated the city's policy of racial harmony and equality—an interest the Sixth Circuit recognized to be "a substantial state interest," relying on *Linmark Associates, Inc. v. Willingboro*, 431 U.S. 85, 94–95, (1977) (prohibition of residential "For Sale" signs to promote stable, racially integrated neighborhoods). The Sixth Circuit commented that "[m]uch more than a speculative causal relationship is required for even though exposure to the 'Sambo's' signs may offend some citizens, the ability of the City 'to shut off discourse solely to protect others from hearing it is dependent on a showing that substantial privacy interests are being invaded in an essentially intolerable manner,' '' 663 F.2d at 695.

Commercial Speech "Related to" Unlawful Activity

An important element of the Supreme Court's current doctrine of commercial speech involves the limitation of constitutional protection to commercial speech that is not "related to '' unlawful activity. The Court formulated this element in the *Central Hudson* standard, as follows:

In commercial speech cases, then, a four-part analysis has developed. At the outset, we must determine whether the expression is protected by the First Amendment. *For commercial speech to come within that provision, it at least must concern lawful activity* and not be misleading. 447 U.S. at 566 (emphasis added)

Although in *Central Hudson*, the Court referred to commercial speech that "concern[s] lawful activity," several other formulations appear in the Supreme Court's opinion to date, and the ambiguities in the doctrine still exist.

Thus, in *Pittsburgh Press Co. v. Human Relations Commission, supra*, 413 U.S. at 388–389, the Court spoke of advertising "proposing" unlawful activity, saying "[w]e have no doubt that a newspaper constitutionally could be forbidden to publish a want ad proposing a sale of narcotics or soliciting prostitutes," 413 U.S. at 388. The Court also considered and similarly rejected a slight variation of that type of advertising in which the newspaper labeled columns of advertisements, concluding that the result would not be different "if the nature of the transaction were indicated by placement under columns captioned 'Narcotics for Sale' and 'Prostitutes Wanted' rather than stated within the four corners of the advertisement," 413 U.S. at 388. The advertising in *Pittsburgh Press* was not precisely of this kind. The Court acknowledged as much in observing that ''[t]he illegality in this case may be less overt,'' *id.* However, the Court declined to distinguish the principles applicable. Pittsburgh Press was found to have violated section 8 (j) of the Pittsburgh ordinance, which made it unlawful for ''any person . . . *to aid . . . in the doing of any act declared to be an unlawful employment practice* by this ordinance,'' (emphasis added). The Human Relations Commission had concluded that the practice of placing want ads for employment in sex-designated columns did aid employers to indicate illegal sex preferences, notwithstanding the Pittsburgh Press's subsequent adoption of the captions ''Jobs–Male Interest,'' ''Jobs–Female Interest'' and ''Male–Female.'' The Court said:

> The advertisements, as embroidered by their placement, signalled that the advertisers were likely to show an illegal sex preference in their hiring decisions. Any First Amendment interest which might be served by advertising an ordinary commercial proposal and which might arguably outweigh the governmental interest supporting the regulation is altogether absent when the commercial activity itself is illegal *and the restriction on advertising is incidental to a valid limitation on economic activity.* 413 U.S. at 389 (Emphasis added.)

Pittsburgh Press thus identifies two related senses in which commercial advertising may concern unlawful activity: (1) commercial advertising may propose unlawful activity, as in the examples where the transaction offered is illegal, and (2) commercial advertising, although not proposing a transaction that is itself unlawful, may in some way facilitate or aid a practice or course of conduct that is illegal. The latter category may be distinguished further into cases where the buyer or other party to the transaction is the potential victim of the practice or course of conduct and cases where the victim of the unlawful practice or course of conduct is not a party to the commercial transaction.

The decision is also significant because it deals with commercial speech that concerns unlawful activity in a context in which the publisher of the advertisement, rather than the advertiser or the potential recipient, was advancing a claim of constitutional protection. In *Pittsburgh Press*, the Court did not give explicit consideration to any further criteria necessary to defeat the First Amendment claim of a third party to the proposed transaction or practice aided by the advertisement. But hypothetical examples can no doubt be produced presenting cases in which the third party's lack of knowledge about or lack of intent to facilitate an unlawful practice or course of conduct might attenuate any connection with the course of conduct, and therefore, as a constitutional matter defeat any claim that the third party could incur civil or criminal liability for the publication.

In *Bigelow v. Virginia*, the Court touched on the same issue of speech related to unlawful conduct when it reversed a publisher's conviction for carrying in a Virginia newspaper an advertisement for an abortion referral service in New York. The Court observed that the placement services advertised in the newspaper were legally provided in New York at that time and that Virginia could neither have regulated the advertiser's activity in New York, nor proscribed the activity in New York, nor prevented Virginia residents from traveling to New York to obtain these services, nor prosecuted them for going there. The advertising was not "related to" activity that was unlawful in the place where it was proposed to be carried out; therefore, the Virginia conviction could not stand. In a footnote, the Court was careful to state that the case did not present any question concerning advertising that is closely related to unlawful activity:

We have no occasion . . . to comment on decisions of lower courts concering regulation of advertising in readily distinguishable fact situations. Wholly apart from the respective rationales that may have been developed by the courts in those cases, their results are not inconsistent with our holding here. In those cases there usually existed a clear relationship between the advertising in question and an activity that the government was legitimately regulating. *See, e.g., United States v. Bob Lawrence Realty, Inc.*, 474 F.2d 115, 121 (5th Cir.), *cert. denied*, 414 U.S. 826 (1973); *Rockville Reminder Inc. v. United States Postal Service*, 480 F.2d 4 (2d Cir. 1973); *United States v. Hunter*, 459 F.2d 205 (4th Cir.), *cert. denied*, 409 U.S. 934 (1972). 421 U.S. at 825 n.10.

The *Bob Lawrence* and *Hunter* decisions cited by the Court in this passage dealt principally with "blockbusting" activities by real estate brokers and racially discriminatory "For Sale" advertising. The *Rockville Reminder* case dealt with the validity of postal regulations proscribing the attachment of hooks to mailboxes for use for newspaper delivery—an issue which the Court subsequently resolved in another case, see, *United States Postal Service v. Council of Greenburgh Civic Association*, 453 U.S. 114, (1981).

The Court also commented on the question presented if "the agency-advertiser's practices, although not then illegal, may *later* have proved to be at least 'inimical to the public interest' in New York," 421 U.S. at 827. That development, the Court said, "would not justify a Virginia statute that forbids Virginians from using in New York the then legal services of a local New York agency," *id*.

In attempting to delineate the manner in which commercial speech might be related to unlawful activity in such a way as to deprive such speech of First Amendment protection, the Court in *Bigelow* stated by contradistinction that the abortion referral service advertising in question was not "*related to* a commodity or service that was then illegal in either Virginia or in New York" and that advertising was not such that it "*furthered* a criminal scheme in Virginia," *id*. at 828. The Court also declined to address a variation on the hypothetical case it discussed in *Pittsburgh Press* involving an advertisement for narcotics. Although in dictum in *Pittsburgh Press*, the Court found no difficulty in concluding that such advertising would not be protected as against regulation or proscription under a state law in the state in which both the advertising and the proposed illegal transaction was to be carried out. The Court in *Bigelow* added that it was "not required to decide here what the First Amendment consequences would be if the Virginia advertisement promoted an activity in New York which was then illegal in New York'' and gave as an example ''an advertisement announcing the availability of narcotics in New York City when the possession and sale of narcotics was proscribed in the State of New York,'' *id.* at 829 n.14.

The Court was also specifically attentive to the problems posed for publications that are distributed in interstate commerce by local attempts to regulate advertising of products or services that are lawful in other states where they are proposed to be sold or delivered, but unlawful in the state or county seeking to impose the restriction on advertising, *id.* at 828–829.

In *Virginia Pharmacy Board,* although the Court did not deal directly with the problems of commercial speech related to unlawful conduct, it touched on that issue only in pointing out that in that case there was ''no claim that the transactions proposed in the forbidden advertisements are themselves illegal in any way,'' 425 U.S. at 772. In *Linmark Associates, Inc. v. Willingboro, supra,* however, the Court was once again confronted tangentially with the interconnection between commercial advertising and unlawful conduct when it invalidated Willingboro's ordinance prohibiting residential ''For Sale'' signs. The *Linmark* case is situated in that line of commercial speech cases which present First Amendment questions in the context of statutory prohibition of racial discrimination in the sale of and leasing of residential properties, panic selling, and blockbusting practices, to which the Supreme Court has referred in at least three of its decisions, *see, Bigelow v. Virginia,* 421 U.S. at 825 n.10; *Virginia Pharmacy Board v. Virginia Citizens Consumer Council,* 425 U.S. at 772–773 (the citation of *United States v. Hunter,* 459 F.2d 205); *Linmark Associates, Inc. v. Willingboro* 431 U.S. at 95 n.9. The Court in *Linmark* was careful to confine its attention, however, to the precise issues then before it and declined to intimate its view on related issues involved in other cases, 431 U.S. at 95 n.9. In particular, the Court took note of the lower court decision in *Barrick Realty, Inc. v. City of Gary,* 491 F.2d 161 (7th Cir. 1974), in which Gary, Indiana's prohibition on ''For Sale'' signs was upheld on a record indicating that such signs were causing ''whites to move *en masse* and blacks to replace them,'' *id.* at 163–164. The *Linmark* Court expressed no view as to ''whether *Barrick Realty* can survive *Bigelow* and *Virginia Pharmacy Board,''* 431 U.S. at 95 n.9.

The *Linmark* decision is significant in this connection for its requirement of a clear connection between commercial advertising and a valid governmental interest. In *Bates,* the Court had merely reiterated the power of government to suppress ''[a]dvertising concerning transactions that are themselves illegal,'' 433 U.S. at 384.

In *Ohralik,* the Court dealt with attorney in-person solicitation that combines commercial speech and conduct. The Court further elaborated its analysis of the requirement that commercial speech, to enjoy First Amendment protection, not be related to unlawful conduct. *Ohralik* dealt with commercial speech that is related to unlawful conduct, not in the sense that the commercial speech proposed a commercial transaction that was illegal where it was to be performed, but rather commercial speech that might be used to further unlawful activity, or that actually does aid an unlawful practice or course of conduct.

Commercial speech may fall into the latter category for two reasons and in two different ways. First, commercial speech may be one constituent element in a broader course of conduct involving conduct components quite distinct from the commercial speech itself. Second, the commercial speech may be conveyed through a medium or means which in itself mixes speech and conduct (expressive conduct), such as draft-card burning. The same principles may apply to both categories, but *Ohralik*, which involved a prohibition of in-person solicitation of legal business by attorneys, involved only the latter variety. These categories potentially implicate two related but distinct strands of conventional First Amendment doctrines emanating respectively from the Supreme Court's decisions in *Giboney v. Empire Storage & Ice Co.*, 336 U.S. 490 (1949) (speech as a constituent element of course of conduct), and *United States v. O'Brien*, 391 U.S. 367 (1968) (mixed speech and expressive conduct). In *Ohralik*, the Court made specific reference to the principle of *Giboney*, pointing out that "it has never been deemed an abridgement of freedom of speech or press to make a course of conduct illegal merely because the conduct was in part initiated, evidenced, or carried out by means of language, either spoken, written or printed," 436 U.S. at 456. Curiously, the Court did not employ the *O'Brien* standard in *Ohralik*, which would appear to be the applicable principle in view of the fact that in-person solicitation brought the appellant's conduct into the *O'Brien* category of mixed speech and conduct.

An understanding of *Giboney* is crucial to an understanding of the exception which the Court has carved out from the commercial speech doctrine for commercial speech that is related to unlawful activity, in the sense that the unlawful course of conduct was in part "initiated, evidenced, or carried out" by means of commercial speech. In *Giboney*, the Court considered the constitutionality of Missouri's use of its state antitrust law forbidding conspiracies in restraint of intrastate commerce to enjoin union members from picketing that was carried on "as an essential and inseparable part of a course of conduct" alleged to be in violation of that state antitrust law. Empire Storage & Ice Company, a producer and seller of ice in Kansas City, instituted an action against the officers and members of the Ice and Coal Drivers and Handlers Local Union No. 953 for an injunction restraining them from picketing Empire's plant. The union's picketing of Empire's plant was part of an organization drive to convince non-union retail ice peddlers to join the union. To break down the independent retail peddlers' resistance to the union, the union adopted a plan designed to make it impossible for non-union peddlers to buy ice to supply their retail customers in Kansas City. Pursuant to that plan, the union attempted to secure an agreement from all the Kansas City wholesale ice distributors that they would not sell ice to non-union peddlers. Empire refused to enter into such an agreement, and the union began to picket Empire's plant. The union's avowed purpose in picketing Empire's plant was to cause Empire to cease selling to the non-union ice peddlers.

When Empire's business fell off by 85 percent, it instituted suit. The union defended its picketing on First Amendment grounds, contending that there was "a labor dispute" existing between Empire and the union, although Empire's employees were not involved in it, and contending that the picketers publicized only the truthful information that Empire was "selling ice to peddlers who are not members of the union," 336 U.S. at 493–494. The union's First Amendment contentions were rejected, and the trial court's injunction was affirmed by the Missouri Supreme Court. The Supreme Court of the United States affirmed the injunction and rejected the union's First Amendment defense. Although the picketers were attempting peacefully to publicize truthful facts, the Court emphasized that "the record here does not permit this publicizing to be treated in isolation," id. at 498. The Court emphasized that "the sole immediate object of the publicizing adjacent to the premises of Empire, as well as the other activities of the appellants and their allies, was to compel Empire to agree to stop selling ice to non-union peddlers." The Court said:

Thus all of appellants' activities—their powerful transportation combination, their patrolling, their formulation of a picket line warning union men not to cross at peril of their union membership, their publicizing—*constituted a single and integrated course of conduct, which was in violation of Missouri's valid law.* 336 U.S. at 498 (Emphasis added.)

The Court rejected the union's contention that the First Amendment extends its immunity to speech or writing "used as an integral part of conduct in violation of a valid criminal statute," *see*, *Eastern States Lumber Dealers Association v. United States*, 234 U.S. 600 (1914) (agreement among competitors to exchange truthful pricing information as part of price-fixing conspiracy); *American Column & Lumber Co. v. United States*, 257 U.S. 377 (1921) (agreement among competitors to exchange truthful pricing information); *NLRB v. Gissel Packing Co.*, 395 U.S. 575, 619 (1969) (employer's alleged predictions of "demonstrable economic consequences" of unionization construed as illegal coercive threat of retaliatory action against employees).

The First Amendment doctrine relating to speech that is "brigaded" with conduct in an unlawful course of conduct of which the speech is an integral part, illustrated in *Giboney*, is conceptually related to the doctrine of *United States v. O'Brien*, 391 U.S. 367 (1968), in which the Court dealt with expressive conduct. O'Brien burned his Selective Service registration certificate before a sizable crowd on the steps of the South Boston Courthouse in order to influence others to adopt his antiwar beliefs. He was convicted of a violation of 50 U.S.C. App. § 462 which makes it unlawful to knowingly destroy, mutilate, alter, or forge a draft card. O'Brien contended that his conviction was unconstitutional because his act of burning his draft card was protected "symbolic speech," and that the freedom of expression which the First Amendment guarantees includes all modes of "communication of ideas by conduct." The Court stated that it could not "accept the view that an apparently limitless variety of conduct can be labeled 'speech' whenever any person engaging in the conduct intends thereby to express an idea,'' 391 U.S. at 376. The Court assumed, without accepting, that the ''communicative element'' in O'Brien's conduct was sufficient to bring into play the First Amendment. The Court said, however:

This Court has held that when ''speech'' and ''nonspeech'' elements are combined in the same course of conduct, a sufficiently important governmental interest in regulating the nonspeech element can justify incidental limitations on First Amendment freedoms. To characterize the quality of the governmental interest which must appear, the Court has employed a variety of descriptive terms: compelling; substantial; subordinating; paramount; cogent; strong. Whatever imprecision inheres in these terms, we think it clear that a governmental regulation is sufficiently justified if it is within the constitutional power of the government; if it furthers an important or substantial governmental interest; *if the governmental interest is unrelated to the suppression of free expression*; and if the *incidental restriction* on alleged First Amendment freedoms is *no greater than is essential to the furtherance of that interest*. (Emphasis added.)

Concluding that each of these criteria was satisfied, the Court upheld O'Brien's conviction.

The precise extent to which the *O'Brien* standard might apply to commercial speech that is mixed with elements of conduct remains to be seen, although a comparison of the *O'Brien* and *Central Hudson* standards would seem to suggest that the *O'Brien* standard might somewhat overstate the protection to which commercial speech is entitled in such a context. The in-person solicitation involved in *Ohralik* involved an element of conduct—the physical presence of a speaker making requests—which altered the normal risks or imminence of harm, as the Court pointed out, 436 U.S. at 457 n.13. An in-person solicitation goes beyond a merely passive communication of acts in that it demands an immediate response without time for full reflection. In *Ohralik*, the Court pointed to general features of in-person solicitation which may be applicable to in-person commercial solicitations of other kinds as well, although there are special features of in-person solicitation of legal employment (layman's lack of familiarity with legal services and the lawyer's special training in the arts of persuasion) which compound the difficulties.

A final decision of significance in connection with the ''related to unlawful activity'' exception to the *Central Hudson* commercial speech doctrine is *Village of Hoffman Estates v. The Flipside*, 455 U.S. 489 (1982), in which the Court considered the constitutionality of a local ''head-shop'' licensing ordinance requiring businesses to obtain a license to sell any items ''designated or marketed for use with illegal cannabis or drugs.'' The Supreme Court upheld the ordinance and rejected any argument that the ordinance unconstitutionally interfered with commercial, drug-related expression incidental to the operation of head shops. The Court stated that if the marketing activity ''is deemed 'speech' then it is speech proposing an illegal transaction, which a government may regulate or ban entirely,'' 455 U.S. at 496.

THE APPLICATION OF ANCILLARY PROCEDURAL AND PROTECTIVE PRINCIPLES OF THE FIRST AMENDMENT TO COMMERCIAL SPEECH

The basic protection afforded to non-commercial speech under the First Amendment has been articulated by the Supreme Court in judicial decisions principally during the period 1910 to date and has been laid down in an intricate set of rules which operate together to define that system of protection. Some of these rules are substantive rules of law that define the governing standard of judicial review of governmental restraints on expression. Other rules are purely procedural in nature but may be equally as effective as substantive rules in specific circumstances, in guaranteeing protection to non-commercial speech, because they define the manner in which freedom of speech issues are litigated in courts. The Supreme Court has repeatedly cautioned that established principles of First Amendment jurisprudence in the area of non-commercial speech do not necessarily apply in straightforward fashion to commercial speech. Those doctrines may not apply at all to commercial speech, or they apply only to a limited extent. In *Friedman v. Rogers, supra*, at 10 n.9, the Court said that the First Amendment principles regarding non-commercial speech "do not extend automatically" to commercial speech:

The application of First Amendment protection to speech that does "no more than propose a commercial transaction," *Pittsburgh Press Co. v. Human Relations Commission*, 413 U.S. 376, 385 (1973), has been recognized generally as a substantial extension of traditional free-speech doctrine which poses special problems not presented by other forms of protected speech.

. . .

Because of the special character of commercial speech and the relative novelty of First Amendment protection for such speech, we act with caution in confronting First Amendment challenges to economic legislation that serves legitimate regulatory interests. *Our decisions dealing with more traditional First Amendment problems do not extend automatically to this as yet uncharted area. See, e.g.,* [Ohralik], at 462 n.20 (overbreadth analysis not applicable to commercial speech). When dealing with restrictions on commercial speech we frame our decisions narrowly, "allowing modes of regulation [of commercial speech] that might be impermissible in the realm of non-commercial expression." *Id.* at 456. 440 U.S. at 11

It would seem to follow that established First Amendment principles should apply, unless "special problems" associated with commercial speech make the application impossible.

Basic First Amendment Principles Concerning Non-Commercial Speech

Eight of the most important First Amendment principles in the area of non-commercial speech are (1) the doctrine of prior restraint; (2) the doctrine of

overbreadth; (3) the "time, place and manner" rule; (4) the Equal Protection/
First Amendment rule; (5) the principles of standing to sue and burden of proof
in First Amendment litigation; (6) the doctrine of compulsory speech; (7) the
special First Amendment principles applicable to the electronic media; and (8)
the rules relating to the status of false speech.

A summary of these principles and an account of the extent to which they
apply to commercial speech complete this summary of the commercial speech
doctrine.

The Doctrine of Prior Restraint

According to Blackstone, the entire content of the English law of liberty of
the press consisted "in laying no previous restraints on publications, and not in
freedom from censure for criminal matters when published," W. Blackstone, 4
Commentaries on the Laws of England 151 (1st ed. 1765–1769 (facsimile,
University of Chicago, 1979). Since the Supreme Court's decision in *Near v.
Minnesota*, 283 U.S. 697 (1931), it has been well established that the First
Amendment will not tolerate governmental regulation of speech in the form of
censorship or prohibition or system of licensure imposed on speech prior to
publication, with the possible exceptions of serious interferences with a war
effort, enforcement of laws against obscenity, and protection against incitement
to acts of violence and the overthrow by force of orderly government, *Citizens
for a Better Austin v. Keefe*, 402 U.S. 415 (1971); *New York Times v. United
States*, 403 U.S. 713 (1971) ("Pentagon Papers" case). In certain instances,
subsequent punishment for the content of speech may be permissible under the
First Amendment, but the prior restraint doctrine makes it clear that the First
Amendment's prohibition against injunctions, cease and desist orders, licensure
problems, and other forms of previous restraints is perhaps the nearest thing to
an absolute in constitutional law.

The question of the applicability of the prior restraint doctrine to commercial
speech remains to be resolved definitively by the Supreme Court. Several decisions in the commercial speech area have involved what would in other contexts
have been found to be illegitimate prior restraints. For example, the Pittsburgh
Human Relations Commission's cease and desist order addressed to the newspaper in the *Pittsburgh Press* case was a kind of prior restraint, as was the New
York Public Service Commission's order addressed to state-regulated electric
utilities in *Central Hudson*. The Supreme Court has on several occasions commented pointedly on the applicability of the prior restraint doctrine to commercial
speech. In *Pittsburgh Press*, an *amicus curiae* argued that "the Commission's
order should be condemned as a prior restraint," 413 U.S. at 389. Although the
Court rejected all the First Amendment arguments in *Pittsburgh Press* on the
ground that the gender-based help-wanted advertising involved there was related
to unlawful conduct, the Court chose to respond separately to the prior restraint
argument. The Court observed that the classic prior restraint doctrine described

by Blackstone barred only a "system of administrative censorship," but took note of the fact that the Court's earlier prior restraint decisions had gone well beyond prohibiting only "administrative censorship." In the *Near* case, for example, the Court had struck down a judicial injunction against further publication of a newspaper that the trial judge had found to be a "public nuisance." The answer to the prior restraint argument in *Pittsburgh Press* was, therefore, not to be found in any pre-existing limitation of the prior restraint doctrine.

The Court listed several reasons (apart from the fact that the Human Relations Commission's order did "not endanger arguably protected speech") why the prior restraint doctrine could not apply. In the first place, in prior decisions the Court had "never held that all injunctions are impermissible" under the prior restraint doctrine, 413 U.S. at 390. The Court observed that the special vice of a prior restraint is that communication will be suppressed, either directly or by inducing excessive caution in the speaker, before an adequate determination that it is unprotected by the First Amendment. The Court stated:

Because the order is based on a continuing course of repetitive conduct, this is not a case in which the Court is asked to speculate as to the effect of publication. *Cf. New York Times Co. v. United States*, 403 U.S. 713 (1971). Moreover, the order is clear and sweeps no more broadly than necessary. And, because no interim relief was granted, the order will not have gone into effect before our final determination that the actions of Pittsburgh Press were unprotected. 413 U.S. at 390

The Court noted that the commission did not possess summary contempt power. Chief Justice Burger, in dissent, questioned the Court's ruling on the prior restraint issue, 413 U.S. at 393. He commented that "the weighty presumption of unconstitutionality of prior restraint of the press seems to be given less regard than we have traditionally accorded it," *id.* at 393. The four dissenting justices (Douglas, Stewart, Burger, and Blackmun) all voted to invalidate the order precisely on the ground that it constituted a prior restraint.

In *Virginia Pharmacy Board*, the Court cautioned that attributes such as the greater objectivity and hardiness of commercial speech "may make it less necessary to tolerate inaccurate statements for fear of silencing the speaker," 425 U.S. at 772 n.24, and also specifically observed, in dictum not essential to the decision, that "they may also make inapplicable the prohibition against prior restraints" in connection with commercial speech, *id.* at 772 n.24. The Court repeated this caution in *Friedman v. Rogers*, 440 U.S. 1, 10 (1978). Neither statement constitutes binding precedent that the prior restraint doctrine does not apply to commercial speech.

In *Central Hudson*, the Court invalidated a Public Service Commission order flatly prohibiting in advance any form of promotional advertising of electric utility service on the ground that the state of New York had failed to establish that blanket prohibition of such advertising was the only feasible regulatory alternative and on the ground that New York had failed to establish a more limited restriction on the content of promotional advertising would not serve adequately the state's interest. The Court proceeded to suggest several other less restrictive alternatives which the State Public Service Commission might have considered. The Court suggested, by way of example, that the commission could attempt to restrict the format and content of Central Hudson's advertising, by requiring that the advertising include information about the relative efficiency and expense of the offered service, under current conditions and in the future. The other alternative the Court suggested was "a system of previewing advertising campaigns," 447 U.S. at 571 n.13. Of course, a system for previewing communications would run afoul of the prior restraint doctrine if such a system were imposed on non-commercial speech. While mentioning the prior restraint doctrine, the Court intimated that such a "system of previewing advertising campaigns" for electric utilities may not pose prior restraint problems in the commercial speech field. The Court said (*id.* at 571 n.13):

The Commission also might consider a system of previewing advertising campaigns to insure that they will not defeat conservation policy. It has instituted such a program for approving "informational" advertising under the Policy Statement challenged in this case. *See, supra,* at 2348. We have observed that commercial speech is such a sturdy brand of expression that traditional prior restraint doctrine may not apply to it. *Virginia Pharmacy Board v. Virginia Citizens Consumer Council,* 425 U.S. at 771–772 n.24. And in other areas of speech regulation, such as obscenity, we have recognized that a prescreening arrangement can pass constitutional muster if it includes adequate procedural safeguards. *Freedman v. Maryland,* 380 U.S. 51 (1965).

Although by these dicta the Supreme Court has clearly intimated that the prior restraint doctrine may be inapplicable to commercial speech, the Court has yet to actually rule on its applicability to commercial speech.

In addition to the foregoing authorities' suggesting that the doctrine of prior restraint "may not" apply to commercial speech, several Civil Rights Act decisions antedate the modern commercial speech doctrine, in which courts entered prior restraints against newspapers for discriminatory apartment rental ads, *see, United States v. Hunter,* 459 F.2d 205 (4th Cir. 1972) ("white home" case); *see also, Head v. New Mexico Board of Examiners,* 374 U.S. 424, 432 n.12 (1963) (injunction restraining newspaper from publishing optometrist's advertising—due process); *Gomper's v. Buck's Stove & Range Co.,* 221 U.S. 418, 439 (1911) (upholding injunction against union newspaper promoting boycott); *Lorain Journal Co. v. United States,* 201 F.Supp. 752 (D.C. Ohio 1962) (injunction prohibiting publisher from accepting or rejecting advertisements of others in violation of antitrust laws). In *FTC v. National Commission on Egg Nutrition,* 517 F.2d 485 (1975), the Seventh Circuit directed an injunction restraining further publication of statements saying that there is no scientific evidence that eating eggs brings on heart disease or heart attacks. Each of these cases, however, fits within one of the categories of unprotected commercial speech, *i.e.*, commercial speech that is an integral part of an unlawful course of conduct, or commercial speech that is false.

Several lower court decisions have taken into consideration the prior restraint aspects of certain forms of regulatory action directed to commercial speech. In *Standard Oil Co. of California v. FTC*, 577 F.2d 653, 662 (9th Cir. 1978), the Court noted that "first amendment considerations dictate that the Commission exercise restraint in formulating remedial orders which may amount to a prior restraint on protected commercial speech." Thus, while the prior restraint doctrine has not been held to apply to commercial speech, the doctrine may have a peripheral effect on questions of the proper scope of remedial orders made by regulatory authorities. In *Standard Oil*, for example, the Court invalidated a blanket order as "wholly unwarranted by the circumstances of the case," 577 F.2d at 662; *see also, Bauer v. Chaussee*, 567 P.2d 448 (Mont. 1977).

In other cases, arguments based on the prior restraint doctrine have been rejected: *D. v. Educational Testing Service*, 87 Misc.2d 657, 386 N.Y.S. 2d 747 (Special Term, N.Y.Co. 1976) (order preventing ETS from mailing notice of concealment of LSAT score because of examinee's large score improvement held not to be a "prior restraint"); *A&M Records, Inc. v. Heilman*, 75 Cal. App. 3d 554, 142 Cal. Rptr. 390 (1977) (restraint on advertising of "pirated" tapes upheld on the ground that advertisements proposed illegal transactions); *Sears Roebuck & Co. v. Federal Trade Commission*, 676 F.2d 385 (9th Cir. 1982) (noting that "doctrinal question whether prior restraint analysis . . . is properly applicable to any commercial speech question remains open" and holding that FTC "may require prior reasonable substantiation of product performance claims after finding violations of the Act''); *Triangle Publications v. Knight-Ridder Newspapers*, 445 F.Supp 875 (S.D. Fla. 1978); *People v. Columbia Research Corp.*, 71 Cal. App. 3d 607, 139 Cal. Rptr. 517 (1977) (mail order "gift" promotion) (comparative ads of newspaper television program listing and *TV Guide* copyright to justify injunctive relief).

A number of other cases have addressed the propriety of regulatory orders affecting commercial advertising in the First Amendment context: *see, Transworld Accounts, Inc. v. FTC*, 594 F.2d 212 (9th Circ. 1979) (Duniway, J., concurring and dissenting) (debt collection practices); *Encyclopedia Britannica, Inc. v. FTC*, 605 F.2d 964, 972–973 (7th Cir. 1979) (door-to-door encylcopedia sales practices modified by requirement of specified notices); *National Commission on Egg Nutrition v. FTC*, 570 F.2d 157 (7th Cir. 1977), *cert. denied*, 439 U.S. 821 (1978) (advertisements denying adverse medical evidence on effects of eating eggs; FTC order directing inclusion of reference to belief of many medical experts that eating eggs increases risk of heart disease, modified to require disclosure only in connection with ads commenting specifically on medical evidence); *Beneficial Corp. v. FTC*, 542 F.2d 611 (3d Cir. 1976), *cert. denied*, 430 U.S. 983 (1977); *Litton Industries, Inc. v. FTC*, 676 F.2d 364 (9th Cir. 1982) (microwave oven ads: First Amendment challenge to order rejected after modification of order); *Original Cosmetics Products, Inc. v. Strachan*, 459

F.Supp. 496 (S.D.N.Y. 1978) (mail stop of "legendary aphrodisiacs with placebo qualities"); *Scott v. Association for Childbirth at Home*, 85 Ill. App. 3d 311 (1980) (advertisements and information regarding childbirth at home); *People v. Sapse*, 104 Cal. App. 3d Supp. 1, 163 Cal. Rptr. 920 (1980) (unlicensed foreign doctor); *Warner-Lambert Co. v. FTC*, 562 F.2d 749 (D.C. Cir. 1977) (challenge to corrective advertising order designed to correct impression created by prior deceptive advertising); *United States v. Reader's Digest Association*, 464 F.Supp. 1037 (D. Del. 1978) (pre–commercial speech doctrine waiver in consent decree); *see*, Note, "Corrective Advertising Orders of the Federal Trade Commission," 85 Harv. L. Rev. 477 (1971); Reich, "Consumer Protection and the First Amendment: A Dilemma for the FTC?" 61 Minn. L. Rev. 705 (1977); Note, "Yes, FTC, There Is a Virginia: The Impact of Virginia State Board of Pharmacy v. Virginia Citizens Consumer Council Inc. on the Federal Trade Commission's Regulation of Misleading Advertising," 57 B. Univ. L. Rev. 833 (1977); Pitofsky, "Beyond Nader: Consumer Protection and the Regulation of Advertising," 90 Harv. L. Rev. 661 (1977); *Better Business Bureau of Houston v. Medical Directors*, 681 F.2d 397 (5th Cir. 1982) (enjoining ads representing that weight reduction center was approved by Better Business Bureau); *People v. Superior Court of Orange County*, 96 Cal. App. 3d 181, 157 Cal. Rptr. 628 (1979) (real estate broker advertising 406 street addresses "sold in 8 days or less").

The Doctrine of Overbreadth

Although the overbreadth doctrine has recently undergone considerable modification even as applied to non-commercial speech, the doctrine is a well-established component of conventional First Amendment law. Statutes that impinge on the exercise of the First Amendment are necessarily drawn by legislatures using general terminology that encompasses a wide variety of instances of individual conduct. Poorly drafted statutes sometimes by their imprecision embrace conduct that is clearly protected by the Constitution and that cannot therefore be constitutionally proscribed. Where the constitutionality of a statute is challenged in a case in which the government is attempting to apply a statute to conduct or expression that is clearly protected by the Constitution, no problems of overbreadth of the statute arise. The Court may simply declare the statute unconstitutional as applied to that protected conduct. The courts are capable in this fashion of eliminating the bad applications which the statute by its terms might have as they arise. Under this so-called as applied method of judicial review, the courts permit a statute to continue to operate where it might do so constitutionally, but uphold the rights of individuals to whom the statute is sought to be applied in instances where such individuals' constitutional rights conflict with the broad terms of the statute.

The courts occasionally have resorted to a more drastic alternative, however, in dealing with such defectively drawn statutes. The courts may declare the statute unconstitutional "on its face" and invalidate the statute in all of its future applications. The statute accordingly becomes a nullity, without force or legal effect. Such facial invalidation of a statute may be appropriate where the terminology of a statute is so broad and its imprecision is so great that, in addition to making unlawful certain areas of conduct which are not constitutionally protected, the statute also by its terms makes unlawful a broad range of conduct that is constitutionally protected. The mere existence of such an overly broad statute "chills" a category of protected expression or conduct.

When the courts exercise the option of ruling on a case-by-case basis that the statute is unconstitutional as applied to a succession of acts that are constitutionally protected, the individual challenges to its application to specific protected conduct, taken together, gradually will redefine the boundaries of the statute, clarify the scope of the law, and confine its scope to the constitutionally permissible sphere of operation. Given the paramount importance of First Amendment rights, this case-by-case method of applied review of a statute may be an unacceptably slow method of clarifying the constitutional scope of the statute, and the interim continuing chill of important rights and interests may be deemed constitutionally intolerable. As a consequence, the courts have sometimes employed the overbreadth doctrine in appropriate cases as a means of immediately invalidating legislation that by its terms applies to many instances of constitutionally protected conduct.

The doctrine has been described[8] as follows:

The newer and more aggressive method of reviewing overbroad laws on their face involves scrutiny to determine whether a statute is too sweeping in coverage—and if so, invalid on its face. *Such review proceeds without regard to the constitutional status of a particular complainant's conduct.* Rather than excise particular invalid applications one by one as they arise, the Court has employed the First Amendment overbreadth doctrine to short circuit the process by invalidating the statute and putting it up to the legislature for redrafting. The doctrine focuses directly on the need for precision in drafting to avoid conflict with First Amendment rights. It may condemn a statute which comprehends a range of applications against privileged activity even though the interests it promotes outweigh the infringement of First Amendment liberties. Furthermore, *the Court has been willing to review the breadth of statutory burdens on expressive activity even in the case of a person whose conduct could constitutionally be burdened.* (emphasis added)

The Supreme Court has recently narrowed the overbreadth doctrine considerably even in its application to non-commercial speech. In *Broadrick v. Oklahoma*, 413 U.S. 601 (1973), the Supreme Court deliberately narrowed the overbreadth doctrine by intimating that the doctrine may be used to invalidate legislation on its face only when a statute is substantially overbroad. In *Broadrick*, the Court observed that "[e]mbedded in the traditional rules governing constitutional adjudication is the principle that a person to whom a statute may constitutionally be applied will not be heard to challenge that statute on the ground that it may conceivably be applied unconstitutionally to others in other situations not before the Court," 413 U.S. at 610, and that "constitutional rights are personal and may not be asserted vicariously," *id*. The Court summarized the doctrine:

In the past, the Court has recognized some limited exceptions to these principles, but only because of the most "weighty countervailing policies." *United States v. Raines*, 362 U.S., at 22–23. One such exception is where individuals not parties to a particular suit stand to lose by its outcome and yet have no effective avenue of preserving their rights themselves. . . . Another exception has been carved out in the area of the First Amendment.

It has long been recognized that the First Amendment needs breathing space and that statutes attempting to restrict or hinder the exercise of First Amendment rights must be narrowly drawn and represent a considered legislative judgment that a particular mode of expression has to give way to other compelling needs of society.

. . .

As a corollary, the Court has altered its traditional rules of standing to permit—in the First Amendment—"attacks on overly broad statutes with no requirement that the person making the attack demonstrate that his own conduct could not be regulated by a statute drawn with the requisite narrow specificity." *Dombrowski v. Pfister*, 380 U.S. at 486. *Litigants, therefore, are permitted to challenge a statute not because their own rights of free expression are violated, but because of a judicial prediction or assumption that the statute's very existence may cause others not before the court to refrain from constitutionally protected speech or expression.*

Such claims of facial overbreadth have been entertained in cases involving statutes which by their terms, seek to regulate "only spoken words." 413 U.S. at 611–612

The Court concluded its summary in *Broadrick* with the observation that the overbreadth doctrine should be confined to cases where the overbreadth of the statute is not only real, but substantial:

It remains a "matter of no little difficulty" to determine when a law may properly be held void on its face and when "such summary action" is inappropriate. *Coates v. City of Cincinnati*, 402 U.S. 611 (1971) (opinion of Black, J.). But the plain import of our cases is, at the very least, that facial overbreadth adjudication is an exception to our traditional rules of practice and that its function, a limited one at the outset, attenuates as the otherwise unprotected behavior that it forbids the State to sanction moves from "pure speech" toward conduct and that conduct—even if expressive—falls within the scope of otherwise valid criminal laws that reflect legitimate state interests in maintaining comprehensive controls over harmful, constitutionally unprotected conduct. Although such laws, if too broadly worded, may deter protected speech in some unknown extent, there comes a point where that effect—at best a prediction—cannot, with confidence, justify invalidating a statute on its face and so prohibiting a State from enforcing the statute against conduct that is admittedly within its power to proscribe. *Cf. Alderman v. United States*, 394 U.S. 165, 174–174 (1969). To put the matter another way, particularly where conduct and not merely speech is involved, we believe that the overbreadth of a statute must not only be real, but substantial as well, judged in relation to the statute's plainly legitimate sweep. *Id*. at 615

Although this revised "substantial overbreadth" doctrine, as reformulated in *Broadrick* and subsequent cases, is of increasingly little significance even in First Amendment litigation involving non-commercial speech, the doctrine still remains a potentially potent one where it is applicable, particularly in cases where no conduct is involved. It is, as the Court has acknowledged, "strong medicine." The question arises, therefore, whether this powerful doctrine applies in the area of commercial speech.

The Supreme Court has addressed the question of the applicability of the overbreadth doctrine to commercial speech on a number of occasions and each time intimated that it will not apply the doctrine in the commercial speech context or at least that the overbreadth doctrine is "inapplicable in certain commercial speech cases," for example, *Metromedia, Inc. v. City of San Diego*, 453 U.S. 490, 504 n.11 (1981); *Central Hudson Gas & Electric Corp. v. Public Service Commission*, 447 U.S. 557, 565 (1980); *Friedman v. Rogers*, 440 U.S. 1, 11 n.9 (1979); *Schaumburg v. Citizens for a Better Environment*, 444 U.S. 620, 634 (1980); *Ohralik v. Ohio State Bar Association*, 436 U.S. 447, 462 n.20 (1978); *Bates v. State Bar of Arizona*, 433 U.S. 350, 381 (1977). The Court's intimations, however, have fallen somewhat short of an explicit holding to this effect.

In *Bates*, which involved professional advertising, the Court refused to apply the overbreadth doctrine to invalidate the state bar regulation prohibiting attorney advertising on the ground that this is not a context in which the doctrine is "necessary to further its intended objective":

Since advertising is linked to commercial well-being, it seems unlikely that such speech is particularly susceptible to being crushed by overbroad regulation. *See, Virginia Pharmacy Board*, at 771–772, n.24. Moreover, concerns for uncertainty in determining the scope of protection are reduced; the advertiser seeks to disseminate information about a product or service that he provides, and presumably he can determine more readily than others whether his speech is truthful and protected. *Ibid.* Since overbreadth has been described by this Court as "strong medicine," which "has been employed sparingly and only as a last resort," *Broadrick v. Oklahoma*, 413 U.S., at 613, we decline to apply it to professional advertising, a context where it is not necessary to further its intended objective. *Cf. Bigelow v. Virginia*, 421 U.S. at 817–818. 433 U.S. at 381

The Court also stated that "the justification for the application of overbreadth analysis applies weakly, if at all, in the ordinary commercial context," 433 U.S. at 380.

The holding of *Bates*, limited as it was to a refusal to apply the overbreadth doctrine to professional advertising, was arguably narrow enough to permit the overbreadth doctrine to be applied in certain other commercial speech contexts. The Court observed only that "in the ordinary commercial context" the justification applies "weakly," if at all. However, if it can be shown that the justification for applying overbreadth analysis does apply in a particular case—for example, that in such a case commercial speech that was protected was likely to be deterred for various reasons—an exception might conceivably be recognized, and the overbreadth doctrine held to be applicable. One such example might be the sale of goods or commodities by a non-profit, charitable organization for the purpose of fund-raising—a context in which the commercial motive is arguably not strong enough to weather heavy-handed governmental regulation.

The Supreme Court's statements in other cases also tend to suggest at least a degree of flexibility on the question whether overbreadth analysis is applicable in the commercial speech context. For example, in *Schaumburg v. Citizens for a Better Environment, supra,* the Court carefully characterized the *Bates* holding rather narrowly, stating that "[w]e have declared the overbreadth doctrine to be inapplicable *in certain commercial speech cases,*" 444 U.S. at 634 (emphasis added).

In *Ohralik,* as the Court specifically pointed out, the appellant did not rely on the overbreadth doctrine, 436 U.S. at 462 n.20. Nonetheless, the Court chose to discuss its possible application to the prohibition of in-person solicitation:

To the extent that appellant charges that the rules prohibit solicitation that is constitutionally protected—as he contends his is—as well as solicitation that is unprotected, his challenge could be characterized as a contention that the rules are overbroad. But appellant does not rely on the overbreadth doctrine under which a person may challenge a statute that infringes protected speech even if the statute constitutionally might be applied to him. *See, e.g., Gooding v. Wilson,* 405 U.S. 518, 520–521 (1972); *United States v. Robel,* 389 U.S. 258, 265–266 (1967); *Dombrowski v. Pfister,* 380 U.S. 479 (1965); *NAACP v. Button,* 371 U.S. 415, 432–433 (1963); *Kunz v. New York,* 340 U.S. 290 (1951). *See generally,* Note, the First Amendment Overbreadth Doctrine, 83 Harv. L. Rev. 844 (1970). On the contrary, appellant maintains that DR 2–103(A) and 2–104(A) could not constitutionally be applied to him.

Nor could appellant make a successful overbreadth argument in view of the Court's observation in *Bates* that "the justification for the application of overbreadth analysis applies weakly, if at all, in the ordinary commercial context." 433 U.S. at 380. Commercial speech is not as likely to be deterred as non-commercial speech, and therefore does not require that added protection afforded by the overbreadth approach. 436 U.S. at 462 n.20

The Court proceeded to assume that overbreadth analysis was applicable, sketched out the overbreadth argument, and then rejected it as unpersuasive. The Court wrote:

Even if the commercial speaker could mount an overbreadth attack, "where conduct and not merely speech is involved . . . the overbreadth of a statute must not only be real, but substantial as well, judged in relation to the statute's plainly legitimate sweep." *Broadrick v. Oklahoma,* 413 U.S. 601, 615 (1973). The Disciplinary Rules here at issue are addressed to the problem of a particular kind of commercial solicitation and are applied in the main context. *Id.*.

The Court pointed out that solicitation is ordinarily defined in the context where an attorney engages in conduct with the hope of pecuniary gain. In *Primus,* the companion case decided the same day as *Ohralik*, the Court had held that a lawyer who engages in solicitation as a form of protected political association generally may not be disciplined without proof of actual wrongdoing that the state constitutionally may proscribe. The Court concluded its analysis by saying:

As these Disciplinary Rules thus can be expected to operate primarily if not exclusively in the context of commercial activity by lawyers, the potential effect on protected, noncommercial speech is speculative. *See, Broadrick, supra* 413 U.S. at 612; see also Note, 83 Harv. L. Rev., *supra*, at 882–884, 908–910. *Id.*

In *Schaumburg*, as noted above, the Court said "it had declared the overbreadth doctrine to be inapplicable in certain commercial speech cases," citing *Bates*, 444 U.S. at 634. Although the Court in its limited reference to "certain commercial speech cases" preserved sufficient flexibility to apply the doctrine in an appropriate commercial context, if any, the Court had no occasion to further define the doctrine's possible application to commercial speech.

In *Central Hudson*, the Court elaborated on that component of its four-part test which requires that "speech restrictions be 'narrowly drawn,' " 447 U.S. at 565. In doing so, however, the Court was careful to point out in a footnote that "[t]his analysis is *not* an application of the 'overbreadth' doctrine." The Court said:

The latter theory permits the invalidation of regulations on First Amendment grounds even when the litigant challenging the regulation has engaged in no constitutionally protected activity. *E.g., Kunz v. New York*, 340 U.S. 290 (1951). The overbreadth doctrine derives from the recognition that unconstitutional restriction of expression may deter protected speech by parties not before the court and thereby escape judicial review.... This restraint is less likely where the expression is linked to "commercial well-being" and therefore is not easily deterred by "overbroad regulation." *Bates v. State Bar of Arizona, supra*, at 381.

In this case, the Commission's prohibition acts directly against the promotional activities of Central Hudson, and to the extent the limitations are unnecessary to serve the State's interest, they are invalid. 447 U.S at 565 n.8

The Court's comments in *Central Hudson* show that it had no occasion in that case to determine whether or to what extent the overbreadth doctrine was ever applicable to commercial speech. The Court in *Central Hudson*, therefore, left this issue open once again.

A more sweeping rejection, in dictum in a plurality opinion, appears in *Metromedia*. Footnote 11 of Justice White's opinion (expressing the views of only four justices) also contained a discussion of the overbreadth doctrine in the context of regulation of billboards. Responding to the California Supreme Court's erroneous determination that the owners of billboard businesses lacked standing to challenge the restrictions, Justice White commented, in rather more comprehensive terms, that "*[w]e have held that the overbreadth doctrine*, under which a party whose own activities are unprotected may challenge a statute by showing that it substantially abridges the First Amendment rights of parties not before the court, *will not be applied in cases involving 'commercial speech.' Bates v. State Bar of Arizona*, 433 U.S. 350, 381 (1977)," (emphasis added). Justice White went on to point out, however, that one with only a "commercial interest" does not, by reason of that, lack standing to challenge the facial validity of a statute on the grounds of its substantial infringement of the First Amendment interest of others, 101 S. Ct. at 2891 n.11. The plurality nonetheless voted to invalidate the San Diego ordinance.

Justice Stevens's dissenting opinion in *Metromedia* is particularly noteworthy for its tacit accusation that the plurality reached its conclusion only by applying some form of the overbreadth doctrine, while at the same time explicitly disavowing it. In support of that view, Justice Stevens emphasized that the plurality had focused its attention on "speculative," "remote," and "hypothetical" claims of on-site advertisers—persons not before the Court—in reaching the conclusion that the anti-billboard ordinance was invalid. He referred to "the plurality's reliance on the overbreadth doctrine to support vicarious standing in this case," 101 S. Ct. at 2911–2913 & n.16. Arguably, the *Metromedia* plurality opinion does offer some support for the applicability of the overbreadth doctrine in litigation resembling *Metromedia*, where the First Amendment interests of absent parties with valid constitutional objections are also implicated in regulations that restrict both commercial and non-commercial speech.

Lower courts have consistently held that the overbreadth doctrine is not applicable to commercial speech, *Amway Service Corp. v. Insurance Commissioner*, 113 Mich. App. 423, 317 N.W. 2d 870 (1982), *leave to appeal denied*, 413 Mich. 892.

The power of the overbreadth doctrine in commercial speech areas, if it were ever to be held applicable, is such that it might permit an advertiser to challenge the constitutionality of a state or federal regulation of advertising that is substantially overbroad even where the advertiser's communication in question was false or misleading, or related to unlawful activity, or was for some other reason unprotected. Since many statutes and regulations touching commercial speech were enacted prior to the Supreme Court's decisions in the commercial speech area, they do not take into account the new standards for judicial review in this area and, therefore, may not survive scrutiny under the *Central Hudson* four-part standard. The potential applicability of the overbreadth doctrine in the commercial speech field could conceivably jeopardize the validity of a substantial body of federal and state legislation.

"Time, Place and Manner" Restrictions and the "Special Format" Principle

Under a well-established principle of First Amendment jurisprudence, content-neutral regulation of the time, place, and manner of protected non-commercial speech is constitutionally valid (1) provided that "alternative channels" for the protected communication are left open; (2) provided that those alternative channels are not prohibitively more expensive, not markedly more inconvenient, and not significantly less effective as a means broadcasting the message; (3) provided that the "time, place and manner" regulation in question promotes a legitimate and adequate governmental purpose; and finally (4) provided that the "time, place and manner" regulation is narrowly drawn and is no broader than necessary. The "time, place and manner" rule simply recognizes that operation of sound trucks in the middle of the night in residential neighborhoods is unacceptable regardless of the importance of the expression; that a demonstration or parade in a busy street at rush hour is unacceptably inconvenient; and that three parades cannot occur on the same street at the same time, *see Kovacs v. Cooper*, 336 U.S. 77 (1949).

The "time, place and manner" rule, however, has its limits. In examining whether a regulation significantly interferes with protected speech, the courts are bound by the countervailing principle that "one is not to have the exercise of his liberty of expression in appropriate places abridged on the plea that it may be exercised in some other place," *Bolger v. Youngs Drug Products Corp.*, 463 U.S. 60, 103 S. Ct. at 2882 n.18; *Schneider v. State*, 308 U.S. 147, 163 (1939); *Virginia Pharmacy Board v. Virginia Consumer Council*, 425 U.S. 748, 757 n.15 (1966).

Unquestionably, a doctrine such as the "time, place and manner" rule, which applies even to non-commercial speech, will be applied to uphold regulations on the time, place, and manner of commercial speech. A question arises, however, whether the "time, place and manner" doctrine must be applied to commercial speech in the same fashion that it is applied to non-commercial speech, or whether, given the common-sense difference between commercial and non-commercial speech, it may be applicable in an even more relaxed version. Specifically, by way of example, must a regulation on the time, place, or manner of commercial speech be content-neutral between different kinds and varieties or may the government distinguish among the relative values of different categories of commercial speech and enact more or less restrictive time, place, and manner regulations for some types of commercial speech depending on the content of the advertising, *e.g.*, depending on the inherent social value of the product or service advertised (prescription drugs versus alcohol, or books versus cosmetics) or depending on the informative value of advertising copy (an advertisement that "Coke is the One" versus advertising specifying the price, precise attributes, and local availability of the product or service)? Must it be content-neutral where different kinds of advertising are inherently susceptible in varying degrees to use in deceptive ways? What role, if any, does the equal protection doctrine play in this respect? Must alternative channels exist in the case of commercial speech, and, if so, are the constraints on the adequacy of such alternative channels as stringent for commercial speech as they are for non-commercial speech? For example, must alternative channels be as effective or as inexpensive as the manner, place, or time eliminated by regulation? Must the governmental interest supporting a "time, place and manner" regulation of commercial speech be as weighty a governmental purpose as that required to support a "time, place and manner" regulation of non-commercial speech?

The Supreme Court has addressed arguments in several commercial speech cases that the state regulation in question was nothing more than a valid "time, place and manner" regulation. Generally, where the Court has applied the "time, place and manner" rule, it has not modified that doctrine. However, the Court has fashioned a related rule for commercial speech for handling content regulation of commercial speech. In *Virginia Pharmacy Board*, the Court specifically stated that "[t]here is no claim . . . that the prohibition on prescription drug price advertising is a mere time, place and manner restriction," 425 U.S. at 771. The Court went on to intimate that the "proper bounds of time, place and manner restrictions on commercial speech" remained an open question:

We have often approved restrictions of that kind provided that they are justified without reference to the content of the regulated speech, that they serve a significant governmental interest, and that in so doing they leave open ample alternative channels for communication of the information. *Compare Grayned v. City of Rockford*, 408 U.S. 104, 116 (1972); *United States v. O'Brien*, 391 U.S. 367, 377 (1968); and *Kovacs v. Cooper*, 336 U.S. 77, 85–87 (1949), with *Buckley v. Valeo*, 424 U.S. 1; *Erznoznik v. City of Jacksonville*, 422 U.S. 205, 209 (1975); *Cantwell v. Connecticut*, 310 U.S. at 304–308; and *Saia v. New York*, 334 U.S. 558, 562 (1948). *Whatever may be the proper bounds of time, place and manner restrictions on commercial speech, they are plainly exceeded by this Virginia statute which singles out speech of a particular content and seeks to prevent its dissemination completely.* 425 U.S. at 771 (emphasis added)

The Court in *Virginia Pharmacy Board* thus specifically rejected Virginia's "time, place and manner" defense of the statute and did so on the grounds that the statute was not content-neutral and that it left open no alternative channel. Although the Court did not touch on this feature, the vice of the Virginia ordinance included the fact that, considered as a "time, place and manner" regulation, the Virginia statute was not reasonably related to any legitimate governmental purpose. Although Virginia pointed to a governmental interest in professionalism of pharmacists which it claimed supported the prohibition of drug price advertising, that governmental interest had no relation to the time or the place or the manner in which Virginia pharmacists might have chosen to advertise drug prices. Advertising at any time, at any place, and in any manner was prohibited.

The Supreme Court also raised and explicitly rejected the proffered "time, place and manner" justification in *Linmark Associates v. Willingboro, supra*, where the Court invalidated a township's ordinance prohibiting residential "For Sale" signs. Respondents argued in that case that Willingboro's ordinance restricted "only one method of communication," 431 U.S. at 93. Although the case involved commercial speech, the fact that the ordinance affected only one manner of communicating the offer of sale of residences in Willingboro "was not without significance to First Amendment analysis, since laws regulating the time, place or manner of speech stand on a different footing from laws prohibiting speech altogether," *id.*

The Court rejected the "time, place and manner" argument in *Linmark* on two grounds. First, the Court took note of a serious question in that case whether "ample alternative channels" for communication existed, pointing out that real estate is not customarily sold through any form of advertising except on-premises "For Sale" signs, newspaper advertising, and listing with real estate agents. The Court found these alternatives unsatisfactory because they are more costly, permit less autonomy, and are less effective. The alternatives were therefore said to be "far from satisfactory," 431 U.S. at 93. The Court here evidently applied to this commercial speech a stringent form of the "time, place and manner" principle and did not in any manner relax the requirement of "ample alternative channels." The Court also relied on the fact that the Willingboro ordinance was not genuinely aimed at the place (front lawns) or the manner (signs). If that were the aim of the ordinance, it was grossly underinclusive— no other signs were regulated. There was no privacy intrusion and no detrimental "secondary effect." The signs were regulated on the basis of content because of their "primary effect"—*i.e.*, they would cause those receiving the information to act upon it. That the township chose to regulate only one available mode by which the "For Sale" message could be communicated did not save the ordinance as a "time, place and manner" regulation. *Linmark* would therefore seem to represent another application of the full strength version of the First Amendment "time, place and manner" rule, rather than a diluted version of that principle redesigned by the Court for special use in commercial speech.

In *Bates v. State Bar of Arizona*, 433 U.S. at 384, where the Court struck down a state bar prohibition on attorney advertising, the Court was careful to point out that "[a]s with other varieties of speech, it follows . . . that there may be reasonable restrictions on the time, place and manner of advertising," but the Court had no occasion to elaborate on the scope of that principle as it might be applied to commercial speech. In *Ohralik*, which dealt with in-person solicitation and where one might have expected the Court to justify the restriction on in-person solicitations explicitly as a valid "time, place and manner" regulation, the Court's opinion curiously does not even so much as mention that principle, although the court upheld the regulation. Instead, the Court surprisingly selected the *Giboney* and *Pittsburgh Press* "speech-related-to-unlawful-conduct" exception as the basis of its decision and fashioned a completely new "special format" doctrine peculiar to the commercial area to the effect that states possess broad powers to require that commercial information appear in a particular form if that is necessary to eliminate its potential for deceptive use. Justice Marshall's concurring opinion, however, mentioned the "time, place and manner" doctrine, saying that "[t]o the extent that in-person solicitation of business may constitutionally be subjected to more substantial state regulation as to time, place and manner than printed advertising of legal services, it is not because such solicitation has 'traditionally' been banned, nor because one form of commercial speech is of less value than another under the First Amendment,'' 436 U.S. at 477. This, however, was not the principle on which the majority rested its decision.

The Court made specific reference in *Friedman v. Rogers, supra,* to the applicability of ''time, place and manner'' regulations to commercial speech, 440 U.S. at 9, but it did not, in upholding the Texas prohibition on advertisement of optometric services using trade names, specifically clarify the manner in which the doctrine might apply to commercial speech. Once again, as in *Ohralik,* the Court chose to approve the state regulation on a broader basis, after balancing the potential for deception of consumers through use of trade names. The ruling in *Friedman* was based on the broader power of states, once again under the special format principle, to require that commercial information ''appear in such a form . . . as is necessary to prevent its being deceptive,'' *Friedman v. Rogers,* 440 U.S. at 16; *Virginia Pharmacy Board,* 425 U.S. at 772 n.24. The strong version of the special format principle which the Court applied in both *Ohralik* and *Friedman,* in circumstances where in a non-commercial speech case one might have anticipated the invocation of the ''time, place and manner'' doctrine, was mentioned in *Central Hudson.* In striking down the Public Service Commission's order, the Court was careful to say that in the commercial speech area ''[t]he government *may ban forms of communication* more likely to deceive the public than to inform it, *Friedman v. Rogers, supra,* at 13, 15–16; *Ohralik v. Ohio State Bar Association, supra,* at 464–465,'' 447 U.S. at 563 (emphasis added).

The special format principle is unique to the commercial speech area. It is a marked departure from the rules applicable to non-commercial speech. As applied to commercial speech, it in effect permits state and federal governments to regulate not only the ''time, place and manner'' but also the form of commercial speech because of the likelihood that the commercial speech may deceive. By contrast, the ''time, place and manner'' principle applicable to non-commercial speech does not recognize as a legitimate justification for regulation of the time, place, or manner of protected non-commercial speech the possibility that the speech is susceptible to deceptive use. The state has no control over the format of political expression. Consistent with the broad command of the First Amendment, no such thing as a ''false idea'' is recognized in the sphere of protected non-commercial speech. Government is prohibited from regulating non-commercial speech on that ground.

If the Court intended to specify the contours of the special format principle in *Central Hudson,* the Court defined a rigorous standard. Where the government has exercised the power to ''ban forms of communication'' or to require that commercial information, if it is to appear, appear in a form specified by the government, the Court has said that such government regulation will pass constitutional muster only when the state is able to show on the basis of prior experience that in other prohibited forms the communication is ''more likely to deceive the public than inform it,'' 447 U.S. at 563. Alternatively, the Court has required that, to justify this approach, the type of advertising in question be shown to be "inherently misleading," *R.M.J.*, *supra*, 455 U.S. 191, 102 S. Ct. 929, 939 (1982).

In *Metromedia*, the plurality opinion specifically rejected San Diego's "time, place and manner" defense of the billboard ordinance, 101 S. Ct. at 2897, pointing out that the San Diego ordinance did not generally ban billboards from communicating information or ideas but permitted various kinds of signs: "Signs that are banned are banned everywhere and at all times," *id*. The plurality appears once again to have applied a "full strength" version of the "time, place and manner" doctrine, rather than a diluted version of the principle designed for commercial speech:

We have observed that time, place and manner restrictions are permissible if "they are justified without reference to the content of the regulated speech, . . . serve a significant governmental interest, and . . . leave open ample alternative channels for the communication of the information." . . . Here, it cannot be assumed that "alternative channels" are available, for the parties stipulated to just the opposite: "Many businesses, politicians and other persons rely upon outdoor advertising because other forms of advertising are insufficient, inappropriate and prohibitively expensive." 101 S. Ct. at 2897.

The *Metromedia* plurality cited the rejection of a similar "time, place and manner" argument in *Linmark* and concluded that the San Diego ordinance, which distinguished in several ways between permissible and impermissible signs at a particular location by reference to their content, simply could not be justified as a "time, place and manner" restriction.

In *R.M.J.*, 455 U.S. 191 (1982), the Court was once again confronted with regulation of attorney advertising and again relied on the special format principle, formulating the principle as follows: "[W]hen the particular content or method of the advertising suggests that it is inherently misleading or when experience has proven that in fact such advertising is subject to abuse, the States may impose appropriate restrictions," 455 U.S. at 203. There are limits to the special format principle, and in *R.M.J.* the Court began to articulate those limits. Although misleading commercial advertising can always be prohibited, the states cannot absolutely prohibit certain types of potentially misleading information if the information also may be presented in a way that is not deceptive, *id*. at 203. Remedies in this area may be no broader than reasonably necessary to prevent the deception. The Court's opinion in *R.M.J.* strongly suggests that no blanket prohibition of commercial expression will ever survive scrutiny if it is not supported by evidence that—short of absolute prohibition—a requirement of "disclaimers or explanation" would not suffice, *id*. at 203.

Generally, content-based regulations cannot be justified as "time, place and manner" regulations. The latter by definition must be content-neutral to be valid. Most frequently in the Supreme Court's decisions to date in this area, where states have sought to regulate the format of commercial expression, the state regulation in question was adopted precisely because of some feature of the content of the commercial expression. Accordingly, in these instances, the conventional "time, place and manner" principle will not apply, and the need arises for a principle that justifies format regulation on the ground of the content of the commercial expression. The novel special format principle which the Court has fashioned for this purpose fulfills this function.

In summary, the Court's recent commercial speech opinions that deal with the "time, place and manner" principle appear to follow one of two alternatives. First, they may apply the "time, place and manner" principle in its conventional form to content-neutral regulations of commercial speech. Where the conventional rule is applied, the Court has not relaxed any elements of the doctrine to make it easier for states or the federal government to enact constitutional "time, place and manner" regulations in the commercial speech area. However, when the basis of governmental regulation of time, place, or manner of commercial speech is based on content and is intended to prevent speech demonstrably susceptible to deceptive use or "inherently deceptive" speech, the Court has fashioned and applied the special format principle, a rule narrowly drawn for application to commercial speech—and one that permits government to ban an entire form of communication that is likely to be deceptive or is likely to lead to the abuses of deceptive advertising, if no less restrictive form of regulation will suffice, or to require that certain disclosures or disclaimers be made in the advertisement.

The Equal Protection/First Amendment Intersection and Commercial Speech

In *Police Dept. of Chicago v. Mosley*, 408 U.S. 92 (1972), the Supreme Court struck down a local ordinance which prohibited picketing, with the exception of picketing related to a labor dispute, within 150 feet of a school building during school hours. Justice Marshall's opinion for the Court, which relied not only on the First Amendment but the equal protection clause as well, announced the rule that "[s]elective exclusions from a public forum may not be based on content alone and may not be justified by reference to content alone," 408 U.S. at 96. If the equal protection clause acts as a further constraint on time, place, and manner restrictions of protected non-commercial speech, the question may fairly be asked whether the same First Amendment/Equal Protection principle applies to commercial speech and, if it does apply, whether it applies with the same force to commercial speech as it does to non-commercial speech. In other words, may the state validly prohibit non-deceptive advertising of one kind or of one product or service while permitting advertising of a different kind or of a different product or service? The Court's decisions have provided a partial answer to this question. Although expressing the views of only four justices, the plurality opinion in *Metromedia* acknowledged that "the city may distinguish between the relative value of different categories of commercial speech," 101 S. Ct. at 2896, and at the same time, citing *Mosley*, said that "the city does not have the same range of choice in the area of non-commercial speech to evaluate the strength of, or distinguish between, various communicative interests," *id*. Of course, the distinction in *Metromedia* was between commercial and non-commercial speech.

In *Ohralik* and *Friedman*, the Court upheld state restrictions on forms of speech based specifically on the content of the commercial expression and on its inherently deceptive character or its susceptibility to abuse for purposes of deception. The Court has also made it clear that, as a general principle, the states have the power, in dealing with forms of expression that are peculiarly susceptible to abuse by deception, to single out modes of expression by content for outright prohibition or regulation. The First Amendment/Equal Protection doctrine, then, obviously does not apply with full force to deceptive commercial speech. Governments may validly consider the content of commercial speech and may prohibit certain forms of commercial speech where the relevant features of its content justify such a step in the public interest.

Beyond the *Ohralik-Friedman* principle, however, may the state, all other things being equal, selectively exclude one type of commercial advertising while permitting another based on the content of the advertising? May the state, for example, limit advertising of cigarettes in ways in which it does not limit advertising of tires or books? May the Federal Trade Commission issue exacting trade practice guides regulating advertising in some industries but not in others?

Analysis of this problem under the equal protection doctrine would ordinarily draw into play the conventional standards of judicial review under the equal protection clause and would raise the question whether the strict scrutiny or rational relationship standard, or some intermediate standard, is applicable. The choice among these competing standards would revolve, in turn, on the question whether the exercise of the right involved is a fundamental right. If the right involved is a fundamental right, the strict scrutiny standard applies, and the state must present a compelling or overriding governmental interest in making the classification on which the differential treatment depends. If the right involved were not a fundamental right, the state need only point to a rational relationship between the classification and the legitimate state objective or interest behind the classification. The Court has always treated First Amendment rights in the non-commercial speech area as fundamental rights. The Court has not yet decided whether the First Amendment right of commercial expression is a fundamental right; therefore, the applicability of a strict scrutiny standard to discriminatory commercial speech regulations is undecided.

Generally, the Court in speaking of fundamental rights has referred to the fundamental rights of individuals. Moreover, it should be recalled that in setting forth the rationale for protecting commercial speech at all, the Court laid heavy (although not exclusive) emphasis on the right of the public to receive commercial advertising rather than on the rights of advertisers to publish. This is not to say that the economic interests of the advertiser have no weight or that they are not part of the rationale for protecting commercial speech. The Court in *Virginia Pharmacy Board* specifically acknowledged and gave weight to the interests of advertisers. Nonetheless, there is some reason to doubt whether the right of commercial expression will be held to be a fundamental right. If commercial speech is not a fundamental right, the strict scrutiny standard of judicial review would be inapplicable, and the governmental interest supporting the discrimination against one form of advertising would not need to be compelling. The state would need to identify only some legitimate purpose and a rational relationship between that purpose and the discriminatory restriction on commercial speech.

The possibility remains, however, that some intermediate level of scrutiny between the strict and rational relationship standards would be applicable to this problem. Supporting this notion is the fact that the *Central Hudson* standard itself requires at least a substantial government interest. If so, it is fair to ask how a lesser standard could be applicable under the equal protection clause.

Standing to Sue and Burden of Proof in First Amendment Litigation

The advent of modern commercial speech doctrine has been accompanied by a marked expansion and sophistication of the rules governing who has the right to sue, or "standing," to challenge restrictions on expression. Generally, in cases involving challenges to the constitutionality of provisions restricting or prohibiting non-commercial speech, the party raising the challenge is typically the speaker whose expression has been forbidden or limited. Putting to one side the slightly expanded notion of standing in cases where the overbreadth doctrine applies, and the standing of an association to raise the First Amendment rights of members, standing to sue in non-commercial speech cases has not proven to be a troublesome issue. In the commercial speech cases, the Supreme Court has already recognized those separate of persons with standing to sue: (1) advertisers, *Bates v. State Bar of Arizona, Friedman v. Rogers, Central Hudson Gas & Electric v. Public Service Commission, Bolger v. Youngs Drug Products Corp.*; (2) newspapers, publishers, and other owners of media through which the advertising is broadcast or published, *Bigelow v. Virginia, Pittsburgh Press Co. v. Human Relations Commission, Metromedia, Inc. v. City of San Diego*, and (3) potential recipients of commercial expression, *Virginia Pharmacy Board v. Virginia Consumers Council.*

Although the Supreme Court has not yet so held, presumably printers and distributors of commercial expression also would be held to have standing to challenge the constitutionality of restrictions on commercial expression, notwithstanding the fact that their only interest may be that of economic gain, *see, Printing Industries of Gulf Coast v. Hill*, 382 F.Supp. 801, 814 (S.D.Tex. 1974), *probable jurisdiction noted*, 419 U.S. 1 (1974), *vacated with instructions to dismiss if moot*, 422 U.S. 937 (1975) (printers have standing to sue); *Smith v. California*, 361 U.S. 147 (1959) (booksellers); *Bantam Books v. Sullivan*, 372

U.S. 58, 64 n.6 (1963) (freedom of press embraces circulation of books as well as publication). This is only a corollary of the more general proposition that "[l]iberty of circulating is as essential to [freedom of press] as liberty of publishing; indeed, without the circulation, the publication would be of little value," *Ex Parte Jackson*, 96 U.S. 727 (1878).

An issue frequently of practical importance in the actual litigation of constitutional and other claims is the allocation of "burden of proof" of the operative facts on which legal rights turn under the substantive legal principles. Although rules regarding allocation of the burden of proof seem procedural, they are often outcome-determinative in the way that substantive rules of law are. Any comprehensive system of rules defining the protection which commercial speech enjoys must specify principles for allocating the burden of proof in litigation over the constitutionality of governmental restrictions in commercial speech. The Supreme Court has spoken on this question most recently in *Bolger v. Youngs Drug Products Corp.*, 463 U.S. 60, 103 S. Ct. at 2882 n.20, where it said: "The party seeking to uphold a restriction on commercial speech carries the burden of justifying it. See *Central Hudson Gas & Electric Corp. v. Public Service Commission of New York*, 447 U.S. 557, 570 (1980); *Linmark Associates, Inc. v. Willingboro*, 431 U.S. 85, 95 (1977)."

The Court's cited remarks in *Central Hudson* and *Linmark* add specificity to the general rule stated in *Bolger*. In *Central Hudson*, the Supreme Court made it clear that with respect to the requirement that the government restriction on commercial speech is "no more extensive than necessary to further the state's interest," the burden remains on the government, 447 U.S. at 570; *see Linmark Associates, Inc., supra*. Although the Court in *Central Hudson* did not specifically so hold, it seems clear that the burden of establishing the substantiality of governmental interests, and the burden to establish that the regulation directly advances the governmental interest asserted, also rests on the government. *Ohralik* is instructive on the issue of burden of proof. In *Ohralik*, the Court made it clear that when the form of expression is peculiarly susceptible to being used in a deceptive way or is "inherently deceptive," the government does not have the burden to prove actual harm in the particular case, but may rely on proof of harm that generally results, 436 U.S. at 466.

It is still not clear, however, which party has the burden to establish that the commercial expression in question "concern[s] lawful activity" and is not "misleading." These are preconditions to the determination that the commercial speech in question is, in fact, constitutionally protected. In the absence of an allegation to the contrary by the government seeking to defend regulation of commercial speech, the Court appears to have been willing to assume that the speech is entitled to constitutional protection.

The Doctrine of Compulsory Speech

It is a well-established principle of First Amendment jurisprudence regarding non-commercial speech that, just as the Constitution places rigid restrictions on the government's power to silence expression, the Constitution likewise will tolerate no effort by government to require citizens to speak. The First Amendment principles relating to compulsory speech are laid down in cases such as *Railway Employees' Department v. Hanson*, 351 U.S. 225 (1956); *International Association of Machinists v. Street*, 367 U.S. 740 (1961); *Lathrop v. Donohue*, 367 U.S. 820 (1961); *Miami Herald Publishing Co. v. Tornillo*, 418 U.S. 241 (1974) (compulsory "right of reply" statute applicable to newspaper was held unconstitutional); *Wooley v. Maynard*, 430 U.S. 705 (1977) (right of Jehovah's Witness to mask state license plate motto "Live Free or Die"). In some of these cases, the Court has held that absent a "compelling" government interest, the states may not force citizens to express their beliefs and opinions or the beliefs or opinions of others, including those of the government.

Do these basic principles apply with the same force and effect in the field of commercial speech? After *Central Hudson* and *Virginia Pharmacy Board*, does the government have the power, for example, to order corrective advertising? Does the government have the power, in apparent contravention of the rule against compulsory speech, to require the publication of specific facts as part of a commercial advertisement? The Supreme Court has specifically held in the commercial speech cases that where a substantial governmental interest requires it, the states may "require that . . . advertisements include information about the relative efficiency and expense of" offered services and products, *Central Hudson Gas & Electric Corp. v. Public Service Commission*, 447 U.S. at 571; *Virginia Pharmacy Board v. Virginia Consumers Council*, *supra*, 425 U.S. at 772; *Friedman v. Rogers* 440 U.S. at 10. In *Virginia Pharmacy Board*, moreover, the Court said that the greater objectivity and hardiness of commercial speech may make it appropriate "to require that a commercial message appear in such a form or *include such additional information, warnings, and disclaimers, as are necessary to prevent its being deceptive*," 425 U.S. at 772 n.24 (emphasis added). In *Bates*, also, the Court was careful not to foreclose the possibility that "some limited supplementation by way of warning or disclaimer or the like, might be required of even an advertisement of the kind ruled upon today so as to assure that the consumer is not misled," 433 U.S. at 384; *cf. Banzhaf v. FCC*, 405 F.2d 1082 (1968), *cert. denied*, 396 U.S. 842 (1969).

This is but another illustration of the concept that in the commercial speech area the courts will frame their decisions narrowly "allowing modes of regulation of commercial speech that might be impermissible in the realm of non-commercial expression," *Friedman v. Rogers*, 440 U.S. at 10 n.9; *Ohralik v. Ohio State Bar Association*, 436 U.S. at 456. It is a principle which has important implications regarding the power of governments to require specific information, to order corrective advertising, and even to preview advertising prior to publication—powers that the government, of course, may never exercise with respect to non-commercial speech.

Commercial Speech and the Electronic Media

In its recent commercial speech cases, the Court has been careful to preserve the special principles that apply even in the non-commercial speech area to communications over the electronic media. In *Bigelow v. Virginia*, 421 U.S. at 825 n.10, for exmple, the Court referred to "the First Amendment ramifications of legislative prohibitions of certain kinds of advertising in the electronic media, where the 'unique characteristics' of this form of communication 'make it especially subject to regulation in the public interest,' " citing among other illustrative cases, *Columbia Broadcasting System, Inc. v. Democratic National Committee*, 412 U.S. 94 (1973). And in *Virginia Pharmacy Board*, 425 U.S. at 773, the Court noted that "the special problems of the electronic broadcast media are . . . not in this case," citing *Capital Broadcast Co. v. Mitchell*, 333 F.Supp. 582 (D.D.C. 1971), *aff'd sub nom.*, *Capital Broadcast Co. v. Acting Attorney General*, 405 U.S. 1000 (1972). The same intimation of special limitations on commercial speech over the electronic media was repeated in *Bates*, 433 U.S. at 384.

There is a considerable history of governmental regulation of the content of advertising over the electronic media, especially with respect to regulation of cigarette advertising. Since the advent of the modern commercial speech doctrine, however, the Supreme Court has had no occasion to address this question directly. To be sure, government regulation of commercial advertising over the electronic media may be as extensive as government regulation of commercial advertising using other media. The unanswered question is whether, by reason of the peculiar features of the electronic media, permissible government regulation in this context may be more extensive than for non-commercial speech.

The Status of False Commercial Speech

In the realm of non-commercial speech, there is no such thing as a "false idea." Apart from obscenity, fighting words, and incitement, which are not conventionally thought of as involving exposition of ideas that may be true or false, only libel and slander constitute a category of speech where the truth or falsity of speech is relevant to the constitutionality of government interference. The truth or falsity of protected non-commercial speech is partially determinative of protection where the publication of defamatory statements concerns individuals, businesses, and products and causes injury. It has sometimes even been said that, even disregarding its potential for causing injury, false speech has no value at all. Thus, in *Virginia Pharmacy Board*, 425 U.S. at 771, the Court said "[u]ntruthful speech, commercial or otherwise, has never been protected for its own sake. *Gertz v. Robert Welch, Inc.*, 418 U.S. 323, 340 (1974); *Konigsberg v. State Bar*, 366 U.S. 36, 49, and n.10 (1961)." In *Gertz*, the Court said that while there is no such thing as a false idea, there is "no constitutional value in false statements of fact":

We begin with the common ground. Under the First Amendment, there is no such thing as a false idea. However pernicious an opinion may seem, we depend for its correction not on the conscience of judges and juries but on the competition of other ideas. *But there is no constitutional value in false statements of fact.* Neither the intentional lie nor the careless error materially advances society's interest in "uninhibited, robust, and wide-open" debate on public issues. *New York Times Co. v. Sullivan*, 376 U.S. at 270 (emphasis added)

The Court likened false statements of fact to "that category of utterances which are 'no essential part of any exposition of ideas, and are of such slight social value as a step to truth that any benefit that may be derived from them is clearly outweighed by the social interest in order and morality,' " 418 U.S. at 340.

Can false factual statements and opinions be a step toward truth? The notion that false speech is of no constitutional value has unquestionable, common sense appeal to support it. But the Court has not always entertained that notion to the exclusion of other sound considerations. In *New York Times v. Sullivan*, 376 U.S. at 279 n.19, for example, the Court cited no lesser authorities than John Stuart Mill and John Milton for the proposition that even false expression has value:

Even a false statement may be deemed to make a valuable contribution to public debate, since it brings about "the clear perception and livelier impression of truth, produced by its collision with error." Mill, *On Liberty* (Oxford: Blackwell, 1947), at 15; *see also* Milton, Areopagitica, in *Prose Works* (Yale, 1959), Vol. II, at 561.

In the area of non-commercial speech, false statements of fact or opinion are said to have no value, but such expression is constitutionally protected unless it constitutes libel or slander. In order to give sufficient breathing space to attempts to state the truth about public figures and public officials, the First Amendment protects false expression so long as it is not communicated with "actual malice," *i.e.*, with knowledge of its falsity or in reckless disregard of its truth or falsity. Merely negligent communication of false statements of this type are often not actionable. The courts have also placed the burden of proof of actual malice on the party contending that the expression is not protected. If non-commercial statements do not concern individuals and accordingly inflict no injury, they are constitutionally protected regardless of their falsity. The government may not be the arbiter of true opinion.

By contrast, the truth or falsity of commercial speech appears to be completely determinative of its protected status. The principal questions that arise in this connection are (1) whether negligently false or deceptive speech is entitled to any constitutional protection at all, and, if so, to what extent; and (2) if false or deceptive commercial speech is sometimes protected, who has the burden to establish that it is not negligently false? In *New York Times Co. v. Sullivan*, the Supreme Court "constitutionalized" the common law of libel and slander. The result was a change in the standard of liability and the allocation of the burdens of proof in this field. Now that the Court has recognized that commercial speech is also protected by the First Amendment, it is fair to ask whether the "constitutionalization" of commercial speech likewise requires the adoption of a more exacting standard of liability or a different allocation of the burdens of proof. Does the First Amendment impose, for example, a *scienter* requirement, akin to the actual malice standard, before false commercial speech may be punished?

In the commercial speech cases to date, the Supreme Court has consistently and completely excepted false commercial speech from the evolving doctrine, without expressly considering this issue. It has repeatedly reaffirmed the power of government to deal with false commercial speech in the conventional, abrupt ways. In *Virginia Pharmacy Board*, there was no claim that prescription drug price advertisements were false or misleading in any way. In dictum, however, the Court was careful to say that untruthful commercial speech is not to be protected for its own sake and stated that it foresaw no obstacle to a state's dealing effectively with the problems of false advertising, 425 U.S. at 771. The Court acknowledged that "much commercial speech is not provably false, or even wholly false, but only deceptive or misleading," *id*.

Footnote 24 of *Virginia Pharmacy Board* is a crucial starting point for any understanding of the status of false advertising under the evolving commercial speech doctrine. After pointing out the greater "objectivity" and "hardiness" of commercial speech, the Court took pains to preserve the false advertising jurisdiction of the Federal Trade Commission and the similar power of the states over false advertising:

Attributes such as these, the greater objectivity and hardiness of commercial speech, may make it less necessary to tolerate inaccurate statements for fear of silencing the speaker. *Compare New York Times Co. v. Sullivan*, 376 U.S. 254 (1964), with *Dun & Bradstreet, Inc., v. Grove*, 404 U.S. 898 (1971). They may also make it appropriate to require that a commercial message appear in such a form, or include such additional information, warnings, and disclaimers, as are necessary to prevent its being deceptive. *Compare Miami Herald Publishing Co. v. Tornillo*, 418 U.S. 241 (1974), with *Banzhaf v. FCC*, 405 F.2d 1082 (1968), *cert. denied sub. nom. Tobacco Institute Inc. v. FCC*, 396 U.S. 842 (1969). *Cf. United States v. 95 Barrels of Vinegar*, 265 U.S. 438, 443 (1924) ("It is not difficult to choose statements, designs and devices which will not deceive").

In *Bates, Ohralik, Friedman*, and *R.M.J.*, the Court was required to address the issue of false advertising. In *Bates*, the Court stated that advertising that is false, deceptive, or misleading "is subject to restraint," 433 U.S. 350. However, the Court specifically left open the factors that govern the degree of governmental interference that might be justifiable, or the manner in which it might be accomplished. The Court acknowledged also that "we recognize that many of the problems in defining the boundary between deceptive and nondeceptive advertising remain to be resolved," 433 U.S. at 384. The opinions in the commercial speech cases nonetheless suggest that at least the following factors may be relevant in circumscribing the power of the states in dealing with the problem of false commercial advertising: (1) the objectivity of the particular commercial speech, (2) the hardiness of speech on that subject by that advertiser or speaker at that time, (3) the nature of the product or service as compared with the sophistication of the audience to which such advertising is directed, (4) the immediacy of a particular communication, (5) the imminence of harm, *Ohralik*, footnote 13, at 457 and (6) the inherent susceptibility of such speech to deceptive abuse.

In *Central Hudson*, the Court stated that the First Amendment's concern for commercial speech is based on "the informational function of advertising." Commercial advertising that does not serve that interest may be suppressed: "[T]here can be no constitutional objection to the suppression of commercial messages that do not accurately inform the public about lawful activity. The government may ban forms of communication more likely to deceive the public than inform it," 447 U.S. at 563. Under current commercial speech doctrine, then, it would appear that the Court recognizes no value whatsoever in false commercial speech, and such expression enjoys no constitutional protection.

With respect to the burden of proof, it is already clear that the state need not show in a particular case that commercial expression was false or injurious in order to punish it, *Ohralik v. Ohio State Bar Association*, 436 U.S. at 467–468. It is enough if the state can demonstrate that the category of commercial expression in general either (1) has been used in the past for deceptive purposes, or (2) has a potential for such use (is "more likely to deceive the public than inform it"), or is (3) inherently deceptive, *Central Hudson*, 447 U.S. at 563; *Friedman v. Rogers*, 440 U.S. at 13–16; *Ohralik*, 436 U.S. at 463–468. The burden of proof that the regulation is no broader than necessary to advance the legitimate interest of preventing fraud or deception, however, remains on the state, *see Bolger v. Youngs Drug Products Corp.*, 463 U.S. 60, 103 S. Ct. at 2882 n.20; *Central Hudson Gas & Electric Corp. v. Public Service Commission*, 447 U.S. 557, 570 (1980); *Linmark Associates, Inc. v. Willingboro*, 431 U.S. 85, 95 (1977). The Court has not yet specifically addressed the procedural nuances that arise from the "constitutionalization" of commercial speech, including the issues relating to allocation of burden of proof of falsity and the possibility of a heightened burden of proof of state of mind, *scienter*, or actual malice.

NOTES

1. *Source Book on Corporate Image and Corporate Advocacy and Advertising*, compiled by the Subcommittee on Administrative Practice and Procedure of the Committee on the Judiciary of the U.S. Senate, 95th Cong., 2nd Session (U.S. Govenment Printing Office, Washington, D.C., 1978).

2. *Ibid.*, pp.1149–1337.

3. Although the Supreme Court in its commercial speech decisions to date has spoken not only of the content of speech but also of what particular forms of expression "do"— as in the formulation of the definition of commercial speech as speech that "does no

more than propose a commercial transaction''—the Court has never explicitly articulated a distinction between a linguistic description and a linguistic or speech act. Such a distinction has been drawn by certain philosophers of the "ordinary language" school and by philosophers of language, most notably by the Oxford philosopher J. L. Austin in his William James Lectures delivered at Harvard University in 1955, edited by J. O. Urmson and published posthumously as *How to Do Things With Words* (Oxford University Press, 1965) and in his philosophical essay "Performative Utterances," published in Austin's *Philosophical Papers* (Oxford University Press, 1961). Discussions and developments of Austin's ideas may also be found, among other places, in John R. Searle's *Speech Acts: An Essay in the Philosophy of Language* (Cambridge University Press, 1969), in volume 2 of John Lyons's *Semantics* (Cambridge University Press, 1977), and in William Alston's *The Philosophy of Language*. In *How to Do Things With Words*, Austin drew a useful distinction between utterances that describe or report facts and so-called performative utterances that have "humdrum verbs in the first person singular present indicative acting," but yet such that they "do not 'describe' or 'report' or constate anything at all, are not 'true or false'; and the uttering of the sentence is, or is part of, the doing of an action, which again would not *normally* be described as saying something," (p. 5).

4. In Lochner v. New York, 198 U.S. 45 (1905).

5. Michael J. Perry, *Modern Equal Protection*, 79 Colum. L. Rev. 1023–1084 at 1074 (1979).

6. The subject of "invisible hand" mechanisms and their implications for state regulation have been discussed by Robert Nozick in *Anarchy, State and Utopia*, 18–22 (1974).

7. T. Schelling, American Economic Review, May 1969, pp. 488–493; *cf.* Nozick, *Anarchy, State and Utopia*, at 20.

8. Note, *The First Amendment Overbreadth Doctrine*, 83 Harv. L. Rev. 844 at 845 (1970).

6

A Summary Review of Decisions on Recurrent Problems Involving Commercial Speech

Having traced the evolution of the modern doctrine of commercial speech, it is useful to survey some of the concrete problems which have arisen to date relating to the extension of the First Amendment to commercial speech. The doctrine has already had ramifications across a wide spectrum of governmental regulation. The survey that follows illustrates the application or non-application of the doctrine in a multitude of areas: billboards, regulation of commercial solicitation at state-owned facilities, door-to-door solicitation, advertising in public places, vehicular signs, distribution of "shopper" advertising newspapers, false commercial advertising, insurance industry advertising relating to jury verdicts, telephone solicitation, solicitation to engage in immoral conduct, newspaper coupon promotion schemes, Krishna evangelism, issues of corporate and securities laws relating to false statements and omissions in corporate registration and proxy statements and the validity of state anti-takeover legislation, federal antitrust law issues of "price signalling," product disparagement and comparative advertising, fair credit reporting laws, government control of product advertising over the electronic media, exportation of commercial information, and regulation of real estate advertising and "blockbusting" legislation.

BILLBOARDS

Each method of communicating ideas, as the Supreme Court has pointed out, generates what is, in effect, a law unto itself,[1] and billboard advertising has always engendered a substantial amount of legislation as well as judicial decisions.

Outdoor Signs

As Justice Clark of the California Supreme Court said in *Metromedia v. City of San Diego*, 164 Cal. Rptr. at 533–534, 610 P.2d at 430–431, "[t]he outdoor sign or symbol is a venerable medium for expressing political, social and commercial ideas. From the poster to the billboard, outdoor signs have played a prominent role throughout American history, rallying support for political and social causes.'' Outdoor billboards are a relatively inexpensive way to broadcast a message to a large number of potential listeners. However, billboards have a severe disadvantage over other forms of communication. They are often perceived to be a nuisance. Billboards are banned not because of the messages they convey, but because the medium itself is thought objectionable, *John Donnelly and Sons v. Campbell*, 639 F.2d 6 (1st Cir. 1980) *aff'd* 453 U.S. 916 (1981). Billboards combine communicative aspects with non-communicative aspects that governments seek to regulate.

Through 1975 the courts had almost universally held that state and local regulation prohibiting off-premises advertising did not infringe on freedom of speech when the government interests outweighed the free speech interests of the owner of the billboards. Balancing the governmental interests in traffic safety and the free speech interests of the billboard owner, the courts almost invariably upheld the regulations. While commercial speech has been afforded less constitutional protection than non-commercial speech, the level of scrutiny for a regulation of commercial speech increased from the ''rational relation'' test to intermediate scrutiny. The new test was set forth by Justice Powell in *Central Hudson*.[2]

Nonetheless, the courts continued to review billboard regulations in much the same manner as they had in the past, *see, Williams v. City and County of Denver*, 622 P.2d 542 (1981). Finally, in *Metromedia*, the U.S. Supreme Court conducted its first plenary consideration of a billboard ordinance under the *Central Hudson* standard. In a plurality opinion, Justice White bifurcated his analysis, examining first the effect of the ordinance on commercial speech, and then its effect on non-commercial speech. In *Metromedia*, San Diego's ordinance banned the use of outdoor, off-premises advertising display signs with twelve exceptions, *see* 453 U.S. at 495 n.3 and Metromedia, the owner of between 500 and 800 outdoor display signs within San Diego, challenged the ordinance.

The Court applied the *Central Hudson* four-part analysis. The restricted communication involved no ''unlawful activity'' nor was it ''misleading.'' It was therefore constitutionally protected commercial expression. The plurality recognized both traffic safety and aesthetics as substantial government goals. Given these governmental interests, the only effective approach, according to the plurality, was outright prohibition. Accordingly, no narrower regulation was possible, and the fourth criterion of the *Central Hudson* standard was satisfied. The plurality held that the record was inadequate to determine whether the prohibition of outdoor billboards would directly promote traffic safety. The court deferred to the local lawmakers since there was no showing that their judgments were unreasonable. With regard to the governmental interest in aesthetics, the plurality classified the interest as ''necessarily subjective, defying objective evaluation,'' *Metromedia v. City of San Diego, supra*, at 510. Since there was no claim of an ulterior motive in suppressing commercial speech, the ordinance was held to pass the *Central Hudson* test.

In the second part of the plurality's bifurcated analysis, however, the Court held that the ordinance was not a "time, place and manner" regulation of non-commercial speech, since outdoor billboards of this type were banned everywhere within the city and at all times. Therefore, the plurality examined the ordinance under the highest level of judicial scrutiny and found it to be unconstitutional as an impermissible restraint on protected speech.

Justice Brennan, joined by Justice Blackmun, concurred in the judgment but disagreed with the plurality's holding that a ban of commercial speech alone would have passed constitutional muster. Justice Brennan viewed the ordinance as a total ban of billboards. The judicial standard for a total ban requires consideration of (1) the substantiality of the government interest asserted, and (2) whether those interests could be served by less intrusive means, 453 U.S. at 528. Since San Diego had, in his view, failed to meet its burden by demonstrating that its interest was genuine and substantial, the ordinance would fail as an unconstitutional ban on commercial speech.

The lack of a clear majority in *Metromedia* on the precise rationale of the judgment allowed the lower courts a degree of leeway. In *Dills v. City of Marietta, Georgia*, 674 F.2d 1377 (1982) *cert. denied* 461 U.S. 905 (1983), an ordinance that restricted the use of portable display signs by limiting the time period of use was held to be an unconstitutional restriction of commercial speech. The court did not consider the effect on non-commercial speech. Applying the *Central Hudson* standard, the court held that time limitations did not directly advance the claimed interests in traffic safety. In fact, the limitation on time period made the signs more noticeable and defeated the traffic safety interest.

In *Metromedia v. Baltimore*, 538 F.Supp. 1183 (D.Md. 1982), an ordinance for urban renewal that contained provisions of the kinds and sizes of outdoor advertising signs permitted with a ban of off-site billboards was held to be an unconstitutional restriction of free speech. The district court followed the *Metromedia* plurality and bifurcated its analysis. Using the *Central Hudson* test, the court held the restriction on commercial speech to be constitutional, but held that the restriction on non-commercial speech did not meet the constitutional requirements.

In *Frumer v. Cheltenham Township*, 709 F.2d 874 (3d Cir. 1983), the court of appeals for the Third Circuit upheld an ordinance that banned temporary signs affixed to utility poles, street signs, or any other structures within the rights-of-way of public streets or highways, as a valid "time, place and manner" regulation.

The Ninth Circuit in *Taxpayers for Vincent v. Members of the City Council*, 682 F.2d 847 (9th Cir. 1982), which dealt with a Los Angeles ordinance prohibiting the posting of signs on public property, added one more criterion to those required for a valid "time, place and manner" regulation. The Ninth Circuit also considered whether the ordinance was the least drastic means of protecting the government interests. This higher level of scrutiny was one the

Third Circuit rejected in *Frumer*. The Supreme Court subsequently reversed the
Ninth Circuit, 104 S. Ct. at 2118 (1984).

The Supreme Court's first plenary consideration of the First Amendment analysis of billboard regulations left four questions in cases concerning validity of
ordinances prohibiting or regulating outdoor advertisement display signs.

1. Whether the ordinance affects both commercial and non-commercial speech (If so,
   then proceed to the next point. If not, proceed to the fourth point);

2. Whether the ordinance is an otherwise valid "time, place and manner" regulation;

3. Whether the ordinance is a total ban subject to the highest level of scrutiny;

4. Whether the regulation of commercial speech passes the *Central Hudson* four-part
   analysis.

REGULATION OF COMMERCIAL SOLICITATION AT
STATE-OWNED FACILITIES

State-Owned Schools

Another recurrent issue has involved the validity of state regulation of commercial solicitation activities at state-owned facilities such as schools, state colleges, and state-owned office buildings. *American Future Systems v. Pennsylvania
State University*, 688 F.2d 907 (3d Cir. 1982)[3] involved the constitutionality of
a state university's regulations concerning commercial activities in the common
areas of its student residence halls. The plaintiffs included the seller of cookware
and several students who favored receiving commercial solicitations for these
products. American Future Systems (AFS) engaged in the sale of cookware,
crystal, and tableware through demonstrations of its merchandise at colleges
throughout the United States. The demonstrations were attended by a student
hostess, invited guests, and a sales representative. The university sought to
restrain these activities by policies that forbade the use of the dormitory common
areas by individuals and groups who are not members of the university community
for commercial activities.

The district court upheld Penn State's regulations insofar as they permitted
demonstrations on college property but prohibited solicitation of sales. The district court upheld the standing of AFS to raise the First Amendment issues,
relying on *Virginia Pharmacy Board*, 464 F.Supp. at 1259. The court also held
the overbreadth doctrine inapplicable, *id.* at 1260. The district court was not
convinced that AFS had a constitutional right to sell its merchandise to college
students in the manner in which it selected as most conducive to sales, by
establishing its representatives on campus. The court likened this conduct to the
in-person solicitations involved in *Ohralik* and rejected AFS's contention, *id* at
1262. The district court denied the injunction sought, and the court of appeals
affirmed, albeit for reasons that differed in some respects from those of the
district court, *American Future Systems, Inc. v. Penn State University*, 618 F.2d

252 (3d Cir. 1980). The court of appeals held that the common areas and lounges of the dormitories were not a public forum and that AFS's group sales impinged on the primary activities of the dormitories and accordingly conflicted with legitimate interests. The Third Circuit also rejected AFS's argument that commercial and non-commercial activities must be treated the same way and that Penn State's policies discriminated improperly against commercial activities, *id.* at 257.

In the second round of the *American Future Systems* litigation, AFS contended that Penn State's prohibition of group demonstrations or sales in an individual dormitory room to a purchaser other than the occupant of the room was unconstitutional. The district court also rejected this contention and denied a preliminary injunction, 510 F.Supp. 98 (M.D. 1981). Thereafter, the district court granted summary judgment for Penn State, 522 F.Supp. 544 (M.D. 1981). The summary judgment was reversed, this time on the ground that Penn State had "failed to show substantial state interest, much less a plausible explanation, for a policy differentiating between the nature of the information contained in the AFS demonstration," 688 F.2d 907, 913. The basis of the reversal, however, appears largely to have been the lack of a sufficient factual record and the Third Circuit remanded the case to the district court for further proceedings. The district court thereafter entered a preliminary injunction against Penn State enjoining the enforcement of its rules banning group sales meetings in individual dormitory rooms. The district court found Penn State's position "illogical" and held that the regulation "[did] not serve any legitimate governmental interest," 553 F.Supp. 1268 at 1281 (1982).

Penn State appealed this ruling, and once more the Court of Appeals for the Third Circuit reversed the district court's findings. The court held that Penn State's regulation " . . . does not unconstitutionally infringe upon either the right of students to receive commercial information in an association with other students or upon the right of AFS to disseminate such commercial information" 752 F.2d 854 (3d Cir. 1984) *cert. den.* 53 U.S.L.W. 3912 (1985).

The Court of Appeals cited *Bolger v. Youngs Drug Product Corp.*, 463 U.S. 60, and *Central Hudson Gas and Electric Corp. v. Public Service Commission*, 447 U.S. 557. The Court first established, using the three-part test outlined in *Bolger,* that AFS's dormitory sales program constituted "commercial" speech, as (1) the speech was an advertisement, (2) it specifically referred to AFS's products, and (3) AFS had an obvious economic motive for the speech, *id.* at 16–19. The Court of Appeals then applied the four-part test set forth in *Central Hudson* to determine the validity of Penn State's restrictions on AFS's commercial speech. Under *Central Hudson*, commercial speech first must be lawful. Regulations affecting lawful commercial speech must reflect a substantial government interest and directly advance that interest while being no more extensive than necessary. The Court of Appeals held that although AFS's speech was lawful, Penn State, as a property-owner *and* educator, had a valid interest in regulating commercial speech in student dormitory rooms. The Court held that Penn State's regulations advanced that interest in a direct and non-excessive manner and thus, by the guidelines of *Central Hudson*, were constitutional, *id.* at 28.

Five members of the court of appeals voted for a rehearing *en banc*, noting in the panel decision "the extension of a judicial concept by a dry and remorseless logic . . . to a position never contemplated by the Supreme Court," 688 F.2d at 918. This vote, however, was insufficient to require a rehearing.

Similar issues have been presented in other cases: *Jacobs v. Board of School Commission*, 490 F.2d 601, 608 (7th Cir. 1973) *vacated* 420 U.S. 128 (1975) (outright prohibition invalidated); *Hernandez v. Hanson*, 430 F.Supp. 1154 (D.Neb. 1977) (outright prohibition of distribution of non-school commercial literature within school held inconsistent with First Amendment); *Peterson v. Board of Education*, 370 F.Supp. 1208 (D.Neb. 1973).

The use of public places for commercial solicitation and advertising has been presented in a number of cases: *Perry v. City of Chicago*, 480 F.Supp. 498 (N.D. Ill. 1979) (city ordinance prohibiting peddling of all articles except newspapers in certain downtown locations held to be a valid "time, place and manner" regulation); *State v. Bloss*, 64 Hawaii 148, 637 P.2d 1117 (Hawaii 1981) (ordinance regulating peddling on streets, sidewalks, and malls invalidated); *Goldstein v. Town of Nantucket*, 477 F.Supp. 606 (D.Mass. 1979) (ordinance restricting musical performances of "Troubadour of Nantucket" invalidated); *O'Brien v. United States*, 444 A.2d 946 (Dist. of Columbia 1982) (ordinance prohibiting distribution of commercial handbills within Metro station); *People v. Remeny*, 387 N.Y.S.2d 415, 40 N.Y. 2d 527, 355 N.E.2d 375 (N.Y. Ct. of Appeals 1976) (ordinance prohibiting distribution of commercial leaflets in public places held to be unconstitutional); *New Jersey v. Today Newspapers*, 183 N.J. Super. 264, 443 A. 2d 787 (1982) (ordinance prohibiting deposit of handbills and "shoppers" on vacant premises invalidated); *Sabin v. Butz*, 515 F.2d 1061, 1065 (10th Cir. 1975) (National Park Ski Slopes); *Philadelphia Newspapers, Inc. v. Borough Council*, 381 F.Supp. 228, 240 (E.D.Pa. 1974) (on-street newspaper boxes).

Krishna Litigation

The Krishna litigation over state fairground regulation of quasi-commercial solicitation provides a further example of the same issues: *Int. Society for Krishna Consciousness v. State Fair of Texas*, 461 F.Supp. 719, 722 (N.D. Tex. 1978); *Int. Society for Krishna Consciousness v. Barber*, 506 F.Supp. 147 (N.D.N.Y. 1980) *rev'd* 650 F.2d 430 (2d Cir. 1981) (New York State Fair); *Int. Society for Krishna Consciousness v. City of Houston*, 482 F.Supp. 852 (S.D. Tex. 1979) *rev'd* 689 F.2d 541 (5th Cir. 1982); *McMurdie v. Doutt*, 468 F.Supp. 766, 768 (N.D.Ohio 1979) (solicitation by Unification Church of Sun Myung Moon in stores); *Fernandes v. Limmer*, 465 F.Supp. 493 (N.D. Tex. 1979)

(Krishna solicitation at airports); *Int. Society for Krishna Consciousness of Western Pennsylvania v. Griffin*, 437 F.Supp. 666 (W.D.Pa. 1977); *Int. Society of Krishna Consciousness v. City of New Orleans*, 347 F.Supp. 945 (E.D.La. 1972) (prohibition of solicitation in French Quarter).

DOOR-TO-DOOR DISTRIBUTION OF COMMERCIAL HANDBILLS, "SHOPPERS," AND SAMPLES OF COMMERCIAL PRODUCTS

The door-to-door distribution of commercial handbills and "throw-away shopper" advertising newspapers has generated a considerable amount of litigation with conflicting results: *Ad World, Inc. v. Township of Doylestown*, 672 F.2d 1136 (3d Cir.), *cert. denied*, 456 U.S. 975 (1982) (invalidating as applied to shopper newspaper; local ordinance prohibiting on-premises deposit without consent); *Commonwealth v. Sterlace*, 481 Pa. 6, 391 A.2d 1066 (Pa. 1978) (upholding ordinance similar to that invalidated in *Ad World, supra*); *People v. Bohnke*, 287 N.Y. 154, 38 N.E. 2d 478 (N.Y. 1941) (upholding ordinance); *H L. Messengers, Inc. v. City of Brentwood*, 577 S.W. 2d 444 (Tenn. 1979) (invalidating ordinance); *Van Nuys Pub. Co. v. City of Thousand Oaks*, 5 Cal. 3d 817, 97 Cal. Rptr. 777, 489 P.2d 809 (1971), *cert. denied*, 405 U.S. 1042 (1972) (invalidating ordinance); *National Delivery Systems, Inc. v. City of Inglewood*, 43 Cal. App. 3d 573, 117 Cal. Rptr. 791 (Cal. 1974); *City of Fredonia v. Chanute Tribune*, 7 Kan.App. 2d 65, 638 P.2d 347 (Kan. Ct. of App. 1981) (ordinance upheld); *Ad Express, Inc. v. Kirvin*, 516 F.2d 195 (2d Cir. 1975); *Sunday Mail, Inc. v. Christie*, 312 F.Supp. 677 (C.D. Cal. 1970); *Buxbom v. City of Riverside*, 29 F.Supp. 3 (S.D. Cal. 1939).

DOOR-TO-DOOR SOLICITATION

Several cases have considered the validity of special regulations governing door-to-door sales solicitations especially those prescribing a "cooling-off period" after a successful sales solicitation, *May v. Colorado*, 636 P.2d 672 (Colo. 1981) (ordinance upheld). These ordinances present examples of the application of the "special format" principle.

REGULATION OF MAIL-ORDER HOME STUDY COURSE SOLICITATION

The Federal Trade Commission's regulations, 16 C.F.R. § 438, entitled "Proprietary Vocational and Home Study Schools" have figured in one challenge under the First Amendment, *see, Katharine Gibbs School v. FTC*, 612 F.2d 658 (2d Cir. 1979) (upholding a requirement that advertiser include dropout information in advertising, sales, and enrollment material).

VEHICULAR SALE SIGNS

A number of cases have considered First Amendment challenges to ordinances prohibiting the owner of a motor vehicle from parking the vehicle for the purpose of selling it, or regulating the use of signs on operational motor vehicles, *see, e.g., People v. Moon*, 89 Cal. App. 3d Supp. 1, 152 Cal. Rptr. 704 (App. Dept. Super. Ct. 1978) (ordinance held unconstitutional); *Arizona v. Jacobson*, 121 Ariz. 65, 588 P.2d 358 (App. Div. Arizona 1978) (ordinance regarding vehicular signs upheld).

ADVERTISING, THE MAILS, AND OBSCENITY

Several federal statutes which touch on the mailability of sexually oriented, non-obscene advertising material have resulted in constitutional challenge. Under 39 U.S.C. § 3008, a recipient of mail may determine "in his sole discretion" that "pandering advertising" is "erotically arousing or sexually provocative" and may request the U.S. Postal Service to direct the sender to refrain from mailing such material to the addressee.[4]

The constitutionality of § 3008 (formerly 39 U.S.C. § 4009) was initially upheld in 1970 in *Rowan v. U.S. Post Office Dept.*, 397 U.S. 728 (1970); *see also, United States v. Pent-R-Books, Inc.*, 538 F.2d 519 (2d Cir. 1976), *cert. denied*, 430 U.S. 906 (1977).

Title 39 U.S.C. § 3010 provides a remedy permitting a recipient of mail to request that no sexually oriented advertisements be mailed to that address.[5] The constitutionality of sections 3010 and 3011 was examined in *United States v. Treatman*, 408 F.Supp. 944 (C.D. Cal. 1976). Insofar as § 3011 allowed injunctions against the mailing of non-obscene matter even to persons who did not object to receiving such mail and as to persons who requested such mail, the statute was unconstitutional.

The constitutionality of 39 U.S.C. § 3001(e)(2), which prohibits the mailing of unsolicited advertisements for contraceptives was dealt with in *Bolger v. Youngs Drug Products*, 463 U.S. 60, 103 S. Ct. 2875 (1983), where the Court held that, as applied to that appellee's advertisements, § 3001 (e)(2) was an unconstitutional restraint on protected commercial speech.

MAIL DETENTION—FALSE REPRESENTATIONS

The constitutionality of 39 U.S.C. § 3007, providing for temporary detention of mail to determine whether it is in violation of 39 U.S.C. §§ 3005 and 3006 was upheld in *U.S. Postal Service v. Athena Products, Ltd.*, 654 F.2d 362 (5th Cir. 1981), *cert. denied*, 456 U.S. 915 (1982).

FALSE REPRESENTATIONS AND MAILABILITY

The constitutionality of Title 39 U.S.C. § 3005, as amended, dealing with the use of a scheme or device for obtaining money or property through the mail by means of false representations,[6] has been upheld in *U.S. Postal Service v. Athena Products, Ltd.*, 654 F.2d 362 (5th Cir. 1981), *cert. denied*, 456 U.S. 915 (1982); *Original Cosmetics Products, Inc. v. Strachan*, 459 F.Supp. 496 (S.D.N.Y. 1978), *aff'd*, 603 F.2d 214 (2d Cir.), *cert. denied*, 444 U.S. 915 (1979).

The constitutionality of this provision has also been upheld, in a doubtful decision, as applied to false representations of literature sold through the mail, *Hollywood House International, Inc. v. Klassen*, 508 F.2d 1276 (9th Cir. 1974).

REAL ESTATE BROKERS, DISCRIMINATORY HOUSING PRACTICES, AND FEDERAL "ANTI-BLOCKBUSTING" LEGISLATION

Several cases have involved the constitutionality of federal statutes touching commercial advertising that are aimed at discriminatory housing practices. Title 42 U.S.C. § 3604 provides:

§ 3604. DISCRIMINATION IN SALE OR RENTAL OF HOUSING.

As made applicable by section 3603 of this title and except as exempted by sections 3603(b) and 3607 of this title, it shall be unlawful:

. . .

(a) To make, print, or publish, or cause to be made, printed, or published any notice, statement, or advertisement, with respect to the sale or rental of a dwelling that indicates any preference, limitation, or discrimination based on race, color, religion, sex, or national origin, or an intention to make any such preference, limitation, or discrimination.

. . .

(b) For profit, to induce or attempt to induce any person to sell or rent any dwelling by representations regarding the entry or prospective entry into the neighborhood of a person or persons of a particular race, color, religion, sex, or national origin. Pub.L. 90–284, Title VIII, § 804, Apr. 11, 1968, 82 Stat. 83; Pub.L. 93–383, Title VIII, § 808(b)(1), Aug. 22, 1974, 88 Stat. 729.

Subsection (c) of this provision was upheld in *United States v. Hunter*, 459 F.2d 205 (4th Cir. 1972), *cert. denied*, 409 U.S. 934 (1972); *Pittsburgh Press v. Human Relations Commission, supra*, which was decided after *Hunter*, would clearly appear to support and require the result reached in *Hunter*, because advertisements within the scope of subsection (c), like the gender-based advertisements in the *Pittsburgh Press* case, aid or facilitate violations of other provisions of the anti-discrimination law.

Subsection (e), dealing with "blockbusting" activities by real estate brokers, was upheld in *United States v. Bob Lawrence Realty, Inc.*, 474 F.2d 115 (5th Cir. 1973), *cert. denied*, 414 U.S. 826 (1973). The continuing validity of the *Bob Lawrence* decision, particularly as applied to truthful statements, may well be doubted, notwithstanding that the statutory provision is supported by important governmental interests. Although its application to in-person solicitations may be permissible upon a rationale similar to that of *Ohralik*, *i.e.*, the susceptibility to deceptive abuses, it may be doubted whether the statute's outright prohibition as applied to truthful, non-deceptive written communications could survive constitutional scrutiny after *Linmark* and *Central Hudson, see, Hawley v. Cuomo*, 91 Misc.2d 13 (396 N.Y.S. 2d 987 (1977), aff'd. 61 App. Div. 2d 1046, 403 N.Y.S. 2d 280 (1978) (vacating order of Secretary of State directing real estate brokers to cease and desist from soliciting listings of property for sale and for purchase in any manner in Kings and Queens Counties, New York). A different result was reached, however, in *Illinois v. C. Betts Realtors, Inc.*, 66 Ill.2d 144 (Ill. 1977) (upholding anti-blockbusting statute) and *Howe v. City of St. Louis*, 512 S.W.2d 127 (Mo. 1974) (upholding anti-blockbusting ordinance).

In another case, *Barrick Realty, Inc. v. City of Gary*, 354 F.Supp. 126 (N.D. Ind. 1973), *aff'd* 491 F.2d 161 (7th Cir. 1974), which like *Linmark* concerned the validity of a local ordinance prohibiting residential "For Sale" signs, the court opined in dictum that federal anti-blockbusting provisions were constitutional. The continuing vitality of the holding of *Barrick Realty*, however, is doubtful in view of the Supreme Court's holding in *Linmark*, with respect to the *Barrick* decision, striking down a Willingboro, New Jersey, ordinance banning residential "For Sale" signs. The Supreme Court in *Linmark* specifically stated: "We express no view as to whether *Barrick Realty* can survive *Bigelow* and *Virginia Pharmacy Board*." An ordinance similar to that invalidated in *Linmark* was invalidated in *Daugherty v. City of East Point*, 447 F.Supp. 290 (N.D.Ga. 1978).

Some communities which have approached the problem of blockbusting practices by means of additional advance licensing restrictions on real estate brokers have found the First Amendment considerations insuperable, *Illinois Association of Realtors v. Village of Bellwood*, 516 F.Supp. 1067 (N.D. Ill. 1981) (invalidating licensure system requiring advance approval of solicitation by "citizens advisory council").

APARTMENT INFORMATION VENDORS

The constitutionality of state legislation regulating apartment information vendors has been presented in several cases. In *Galaxy Rental Service, Inc. v. New York*, 108 Misc.2d 237, 437 N.Y.S. 2d 854 (1981), *rev'd* 88 App. Div. 2d 99, 452 N.Y.S. 2d 921 (New York 1982), the Supreme Court for Erie County, New York, upheld the constitutionality of Real Property Law, 446-b, subdivisions 3 and 4, and section 446-c (subd. 5, paras. [a] and [b]), and certain regulations of the New York Secretary of State, 19 N.Y.C.R.R. 190.1, 190.2, 190.5, 190.6, and 190.8, relating to the licensing and regulation of apartment information vendors. These provisions, which are calculated to prevent intentionally fostered deception of consumers through the supply of false information concerning the availability, cost, and habitability of apartments, must be justified, if at all, on the basis of the inherently deceptive nature of the information or on the basis of experience with information vendors of this type. The appellate division reversed, 88 App. Div. 2d 99, 452 N.Y.S. 2d 921 (1982), holding that New York's regulation failed to pass constitutional standards, in that the state had made an insufficient showing that its interests could not be advanced by less restrictive means. It is doubtful that any outright prohibition would survive constitutional scrutiny under *Central Hudson*, cf. *Ohio v. Renalist, Inc.*, 56 Ohio St.2d 276 , 383 N.E. 2d 892 (Ohio 1978).

THE COMMERCIAL SPEECH DOCTRINE AND CORPORATE SECURITIES

Misleading Statements and Omissions in Proxy Statements and Prospectuses and the Scope of the Doctrine under the Federal Securities Laws

The question of the constitutionality of federal and state laws that prohibit misleading statements and omissions in proxy statements and offering circulars does not appear to be a serious issue.

Assuming information in proxy statements and prospectuses is commercial speech, recent Supreme Court decisions indicate that misleading statements they contain receive no First Amendment protection. In *Friedman v. Rogers*, 440 U.S. 1 (1979), the Court held that even speech which has only a potential to mislead may be regulated. In that case, the Court upheld a Texas ban on the use of trade names by optometrists. The Court feared the "significant possibility that trade names will be used to mislead the public." According to the *Central Hudson* test, for commercial speech to receive constitutional protection "it at least must concern lawful activity and not be misleading," 447 U.S. at 566. By implication, speech that is related to unlawful activity and misleading speech enjoy no protection under the First Amendment. Misleading or false statements in proxy statements and registration statements arguably fall in both categories, in that they are related to unlawful activity in the *Giboney* sense of being an integral part of an unlawful course of conduct, and they are false, misleading, or deceptive.

Post–*Central Hudson* decisions reaffirm the principle that misleading commercial speech receives no constitutional protection. *In re R.M.J.*, 455 U.S. 191 (1982), the Court set down more general standards concerning misleading and potentially misleading commercial speech. The Court held that lawyer advertising which is actually or inherently misleading may be flatly banned. When the state's claim is that a particular advertisement is potentially misleading, the state may not automatically prohibit it completely but must show that its regulation is "no broader than reasonably necessary to prevent the deception," 455 U.S. at 203.

These decisions support the proposition that misleading statements in proxy statements and prospectuses are not protected by the First Amendment if they are considered to be commercial speech. However, the distinction betwen the "potentially misleading" and the "inherently misleading" referred to in *R.M.J.*, 455 U.S. 191 (1982), suggests that the same distinction might be drawn in securities litigation. If a statement in a prospectus or proxy statement is only potentially misleading as opposed to misleading, the *R.M.J.* test for potentially misleading advertising may be applied, *i.e.*, the state must show that its regulation is "no broader than reasonably necessary to prevent the deception." Thus, regulations prohibiting potentially misleading statements in proxy statements and prospectuses may have to be narrowly drawn to withstand First Amendment scrutiny.

A question arises concerning securities act provisions that prohibit omissions in proxy statements and prospectuses. It is unlikely that the right to silence extends to the disclosure of factual matters in such documents. An argument that the government cannot prohibit omissions in proxy statements and prospectuses is tantamount to an argument that the government must allow concealment of information because of a fear that shareholders and potential shareholders might react adversely to the truth, *see* Farber, "Commercial Speech and First Amendment Theory," 74 N.W.U.L. Rev. 372–408 (1979).

A question also arises whether information in proxy statements and prospectuses falls within the ill-defined realm of commercial speech at all. The Supreme Court has yet to provide a precise definition of commercial speech. Recent decisions have not clarified the concept.

In *Central Hudson*, the majority spoke of two different definitions of commercial speech: one defining such speech as any expression which does no more than "propose a commercial transaction," and the other defining commercial speech as any speech which is "related solely to the economic interests of the speaker and its audience." The second definition is problematic because it could conceivably include within the commercial speech classification speech which has political or socioeconomic undertones, *e.g.*, the union leader's speech mentioned in Justice Stevens's concurrence in *Central Hudson*. As noted above, the post–*Central Hudson* cases have not cleared up this definitional problem. In *Bolger v. Youngs Drug Products*, 463 U.S. 60, 103 S. Ct. 2875 (1983), for example, the Court failed to give a precise definition of commercial speech. The Court stated that the fact that speech "links a product to a curent public debate" is not automatically sufficient to remove it from the realm of commercial speech and left open the possibility that speech that does not refer to a specific product could nonetheless constitute commercial speech.

Given the absence of a clear definition of commercial speech, the status of proxy statements and prospectuses as commercial speech remains unclear. Both proxy statements and prospectuses "relate to the economic interests of the speaker and its audience." If they do fall within the commercial speech category, federal and state regulations which prohibit misleading statements and omissions are probably valid.

A different question that may be raised is whether the constitutionalization of commercial speech also constitutionalizes the standards of liability under these laws. For example, is a *scienter* requirement for securities violations constitutionally required, in the same way that constitutionalization of the libel field resulted in the "actual malice" standard, requiring in public figure and public official cases, at least, proof of knowing falsity or proof of reckless indifference to truth or falsity?

Securities and Exchange Commission Enforcement and Regulatory Programs

It has been acknowledged by at least one commissioner of the Securities and Exchange Commission that certain aspects of the SEC's enforcement and regulatory program "could prove open to constitutional attack if the Supreme Court were to expand First Amendment protection for commercial speech." Commissioner Roberta S. Karmel, in a September 14, 1979, speech, "The Tension Between the First Amendment and the Federal Securities Laws,"[7] pointed out that "[t]he SEC's mandated disclosure requirements coupled with the antifraud provisions of the federal securities laws effect a chill on free speech by public companies." In addition, the commissioner observed that the regulation requirement for public offerings "often acts as a prior restraint on such speech."

The evolution of the modern commercial speech doctrine has altered regulatory perspectives, and SEC decision making after the commercial speech cases has involved some degree of First Amendment issues. Commissioner Karmel cited two specific examples: the adoption of expanded investment company advertising in a less restrictive form than had been proposed initially, and the withdrawal of the SEC's Statement of Policy on Advertising. The commissioner commented that "[a]lthough it was possible that the Statement of Policy did not violate constitutional proscription the commercial free speech cases expanding First Amendment protection at least raised a question about the propriety of this type of regulatory approach to advertising," *id.*

In Release No. 33–6116, August 31, 1979, the commission adopted Rule 434d, which expanded the scope and content of investment company sales literature to permit the use of advertising in the form of an "omitting prospectus." Under the 1979 revision of Rule 434d, investment companies were permitted to advertise over radio and television and in any *bona fide* newspaper or magazine. The 1979 rule did not allow advertising by means of direct mailings which the SEC determined could have "a greater potential than newspaper or magazine advertisements for supplanting the full § 10 (a) prospectus as the primary selling document," according to the SEC release.

On March 8, 1979, in Release No. 1C-10621, the SEC withdrew its 28–year-old Statement of Policy on investment company advertising, adopted in 1950.[8]

The Constitutionality of State Anti-Takeover Statutes and Tender-Offer Procedures in the Light of the Commercial Speech Doctrine

Another emerging issue concerns the effect of state tender-offer procedures and anti-takeover statutes on First Amendment commercial speech interests. In *Kennecott Corp. v. Smith*, 637 F.2d 181 (3rd Cir. 1980), Judge Adams recognized the fact that this type of regulation often prevents corporations from disseminating information and thus might present First Amendment commercial speech problems. Because *Kennecott* dealt only with granting a preliminary injunction to enjoin the enforcement of the New Jersey Corporation Takeover Bid Disclosure Law, the Court had no occasion to resolve these potential constitutional problems. The Court observed, however:

Because the New Jersey scheme has operated in this case to prevent Kennecott from disseminating information that it is entitled under federal statutes and regulations to convey, it may also be difficult to reconcile the effect of the New Jersey provisions with the recently expanded scope of First Amendment protection for commercial speech. *See, Central Hudson Gas & Electric Corp. v. Public Service Commission*, 447 U.S. 557, 100 S. Ct. 2343, 65 L.Ed. 2d 341 (1980); *Virginia State Board of Pharmacy v. Virginia Citizens Consumer Council, Inc.*, 425 U.S. 748, 96 S.Ct. 1817, 48 L.Ed. 2d 346 (1976). The thrust of the commercial speech doctrine is that if purchasers, or in this case the target shareholders, have full information on the purchase terms and implications, "the rational decision making that fosters self-government in the economic sphere" will be facilitated. The Supreme Court—1979 Term, 94 Harv. L. Rev. 75, 165 (1980). Thus, the recent Supreme Court cases indicate that "[t]he state cannot control commercial speech as an incident to its control over the economic operations of a corporation. Economic regulation is presumptively valid because it arises from and is subject to correction by an unfettered political process. Because it restricts the flow of information by which the public becomes aware of, and acts to change legislation, regulation of expression cannot be similarly justified." *Id.* at 167. 637 F.2d at 190 n.10

Arguments exist which might support the proposition that tender-offer procedures violate free speech rights. These procedures often prohibit corporations from disseminating information to target shareholders. One of the main reasons for protecting commercial speech is to further the free flow of information, *see, Central Hudson Gas & Electric Corp. v. Public Service Commission*, 447 U.S. 557 (1980). The Court in *Virginia Pharmacy Board* stated that "[p]eople will perceive their own best interests if only they are well informed, and . . . the best means to that end is to open the channels of communication, rather than to close them," *Virginia Pharmacy Board v. Virginia Consumer Council*, 425 U.S. 748, 770 (1976). Thus, it might be argued that recent Supreme Court decisions support the proposition that shareholders of a target corporation should be able to receive full information on purchase terms and that state tender-offer procedures and anti-takeover statutes which impede them from securing this information are unconstitutional.

Mandatory State Registration of Securities Brokers and the First Amendment

Recent state and federal cases have held that state regulations requiring the registration of securities brokers do not violate the First Amendment or any other section of the Constitution, *see, Knott v. Minge*, 119 Fla. 515, 160 So. 670 (1935); *State v. Henderson*, 156 N.W.2d 700 (1968); *Underhill Associates, Inc. v. Bradshaw*, 674 F.2d 293 (4th Cir. 1982). For example, in *Underhill*, the court held that the registration provisions of the Virginia Securities Act did not violate the First Amendment. The court viewed the registration requirement as an economic regulation and ruled that any inhibition on the right to advertise was merely an incidental effect of observing the legitimate economic regulation.

The SEC and Commercial Investor Newsletters

The SEC has instituted several proceedings involving publishers of non–*bona fide* commercial investor newsletters in which important First Amendment issues have been presented, *see, Securities & Exchange Commission v. Wall Street Transcript Corp.*, 422 F.2d 1371 (2d Cir. 1970), *cert. denied* 398 U.S. 958 (1970); *SEC v. Lowe*, 725 F.2d 892 (2d Cir. 1984), *rev'd*, 53 U.S.L.W. 4705 (June 10, 1985).

Although the Supreme Court granted certiorari in *Lowe v. S.E.C.* to decide the constitutional question whether an injunction against publication and distribution of petitioner's newsletter was prohibited by the First Amendment, the Court avoided the constitutional question and held instead that the newsletter in question fell within an exclusion in the Investment Advisers Act of 1940 for "the publisher of any bona fide newspaper, news magazine or business or financial publication of general and regular circulation." The Court held the newsletters exempt because they "do not offer individualized advice attuned to any specific portfolio or to any client's particular needs," 53 U.S.L.W. 4705 (1985). Three justices concurred in the judgment of reversal, but on the ground that the statute is unconstitutional.

THE ANTITRUST LAWS AND COMMERCIAL SPEECH

"Price Signalling" and the Commercial Speech Doctrine

It has sometimes been suggested that the federal antitrust laws, specifically sections 1 and 2 of the Sherman Act and section 45 of the Federal Trade Commission Act, 15 U.S.C. §§ 1 and 2, and 15 U.S.C. § 45, are broad enough to embrace the notion of "price signalling" by manufacturers and sellers.

"Price signalling, " in the government's view, occurs in "shared monopoly" situations, *i.e.*, in industries dominated by a few firms.[9] The antitrust division has suggested on several occasions that some firms in such concentrated industries publicly signal their pricing decisions (or other competitive moves) to each other by placing announcements in the business or trade press. The division has said that some statements made by such large firms are intended to communicate pricing decisions, not to the public or to their customers, but to each other. At various times, the division has announced its intention to file suit when it concludes that the net result of such public exchanges of information is an agreement among competitors to fix prices.[10]

The division has expressed the belief that price signalling is a mechanism that firms in an oligopoly employ to reach an understanding between or among themselves to refrain from competition and to act interdependently. In its view, the issuance of detailed price books months in advance of proposed price changes, or the joint adoption of a uniform delivered price system, are among the mechanisms that the division believes are used by the companies to implement their decision not to compete with each other.[11]

The Division has stated that its search for signalling behavior in concentrated industries does not, in its view, implicate First Amendment problems. The division's approach is based on its belief that the antitrust laws are intended to deal with "anti-competitive consequences" and that price signalling is not protected by the First Amendment if it results in a forbidden consequence, such as price-fixing.[12] The First Amendment does not protect conspiracies to set prices where the competitors orally agree in private. The division believes that "[c]ollusion is no less objectionable when the vehicle for agreement is a billboard or a magazine instead of the backside of a menu at an airport motel."[13]

The division has acknowledged that what it refers to as "shared monopoly" (defined as "a few business organizations acting collectively as a true monopoly")[14] does not fall within either section 1 or 2 of the Sherman Act. Section 1 conspiracies and section 2 conspiracies to monopolize usually depend on price-fixing through direct personal contact—a factor which is absent in price signalling. From a section 2 perspective, the division believes that a group of dominant firms that together maintain similar prices and terms of sale, reducing production instead of price when demand is slack, but behaving competitively when a new competitor appears, can and do have the same effect on the market and on competition as single-firm monopolization. In other words, although no one firm may possess monopoly power, in the aggregate they act as—and thus, in the government's view, may be treated as—a monopolist.

The Price Signalling Theory as Applied in the 1976 Modification to the General Electric–Westinghouse Consent Decree

The December 1976 modification to the 1962 final judgment in the electrical equipment conspiracy cases addresses itself to price signalling in the domestic turbine-generator industry. It is, however, important to bear in mind that the domestic turbine-generator industry is essentially a duopoly in which General Electric and Westinghouse together account for nearly all production.

The government admitted that an exhaustive investigation in the mid-1970s was unable to uncover any evidence that the elimination of price competition in the production and sale of turbine-generators was the result of "direct, covert communication."[15] Instead, the government contended that price stability in the industry since the 1962 decree was "the result of identical policies deliberately adopted and published" by the two defendants, 42 Fed. Reg. 17006. Specifically, the government contended that "the nature and content of the public communication of pricing intentions and the mechanics of the pricing system" were employed by General Electric and Westinghouse to assure each other that they would not deviate from published price levels. The government asserted that an agreement to stabilize prices in violation of the Sherman Act was contained within the defendants' "public exchange of assurances, with such intent," *Id*.

The government, in short, believed that "the publication and communication to third parties of detailed prices and other price-related information, coupled with public statements regarding future pricing intentions, permitted each manufacturer to know the price that the other would offer in individual transactions involving turbine generators," thus suppressing price competition between them, 42 Fed. Reg. at 17007. The modification of the final judgment, therefore, takes a number of different approaches that together are designed "to limit direct and indirect communication by each manufacturer to the other," *Id*.

The terms of the modification are designed to accomplish four results: (1) a prohibition of "the kind of public statement of pricing policy that is actually intended to signal or communicate an invitation from one manufacturer to the other to eliminate various elements of competition"; (2) a prohibition of "certain specific practices that served to police or reinforce the manufacturers' agreement" (*e.g.*, a "price protection" policy and the publication of outstanding quotations); (3) a prohibition of "the nature and quantity of price and price-related information publicly disseminated by each manufacturer from which a general pricing policy or strategy can be inferred"; and (4) a prohibition of "the examination by each manufacturer of price-related documents that the other manufacturer may legitimately distribute to individual customers, from which the one manufacturer might infer the pricing policy or strategy of the other," *Id*. The government, in short, sought to restore price competition by forbidding defendants (1) from making public statements, (2) from certain specific practices, (3) from disseminating price information, and (4) from examining the other's price information in the hands of customers.

It is evident that the government has adopted the approach that it can legitimately and legally curtail a firm's public statements regarding pricing, if it can couple these public statements with other, specific practices engaged in by the firm, and from the totality of which it can infer an intention on the part of the firm to enter into and maintain an agreement with its rivals to fix prices. Under this theory, public statements, without more, are insufficient to create a price-fixing agreement. The inference that a firm's public statements are intended to signal prices is found in specific acts and practices which, coupled with its public announcements, suggest such a course of conduct.

The government has acknowledged that if it attacks price signalling as being illegal under either section 1 or section 2 of the Sherman Act, it encounters First Amendment questions. Thus, when John H. Shenefield, the former Assistant Attorney General in charge of the antitrust division, was asked at a congressional hearing about the division's initiatives in the shared monopoly area, his testimony recognized that First Amendment rights might be abridged by such an attack on price signalling:

Now, there is a third area that, I regret to say I cannot go into any great detail, but it is characterized by the kinds of events that happened recently in the steel industry where you have public announcements back and forth. One is concerned obviously not in thinking about the application of the antitrust laws to that kind of conduct, *you are very much in danger of trampling upon first amendment rights*, and that is at least something we are very much concerned about.[16] (Emphasis added.)

However, on March 10, 1978, Shenefield minimized the First Amendment difficulties. In a speech given that day, he said:

[E]ver since I started discussing the possibility of challenging signalling behavior by which shared monopolies may communicate pricing intentions through public media, I have been accused of defiling the First Amendment. . . . To call this vein of commentary silly would be to grant it too much dignity.[17]

From this radical shift in perspective it can be concluded that the government has reformulated its concept of shared monopoly to focus primarily on conduct[18] by oligopolistic firms, rather than on their speech *per se*. Such an approach would, of course, place the government's theory squarely in line with the "speech plus" doctrine adumbrated in *Giboney*, 336 U.S. at 502, and would constitute an attempt to avoid the constitutional infirmities that would attend any attempt to prohibit signalling alone.

Thus, the modification to the *General Electric–Westinghouse* decree (see *supra*) sought to eliminate not public statements of pricing policy alone, but also to "enjoin the use of policing tools such as the price protection policy; prohibit the public dissemination of price and price-related information from which a general pricing policy or strategy can be inferred; and prohibit the manufacturers from examining each other's bids to individual customers."[19]

The Giboney Doctrine

As noted in chapter 5, in *Giboney v. Empire Storage & Ice Co.*, 336 U.S. 490 (1949), the Court unanimously affirmed a state court injunction prohibiting a union of retail ice peddlers from forcing a wholesaler to refrain from selling ice to non-union peddlers. The injunction was based on the grounds that the union's activities were an attempt to force the wholesaler to violate state antitrust law by joining other ice distributors in boycotting the non-union peddlers.

Giboney and its progeny—*Hughes v. Superior Court*, 339 U.S. 460 (1950); *Teamsters Local 309 v. Hanke*, 339 U.S. 470 (1950); and *Building Service Employees Local 262 v. Gazzam*, 339 U.S. 532 (1950)—have been said to stand only for the proposition that it is constitutional for a state to restrain "picketing [which was] for the purpose of forcing the person picketed to violate the law and public policy of the state," *Teamsters Local 309 v. Hanke*, 339 U.S. 470, 481. Justice Minton, dissenting in *Hanke*, argued that peaceful picketing and truthful publicity are absolutely protected from state regulation under the First Amendment, *id.* at 484.

Finally, *Teamsters Local 695 v. Vogt, Inc.*, 354 U.S. 284 (1957), upheld the constitutionality of an injunction prohibiting union picketing aimed at coercing an employer to interfere with his employees' right to choose whether or not to join the union. The *Vogt* decision must be read to hold that, although picketing is partly communicative (*see Hughes v. Superior Court*, 339 U.S. 460, 464 (1950), its primary emphasis is on other, non-speech activities. Picketing, then, involves an intermingling of speech and conduct and is distinguished from "purer" speech forms entitled to more protection under the First Amendment.[20] These non-speech elements of picketing transform the activity into "speech plus" and thereby justify government regulation that would be unconstitutional when applied to pure speech, *see Cox v. Louisiana*, 379 U.S. 536, 555 (1965).

There is an analogy between peaceful labor picketing and the government's theory of shared monopoly implemented by price signalling. Shared monopoly involves corporate speech (price signalling) plus further actions by the corporations. It comprises "speech plus" in the same way peaceful picketing does, which is a mixture of speech and conduct combined.

The dichotomy of speech versus conduct that appears in the Supreme Court's decisions on labor picketing has been criticized as being "question-begging," *see, e.g.*, Ely, "Flag Desecration: A Case Study in the Rules of Categorization and Balancing in First Amendment Analysis," 88 Harv. L. Rev. 1482, 1494–96 (1975); Henkin, "The Supreme Court, 1967 Term—Forward: On Drawing Lines," 82 Harv. L. Rev. 63, 79 (1968); Kalven, "The Concept of the Public Forum: *Cox v. Louisiana*," 1965 Sup. Ct. L. Rev. 1. And, indeed, the Court's more recent First Amendment decisions raise doubt whether it will continue to adhere to its speech versus conduct analysis. In *United States v. O'Brien*, 391 U.S. 367 (1968), the Court upheld a prosecution for draft card burning despite the contention that the conduct was constitutionally protected as symbolic speech. In *O'Brien*, the Court shifted its concern from the nature of the activity being regulated—that is, from whether the activity was speech, conduct, or a hybrid[21]— to the nature of the state's interest in effecting the regulation.[22] Under the *O'Brien* standard, "a government regulation is sufficiently justified . . . if it furthers an important or substantial governmental interest [that] is unrelated to the suppression of free expression," 391 U.S. at 377. The crucial question *O'Brien* poses is whether the communicative significance of the regulated activity is relevant to the state interest underlying the regulation. Where the governmental interest is unrelated to the activity's expressive content and the restriction on speech is merely incidental to the state's objective, the regulation may be justified by demonstrating that it satisfies a reasonable balancing test, *i.e.*, that "the incidental restriction on alleged First Amendment freedoms is no greater than is essential to the furtherance of that interest," 391 U.S. at 377.

RESTRAINTS ON EXPORTATION OF COMMERCIAL INFORMATION

The First Amendment commercial speech doctrine has been invoked in the complex field of international transborder data flow, in cases involving the exportation without a license of technical data relating to articles on the Munitions List 22 U.S.C. § 1934 (repealed 1976) and 22 U.S.C. § 2778.

In *United States v. Edler Industries, Inc.*, 579 F.2d 516 (9th Cir. 1978), the Ninth Circuit upheld a version of this restriction on export of technology in the face of a First Amendment commercial speech challenge, *see also*, M. Feldman, "Commercial Speech, Transborder Data Flows and the Right to Communicate Under International Law," 17 International Lawyer, 87 (1983).

COMMERCIAL TELEPHONE CALLS—"JUNK" TELEPHONE CALLS

A number of states, as well as the federal government have enacted statutes that prohibit the making of harassing telephone calls, and these statutes have engendered some First Amendment challenges, *see*, "Validity, Construction and Application of State Criminal Statute Forbidding Use of Telephone to Annoy or Harass," 95 A.L.R. 3d 411 (1979); *New Jersey v. Finance American Corporation*, 182 N.J. Super. 33, 440 A. 2d 28 (1981) (rejecting First Amendment challenge); *Walker v. Dillard*, 523 F.2d 3 (4th Cir. 1975), *cert. denied*, 423 U.S. 906 (1975); *People v. Klick*, 66 Ill. 2d 269, 362 N.E. 2d 329 (Sup. Ct. 1977); *State v. Keaton*, 371 So.2d 86 (Fla. Sup.Ct. 1979); *State v. Blair*, 287 Or. 519, 601 P.2d 766 (Sup.Ct. 1979); *State v. Anonymous*, 34 Conn. Super. 689, 389 A.2d 1270 (Super.Ct.App. 1978); *Gormley v. Conn. State Dept. of Prob. Dir.*, 632 F.2d 938 (2d Cir. 1980), *cert. denied*, 449 U.S. 1023 (1980); *Von Lusch v. State*, 39 Md. App. 517, 387 A.2d 306 (Ct.App. 1978); *State v. Hagen*, 27 Ariz. App. 722, 558 P.2d 750 (Ct.App. 1976).

NEWSPAPER COUPON AND PYRAMID OR CHAIN PROMOTION SCHEMES

The commercial speech exception was invoked unsuccessfully by the vendor of a newspaper, the *Crime Snooper*, which contained a coupon through which readers could win a cash prize if they selected the proper horse in connection with a race held on the day of selection. By the date of decision over 700 copies of the paper had been sold but no "bettor" had won. An action to restrain enforcement of gambling paraphernalia laws failed, *Ingram v. City of Chicago*, 544 F.Supp. 654 (N.D. Ill. 1982).

Companies using chain distribution schemes encountering regulatory action have also invoked the commercial speech doctrine, *see, Holiday Magic, Inc. v. Warren*, 357 F.Supp. 20 (E.D. Wis. 1973), (*vacated*) 497 F.2d, 687, 695 (7th Cir. 1974); *Space Age Products, Inc. v. Gilliam*, 488 F.Supp. 775 (D.Del. 1980).

PRICE ADVERTISING SIGNS

A number of cases have considered the validity of regulations on price advertising by sign, *see, New York v. Mobil Oil Corp.*, 48 N.Y.2d 192, 397 N.E.2d 724 (gas station signs); *H&H Operations, Inc. v. Peachtree City*, 248 Ga. 500, 283 S.E. 2d 867 (1981).

THE COMMERCIAL SPEECH DOCTRINE AND CREDIT REPORTING

In 1970, Congress enacted the Fair Credit Reporting Act, 15 U.S.C. §§1681-1681t, to protect subjects of credit reports. Several states have enacted similar statutes and they have provoked considerable constitutional controversy. See *Equifax Services, Inc. v. Cohen*, 420 A.2d 189 (Me. 1980), *cert. denied*, 450 U.S. 916 (1981) (invalidating several sections of the Maine Fair Credit Reporting Act); *Hood v. Dun & Bradstreet*, 486 F.2d 25 (5th Cir. 1973), *cert. denied*, 415 U.S. 985 (1974); *Roemer v. Retail Credit Co.*, 44 Cal. App. 2d 926, 119 Cal.Rptr. 82 (1975); *Millstone v. O'Hanlon Reports, Inc.*, 528 F.2d 829 (8th Cir. 1976), *Wortham v. Dun & Bradstreet, Inc.*, 399 F.Supp. 633 (S.D. Tex. 1975), *aff'd without opinion*, 537 F.2d 1142 (5th Cir. 1976); See, Comment, "The New Commercial Speech and the Fair Credit Reporting Act," 130 U.Pa.L.Rev. 131 (1981).

In *Dun & Bradstreet v. Greenmoss Builders, Inc.*, _____ U.S. _____, 53 U.S.L.W. 4866 (June 26, 1985), a libel case, the Supreme Court sharply divided in highly provocative opinions on the important question whether credit reports are "commercial speech," but the issue appears to remain unresolved.

Justice Powell and two concurring justices suggested a radical expansion of the category of commercial speech to include *all* speech "solely in the individual interest of the speaker and its specific business audience," 53 U.S.L.W. at 4869. But four justices stated that "[c]redit reporting is not 'commercial speech' as this Court has defined the term," 53 U.S.L.W. at 4877 (dissenting opinion of Brennan, J.).

INSURANCE COMPANY ADVERTISING CONCERNING THE CONNECTION BETWEEN JURY VERDICTS AND INSURANCE PREMIUMS

A number of cases have raised the question whether insurance company advertisements which relate to the connection between high jury verdicts in personal injury cases and high insurance premiums are constitutionally protected, and whether such speech is commercial speech. *See, Quinn v. Aetna Life & Casualty Co.*, 96 Misc. 2d 545, 409 N.Y.S. 2d 473 (1978); *Naylor v. Case & McGrath, Inc.*, 585 F.2d 557 (2d Cir. 1978); *Rutledge v. Liability Insurance Industry*, 487 F.Supp. 5 (W.D. La. 1979).

ADVERTISEMENT AND SOLICITATION OF LAWFUL BUT SOCIALLY DISAPPROVED ACTIVITIES

A number of cases have considered the constitutionality of local ordinances designed to suppress socially disapproved activities.

Massage Parlors, Solicitation for Prostitution, and Advertisements for Prostitution

A local ordinance of Davenport, Iowa, regulating "massage parlors" led to a constitutional challenge of certain restrictions on advertising of massage parlors. In *MRM, Inc. v. City of Davenport*, 290 N.W.2d 338 (Iowa 1980), the Supreme Court addressed the constitutionality of the Davenport "Massage Establishment and Massage Services Ordinance":

No massage establishment granted a license under the provision of this Article shall place, publish or distribute or cause to be placed, published or distributed any advertising matter that depicts any portion of the human body that would reasonably suggest to prospective patrons that any service is available other than those services as described in Section 18.-05–1 in this Chapter, nor shall any massage establishment indicate in the text of such advertising that any service is available other than those services as described in Section 18.-05–1 in this Chapter.

Since other sections of the ordinance confined the services provided by such establisments to certain defined activities, the Court regarded the advertising provision "as one designed to prevent misrepresentation to the consuming public," 290 N.W.2d at 345. The Court also rejected a challenge to this provision on the ground of the vagueness, after adopting a narrower reading of the ordinance in accordance with which the words "reasonably suggest" denote a specific depiction of sexual or genital parts as defined by the ordinance.

In *Wisconsin v. Johnson*, 108 Wis. 2d 703, 324 N.W.2d 447 (Wisconsin App. 1982), the court upheld a conviction for solicitation for prostitution under Wisconsin Stats. § 944.32. Under the guise of auditioning a woman as a model, the defendant took nude photographs and stated that "while she could make $100 an hour as a model, she could make $200 an hour if she would perform a sex act with the photographer." Johnson assured her that he "had a clientele" and that the clients need not know her real name. The defendant attacked the statute as unconstitutionally overbroad and vague on its face, asserting that the solicitation was constitutionally protected commercial speech. The court rejected this contention, pointing out that "[s]peech that is 'no more than a proposal of possible employment' is a 'classic example of commercial speech' and may be subject to government regulation where the transaction is illegal in any way," 324 N.W.2d at 450.

Citing *Village of Hoffman Estates v. The Flipside, supra*, 455 U.S. 489, 102 S. Ct. at 1192, the court held that speech proposing an illegal commercial transaction may be banned entirely, and since prostitution is illegal, the solicitation to engage in prostitution was entitled to no protection. The court observed that "[e]ven assuming that one might hypothesize a speaker who recruits others for prostitution out of purely political motives, this court is not persuaded beyond a reasonable doubt that section 944.32, reaches a substantial amount of constitutionally protected conduct," 324 N.W.2d at 450. The defendant's argument that his remarks failed to meet the two-pronged "imminence" requirement set forth in *Brandenburg v. Ohio*, 395 U.S. 444 (1969), *i.e.*, that the "advocacy" (1) be directed to inciting or producing imminent lawless action and (2) be likely to incite or produce such action, was rejected. The court held that the *Brandenburg* criteria did not apply to unprotected expression and that Johnson employed "purely commerical speech that proposed an illegal transaction," 324 N.W.2d at 451; *see, State v. Gaither*, 236 Ga. 497, 224 S.E. 2d 378 (Ga. 1976).

A somewhat different issue was presented in *United States v. Moses*, 339 A.2d 46 (Dist.Col.Ct.App. 1975), *cert. denied* 426 U.S. 920 (1976), in which the court rejected a First Amendment challenge to a District of Columbia law prohibiting solicitation by prostitutes. Congress chose not to prohibit prostitution, although adultery, fornication, and sodomy were illegal in the District. The court, however, did not rely on the illegality of the acts under the latter provisions, 339 A.2d at 50 n.5. Instead, the court rested its conclusion on the government's authority to regulate business activities that are lawful. The court's reasoning in this case appears to be of doubtful validity in light of *Central Hudson*.

Related issues, which did not, however, involve commercial speech, were presented in *State v. Phipps*, 58 Ohio St.2d 271, 389 N.E. 2d 1128 (1979), dealing with the constitutionality of a statute prohibiting "solicit[ing] a person of the same sex to engage in sexual activity with the offender, when the offender knows such solicitation is offensive to the other person, or is reckless in that regard."

In *Princess Sea Industries, Inc. v. Nevada* , 97 Nev. 534, 635 P.2d 281 (Nev. 1981), *cert. denied* 456 U.S. 926 (1982), the Nevada Supreme Court upheld the constitutionality of a statute purporting to regulate advertising of houses of prostitution in Nevada, by local option. The challenged provision prohibited such advertising "in any county, city or town where prostitution is prohibited by local ordinance or where the licensing of a house of prostitution is prohibited by state statute" (NRS 201.430[2]). Prostitution is lawful in some counties of Nevada. A substantial amount of the business of the southern Nevada brothels is derived from Clark County where Las Vegas is located. The owner of "The Chicken

Ranch'' brothel in Nye County, Nevada (situated sixty-five miles northwest of Las Vegas), and two newspaper publishing concerns contended that the advertising was protected commercial speech advertising lawful transactions in a nondeceptive manner.

In a cursory opinion, the court rejected this argument. The concurring opinion of Justice Manoukian, however, grappled with ''the important First Amendment issue'' of the appeal, 635 P.2d at 283–287. The concurrence distinguishes the *Bigelow* decision on the grounds that ''the advertisement of prostitution does not pertain to fundamental constitutional interests as does the advertisement of abortion'' and that no interstate regulation was involved. Balancing the state's interest in maintaining an ''atmosphere of decency and sound morals'' and in ''counteracting the deleterious effect prostitution may have on the public welfare,'' Justice Manoukian upheld the statute. Since Nevada had the power to suppress prostitution entirely, the state could suppress the advertising of it, no matter how truthful the advertising or lawful the conduct proposed in the county where the activity was to occur. Notwithstanding the Supreme Court's dictum in *Pittsburgh Press Co. v. Human Relations Commission*, 413 U.S. 376, 388 (1973), ''a newspaper constitutionally could be forbidden to publish a want ad proposing a sale of narcotics or soliciting prostitutes,'' the correctness of the Nevada court's reasoning may be doubted under the unique status of prostitution under Nevada law, *see*, Note, 1983 Det. C.L. Rev. 1613.

Liquor Advertising in Partially Dry States

Another similar case involves the constitutionality of blanket prohibitions on liquor advertising in states in which some counties are ''dry,'' by local option, and some counties are ''wet,'' *Dunagin v. City of Oxford*, 489 F.Supp. 763 (N.D. Miss. 1980), *rev'd* 701 F.2d 335 (5th Cir. 1983), *vacated and district court decision reinstated*, 718 F.2d 738 (5th Cir. 1983) (*en banc*) *cert. denied* ____U.S. ____104 S. Ct. 3553; *Memphis Publishing Co. v. Leech*, 539 F.2d 405 (W.D. Tenn. 1982); *Lamar Outdoor Advertising, Inc. v. Mississippi State Tax Commission*, 539 F.Supp. 817 (S.D.Miss. 1982), *rev'd*, 718 F.2d 738 (1983) (*en banc*) *cert. denied* ____U.S. ____, 104 S. Ct. 3553 (1984) (upholding ban on liquor advertising statewide).

Advertisement of Caloric Content of Wine

In *Taylor Wine Co., Inc. v. Department of Treasury*, 509 F.Supp. 792 (D.D.C. 1981), the court considered the validity of a Treasury Department regulation prohibiting inclusion of caloric information on wine labels by using the word ''light.''

Regulation of Liquor Retailer Advertising

In *Oklahoma Alcoholic Beverage Control Board v. Burris*, 626 P.2d 1316 (Okl. 1980), the Oklahoma Supreme Court upheld strict limitations on store advertising by licensed liquor retailers, *See also, Opinion of the Justices to the Senate*, 373 Mass. 888, 366 N.E. 2d 1220 (Mass. 1977) (right to publish liquor prices by handbill or newspaper outside the licensed premises).

ISSUES OF COMMERCIAL SPEECH UNDER THE BOYCOTT PROVISIONS OF THE EXPORT ADMINISTRATION ACT, 50 U.S.C. § 2401 *et seq.*

The Export Administration Act, 50 U.S.C. § 2401(a)(1), makes it unlawful "to comply with, further, or support any boycott fostered or imposed by a foreign country against a country which is friendly to the United States." The boycott of the League of Arab States against Israel and companies doing business with Israel, formed on December 11, 1954, presented certain commercial speech issues in *Briggs & Stratton Corp. v. Baldridge*, 539 F.Supp. 1307 (E.D. Wis. 1982); *aff'd* 728 F.2d 915 (7th Cir.), *cert. denied* ____U.S. ____, 105 S. Ct. 106 (1984); *see also*, 544 F.Supp. 667 (E.D. Wis. 1982). Under the Arab boycott "principles" a company may be blacklisted if it trades with Israel. In order to determine which companies are trading with Israel and therefore may be eligible for blacklisting, the Central Boycott Office in Damascus, Syria, mailed questionnaires to be answered by certain companies requesting information about trade between the companies and Israel. The regulations under the act prohibited companies from answering such questionnaires. Briggs & Stratton contended that it possessed a First Amendment right to answer the questionnaire, the regulations notwithstanding. Briggs founded this argument on First Amendment commercial speech rights. The court rejected these arguments, 539 F.Supp. at 1317, concluding that the regulation complied with the *Central Hudson* standard, in that it was supported by a strong governmental interest and was no more restrictive than necessary, 539 F.Supp. at 1319.

CONSTITUTIONALITY OF PROHIBITION OF PUBLISHING LIKENESS OF UNITED STATES CURRENCY, 18 U.S.C. § 474

In *Time, Inc. v. Regan*, 539 F.Supp. 1371 (S.D.N.Y. 1982), the court considered the constitutionality of the federal statute that prohibits any likeness of United States currency to be published. The court analyzed this as a protected form of commercial speech and invalidated the government's attempt to prevent *Time* from using the format of currency of the United States. This result was affirmed in part and reversed in part by the Supreme Court, which held that the purpose requirement of 18 U.S.C. § 504 is unconstitutional, but upholding the color and size limitations of 18 U.S.C. §§ 474 and 504, 104 S. Ct. 3262 (1984).

COMMERCIAL SPEECH AND THE ELECTRONIC MEDIA

The Supreme Court has repeatedly cautioned in the modern commercial speech decisions that special First Amendment rules are applicable to the electronic media by reason of the peculiar features of those media. In particular, the question has arisen whether Congress and the Federal Communications Commission (FCC) have the power to prohibit altogether certain truthful advertising of products that are harmful, although lawful to purchase and use, and whether Congress may require, in conjunction with such advertising, that certain disclosures regarding the health hazards posed by certain products be made. The Supreme Court has not yet dealt with these issues, and the principal decisions of the lower courts dealing with these issues antedate the most recent decision defining the modern commercial speech doctrine.

The principal decisions of the lower courts concerning these questions have concerned the Federal Cigarette Labelling and Advertising Act, 15 U.S.C. § 1331 *et seq.*, requiring a cautionary notice on each package of cigarettes, and the Public Health Cigarette Smoking Act of 1969, *see, Capital Broadcasting Co. v. Mitchell*, 333 F. Supp. 582 (D.D.C. 1971) *aff'd* 405 U.S. 1000 (1972); *Banzhaf v. FCC*, 405 F.2d 1082 (D.C. Cir. 1968), *cert. denied* 396 U.S. 842 (1969); *see also, Columbia Broadcasting System, Inc. v. Democratic National Committee*, 412 U.S. 94 (1973) (refusal to accept political advertising); *FTC v. Carter*, 464 F.Supp. 633 (D.D.C. 1979), *aff'd* 636 F. 2d 781 (D.C. Cir. 1980) (FTC investigation of cigarette advertising).

The validity of FCC regulation of the broadcast of state-run lottery information was addressed in *New York State Broadcasters Assn. v. United States*, 414 F.2d 990 (2d Cir. 1969).

STATE RETALIATION FOR PRIVATE COMMERCIAL SPEECH

In a doubtful decision, the *Valentine v. Chrestensen* doctrine was applied as late as 1975 to defeat a claim by a graduate student of state retaliation for the student's exercise of First Amendment rights relating to commercial speech in *Stevenson v. Board of Regents of Univ. of Texas*, 393 F.Supp. 812 (W.D. Texas 1975).

VALIDITY OF TAXES ON COMMERCIAL SPEECH

The history of the First Amendment has established that one of its central purposes was the elimination of all forms of previous restraints, licensing systems, and taxes on protected speech. The question has arisen in at least one case whether a tax levied on commercial speech conflicts with the First Amendment, *see, Grosjean v. American Press Co.*, 297 U.S. 233 (1936); *Murdock v. Pennsylvania*, 319 U.S. 105 (1943); *Follett v. Township of McCormick*, 321 U.S. 573 (1944).

In *Sears Roebuck & Co. v. State Department of Revenue*, 97 Wash. 2d 260, 643 P.2d 884 (1982), *appeal dismissed*, 459 U.S. 803 (1982), the Supreme Court of Washington held that a use tax applied to catalogs shipped directly to Sears stores and then distributed over the counter or otherwise was not unconstitutional as a restriction on commercial speech.

Several earlier decisions had reached a similar result, *Steinbeck v. Gerosa*, 4 N.Y.2d 302, 151 N.E. 2d 170, 175 N.Y.S. 2d 1, *appeal dismissed*, 358 U.S. 39 (1958), in which it was decided that a general tax which only tangentially affects constitutionally protected speech is valid. However, each taxing provision must be examined on its own merits to determine whether the First Amendment is infringed by such provisions. In *Minneapolis Star & Tribune v. Minn. Com'r of Rev.*, 460 U.S. 575, 103 S. Ct. 1365 (1983), however, the Supreme Court held unconstitutional the Minnesota "ink and paper" tax as an abridgement of First Amendment rights, because the tax singled out the press for special tax treatment.

CONSUMER INFORMATIONAL PICKETING AND THE COMMERCIAL SPEECH DOCTRINE

The commercial speech doctrine has figured in situations involving the protected status of picketing of particular businesses by consumer organizations designed to alert the public to certain sales and refund practices and the quality of merchandise of particular retailers. Thus, in *Concerned Consumers League v. O'Neill*, 371 F.Supp. 644 (E.D. Wis. 1974), the court held that informational picketing of this type is constitutionally protected, 371 F.Supp. at 647.

NOTES

1. Metromedia Inc. v. City of San Diego, 453 U.S. 490, 501 (1981) (opinion of Justice White).

2. Central Hudson Gas and Electric Corp. Public Service Commission, 447 U.S. at 566.

3. The courts issued several earlier opinions in the case, *see also*, 464 F.Supp. 1252 (M.D.Pa. 1972); 510 F.Supp. 983 (M.D.Pa. 1981); 522 F.Supp. 544 (M.D.Pa. 1982); 618 F.2d 252 (3d Cir. 1980).

4. 39 U.S.C. § 3008 provides:

§ 3008. PROHIBITION OF PANDERING ADVERTISEMENTS.

(a) Whoever for himself, or by his agents or assigns, mails or causes to be mailed any pandering advertisement which offers for sale matter which the addressee in his sole discretion believes to be erotically arousing or sexually provocative shall be subject to an order of the Postal Service to refrain from further mailings of such materials to designated addresses thereof.

(b) Upon receipt of notice from an addressee that he has received such mail matter, determined by the addressee in his discretion to be of the character described in subsection (a) of this section, the Postal Service shall issue an order, if requested by the addressee, to the sender thereof, directing the sender and his agents or assigns to refrain from further mailings to the named addressees.

. . .

(c) Upon request of any addressee, the order of the Postal Service shall include the names of any of his minor children who have not attained their nineteenth birthday, and who reside with the addressee.

(d) The provisions of subchapter II of chapter 5, relating to administrative procedure, and chapter 7, relating to judicial review, of title 5, shall not apply to any provisions of this section.

(i) [*sic*] For purposes of this section:

(1) mail matter, directed to a specific address covered in the order of the Postal Service, without designation of a specific addressee thereon, shall be considered as addressed to the person named in the Postal Service's order; and

(2) the term "children" includes natural children, stepchildren, adopted children and children who are wards of or in custody of the addressee or who are living with such addressee in a regular parent-child relationship.

Publ. L. 91–375, Aug. 12, 1970, 84 Stat. 748.

5. 39 U.S.C. § 3010 provides:

§ 3010. MAILING OF SEXUALLY ORIENTED ADVERTISEMENTS.

(a) Any person who mails or causes to be mailed any sexually oriented advertisement shall place on the envelope or cover thereof his name and address as the sender thereof and such mark or notice as the Postal Service may prescribe.

(b) Any person, on his own behalf or on the behalf of any of his children who has not attained the age of 19 years and who resides with him or is under his care, custody, or supervision, may file with the Postal Service a statement, in such form and manner as the Postal Service may prescribe, that he desires to receive no sexually oriented advertisements through the mails. The Postal Service shall maintain and keep current, insofar as practicable, a list of the names and addresses of such persons and shall make the list (including portions thereof or changes therein) available to any person, upon such reasonable terms and conditions as it may prescribe, including the payment of such service charge as it determines to be necessary to defray the cost of compiling and maintaining the list and making it available as provided in this sentence. No person shall mail or cause to be mailed any sexually oriented advertisement to any individual whose name and address has been on the list for more than 30 days.

(c) "Sexually oriented advertisement" means any advertisement that depicts, in actual or simulated form, or explicitly describes, in a predominantly sexual context, human genitalia, any act of natural or unnatural sexual intercourse, any act of sadism or masochism, or any other erotic subject directly related to the foregoing. Material otherwise within the definition of this subsection shall be deemed not to constitute a sexually oriented advertisement if it constitutes only a small and insignificant part of the whole of a single catalog, book, periodical, or other work the remainder of which is not primarily devoted to sexual matters.

Pub.L. 91–374, Aug. 12, 1970, 84 Stat. 749.

6. 39 U.S.C. § 3007 provides:

(a) In preparation for or during the pendency of proceedings under sections 3005 and 3006 of this title, the United States district court in the district in which the defendant receives his mail shall, upon application therefore by the Postal Service and upon a showing of probable cause to believe either section is being violated, enter a temporary restraining order and preliminary injunction pursuant to rule 65 of the Federal Rules of Civil Procedure directing the detention of the defendant's incoming mail by the postmaster pending the conclusion of the statutory proceedings and any appeal therefrom. The district court may provide in the order that the detained mail be open to examination by the defendant and such mail be delivered as is clearly not connected with the alleged unlawful activity. An action taken by a court hereunder does not affect or determine any fact at issue in the statutory proceedings.

39 U.S.C. § 3005 provides:

(a) Upon evidence satisfactory to the Postal Service that any person is engaged in conducting a scheme or device for obtaining money or property through the mail by means of false representations, including the mailing of matter which is nonmailable under section 3001(d) of this title, or is engaged in conducting a lottery, gift enterprise, or scheme for the distribution of money or of real or personal property, by lottery, chance, or drawing of any kind, the Postal Service may issue an order which:

(1) directs the postmaster of the post office at which mail arrives, addressed to such a person or to his representative, to return such mail to the sender appropriately marked as in violation of this section, if the person, or his representative, is first notified and given reasonable opportunity to be present at the receiving post office to survey the mail before the postmaster returns the mail to the sender;

(2) forbids the payment by a postmaster to the person or his representative of any money order or postal note drawn to the order of either and provides for the return to the remitter of the sum named in the money order or postal note; and

(3) requires the person or his representative to cease and desist from engaging in any such scheme, device, lottery, or gift enterprise.

For purposes of the preceding sentence, the mailing of matter which is nonmailable under such section 3001(d) by any person shall constitute prima facie evidence that such person is engaged in conducting a scheme or device for obtaining money or property through the mail by false representations.

(b) The public advertisement by a person engaged in activities covered by subsection (a) of this section, that remittances may be made by mail to a person named in the advertisement, is prima facie evidence that the latter is the agent or representative of the advertiser for the receipt of remittances on behalf of the advertiser. The Postal Service may ascertain the existence of the agency in any other legal way satisfactory to it.

(c) As used in this section and section 3006 of this title, the term ''representative'' includes an agent or representative acting as an individual or as a firm, bank, corporation, or association of any kind.

(d) Nothing in this section shall prohibit the mailing of (1) a newspaper of general circulation containing advertisements, lists of prizes, or information concerning a lottery conducted by a State acting under authority of State law, published in that State, or in an adjacent State which conducts such a lottery, (2) tickets or other materials concerning such a lottery within that State to addresses within that State, or (3) an advertisement promoting the sale of a book or other publication, or a solicitation to purchase, or a purchase order for any such publication, if (A) such advertisement, solicitation, or purchase order is not materially false or misleading in its description of the publication; (B) such advertisement, solicitation, or purchase order contains no material misrepresentation of fact: Provided, however, that no statement quoted or derived from the publication shall constitute a misrepresentation of fact as long as such statement complies with the requirements of subparagraphs (A) and (C); and (C) the advertisement, solicitation, or purchase order accurately discloses the source of any statements quoted or derived from the publication. Paragraph (3) shall not be applicable to any publication, advertisement, solicitation, or purchase order which is used to sell some other product in which the publisher or author has a financial interest as part of a commercial scheme. For the purposes of this subsection, ''State'' means a State of the United States, the District of Columbia, the Commonwealth of Puerto Rico, and any territory or possession of the United States.

As amended Pub.L. 98–186, § 2, Nov. 30, 1983, 97 Stat. 1315.

7. 521 Securities Regulation & Law Report, September 26, 1979, pp. A 16–17.

8. *See* Release Nos. 33–5862 (Sales Literature for Mutual Funds), 33–6034, 34–15621, 1C-9916, 1C-10621.

9. The background of the "price signalling" concept can be traced to the 1958 Hearings on Administered Prices before the Subcommittee on Antitrust and Monopoly, Senate Committee on the Judiciary, 85th Cong. 2d Sess., and specifically Part 8 of these hearings, which took place on August 5 and 6, 1958. Victor Hansen, then Assistant Attorney General, Antitrust Division, testified at length on the division's ongoing program of antitrust scrutiny of the steel industry (at 4377–4421). *See also*, the articles contained in the Hearings: "Armco Steel Says it Will Try to Hike Prices After July 1 Pay Rise," *Wall Street Journal*, May 22, 1958; "Building Costs to Climb," *Steel Magazine*, June 2, 1958; "Alan Wood to Boost Steel $6 a Ton," *Wall Street Journal*, June 26, 1958; "J.&L. Says it Won't Lead on Steel Price Hike," *Wall Street Journal*, June 27, 1958; "Three Steel Concerns Lift Their Prices," *N.Y. Times*, July 31, 1958; "Republic, Jones & Laughlin Join Armco in Boosting Steel Prices," *Wall Street Journal*, July 31, 1958; "More Steel Makers Join in Price Rise," *N.Y. Journal of Commerce*, July 31, 1958; "Escalators Pass on Metal Pass Hikes." *Washington Post and Times Herald*, August 1, 1958; "Another Round—Steel, Aluminum Price Increases Sure to Spur Hikes on Metal Products," *Wall Street Journal*, August 1, 1958; "Spirals and Specters," *Washington Post*, August 5, 1958.

10.

"Another high priority in the Antitrust Division at the present time is the so-called shared monopoly problem. In industries dominated by a few firms, it is possible to conclude that there is too much good fellowship and too little competition. Greater concern seems to be paid to the interests of the group rather than to the interests of the individual firms. In short, such industries appear to be achieving the same results one would expect in the case of a single firm monopoly, such as maintaining prices at high levels or excluding new entrants. There are not the inevitable results of a complex economy.

One area of concerted industry behavior of particular concern is public signalling of pricing decisions or other competitive moves. The classic price-fixing conspiracy generally involves clandestine meetings, follow-up communications, and elaborate machinery for ensuring group solidarity. In groups of often-contentious small businessmen this machinery may be necessary; it may not be necessary in a mature concentrated industry. One reads the business or trade press and is hard-pressed to escape the conclusion that some of the statements attributed to large firms or their spokesmen are meant not for the public or for their customers but for the competition.

In a variety of ways, notably through standardization of price lists and the like, the orchestration of an industry's price and production behavior can be accomplished. Public dissemination of elaborate pricing catalogs, public assurances that list prices are being adhered to, and complex price protection clauses that impose severe penalties for charging an off-list price can contribute to making an industry non-competitive. And through publicly-exchanged statements it sometimes looks as though members of a concentrated industry are dickering over who's going to go up in price next, when and by how much. When we conclude that the net result of such public exchanges of information is an agreement among competitors, we will file suit.

"Current Trends in Antitrust Enforcement: A Prosecutor's Perspective." Remarks by William E. Swope, Director of Operations, Antitrust Division, 1978 Southeastern Corporate Law Institute, Point Clear, Alabama, April 22, 1978 (hereafter Swope Remarks).

11.

Another initiative of the Antitrust Division, and again a particular interest of the Attorney General, is in an area often referred to as "shared monopoly." This term refers to the phenomenon of a small number of firms in a concentrated industry acting interdependently to achieve the same results that flow from monopolization—for example, raising prices above competitive levels or excluding new entrants. . . .

The area of our current interest goes beyond a theoretical analysis of behavior of firms in an oligopoly, and includes an attempt to understand how some firms reach an understanding between or among themselves to act interdependently and not to compete. The means to this end might be issuance of detailed price books months in advance of proposed price changes or joint adoption of uniform delivered price system or similar facilitating mechanisms. An interesting common characteristic of this type of conduct is that it is often only rationally explainable in business terms as part of joint, rather than individual, behavior.

Certainly, where the end result is anticompetitive and the firms have engaged in behavior that facilitates the achievement of that harmful result, one is hard pressed to say, due to the absence of a classic hotel-room type of agreement, that such a result is clearly beyond the reach of the Sherman Act, noted for its remarkable breadth, or contrary to Congress' intent in passing it.

"Recent Developments and New Directions in Antitrust: An Antitrust Division Perspective." Remarks by Timothy G. Smith, Special Assistant to the Assistant Attorney General, Antitrust Division, Annual Antitrust Symposium, Lewis and Clark Law School, Portland, Oregon, February 24, 1978 (hereafter Smith Remarks).

12. "The Future Is Now." Remarks by John H. Shenefield, Assistant Attorney General, Antitrust Division, before the Federal Bar Association, Washington, D.C., March 10, 1978 (hereafter Shenefield "Future" Remarks).

13. "Antitrust and Evolution: New Concepts for New Problems." Remarks by John H. Shenefield, before the Eleventh New England Antitrust Conference, Boston, Massachusetts, November 18, 1977 (hereafter Shenefield "New Concepts" Remarks).

14. Shenefield "New Concepts" Remarks, *supra*, n.20.

15. United States v. General Electric Company and Westinghouse Electric Company, No. 28228 (E.D.Pa.): Plaintiff's Memorandum in Support of a Proposed Modification to the Final Judgment (December 10, 1976), 42 Fed.Reg. 17005, 17006.

16. Hearing before the Subcommittee on Monopolies and Commercial Law of the Committee on the Judiciary, House of Representatives, 95th Cong., 1st Sess., on H.R. 6001 (Clayton Act Amendment), June 16, 1977, at 30.

17. Shenefield "Future" Remarks, *supra*, n.19.

18. Such *conduct*—as opposed to "pure" speech in the form of price signalling—would consist of, *inter alia*, "public dissemination of elaborate pricing catalogues, public assurances that list prices are being adhered to, and complex price protection clauses that impose severe penalties for charging an off-list price" (Swope Remarks, *supra*, n.17), or, as "means to [an] end," the "issuance of detailed price books months in advance of proposed price changes or joint adoption of uniform delivered price system or similar facilitating mechanisms." (Smith Remarks, *supra*, n.13).

19. Address by Attorney General Bell before the Harvard Law Review, March 19, 1977, reprinted at 806 A.T.R.R. F-1, F-3.

20. "[W]e must start with the fact that while picketing has an ingredient of communication it cannot dogmatically be equated with the constitutionally protected freedom of speech," Teamsters Local 309 v. Hanke, 339 U.S. 470, 474 (1950) (plurality opinion).

21. "Picketing is indeed a hybrid," Teamsters Local 309 v. Hanke, 339 U.S. 470, 479 (1950) (Frankfurter, J.).

22. The older cases sought to identify whether expression or conduct was being regulated, *see, e.g.*, Cox v. Louisiana, 379 U.S. 536, 563 (1965); NAACP v. Button, 371 U.S. 415, 454 (1963) (Harlan, J., dissenting); Hughes v. Superior Court, 339 U.S. 460, 464–65 (1950).

PART II

Corporate Political Speech

7

Corporate Political Speech and the First Amendment

The preceding chapters have traced the evolution of constitutional protection for commercial speech of business entities. As the Supreme Court decisions in the field of commercial speech reflect, one of the primary interests protected by extending the First Amendment to commercial advertising is the interest of citizens who desire to receive commercial information about the price, quality, attributes, and availability of goods and services. Of course, the economic interests of the advertiser and of society as a whole in this information have been accorded weight as well, but recognition of the rights of recipients appears to have been the crucial step in the evolution of the modern commercial speech doctrine.

The same recognition of the rights of listeners lies at the heart of the Supreme Court's simultaneous recognition during the 1970s of the protected status of political speech by corporations and other businesses. Probably the single most influential passage in the writings of modern political theorists, with respect to the Supreme Court's interpretation of the First Amendment since the *New York Times Co. v. Sullivan* decision in 1964, is Alexander Meiklejohn's discussion of the necessity for the First Amendment in a representative democracy.[1] This passage from Meiklejohn's writings, which has been repeatedly cited by the Supreme Court, is essential to an understanding of the prevailing approach to the First Amendment by the Supreme Court. Meiklejohn used the model of the New England town meeting to explain why there must be a First Amendment to protect all speech concerning public issues and affairs:

The difficulties of the paradox of freedom as applied to speech may perhaps be lessened if we now examine the procedure of the traditional American town meeting. That institution is commonly, and rightly, regarded as a model by which free political procedures may be measured. It is self-government in its simplest, most obvious form.

In the town meeting the people of a community assemble to discuss and to act upon matters of public interest—roads, schools, poorhouses, health, external defense, and the like. Every man is free to come. They meet as political equals. Each has a right and a duty to think his own thoughts, to express them, and to listen to the arguments of others. The basic principle is that the freedom of speech shall be unabridged. And yet the meeting cannot even be opened unless, by common consent, speech is abridged. A chairman or moderator is, or has been, chosen. He "calls the meeting to order." And the hush which follows that call is a clear indication that restrictions upon speech have been set up. The moderator assumes, or arranges, that in the conduct of the business, certain rules of order will be observed. Except as he is overruled by the meeting as a whole, he will enforce those rules. His business on its negative side is to abridge speech. For example, it is usually agreed that no one shall speak unless "recognized by the chair." Also, debaters must confine their remarks to "the question before the house." If one man "has the floor," no one else may interrupt him except as provided by the rules. The meeting has assembled, not primarily to talk, but primarily by means of talking to get business done. And the talking must be regulated and abridged as the doing of the business under actual conditions may require. If a speaker wanders from the point at issue, if he is abusive or in other ways threatens to defeat the purpose of the meeting, he may be and should be declared "out of order." He must then stop speaking, at least in that way. And if he persists in breaking the rules, he may be "denied the floor" or, in the last resort, "thrown out" of the meeting. The town meeting, as it seeks for freedom of public discussion of public problems, would be wholly ineffectual unless speech were thus abridged. It is not a Hyde Park. It is a parliament or congress. It is a group of free and equal men, cooperating in a common enterprise, and using for that enterprise responsible and regulated discussion. It is not a dialectical free-for-all. It is self-government.

These speech-abridging activities of the town meeting indicate what the First Amendment to the Constitution does not forbid. When self-governing men demand freedom of speech they are not saying that every individual has an unalienable right to speak whenever, wherever, however he chooses. They do not declare that any man may talk as he pleases, when he pleases, about what he pleases, about whom he pleases, to whom he pleases. The common sense of any reasonable society would deny the existence of that unqualified right. No one, for example, may, without consent of nurse or doctor, rise up in a sickroom, to argue for his principles or his candidate. In the sickroom, that question is not "before the house." The discussion is, therefore, "out of order." To you who now listen to my words, it is allowable to differ with me, but it is not allowable for you to state that difference in words until I have finished my reading. Anyone, who would thus irresponsibly interrupt the activities of a lecture, a hospital, a concert hall, a church, a machine shop, a classroom, a football field, or a home, does not thereby exhibit his freedom. Rather, he shows himself to be a boor, a public nuisance, who must be abated, by force if necessary.[2]

After explaining in this fashion, what, in legal terms, would be described as the "time, place and manner" rule, Meiklejohn next took up the question precisely what the First Amendment does not permit and why. In Meiklejohn's view, the "point of ultimate interest" in any system of self-government is "the minds of the hearers, because the 'final' aim of the meeting is the voting of wise decisions." From this, Meiklejohn deduced the right of freedom of discussion:

What, then, does the First Amendment forbid? Here again the town meeting suggests an answer. That meeting is called to discuss and, on the basis of such discussion, to decide matters of public policy. For example, shall there be a school? Where shall it be located? Who shall teach? What shall be taught? The community has agreed that such questions as these shall be freely discussed and that, when the discussion is ended, decision upon them will be made by vote of the citizens. *Now, in that method of political self-government, the point of ultimate interest is not the words of the speakers, but the minds of the hearers. The final aim of the meeting is the voting of wise decisions.* The voters, therefore, must be made as wise as possible. The welfare of the community requires that those who decide issues shall understand them. They must know what they are voting about. And this, in turn, requires that so far as time allows, all facts and interests relevant to the problem shall be fully and fairly presented to the meeting. *Both facts and interests must be given in such a way that all the alternative lines of action can be wisely measured in relation to one another.* As the self-governing community seeks, by the method of voting, to gain wisdom in action, it can find it only in the minds of its individual citizens. If they fail, it fails. That is why freedom of discussion for those minds may not be abridged. (emphasis added)

Meiklejohn summarized the import of his deductions as follows:

The First Amendment, then, is not the guardian of unregulated talkativeness. It does not require that, on every occasion, every citizen shall take part in public debate. . . . What is essential is not that everyone shall speak, but that everything worth saying shall be said. . . . No speaker may be declared "out of order" because we disagree with what he intends to say. And the reason for this equality of status in the field of ideas lies deep in the very foundations of the self-governing process. *When men govern themselves, it is they—and no one else—who must pass judgment upon un-wisdom and unfairness and danger. And that means that unwise ideas must have a hearing as well as wise ones, unfair as well as fair, dangerous as well as safe, un-American as well as American. Just so far as, at any point, the citizens who are to decide an issue are denied acquaintance with information or opinion or doubt or disbelief or criticism which is relevant to that issue, just so far the result must be ill-considered, ill-balanced planning for the general good. It is that mutilation of the thinking process of the community against which the First Amendment to the Constitution is directed. The principle of the freedom of speech springs from the necessities of the program of self-government.* It is not a Law of Nature or of Reason in the abstract. It is a deduction from the basic American agreement that public issues shall be decided by universal suffrage.[3]

It would be difficult to overestimate the importance of Meiklejohn's ideas for modern First Amendment interpretation, because they have been cited more than two dozen times in Supreme Court opinions, as well as an almost equal number of times by the courts of appeals. They are the theoretical foundation of the doctrine of "listener's rights," which in turn is the foundation of both First Amendment protection of commercial speech and First Amendment protection for corporate speech addressed to political and public questions. Meiklejohn concluded his elementary civics lesson with this observation:

If, then, on any occasion in the United States it is allowable to say that the Constitution is a good document it is equally allowable, in that situation, to say that the Constitution is a bad document. If a public building may be used in which to say, in time of war, that the war is justified, then the same building may be used in which to say that it is not justified. If it be publicly argued that conscription for armed service is moral and necessary, it may likewise be publicly argued that it is immoral and unnecessary. If it may be said that American political institutions are superior to those of England or Russia or Germany, it may, with equal freedom, be said that those of England or Russia or Germany are superior to ours. *These conflicting views may be expressed, must be expressed, not because they are valid, but because they are relevant. If they are responsibly entertained by anyone, we, the voters, need to hear them. When a question of policy is "before the house," free men choose to meet it not with their eyes shut, but with their eyes open. To be afraid of ideas, any idea, is to be unfit for self-government. Any such suppression of ideas about the common good, the First Amendment condemns with its absolute disapproval. The freedom of ideas shall not be abridged.*[4] (emphasis added)

Acceptance of Meiklejohn's ideas played a significant role in the evolution of the modern commercial speech doctrine, *see, Virginia Pharmacy Board v. Virginia Consumer Council, supra*, 425 U.S. at 765 n.19 (citing Meiklejohn). The same ideas, in Meiklejohn's specific formulation of them, seem to have played a considerable role in the decisional process that led to the recognition that the First Amendment protects the expression of corporations and businesses on public affairs and political issues, *Consolidated Edison Co. v. Public Service Commission, supra*, 447 U.S. at 534 n.3. (citing Meiklejohn's views); *First National Bank of Boston v. Bellotti*, 435 U.S. 765, 777 n.11 (1978) (citing A. Meiklejohn, "Free Speech and Its Relation to Self-Government," 24–26 [1948]).

Part II of this book will consider some of the judicial decisions that deal with the constitutionality of governmental restrictions that prohibit corporations and other business entities from engaging in public debate on governmental and political issues, or limit their ability to do so. Corporate involvement in politics can take a wide variety of forms, which may be lawful or unlawful depending on the jurisdiction in which it is done. Some of the most typical areas of corporate involvement are (1) making political contributions from the general corporate treasury to candidate political committees, political action committees (PACs), and national political parties, (2) financing the formation and administration of PACs, which solicit political contributions from corporate executive and administrative personnel, employees, and stockholders and, in turn, make contributions to the political committee's candidates, other PACs, or national political parties, (3) making available to candidates corporate property and facilities, *e.g.*, to address corporate employees and others, or for political receptions, or the loan of employees for political purposes, as well as a wide variety of similar in-kind contributions, and (4) making independent expenditures of funds from the corporate treasury for the purpose of paying for advertising to publicize the position of the corporation on public issues or on ballot or referendum questions, or to advocate the election or defeat of a specified candidate for public office or political party, or to encourage voters to vote or to encourage those eligible to do so to register and vote ("get-out-the-vote" campaigns), or simply to educate the public concerning the voting records of incumbent candidates for public office.

Although some constitutional questions exist with respect to governmental regulation of all of these corporate political activities, *e.g.*, prohibitions on corporate political contributions, the First Amendment issues discussed here will center on governmental restrictions on the last category of corporate political activities—that is, on those which most clearly interfere with the rights of citizens to have access to all viewpoints and to information from all segments of society, which therefore pose most directly the fundamental constitutional questions of First Amendment protection for corporate political speech.

What follows is a brief historical sketch of federal and state regulation of corporate expenditures for political speech, followed in turn by a review of the principal judicial decisions dealing with the constitutionality of governmental restrictions on the major forms of corporate political activity involving the expenditure of corporate treasury funds, *i.e.*, expenditure of corporate funds to advocate positions on ballot or referendum issues, to advocate positions on general public questions not the subject of a referendum, to advocate the election or defeat of a specific candidate or political party, or to mount a "get-out-the-vote" campaign.

Many of the constitutional issues surrounding governmental regulation of these corporate activities are similar to the constitutional issues which arise in connection with governmental regulation of the same activities on the part of labor unions. Indeed, in many instances, the pertinent state or federal statutory provisions deal with both corporate and labor union (unincorporated association) activities. The issues are similar, but they are not identical. It has been observed that the use of general labor union dues for political purposes can result in a form of compulsory speech by union members who by reason of union shop provisions are obliged to pay dues, therefore, indirectly, making expenditures for political purposes with which they may disagree. When state or federal statutes sanction union shop arrangements, the use of union general treasury funds created by such compulsory exactions may raise serious constitutional questions, *see, Abood v. Detroit Board of Education*, 431 U.S. 209 (1977); *Cort v. Ash*, 422 U.S. 66, 81 n.13 (1975); *Lathrop v. Donohue*, 367 U.S. 820 (1961); *International Association of Machinists v. Street*, 367 U.S. 740 (1961); *Railway Employees' Department v. Hanson*, 351 U.S. 225 (1956). The issues surrounding labor union involvement in similar expressive political activities are perhaps distinguishable and are, therefore, not directly dealt with here, except to the extent that they comprise part of the same background of judicial interpretation of the key statutory provisions relating to corporate political activities.

HISTORICAL BACKGROUND OF FEDERAL AND STATE LEGISLATION RESTRICTING CORPORATE POLITICAL ACTIVITIES

The current federal statute which prohibits corporations from making expenditures in connection with federal elections that are designed to influence the outcome of elections is 2 U.S.C. § 441b which provides, in relevant part:

§ 441b. CONTRIBUTIONS OR EXPENDITURES BY NATIONAL BANKS, CORPORATIONS, OR LABOR ORGANIZATIONS.

(a) It is unlawful for any national bank, or any corporation organized by authority of any law of Congress, to make a contribution or expenditure in connection with any election to any political office, or in connection with any primary election or political convention or caucus held to select candidates for any political office, or for any corporation whatever, or any labor organization, *to make a contribution or expenditure in connection with any election* at which presidential and vice presidential electors or a Senator or Representative in, or a Delegate or Resident Commissioner to, Congress are to be voted for, or in connection with any primary election or political convention or caucus held to select candidates for any of the foregoing offices, or for any candidate, political committee, or other person knowingly to accept or receive any contribution prohibited in this section, or any officer or any director of any corporation or any national bank or any officer of any labor organization to consent to any contribution or expenditure by the corporation, national bank, or labor organization, as the case may be, prohibited by this section.

. . .

(2) For purposes of this section and section 791(h) of Title 15, *the term "contribution or expenditure" shall include* any direct or indirect payment, distribution, loan advance, deposit, or gift of money, or any services, or anything of value (except a loan of money by a national or state bank made in accordance with the applicable banking laws and regulations and in the ordinary course of business) *to any candidate, campaign committee, or political party or organization, in connection with any election* to any of the offices referred to in this section, but shall not include (A) communications by a corporation to its stockholders and executive or administrative personnel and their families or by a labor organization to its members and their families on any subject; (B) nonpartisan registration and get-out-the-vote campaigns by a corporation aimed at its stockholders and executive or administrative personnel and their families, or by a labor organization aimed at its members and their families; and (C) the establishment, administration, and solicitation of contributions to a separate segregated fund to be utilized for political purposes by a corporation, labor organization, membership organization, cooperative, or corporation without capital stock. (emphasis added)

This provision, which prohibits both "contributions" and "expenditures," had its origins in the Tillman Act of 1907,[5] which was aimed at preventing large corporations and national banks from making direct money contributions to the campaigns of candidates for federal election. The Tillman provision was enacted at the behest of President Theodore Roosevelt, whose Democratic opponent in 1904 was notoriously well financed by corporate contributions. During the 1890s, a number of states had also enacted prohibitions against corporate contributions or laws requiring such contributions to be made public. President Theodore Roosevelt, in his annual message to Congress on December 5, 1905, made this recommendation:

All contributions by corporations to any political committee or for any political purpose should be forbidden by law; directors should not be permitted to use their stockholders' money for such purposes; and moreover, a prohibition of this kind would be, as far as it went, an effective method of stopping the evils aimed at in corrupt practices acts. 40 Cong. Rec. 96

A joint committee—the Armstrong Committee—of the New York legislature under the guidance of Charles Evans Hughes reported in 1906 that one insurance company alone had contributed $50,000 to a national campaign committee in 1904 and had given substantial amounts in preceding presidential campaigns. The Armstrong Committee recommended that insurance company contributions be prohibited.[6]

As originally enacted, the Tillman Act provision prohibited only direct money contributions and did not purport to limit the ability of corporations to spend money to express their views on political issues, or even expressly to advocate the election or defeat of a particular candidate for federal elections. The Tillman Act was enacted by Congress based on its constitutional powers to regulate federal elections conferred by Article I, Section 4, and Article II, Section 1, of the Constitution, which authorize Congress to regulate "[t]he Times, Place and Manner of Holding Elections for Senators and Representatives" and "to determine the time of choosing the electors, and the day on which they shall give their votes" in connection with presidential elections. The Supreme Court had construed general congressional powers in this area of regulation in *United States v. Classic*, 313 U.S. 299 (1941); *Burroughs and Cannon v. United States*, 290 U.S. 534 (1934); *United States v. Mosley*, 238 U.S. 383 (1915); *Ex Parte Yarbrough*, 110 U.S. 651 (1884); *Ex Parte Siebold*, 100 U.S. 371 (1880).

The constitutionality of the Tillman Act's prohibition of corporate contributions was challenged, and the statute was upheld as early as 1916, *United States v. United States Brewers' Association*, 239 F. 163 (W.D. Pa. 1916).

One of the principal evils which the legislation was designed to curb was the corruption of the political process created when large corporate contributions to political campaigns were made to create a "debt" owed by the candidate to the corporations for their political sponsorship. During the hearings before the House Committee on the Election of the President, March 12, 1906, Representative Perry Belmont quoted a statement by the Secretary of State which identified the problem Congress intended to cure:

The idea is to prevent . . . the great railroad companies, the great insurance companies, the great telephone companies, the great aggregations of wealth from using their corporate funds, directly or indirectly, to send members of the legislature to these halls in order to vote for their protection and the advancement of their interests as against those of the public.

It strikes at a constantly growing evil which has done more to shake the confidence of the plain people of small means of this country in our political institutions than any other practice which has ever obtained since the foundation of our Government. And I believe that the time has come when something ought to be done to put a check to the giving of

$50,000 or $100,000 by a great corporation toward political purposes upon the understanding that a debt is created from a political party to it.

A proposal was made in 1909 to extend the application of the Tillman Act's prohibition on corporate contributions to political contributions by corporations, not only to federal elections, but also to elections of state legislatures, since at that time United States senators were elected by state legislatures. In support of that measure, Congressman Hardy stated the purpose and utility of the law:

The time has been reached when the great power in this Government may be money and not conscience, and I believe that it is as absolutely necessary to prevent the contribution by big corporations of money for the purpose of electing legislators who may elect Senators as it is to prevent the contribution of money by the State legislatures. I make the amendment with a view of purification of the ballot box. 42 Cong. Rec. 696

The basic federal prohibition of corporate political contributions contained in the Tillman Act was the subject of numerous amendments between 1907 and the present day.[7] The provision was incorporated in the Federal Corrupt Practices Act of 1925.[8] The provision was also extended and made applicable to labor union political contributions in 1943 by a provision of the War Labor Disputes Act.[9] The debates preceding passage of the 1925 act emphasized the purposes of the act. Senator Robinson stated:

We all know . . . that one of the great political evils of the time is the apparent hold on political parties which business interests and certain organizations seek and sometimes obtain by reason of liberal campaign contributions. Many believe that when an individual or association of individuals makes large contributions for the purpose of aiding candidates of political parties in winning the elections, they expect, and sometimes demand, and occasionally, at least, receive, consideration by the beneficiaries of their contributions which not infrequently is harmful to the general public interest. It is unquestionably an evil which ought to be dealt with and dealt with intelligently and effectively. 65 Cong. Rec. 9507–9508

During the hearings on the 1943 amendment, the desirability of a prohibition of political contributions by labor unions was emphasized because substantial contributions by labor organizations to campaigns of candidates for high office were thought to have given labor unions undue influence and control over successfully supported candidates.[10] A prohibition against labor union political contributions was passed over President Franklin F. Roosevelt's veto.

The key provision of the statute—the provision that prohibits corporate and labor union "expenditures" as well as "contributions," in connection with federal elections—was enacted by Congress as part of the Taft-Hartley Labor Management Relations Act of 1947.[11] This amendment also expanded the coverage of the statute to campaigns for nomination as well as for election. The history and meaning of the expenditure provision is the crucial question, because it is the expenditure provision of the law—which remains in effect today as 2 U.S.C. § 441b, quoted above—that acts as a significant potential legal restraint upon the use of general corporate treasury funds for the purpose of commenting favorably or adversely on the qualifications of candidates for federal office, or advocating the election or defeat of specific federal candidates. Since speech concerning the qualifications of candidates for federal office and the wisdom of the measures which they propose or with which they have associated themselves lies at the very core of the protection which the First Amendment was adopted to guarantee, 2 U.S.C. § 441b acts as a very significant restraint on corporate political speech that would be constitutionally protected if it were undertaken by an individual citizen.

The history of the expenditure provision is found in certain of the hearings which followed congressional elections in the 1940s. The full story is recounted in the Supreme Court's opinion in *United States v. United Auto Workers*, 352 U.S. 567, 577–583 (1957). Although lengthy, it is essential to an appreciation of what Congress did when it enacted the expenditure provision of this law. Justice Frankfurter described the introduction of the bill to control labor union and corporate expenditures in connection with federal elections and began by quoting Senator Bankhead's speech on the floor of the United States Senate:

In offering § 313 from the Senate floor Senator Bankhead said:

"We all know that money is the chief source of corruption. We all know that large contributions to political campaigns not only put the political party under obligation to the large contributors, who demand pay in the way of legislation, but we also know that large sums of money are used for the purpose of conducting expensive campaigns through the newspapers and over the radio; in the publication of all sorts of literature, true and untrue; and for the purpose of paying the expenses of campaigners sent out into the country to spread propaganda, both true and untrue." 86 Cong. Rec. 2720

The need for unprecedented economic mobilization propelled by World War II enormously stimulated the power of organized labor and soon aroused its ranks. Wartime strikes gave rise to fears of the new concentration of power represented by the gains of trade unionism. And so the belief grew that, just as the great corporations had made huge political contributions to influence governmental action or inaction, whether consciously or unconsciously, the powerful unions were pursuing a similar course, and with the same untoward consequences for the democratic process. Thus, in 1943, when Congress passed the Smith-Connally Act to secure defense production against work stoppages, contained therein was a provision extending to labor organizations, for the duration of the war, § 313 of the Corrupt Practices Act. 57 Stat. 163, 167.

The testimony of Congressman Landis, author of this measure, before a subcommittee of the House Committee on Labor makes plain the dominant concern that evoked it:

"The fact that a hearing has been granted is a high tribute to the ability of the Labor Committee to recognize the fact that public opinion toward the conduct of labor unions is rapidly undergoing a change. The public thinks, and has a right to think, that labor unions, as public institutions, should be granted the same rights and no greater rights than any other public group. My bill seeks to put labor unions on exactly the same basis, insofar as their financial activities are concerned, as corporations have been on for many years.

. . .

"One of the matters upon which I sensed that the public was taking a stand opposite to that of labor leaders was the question of the handling of funds of labor organizations. The public was aroused by many rumors of huge war chests being maintained by labor unions, of enormous fees and dues being extorted from war workers, of political contributions to parties and candidates which later were held as clubs over the head of high Federal officials.

. . .

"The source of much of the national trouble today in the coal strike situation is that ill-advised political contribution of another day [referring, apparently, to the reported contribution of over $400,000 by the United Mine Workers in the 1936 campaign, *see* S. Rep. No. 151, 75th Cong., 1st Sess.]. If the provision of my bill against such an activity has [*sic*] been in force when that contribution was made, the Nation, the administration, and the labor unions would be better off." Hearings before a Subcommittee of the House Committee on Labor on HR 804 and HR 1483, 78th Cong., 1st Sess. 1, 2, 4 (352 U.S. at 577–579)

Justice Frankfurter continued:

Despite § 313's wartime application to labor organizations Congress was advised of enormous financial outlays said to have been made by some unions in connection with the national elections of 1944. The Senate's Special Committee on Campaign Expenditures investigated, *inter alia*, the role of the Political Action Committee of the Congress of Industrial Organizations. The Committee found "no clear-cut violation of the Corrupt Practices Act on the part of the Political Action Committee" on the ground that it had made direct contributions only to candidates and political committees involved in state and local elections and federal primaries, to which the Act did not apply, and had limited its participation in federal elections to political "expenditures," as distinguished from "contributions" to candidates or committees. S. Rep. No. 101, 79th Cong., 1st Sess. 23. The Committee also investigated, on complaint of Senator Taft, the Ohio C.I.O. Council's distribution to the public at large of 200,000 copies of a pamphlet opposing the re-election of Senator Taft and supporting his rival. In response to the C.I.O.'s assertion that this was not a proscribed "contribution" but merely an "expenditure of its own funds to state its position to the world, exercising its right of free speech . . . ," the Committee requested the Department of Justice to bring a test case on these facts. *Id.* at 59. It also recommended extension of § 313 to cover primary campaigns and monitoring conventions. *Id.* at 81. A minority of the Committee, Senators Ball and Ferguson, advocated further amendment of § 313 to proscribe "expenditures" as well as "contributions" in order to avoid the possibility of emasculation of the statutory policy through a narrow judicial construction of "contributions." *Id.* at 83. (*Id.* at 579–580)

Justice Frankfurter also pointed to a 1945 report:

The 1945 Report of the House Special Committee to Investigate Campaign Expenditures expressed concern over the vast amounts that some labor organizations were devoting to politics:

"The scale of operations of some of these organizations is impressive. Without exception, they operate on a Nation-wide basis; and many of them have affiliated local organizations. One was found to have an annual budget for 'educational' work approximating $1,500,000, and among other things regularly supplies over 500 radio stations with 'briefs for broadcasters.' Another, with an annual budget of over $300,000 for political 'education,' has distributed some 80,000,000 pieces of literature, including a quarter million copies of one article. Another representing an organized labor membership of 5,000,000 has raised $700,000 for its national organizations in union contributions for political 'education' in a few months, and a great deal more has been raised for the same purpose and expended by its local organizations." HR Rep. No. 2093, 78th Cong., 2d Sess. 3 (*Id.* at 580–581)

Justice Frankfurter wrote:

Like the Senate Committee, it advocated extension of § 313 to primaries and nominating conventions, *Id.* at 9, and noted the existence of a controversy over the scope of "contribution." *Id.* at 11. The following year the House Committee made a further study of the activities of organizations attempting to influence the outcome of federal elections. It found that the Brotherhood of Railway Trainmen and other groups employed professional political organizers, sponsored partisan radio programs and distributed campaign literature. HR Rep. No. 2739, 79th Cong., Sess. 36, 37. It concluded that:

"The intent and purpose of the provision of the act prohibiting any corporation or labor organization making any contribution in connection with any election would be wholly defeated if it were assumed that the term 'making any contribution' related only to the donating of money directly to a candidate, and excluded the vast expenditures of money in the activities herein shown to be engaged in extensively. Of what avail would a law be to prohibit the contributing direct to a candidate and yet permit the expenditure of large sums in his behalf?

"Accordingly, to prevent further evasion of the statutory policy, the Committee attached to its recommendation that the prohibition of contributions by labor organizations be made permanent the additional proposal that the statute 'be clarified so as to specifically provide that expenditures of money for salaries to organizers, purchase of radio time, and other expenditures by the prohibited organizations in connection with elections, constitute violations of the provisions of said section, whether or not said expenditures are with or without the knowledge or consent of the candidates.' "
Id. at 46. *Id.* at 581–582 (italics omitted)

Justice Frankfurter described the 1947 investigation of the senatorial campaigns:

Early in 1947 the Special Committee to Investigate Senatorial Campaign Expenditures in the 1946 elections, the Ellender Committee, urged similar action to "plug the existing loophole," S. Rep. No. 1, Part 2, 80th Cong., 1st Sess. 38–39, and Senator Ellender introduced a bill to that effect.

Shortly thereafter, Congress again acted to protect the political process from what it deemed to be the corroding effect of money employed in elections by aggregated power. *Section 304 of the labor bill introduced into the House by Respresentative Hartley in 1947, like the Ellender bill, embodied the changes recommended in the reports of the Senate and House Committees on Campaign Expenditures. It sought to amend § 313 of the Corrupt Practices Act to proscribe any "expenditure" as well as "any contribution," to make permanent § 313's application to labor organizations and to extend its coverage to federal primaries and nominating conventions.* The Report of the House Committee on Education and Labor, which considered and approved the Hartley bill, merely summarized § 304, HR Rep. No. 245, 80th Cong., 1st Sess. 46, and this section gave rise to little debate in the House. *See* 93 Cong. Rec. 3428, 3522. Because no similar measure was in the labor bill introduced by Senator Taft, the Senate as a whole did not consider the provisions of § 304 until they had been adopted by the Conference Committee. In explaining § 304 to his colleagues, Senator Taft, who was one of the conferees, said:

> "I may say that the amendment is in exactly the same words which were recommended by the Ellender committee, which investigated expenditures by Senators in the last election. . . . In this instance the words of the Smith-Connally Act have been somewhat changed in effect so as to plug up a loophole which obviously developed, and which, if the courts had permitted advantage to be taken of it, as a matter of fact, would absolutely have destroyed the prohibition against political advertising by corporations. If 'contribution' does not mean 'expenditure,' then a candidate for office could have his corporation friends publish an advertisement for him in the newspapers everyday for a month before election. I do not think the law contemplated such a thing, but it was claimed that it did, at least when it applied to labor organizations. So, all we are doing here is plugging up the hole which developed, following the recommendation by our own Elections committee, in the Ellender bill." 93 Cong. Rec. 6439.

After considerable debate, the conference version was approved by the Senate, and the bill subsequently became law despite the President's veto. 352 U.S. at 382–383 (emphasis added)

Justice Frankfurter's account of the purposes and the history of the federal restriction on corporate expenditures in connection with an election is the accepted account of this development.

UNITED STATES v. CIO—CONSTITUTIONAL CHALLENGE TO THE EXPENDITURE PROVISION

In order to plug a loophole in the previous statutory provision, therefore, Congress enacted a specific prohibition against expenditures (as well as contributions) by corporations and labor unions that were designed to influence the outcome of federal elections.

The Congress of Industrial Organizations reacted almost immediately to the enactment of the law by bringing a test case to challenge the constitutionality of this restriction on expenditures to comment on the qualifications of candidates for federal office. The CIO placed an article in its weekly house publication called the *CIO News*, which was financed by the CIO. The page one article carried a statement by the president of the CIO urging all members of the CIO to vote for a congressional candidate in Maryland at a special election to be held July 15, 1947. The statement also referred specifically to the prohibition contained in the recently enacted federal statute but said that the CIO's published endorsement of the candidate was carried at CIO expense in spite of the statute and with the conviction that the expenditure provision of the statute was unconstitutional. The union and its president were indicted in the District of Columbia and moved to dismiss the indictment on the ground that the statute was unconstitutional on its face and as applied to the union's expenditure for the article appearing in the *CIO News*. The district court dismissed the indictment, holding that the statute was unconstitutional.

The Supreme Court accepted the government's direct appeal and unanimously affirmed the dismissal of the indictment. The Supreme Court majority, however, avoided the constitutional questions and held instead that the indictment simply did not state an offense under the act, *United States v. CIO*, 335 U.S. 106 (1948). According to the majority, the purposes of the original enactment were (1) to destroy the influence over elections which corporations exercised through financial contributions, and (2) to prevent the use of corporate shareholders' money for contributions to political parties without their consent. The Court found in the Senate debates concerning the expenditure provision of the law "definite indication that Congress did not intend to include within the coverage of the section as an expenditure the costs of the publication described in the indictment." In particular, the majority relied upon a colloquy in the Senate debates between senators Taft and Barkley to the effect that the expenses involved in "the publication of a corporation which, day after day, takes a position against one candidate and in favor of another candidate" in its editorials were not intended to constitute expenditures within the meaning of the act, 335 U.S. at 116–117. This specific example was followed in the legislative debates by another pertinent example, given by a congressman to Senator Taft, by way of elucidating the meaning of the new expenditure prohibition:

Let us suppose a labor organization publishes a newspaper for the information and benefit of its members, and let us suppose that it is published regularly, whether daily or weekly or monthly, and is paid for from a fund created by the payment of dues into the organization it represents. Let us assume that the newspaper is not sold on the streets, and let us assume further that a certain subscription by the month or by the year is not charged for the newspaper. Does the Senator from Ohio advise us that under this measure such a newspaper could not take a position with respect to any candidate for public office without violating this measure? 335 U.S. at 117–118

Senator Taft answered that such a publication would violate the act, at least if the newspaper was prepared and distributed and circulated by means of the expenditure of union funds. But this example was sharpened to center on the actual practice of labor union in-house publications for distribution to members. One senator asked:

In the case of most union papers, as I understand, the subscriptions from the union members are collected along with the dues, but they are an earmarked portion of the dues which the union collects and remits to the paper in the form of subscriptions. I take it that would be in a different category from the case where the union makes a blanket subscription and an appropriation out of union dues. 335 U.S. quoted at 118

Senator Taft acknowledged that such a newspaper, if already a going concern, could lawfully do so. The Supreme Court majority concluded from this excerpt from the legislative debates or from other considerations, that the statute did not even apply to the *CIO News*, and the majority noted that it was bound to construe the statute "to avoid a danger of unconstitutionality," 335 U.S. at 120–121. In a highly significant and historically important passage, the *CIO* majority said:

If § 313 were construed to prohibit the publication, by corporations and unions in the regular course of conducting their affairs, of periodicals advising their members, stockholders or customers of danger or advantage to their interests from the adoption of measures or the election to office of men, espousing such measures, *the gravest doubt would arise in our minds as to its constitutionality. Id.* at 121 (emphasis added)

The statements in the legislative debate pointing to a narrower meaning, in addition to the principle of statutory construction favoring interpretations of statutes that avoid constitutional problems, motivated the Court to hold that the statute, properly construed, did *not* apply to the editorial in the *CIO News* and that the indictment, therefore, did not state an offense and should be dismissed.

The balance of the majority opinion contains a number of very important statements, which played an important role in future legislative enactment in this area:

It is one thing to say that trade or labor union periodicals published regularly for members, stockholders or purchasers are allowable under § 313 and quite another to say that in connection with an election occasional pamphlets or dodgers or free copies widely scattered are forbidden.

. . .

We express no opinion as to the scope of this section where different circumstances exist and none upon the constitutionality of the section. 335 at 122–124

The *CIO* majority, in dictum, therefore carved out several important categories of communications by corporations and labor unions—categories to which the statute, if applied, would pose grave constitutional questions—communications to (1) "stockholders," (2) "members," and (3) "customers" or "purchasers." Some of these categories have remained important exceptions in later amendments to the federal election campaign laws. Thus, expenditures for certain communications by labor unions to their members, and certain communications to stockholders and employees are specifically made exempt from the act, 2 U.S.C. § 441b, quoted above.

Curiously, however, Congress failed in later attempts to codify the Supreme Court's statements in *CIO* explicitly to exempt expenditures for communications with customers, notwithstanding the fact that the Supreme Court had specifically referred to that category of communications.

In an eloquent, separate concurring opinion, Justice Rutledge, joined by Justices Black, Douglas, and Murphy, explained why they believed the expenditure provision to be unconstitutional. To those members of the Court, the majority had so interpreted the statute that the facts critical to the applicability of the statute were whether others than union members receive free copies of the publication and whether the publication is "in regular course" or only in casual and occasional distributions, and, in the latter case, even circulation limited to the membership would fall within the prohibition. According to the concurring justices, the crucial statutory words are "expenditure" and "in connection with"; and these terms were so comprehensive in scope that the provision was unconstitutional.

From the congressional debates' "veritable fog of contradictions relating to specific possible applications," Justice Rutledge wrote that three principal objectives could be discerned: (1) to reduce what had come to be regarded in the light of recent experience as the undue influence of labor unions upon federal elections (the "undue influence" rationale); (2) to preserve the purity of such elections and of official conduct ensuing from the choices made in them against the use of aggregated wealth by union as well as corporate entities (the "purity of elections" rationale); and (3) to protect union members holding political views contrary to those supported by the union from use of funds contributed by them to promote acceptance of those opposing views (the "minority protection" rationale). Justice Rutledge's concurring opinion analyzed the legitimacy of each of these purposes, and the following lengthy passage has become part of the essential background for understanding the federal election laws. First, Justice Rutledge examined the "undue influence" rationale:

If the evil is taken to be the corruption of national elections and federal officials by the expenditure of large masses of aggregated wealth in their behalf, the statute is neither so phrased nor so limited, even in its legislative construction. Indeed the Government does not explicitly argue corruption *per se* arising from union expenditures for publication in the same sense as gave rise to the original and later legislation against corporate contributions down to the War Labor Disputes Act of 1943. And very little in the legislative history directly suggests this evil, although there are inferences implicit in some statements that it was not entirely out of mind. So also with the Government's argument.

The Government stresses the "undue influence" of unions in making expenditures by way of publication in support of or against candidates and political issues involved in the campaign rather than corruption in the gross sense. It maintains that large expenditures

by unions in publicizing their official political views bring about an undue, that is sup-
posedly a disproportionate, sway of electoral sentiment and official attitudes. In short,
the ''bloc'' power of unions has become too great, in influencing both the electorate and
public officials, to permit further expenditure of their funds in directly and openly publicizing their political views. And the asserted evil is to be uprooted by prohibition of
union expenditures as such, not by regulation specifically drawn to meet it.

There are, of course, obvious differences between such evils and those arising from
the grosser forms of assistance more usually associated with secrecy, bribery and corruption, direct or subtle. But it is not necessary to stop to point these out or discuss them,
except to say that any asserted beneficial tendency of restrictions upon expenditures for
publicizing political views, whether of a group or of an individual, is certainly counter-
balanced to some extent by the loss for democratic processes resulting from the restrictions
upon free and full public discussion. The claimed evil is not one unmixed with good.
And its suppression destroys the good with the bad unless precise measures are taken to
prevent this.

The expression of bloc sentiment is and always has been an integral part of our
democratic electoral and legislative processes. They could hardly go on without it. Moreover, to an extent not necessary now to attempt delimiting, that right is secured by the
guaranty of freedom of assembly, a liberty essentially coordinate with the freedoms of
speech, the press, and conscience. *Cf. Bowe v. Secretary of Commonwealth*, 320 Mass.
230, 251, 252, 69 N.E.2d 115, 167 A.L.R. 1447. It is not by accident, it is by explicit
design, as was said in *Thomas v. Collins, supra*, 323 U.S. at 530, 89 L.Ed. 440, 65 S.
Ct. 315, that these freedoms are coupled together in the First Amendment's assurance.
They involve the right to hear as well as to speak, and any restriction upon either attenuates
both.

There is therefore an effect in restricting expenditures for the publicizing of political
views not inherently present in restricting other types of expenditure, namely, that it
necessarily deprives the electorate, the persons entitled to hear, as well as the author of
the utterance, whether an individual or a group, of the advantage of free and full discussion
and of the right of free assembly for the purpose. 335 at 142–144

Justice Rutledge pointed out the central role of political speech in democratic
government:

The most complete exercise of those rights is essential to the full, fair and untrammeled
operation of the electoral process. To the extent they are curtailed the electorate is deprived
of information, knowledge and opinion vital to its function. To say that labor unions as
such have nothing of value to contribute to that process and no vital or legitimate interest
in it is to ignore the obvious facts of political and economic life and of their increasing
interrelationship in modern society. *Cf. DeMille v. American Federation of Radio Artists*,
31 Cal.2d 139, 187 P.2d 769. That ostrichlike conception, if enforced by law, would
deny those values both to unions and thus to that extent to their members, as also to the
voting public in general. To compare restrictions necessarily resulting in this loss for the
public good to others not creating it is to identify essentially different things. The cases
are not identical. The loss inherent in restrictions upon expenditures for publicizing views
is not necessarily involved in other expenditures. *Id.* at 144

The concurring justices questioned especially the flat prohibition on expenditures:

If therefore it is an evil for organized groups to have unrestricted freedom to make expenditures for directly and openly publicizing their political views and information supporting them, but *cf. Bowe v. Secretary of Commonwealth, supra*, 320 Mass. at 252, 69 N.E.2d at page 130, 167 A.L.R. 1447, it does not follow that it is one which requires complete prohibition of the right. *Ibid.* That is neither consistent with the Amendment's spirit and purpose, *ibid.*, nor essential to correction of the evil, whether it be considered corruptive influence or merely influence of undue or disproportionate political weight. *Id.* at 145

Justice Rutledge exposed the fallacy of the "undue influence" rationale:

It is not necessary now to consider whether restricting the rights of individuals, singly or in organized relationships, to publicize their political views, rights often essential to their survival and always to their well being, can be accommodated, in some instances, with the Amendment's purpose or justified because in legislative judgment those persons unless restricted acquire "undue influence" in the electoral process. For "undue influence" in this connection may represent no more than convincing weight of argument fully presented, which is the very thing the Amendment and the electoral process it protects were intended to bring out. And one may question how far legislators may go in accurately assessing undue or disproportionate weight as distinguished from making substantially accurate findings and conclusions concerning corruption.

But even if the right to sway others by persuasion is assumed to be subject to some curtailment, in the interest of preventing grossly unbalanced presentations, that right cannot be wholly denied, *Bowe v. Secretary of Commonwealth, supra*, 320 Mass. at 252, 69 N.E.2d at page 130, 167 A.L.R. 1447; nor can it be restricted beyond what is reasonably and clearly necessary to correct an evil so gross and immediate that the correction indubitably outweighs the loss to the public interest resulting from the restriction.

Here the restriction in practical effect is prohibition, not regulation, when it is considered with respect to the objects of suppressing corruption and "undue influence." It is not a limitation, it is a prohibition upon expenditure of union funds in connection with a federal election. Unions can act and speak today only by spending money, as indeed is true of nearly every organization and even of individuals if their action is to be effective. As was said in the course of the Senate debates, the interdiction applies to "a dollar, or 50 cents, or $500 or $1,000." 93 Cong. Rec. 6438. There is no showing, legislative or otherwise, of corruption so widespread or of "undue influence" so dominating as could possibly justify so absolute a denial of these basic rights. The statute, whether in terms or as given meaning by the legislative history, is not narrowly drawn to meet the precise evils of corruption or "undue influence," if these were the controlling objects of the legislation. 335 U.S. at 145–146

Justice Rutledge's logic also dispatched the "minority protection" rationale, which the government offered in defense of the statutory provision:

As has been stated, it was the "minority protection" idea which became the dominantly stressed one in the Senate debates, although at the most § 313 on its face gave only slight suggestion of this purpose. Nor was there indication in the section's terms that its prohibition turns on the source from which the funds expended were derived. The language bearing on this was "expenditure in connection with an election" and no more. Literally all union expenditures in that connection were outlawed. There is not a word to suggest that unions could spend their funds in that manner if contributed expressly for the purpose or derived from such sources as advertising revenues, subscriptions, etc., received in connection with publication of a paper in regular course or otherwise. The limitation of the prohibition to funds received generally, *i.e.*, without specific designation for use in political publicity, is almost wholly a construction of the Senate sponsor, so far as appears from the legislative history.

Notwithstanding accepted canons of statutory construction, it certainly would be going far to expect laymen, or even lawyers, to read a statute so lacking in specificity concerning its basic criterion with any semblance of understanding of its limitations.

The lawyer might indeed read the Congressional Record and conclude that the source of the funds used was the crux. But even he would be left in broad and deep doubt whether it would turn multitudinous situations one way or the other. If the section is taken nevertheless to have been intended to draw the sponsor's line of distinction, the restriction it makes remains a drastic one. The effect is not merely one of minority protection. It is also one of majority prohibition. *Cf. DeMille v. American Federation of Radio Artists*, 31 Cal.2d 139, 187 P.2d 769, *supra*. Under the section as construed, the accepted principle of majority rule which has become a bulwark, indeed perhaps the leading characteristic, of collective activities is rejected in favor of atomized individual rule and action in matters of political advocacy. *Ibid*. Union activities in political publicity are confined to the use of funds received from members with their explicit designation given in advance for the purpose. Funds so received from members can be thus expended and no others. Even if all or the large majority of the members had paid dues with the general understanding that they or portions of them would be so used, but had not given explicit authorization, the funds could not be so employed. And this would be true even if all or the large majority were in complete sympathy with the political views expressed by the union or on its behalf with any expenditure of money, however small.

. . .

The section does not merely deprive the union of the principle of majority rule in political expression. *Cf. DeMille v. American Federation of Radio Artists*, *supra*. It rests upon the presumption that the majority are out of accord with their elected officials in political viewpoint and its expression and, where that presumption is not applicable, it casts the burden of ascertaining minority or individual dissent not upon the dissenters but upon the union and its officials. The former situation may arise, indeed in one notable instance has done so. But that instance hardly can be taken to be a normal or usual case. Unions too most often operate under the electoral process and the principle of majority rule. Nor in the latter situation does it seem reasonable to presume dissent from mere absence of explicit assent, especially in view of long-established union practice. 335 U.S. at 146–149

Justice Rutledge's conclusion was this:

A statute which, in the claimed interest of free and honest elections, curtails the very freedoms that make possible exercise of the franchise by an informed and thinking electorate, and does this by indiscriminate blanketing of every expenditure made in connection with an election, serving as a prior restraint upon expression not in fact forbidden as well as upon what is, cannot be squared with the First Amendment. *Id*. at 155

The expenditure provision thus escaped being struck down as unconstitutional by the Supreme Court in *CIO* by only one vote. Its constitutionality was tested in the labor union context described in the following sections.

UNITED STATES v. UAW—THE CONSTITUTIONALITY OF THE EXPENDITURE PROVISION AS APPLIED TO PAID POLITICAL ADVERTISING REGARDING CANDIDATES BROADCAST TO THE PUBLIC AT LARGE

The constitutionality of the expenditure provision was tested again in 1957 in *United States v. UAW*, 352 U.S. 567 (1957), which arose out of the indictment of a labor union for using general treasury funds to broadcast over public television station WJBK, Detroit, a paid political advertisement which urged and endorsed selection of certain persons to be candidates for representative and senator to the United States Congress and "included expressions of political advocacy intended by defendant to influence the electorate and to affect the results of the election," 352 U.S. at 584.

The union contended that the statute did not apply to these facts and that, if it did, it was unconstitutional. The district court dismissed the indictment. On appeal by the government, the Supreme Court reversed and reinstated the indictment, by a vote of six to three. The majority declined to decide the constitutional question presented because no factual record had yet been made and opted to address the important constitutional questions involved only after a trial.

According to the majority, the crucial questions of applicability of the expenditure provision were (1) whether the broadcast reached the public at large or only those affiliated with the union, and (2) whether the broadcast constituted "active electioneering" or simply stated "the record of particular candidates on economic issues," 352 U.S. at 592. According to Justice Frankfurter's majority opinion, "The evil at which Congress has struck in § 313 is the use of corporation or union funds to influence the public at-large to vote for a particular candidate or a particular party," 352 U.S. at 589.

Justices Douglas and Black and Chief Justice Warren dissented and, in an opinion by Justice Douglas, again stated their view that the expenditure provision was unconstitutional. Justice Douglas wrote:

We deal here with a problem that is fundamental to the electoral process and to the operation of our democratic society. It is whether a union can express its views on the issues of an election and on the merits of the candidates, unrestrained and unfettered by the Congress. The principle at stake is not peculiar to unions. It is applicable as well to *associations of manufacturers*, retail and wholesale trade groups, consumers' leagues, farmers' unions, religious groups and every other association representing a segment of American life and taking an active part in our political campaigns and discussions. It is as important an issue as has come before the Court, for it reaches the very vitals of our system of government. 352 U.S. at 593 (Emphasis added.)

Justice Douglas's dissenting opinion contains a strong defense of First Amendment rights in the context of advocacy of candidates in federal elections and debate concerning their qualifications and repeats many of the considerations governing the constitutionality of the statute that were aired in *United States v. CIO*. Justice Douglas wrote:

The Act, as construed and applied, is a broadside assault on the freedom of political expression guaranteed by the First Amendment. It cannot possibly be saved by any of the facts conjured up by the Court. The answers to the questions reserved are quite irrelevant to the constitutional questions tendered under the First Amendment. (emphasis added)

The majority's decision in *UAW* kept the constitutional issues open and un-resolved. The Court's opinion is also important because it contains the germ of the "active electioneering" standard for violation of the statute which later became the prevailing judicial interpretation of the expenditure provision.

THE "ACTIVE ELECTIONEERING" STANDARD

After *United States v. UAW, supra*, the lower federal courts faced the issue of statutory construction of the expenditure provision in several cases and applied the "active electioneering" test implied in the Supreme Court majority decision in *UAW*. The term "active electioneering" appears to have been borrowed by Justice Frankfurter from page 51 of the government's brief in *United States v. UAW*, where the government had contended: "It is only when the union un-dertakes active electioneering, on behalf of particular federal candidates and designed to reach the public at large" that the expenditure prohibition is violated. On the basis of the language in the majority opinion in that case suggesting the constitutional relevance of the concept of active electioneering, the lower courts employed a test for determining the legality of expenditures for advertising under § 610, with the aim of avoiding serious constitutional problems. Under these cases construing the expenditure provision of § 610, only expenditures for ad-vertising in the nature of active electioneering are deemed illegal under § 610.

Thus, applying the active electioneering test, in *United States v. Lewis Food Company*, 236 F.Supp. 849 (S.D. Cal. 1964), the district court dismissed an indictment under what was then codified as 18 U.S.C. § 610 which charged that the defendant corporation had made expenditures totalling $9,523.68 to publish an advertisement entitled "Important Notice to Voters" in at least fourteen newspapers. The advertisement in question listed by name two United States Senators, thirty members of the House of Representatives, forty California State Senators, and eighty California State Assemblymen. Next to each legislator's name appeared a "rating" expressed as a percentage, which the text of the advertisement explained showed "the percentage of his votes cast in favor of constitutional principles." The advertisement stated that "100% is perfect." Twenty-eight legislators identified as Democrats received scores of zero. No legislator identified as a Republican received a score of zero.

The Supreme Court remanded the government's appeal of the dismissal of the indictment to the court of appeals for the Ninth Circuit, 381 U.S. 908 (1965). Although reversal followed, in the court of appeals, *United States v. Lewis Food Company*, 366 F.2d 710 (9th Cir. 1966), the government conceded, and the court of appeals held, that an expenditure for advertising does not fall within the purview of § 610 unless the advertisement is in the nature of "active electioneering," 366 F.2d at 712.

The active electioneering test was also applied in *United States v. Anchorage Central Labor Council*, 193 F.Supp. 504 (D. Alaska, 1961), where it was held that no offense was stated under 18 U.S.C. § 610 by an indictment charging that the defendants made expenditures for four fifteen-minute television broadcasts, intended to reach the general public, which "criticized the fitness of three of the candidates for Senator and Representative upon their 'record,' " *cf. also, United States v. National Committee for Impeachment*, 469 F.2d 1135 (2d Cir. 1972); *Schwartz v. Romnes*, 495 F.2d 844 (2d Cir. 1974).

CORT v. ASH

The Supreme Court once again had an opportunity to address the statutory construction issue as well as the constitutional issues surrounding what was then 18 U.S.C. § 610 and is now codified as 2 U.S.C. § 441b, when it granted certiorari in *Cort v. Ash*, 422 U.S. 66 (1975), a stockholder suit against directors of a corporation that had published a paid editorial advertisement in a number of newspapers and magazines. The Supreme Court reached only the question whether a private right of action against the corporation existed under this federal criminal provision and therefore did not decide either the constitutional questions or the questions concerning statutory construction.

A stockholder's action was filed against Bethlehem Steel Corporation and its directors in the United States District Court for the Eastern District of Pennsylvania on September 28, 1972, on the eve of the 1972 Presidential election. The original complaint alleged that the directors of Bethlehem had authorized an expenditure for an advertisement and charged that such expenditure was in violation of 18 U.S.C. § 610, as amended by the FECA, P.L. 92–225, 86 Stat. 3. Count II of the original complaint charged that the expenditure was *ultra vires* and illegal under Delaware law. The complaint sought injunctive relief, including an order that defendants place "corrective advertising at their own expense in national media," and compensatory and punitive damages in favor of Bethlehem, together with costs.

The district court denied the plaintiff's application for a temporary restraining order on October 13, 1972. The stockholder's motion for a preliminary injunction was also denied, *Ash v. Cort* 350 F.Supp. 227 (E.D. Pa. 1972).

The stockholder appealed this ruling to the court of appeals for the Third Circuit which, after oral argument, affirmed, *per curiam*, the order of the district court denying his motion for a preliminary injunction, *Ash v. Cort*, 471 F.2d 811 (3d Cir. 1973). Bethlehem thereafter moved in the district court to require the posting of a bond for security for expenses, and the district court entered an order granting the motion for security for expenses with regard to the cause of action under Delaware law, alone, directing plaintiff to post a bond as security for expenses. At the same time, however, the district court granted the stockholder leave to amend the complaint by eliminating the claim under Delaware law set forth in Count II of the complaint, which the stockholder did. Bethlehem thereafter moved for summary judgment on the federal claim in Count I based on 18 U.S.C. § 610, on the grounds that a stockholder has no private right of action for alleged violations of 18 U.S.C. § 610, that § 610 was inapplicable to the advertising in question, and that, if held to be applicable, § 610 is unconstitutional as applied.

The district court granted the motion for summary judgment against the stockholder. A divided panel of the court of appeals for the Third Circuit reversed the judgment of the district court. The court of appeals held, in an opinion expressing the views of only two judges of the panel, that a registered voter or a stockholder has an "implied" private right of action under § 610 notwithstanding congressional silence on the question in the legislative debates and committee reports. Notwithstanding the unanimous affirmance of dismissal of the indictment in *United States v. CIO, supra*, where four justices had stated that this provision "cannot be squared with the First Amendment," 335 U.S. at 155, and the views of three Supreme Court justices in *United States v. United Auto Workers, supra*, that § 610 is a "broadside assault on the freedom of political expression guaranteed by the First Amendment," 352 U.S. at 598, the majority held that an expenditure by a corporation or a labor union for advertising which did not mention the name of any political party or the name of any candidate for election to federal office may nevertheless fall within the scope of § 610, 496 F.2d 416 (1974). The majority declined to reach the constitutional issues presented. The Supreme Court reversed on the implied private right of action ground, and the case was dismissed, without reaching the constitutional questions presented.

Cort v. Ash accordingly stands for the important principle that there is no private right of action by a stockholder against a corporation or its directors under 18 U.S.C. § 610, or what is now 2 U.S.C. § 441b.

BUCKLEY v. VALEO AND THE FEDERAL ELECTION CAMPAIGN ACT OF 1971, AS AMENDED

The Federal Election Campaign Act (FECA) of 1971 and the several amendments to that act during and in the aftermath of the Watergate era of the 1970s constituted the first comprehensive federal legislation dealing with election campaign financing since the enactment of the Federal Corrupt Practices Act of 1925. In broad terms, the FECA contained the following provisions: (1) individual political contributions were limited to $1,000 to any single candidate per election, with an overall annual limitation of $25,000 by any contributor; independent expenditures by individuals and groups "relative to a clearly identified candidate" were limited to $1,000 a year; campaign spending by candidates for various federal offices and spending for national conventions by political parties were subject to prescribed limits; (2) contributions and expenditures above certain threshold levels were required to be reported and publicly disclosed; (3) a system for public funding of Presidential campaign activities was established; and (4) a Federal Election Commission (FEC) was established to administer and enforce the act.

The original prohibition of corporate expenditures (as well as contributions) in connection with federal elections was incorporated in the FECA with certain amendments and new definitions which are not significant here. The term "expenditure" as used in the FECA was defined generally to include

(i) any purchase, payment, distribution, loan, advance, deposit, or gift of money or anything of value, *made by any person for the purpose of influencing any election for federal office*; and

(ii) a written contract, promise, or agreement to make an expenditure. (Emphasis added.)

The act, however, specifically provides that the term "expenditure" does not include

(i) any news story, commentary or editorial distributed through the facilities of any broadcasting station, newspaper, magazine or other periodical, publication, unless such facilities are owned or controlled by any political party, political committee, or candidate;

(ii) nonpartisan activity designed to encourage individuals to vote or to register to vote;

The definition of "expenditure" as used in the FECA also specifically excludes certain of the expenditures to which the Supreme Court majority in the *CIO* case had commented that prohibition would raise "the gravest doubt . . . as to its constitutionality." These exemptions included communications by a corporation to its stockholders and executive or administrative personnel:

(iii) any *communication* by any membership organization or corporation to its members, *stockholders, or executive or administrative personnel*, if such membership organization or corporation is not organized primarily for the purpose of influencing the nomination for election, or election, of any individual to Federal office, except that the costs incurred by a membership organization (including a labor organization) or by a corporation directly attributable to a communication expressly advocating the election or defeat of a clearly identified candidate (other than a communication primarily devoted to subjects other than the express advocacy of the election or defeat of a clearly identified candidate), shall, if such costs exceed $2000 for any election, be reported to the Commission in accordance with section 304(a)(4)(A)(i), and in accordance with section 304(a)(4)(A)(ii) with respect to any general election. (emphasis added)

The issues in *Buckley v. Valeo* included the constititonality of (1) limitations on campaign expenditures by individuals, by candidates (of their own money) and in a political campaign; (2) limitations on the amounts of contributions; (3) reporting requirements; (4) the provisions of the FECA relating to federal financing of national political conventions, presidential primary campaigns, and presidential election campaigns; and (5) the composition of the Federal Election Commission. *Buckley v. Valeo* did not present directly the question of the constitutionality of the prohibition of corporate and labor union expenditures to finance speech and publication to advocate the election or defeat of a specifically identified candidate for federal office. Nonetheless, the Supreme Court's decision in *Buckley v. Valeo* touches on issues which lie at the core of that question. Thus, the Supreme Court's opinion in *Buckley v. Valeo* reaffirmed a number of basic premises of relevant First Amendment jurisprudence. At the heart of the discussion is the ''Meiklejohnian'' conception of the First Amendment as protecting the rights of citizens to *receive* uncensored information and viewpoints from all sources concerning the qualifications of political candidates and the wisdom of specific governmental policies. The Supreme Court wrote the following in *Buckley v. Valeo*:

The Act's contribution and expenditure limitations operate in an area of the most fundamental First Amendment activities. *Discussion of public issues and debates on the qualifications of candidates are integral to the operation of the system of government established by our Constitution.* The First Amendment affords the broadest protection to such political expression in order ''to assure the unfettered interchange of ideas for the bringing about of political and social changes desired by the people.'' *Roth v. United States*, 354 U.S. 476, 484 (1957). Although First Amendment protections are not confined to ''the exposition of ideas,'' *Winters v. New York*, 333 U.S. 507, 510 (1948), ''there is practically universal agreement that a major purpose of th[e] Amendment was to protect the free discussion of governmental affairs, . . . of course includ[ing] discussions of candidates. . . .'' *Mills v. Alabama*, 384 U.S. 214, 218 (1966). This no more than reflects our ''profound national commitment to the principle that debate on public issues should be uninhibited, robust, and wide-open,'' *New York Times Co. v. Sullivan*, 376 U.S. 254, 270 (1964). In a republic where the people are sovereign, *the ability of the citizenry to make informed choices among candidates for office is essential*, for the identities of those who are elected will inevitably shape the course that we follow as a nation. As the Court observed in *Monitor Patriot Co. v. Roy*, 401 U.S. 265, 272 (1971), ''*it can hardly be doubted that the constitutional guarantee has its fullest and most urgent application precisely to the conduct of campaigns for political office.*'' (emphasis added)(424 U.S. at 14)

On the basis of these premises, the Supreme Court invalidated certain of the FECA's provisions restricting expenditures in connection with federal elections. The Court reasoned:

A restriction on the amount of money a person or group can spend on political communication during a campaign necessarily reduces the quantity of expression by restricting the number of issues discussed, the depth of their exploration, and the size of the audience reached. This is because virtually every means of communicating ideas in today's society requires the expenditure of money. The distribution of the humblest handbill or leaflet entails printing, paper, and circulation costs. Speeches and rallies generally necessitate hiring a hall and publicizing the event. The electorate's increasing dependence on television, radio, and other mass media for news and information has made these expensive modes of communication indispensable instruments of effective political speech.

The expenditure limitations contained in the Act represent substantial rather than merely theoretical restraints on the quantity and diversity of political speech. The $1,000 ceiling on spending "relative to a clearly identified candidate," 18 U.S.C. § 608(e)(1), would appear to exclude all citizens and groups except candidates, political parties and the institutional press from any significant use of the most effective modes of communication. Although the Act's limitations on expenditures by campaign organizations and political parties provide substantially greater room for discussion and debate, they would have required restrictions in the scope of a number of past congressional and Presidential campaigns and would operate to constrain campaigning by candidates who raise sums in excess of the spending ceiling. (Footnotes omitted and emphasis added.)(424 at 19–20)

The Court rejected the "auditory analogy" that has always figured in discussions of the constitutionality of restrictions on expenditures for political advertising. In footnote 17, the Court said:

The nongovernmental appellees argue that just as the decibels emitted by a sound truck can be regulated consistent with the First Amendment, *Kovacs, supra*, the Act may restrict the volume of dollars in political campaigns without impermissibly restricting freedom of speech. See Freund, Commentary in A. Rosenthal, Federal Regulation of Campaign Finance: Some Constitutional Questions 72 (1971). *This comparison underscores a fundamental misconception.* The decibel restriction upheld in *Kovacs* limited the *manner* of operating a sound truck, but not the extent of its *proper* use. By contrast, the Act's dollar ceilings restrict the extent of the reasonable use of virtually every means of communicating information. As the *Kovacs* Court emphasized, the nuisance ordinance only barred sound trucks from broadcasting "in a loud and raucous manner on the streets," 336 U.S. at 89, and imposed "no restriction upon the communication of ideas or discussion of issues by the human voice, by newspapers, by pamphlets, by dodgers" or by sound trucks operating at a reasonable volume. *Ibid. See, Saia v. New York*, 334 U.S. 558, 561–562 (1948). 424 at n.17 (emphasis added)

The Court determined that the FECA's expenditure ceilings imposed "direct and substantial restraints on the quality of political speech," and that a primary effect of the expenditure limitations was to restrict the quantity of campaign speech by individuals, groups, and candidates. The Court concluded that *"[t]he re-strictions, while neutral as to the ideas expressed, limit political expression 'at the core of our electoral process and of First Amendment freedoms.'* "

The Court struck down the prohibition of expenditures for speech by any person during one year "relative to a clearly identified candidate," noting that this provision would make it a federal criminal offense for a person to place a single one-quarter page advertisement relative to a clearly identified candidate in a major metropolitan newspaper. In the course of holding that this provision was unconstitutional, the Court had occasion to clarify the statutory term "relative to a clearly identified candidate," which also appears in other operative provisions of the FECA and is important to the interpretation of the scope of the prohibition of expenditures by corporations and labor unions. In particular, the Court said, in addressing a challenge to the act on the ground of unconstitutional "vagueness": "This context clearly permits, if indeed it does not require, the phrase *'relative to'* a candidate to be read to mean *'advocating the election or defeat of a candidate"* 424 U.S. at 42 (emphasis added).

But the Court's clarification of that term did not entirely eliminate the vagueness of the expenditure ceiling, "[f]or the distinction between discussion of issues and candidates and advocacy of election or defeat of candidates may often dissolve in practical application." The Court specifically mentioned and discussed the problems which arise when candidates are intimately tied to and associated with positions on particular issues involving legislative proposals and governmental action. An advertisement criticizing a particular position on a specific public issue might be read, under specific circumstances, as a criticism of some candidate associated with a contrary position. The Court commented in footnotes 51 and 52 on the interpretation of the act's terminology of "clearly identified" candidates and advocacy of the election or defeat of a candidate:

The constitutional deficiencies described in *Thomas v. Collins* can be avoided only by reading § 608(e)(1) as limited to communications that include *explicit words of advocacy of election or defeat of a candidate*, much as the definition of "clearly identified" in § 608(e)(2) requires that an *explicit and unambiguous reference to the candidate* appear as part of the communication.[51]

---

51. Section 608(e)(2) defines "clearly identified" to require that the candidate's *name, photograph* or *drawing*, or other unambiguous reference to his identity appear as part of the communication. *Such other unambiguous reference would include use of the candidate's initials* (*e.g.*, Ike), *his office* (.*e.g.*, the President or the Governor of Iowa), or *his status* as a candidate (*e.g.*, the Democratic Presidential nominee, the senatorial candidate of the Republican Party of Georgia). 424 U.S. at 43 and n.51 (emphasis added)

The Court went on to add the following:

We agree that in order to preserve the provision against invalidation on vagueness grounds, § 608(e)(1) must be construed to apply only to expenditures for communications that *in express terms advocate the election or defeat of a clearly identified candidate for federal office.*[52]

52. This construction would restrict the application of § 608 (e)(1) to communications containing *express words of advocacy of election or defeat,* such as "vote for," "elect," "support," "cast your ballot for," "Smith for Congress," "vote against," "defeat," "reject". (424 U.S. 44 and n.52)(emphasis added)

Having, by the adoption of narrowing constructions of the key, operative terms of the act, solved the "vagueness" objection to the expenditure ceiling provisions of the FECA, the Court proceeded nonetheless to reject the justifications for the limitations on First Amendment grounds. The first ground was pragmatic:

We find that the governmental interest in preventing corruption and the appearance of corruption is inadequate to justify § 608(e)(1)'s ceiling on independent expenditures. First, assuming *arguendo* that large independent expenditures pose the same dangers of actual or apparent *quid pro quo* arrangements as do large contributions, § 608(e)(1) does not provide an answer that sufficiently relates to the elimination of those dangers. Unlike the contribution limitations' total ban on the giving of large amounts of money to candidates, § 608(e)(1) prevents only some large expenditures. *So long as persons and groups eschew expenditures that in express terms advocate the election or defeat of a clearly identified candidate, they are free to spend as much as they want to promote the candidate and his views.* The exacting interpretation of the statutory langauge necessary to avoid unconstitutional vagueness thus undermines the limitation's effectiveness as a loophole-closing provision by facilitating circumvention by those seeking to exert improper influence upon a candidate or officeholder. *It would naively underestimate the ingenuity and resourcefulness of persons and groups desiring to buy influence to believe that they would have much difficulty devising expenditures that skirted the restriction on express advocacy of election or defeat but nevertheless benefited the candidate's campaign.* Yet no substantial societal interest would be served by a loophole-closing provision designed to check corruption that permitted unscrupulous persons and organizations to expend unlimited sums of money in order to obtain improper influence over candidates for elective office. *Compare, Mills v. Alabama,* 384 U.S. at 220. 424 U.S. at 45

The Court's second reason directly challenged the idea that independent advocacy created any real danger of corruption of candidates, compared to the danger of corruption associated with very large campaign contributions:

Second, quite apart from the shortcomings of § 608(e)(1) in preventing any abuses generated by large independent expenditures, *the independent advocacy restricted by the provision does not presently appear to pose dangers of real or apparent corruption comparable to those identified with large campaign contributions.* The parties defending § 608(e)(1) contend that it is necessary to prevent would-be contributors from avoiding the contribution limitations by the simple expedient of paying directly for media advertisements or for other portions of the candidate's campaign activities. They argue that expenditures controlled by or coordinated with the candidate and his campaign might well have virtually the same value to the candidate as a contribution and would pose similar dangers of abuse. Yet such controlled or coordinated expenditures are treated as contributions rather than expenditures under the Act. Section 608(b)'s contribution ceilings rather than § 608(e)(1)'s independent expenditure limitation prevent attempts to circumvent the Act through prearranged or coordinated expenditures amounting to disguised contributions. By contrast, § 608(e)(1) limits expenditures for express advocacy of candidates made totally independently of the candidate and his campaign. *Unlike contributions, such independent expenditures may well provide little assistance to the candidate's campaign and indeed may prove counterproductive.* The *absence of prearrangement* and coordination of an expenditure with the candidate or his agent not only undermines the value of the expenditure to the candidate, *but also alleviates the danger that expenditures will be given as a quid pro quo for improper commitments from the candidate.* Rather than preventing circumvention of the contribution limitations, § 608(e)(1) severely restricts all independent advocacy despite its substantially diminished potential for abuse. 424 at 45–47 (footnote omitted and emphasis added)

The Court therefore concluded that the expenditure ceiling was constitutionally unjustifiable:

While the independent expenditure ceiling thus fails to serve any substantial governmental interest in stemming the reality or appearance of corruption in the electoral process, it heavily burdens core First Amendment expression. For the First Amendment right to " 'speak one's mind on all public issues' " includes the right to engage in " 'vigorous advocacy' no less than 'abstract discussion.' " *New York Times Co. v. Sullivan*, 376 U.S. at 269, quoting *Bridges v. California*, 314 U.S. 252, 270 (1941), and *NAACP v. Button*, 371 U.S. at 429. *Advocacy of the election or defeat of candidates for federal office is no less entitled to protection under the First Amendment than the discussion of political policy generally or advocacy of the passage or defeat of legislation.* 424 at 47–48 (emphasis added)

Although it did not address the constitutionality of the federal prohibition on corporate expenditures for political purposes, *Buckley v. Valeo* is an important decision for corporate political and issue advocacy advertising for two reasons. First, in *Buckley*, the Court gave clearer meaning to key provisions of the FECA which define the circumstances under which an advertisement by a corporation that addresses political issues might fall within the scope of the FECA and the corporate expenditure to publish it constitute an unlawful expenditure. Second, the Court's discussion affirmed basic First Amendment principles and extended their reach to the "corrupt practices" area. In this respect, what the Court said about the constitutional deficiencies of the limitations on independent expenditures may be equally applicable to the statutory restriction on corporate expenditures for the purpose of advocating the election or defeat of a clearly identified candidate—expenditures that are currently prohibited by 2 U.S.C. § 441b. In short, the reasoning of *Buckley v. Valeo* throws into serious question the constitutionality of the restriction in 2 U.S.C. § 441b on such expenditures. If a

$1,000 *limitation* is unconstitutional, how can § 441b's outright prohibition be justified?

It can be argued that corporations, unlike individuals, do not enjoy First Amendment rights. Corporations are creatures of state or federal law and enjoy only limited consitutional and civil rights. But the Meiklejohnian basis of the Court's reasoning in *Buckley v. Valeo* suggests that such a narrow conception of the First Amendment is not consistent with the broader purposes of the First Amendment. If the source of protection of corporate political speech were—like the primary source of corporate comercial speech—not rooted in the rights of corporations, but in the rights of citizens to hear and receive information and viewpoints from all sources, how can a flat restriction on corporate expenditures for the purpose of advocating the election or defeat of candidates be squared with the First Amendment?

When *Buckley v. Valeo* was decided in January 1976, the Court was already well on its way to recognizing the rights of citizens to *hear* as the doctrinal basis for protecting corporate speech. Four months later, on May 24, 1976, the Court decided *Virginia Pharmacy Board*, which adopted a sweeping Meiklejohnian rationale for protecting commercial speech. *Linmark* and *Bates* followed in 1977. If the Meiklejohnian reasoning of the commercial speech cases were applied to support constitutional protection for corporate political speech, in addition to corporate commercial speech, since the First Amendment interest of potential recipients of political speech lies at the very core of the First Amendment and eclipses by far the constitutional value of commercial speech, all that the Court had said regarding protection of corporate commercial speech would appear to apply with even greater force to corporate political speech.

This was the step which the Supreme Court took in 1978 in *First National Bank of Boston v. Bellotti*, 435 U.S. 765 (1978).

BELLOTTI AND CORPORATE EXPENDITURES FOR SPEECH IN CONNECTION WITH BALLOT AND REFERENDUM ISSUES

In the aftermath of *CIO*, *UAW*, and *Buckley v. Valeo*, the principal surviving rationale for continued federal and state restrictions on corporate contributions in connection with elections at which candidates are elected was the danger that a contribution to a candidate might be perceived to require a quid pro quo by the candidate or party if elected to office, corrupting the officeholder's independent service of the public for the common good. The same rationale was believed to apply to expenditures by corporations for advertising to advocate the election or defeat of a clearly identified candidate. Where a ballot issue or referendum hangs in the balance, however, the same rationale for prohibiting corporate expenditures applies weakly, if at all. There is no candidate. A restriction on corporate expenditures for advertising favoring one side or the other of a ballot issue serves only to restrict the quantity and quality of the information and viewpoint to which citizens may have access in deciding the wisdom of specific governmental policies that are put before them for direct democratic determination. The conflict of the Meiklejohnian interpretation of the First Amendment with such restrictions is stark.

Bellotti involved the constitutionality of a Massachusetts statute which forbade certain expenditures by banks and corporations for the purpose of influencing the vote on referendum issues, other than issues materially affecting any of the business, property, or assets of the corporation making the expenditure. The Supreme Judicial Court of Massachusetts upheld the constitutionality of the statute. The Supreme Court of the United States, by a narrow 5 to 4 vote, struck down the Massachusetts statute.

The majority first rejected the manner in which the Massachusetts court had framed the question, *i.e.*, whether corporations "have First Amendment rights":

[1b] The court below framed the principal question in this case as whether and to what extent corporations have First Amendment rights. We believe that the court posed the wrong question. The Constitution often protects interests broader than those of the party seeking their vindication. The First Amendment, in particular, serves significant societal interests. *The proper question therefore is not whether corporations "have" First Amendment rights and, if so, whether they are coextensive with those of natural persons. Instead, the question must be whether § 8 abridges expression that the First Amendment was meant to protect. We hold that it does.* 435 U.S. at 775–775 (emphasis added)

This step in the Court's reasoning is only that which is required by the thoroughgoing Meiklejohnian conception of the First Amendment set forth in Meiklejohn's influential book, *Free Speech and Its Relation to Self-Government*, in the same passage quoted previously in this chapter.

The Court held that the category of speech involved in the bank's proposed speech was entitled to the highest degree of protection, since it was addressed to public issues:

The speech proposed by appellants is at the heart of the First Amendment's protection.

"The freedom of speech and of the press guaranteed by the Constitution embraces at the least the liberty to discuss publicly and truthfully all matters of public concern without previous restraint or fear of subsequent punishment. . . . Freedom of discussion, if it would fulfill its historic function in this nation, must embrace all issues about which information is needed or appropriate to enable the members of society to cope with the exigencies of their period." *Thornhill v. Alabama*, 310 U.S. 88, 101–102, 84 L.Ed. 1093, 60 S. Ct. 736 (1940)

The referendum issue that appellants wish to address falls squarely within this description. In appellants' view, the enactment of a graduated personal income tax, as proposed to be authorized by constitutional amendment, would have a seriously adverse effect on the economy of the State. See n.4, *supra*. The importance of the referendum issue to the people and government of Massachusetts is not disputed. 435 U.S. at 776

Once again, the majority made explicit its reliance on the critical passage of Meiklejohn's book, in holding that "the inherent worth of the speech in terms of its capacity for informing the public *does not depend upon the identity of its source*, whether corporation, association, union, or individual":

As the Court said in *Mills v. Alabama*, 384 U.S. 214, 218 16 L.Ed. 2d 484, 86 S. Ct. 1434 (1966), "there is practically universal agreement that a major purpose of the [the First] Amendment was to protect the free discussion of governmental affairs." If the speakers here were not corporations, no one would suggest that the State could silence their proposed speech. It is the type of speech indispensable to decision making in a democracy,[11] and this is no less true because the speech comes from a corporation rather than an individual.[12]

---

11. Freedom of expression has particular significance with respect to government because "[i]t is here that the state has a special incentive to repress opposition and often wields a more effective power of suppression." T. Emerson, Toward a General Theory of the First Amendment 9 (1976). See also A. Meiklejohn, Free Speech and Its Relation to Self-Government 24–26 (1948).

12. The individual's interest in self-expression is a concern of the First Amendment separate from the concern for open and informed discussion, although the two often converge. See G. Gunther, Cases and Materials on Constitutional Law 1044 (9th ed. 1975); T. Emerson, The System of Freedom of Expression 6 (1970). The Court has declared, however, that "speech concerning public affairs is more than self-expression; it is the essence of self-government." *Garrison v. Louisiana*, 379 U.S. 64, 74–75, 13 L.Ed. 2d 125, 85 S. Ct. 209 (1964). And self-government suffers when those in power suppress competing views on pubic issues "from diverse and antagonistic sources." *Associated Press v. United States*, 326 U.S. 1, 20, 89 L.Ed. 2013, 65 S. Ct. 1416 (1945), quoted in *New York Times Co. v. Sullivan*, 376 U.S. 254, 266, 11 L.Ed. 2d 686, 84 S. Ct. 710, (1964). *The inherent worth of the speech in terms of its capacity for informing the public does not depend upon the identity of its source, whether corporation, association, union, or individual.* 435 U.S. at 777 (emphasis added)

The majority found it unnecessary "to survey the outer boundaries of the First Amendment's protection of corporate speech, or address the abstract question whether corporations have the full measure of rights that individuals enjoy under the First Amendment," 435 U.S. at 777. The Court unraveled the contentions regarding corporate constitutional rights and then turned to the societal interest. In the course of doing so, the majority related the Court's commercial speech cases to the question of corporate political speech and turned Massachusetts's argument back against it:

Nor do our recent commercial speech cases lend support to appellee's business interest theory. They illustrate that the First Amendment goes beyond protection of the press and the self-expression of individuals to prohibit government from limiting the stock of information from which members of the public may draw. *A commercial advertisement is constitutionally protected not so much because it pertains to the seller's business as because it furthers the societal interest in the "free flow of commercial information." Virginia State Board of Pharmacy v. Virginia Citizens Consumer Council*, 425 U.S. 748, 764, 48 L.Ed. 2d 346, 96 S. Ct. 1817 (1976); see *Linmark Associates, Inc. v. Willingboro*, 431 U.S. 85, 95, 52 L.Ed. 2d 155, 97 S. Ct. 1614 (1977). 435 at 783 (emphasis added)

The majority rejected the proposed governmental interests as insufficient to outweigh the value of the political speech. In doing so, the Court held that to support such a restriction, the governmental interest must be "compelling." The Court applied the rigorous "strict scrutiny" standard of judicial review:

Appellee nevertheless advances two principal justifications for the prohibition of corporate speech. The first is the State's interest in sustaining the active role of the individual citizen in the electoral process and thereby preventing diminution of the citizen's confidence in government. The second is the interest in protecting the rights of shareholders whose views differ from those expressed by management on behalf of the corporation. However weighty these interests may be in the context of partisan candidate elections, they either are not implicated in this case or are not served at all, or in other than a random manner, by the prohibition in § 8. 435 U.S. at 787

In an important footnote, the Court related the Massachusetts law to other federal and state statutes prohibiting or limiting corporate expenditures for advertising expressly relating to candidates—provisions such as 2 U.S.C. § 441b. With respect to such statutes, the Court commented in dictum that "Congress might well be able to demonstrate the existence of a danger of real or apparent corruption in independent expenditures by corporations *to influence candidate elections*":

26. In addition to prohibiting corporate contributions and expenditures for the purpose of influencing the vote on a ballot question submitted to the voters, § 8 also proscribes corporate contributions or expenditures "for the purpose of aiding, promoting or preventing the nomination or election of any person to public office, or aiding, promoting, or antagonizing the interests of any political party." See n.2, *supra*. In this respect, the statute is not unlike many other state and federal laws regulating corporate participation in partisan candidate elections. *Appellants do not challenge the constitutionality of laws prohibiting or limiting corporate contributions to political candidates or committees, or other means of influencing candidate elections. Cf. Pipefitters Local Union No. 562 v. United States*, 407 U.S. 385, 33 L.Ed. 2d 11, 92 S. Ct. 2247 (1972); *United States v. Automobile Workers*, 352 U.S. 567, 1 L.Ed. 2d 563, 77 S. Ct. 529 (1957); *United States v. CIO*, 335 U.S. 106, 92 L.Ed. 1849, 68 S. Ct. 1349 (1948). About half of these laws, including the federal law, 2 U.S.C. § 441b (1976 ed.) [2 U.S.C.S. § 441b] (originally enacted as the Federal Corrupt Practices Act, 34 State 864), by their terms do not apply to referendum votes. Several of the others proscribe or limit spending for "political" purposes, which may or may not cover referenda. *See Schwartz v. Rommes*, 495 F.2d 844 (CA2 1974).

The overriding concern behind the enactment of statutes such as the Federal Corrupt Practices Act was the problem of corruption of elected representatives through the creation of political debts. See *United States v. Automobile Workers, supra*, 352 U.S. at 570–575, 77 S. Ct. 530–533; *Schwartz v. Romnes, supra*, at 849–851. The importance of the governmental interest in preventing this occurrence has never been doubted. The case before us presents no comparable problem, and our consideration of a corporation's right to speak on issues of general pubic interest implies no comparable right in the quite different context of participation in a political campaign for election to public office. Congress might well be able to demonstrate the existence of a danger of real or apparent corruption in independent expenditures by corporations to influence candidate elections. *Cf. Buckley v. Valeo, supra,* 424 U.S. at 46, 96 S. Ct. 612; Comment, The Regulation of Union Political Activity: Majority and Minority Rights and Remedies, 126 U. Pa. L. Rev. 386, 408–410 (1977). 435 at 788 n.26 (emphasis added)

The Court thus rejected both the danger that corporations might "drown out" speech from other sources (the "undue influence" rationale of *CIO* and *UAW*) and the interests of corporate shareholders (the "minority protection" rationale discussed in *CIO* and *UAW*).

With respect to the danger that treasury funds would be used to advocate views at odds with those of some stockholders, the Court noted that the statute was underinclusive because it did not regulate corporate expenditures for lobbying and did not restrict corporate expenditures for advertising addressed to public issues that were not the subject of a referendum. The statute also prohibited corporate expenditures for advertising even if the stockholders unanimously voted their approval for such an expenditure.

In an important footnote, moreover, the majority rejected the application to the corporate context of the "compelled" speech issue presented in labor union contexts such as *Abood v. Detroit Board of Education*, 431 U.S. 209 (1977). A shareholder is free to sell his or her stock:

Appellee does not explain why the dissenting shareholder's wishes are entitled to such greater solicitude in this context than in many others where equally important and controversial corporate decisions are made by management or by a predetermined percentage of the shareholders. Mr. Justice White's repeatedly expressed concern for corporate shareholders who may be "coerced" into supporting "causes with which they disagree" apparently is not shared by appellants' shareholders. Not a single shareholder has joined appellee in defending the Massachusetts statute or, so far as the record shows, has interposed any objection to the right asserted by the corporations to make the proscribed expenditures. 435 U.S. 794 n.34

The majority distinguished the *Abood* and *Machinists* cases as involving only the issues of union political activity in circumscribed situations:

The dissent of Mr. Justice White relies heavily on *Abood v. Detroit Board of Education*, 431 U.S. 209, 52 L.Ed. 2d 261, 97 S. Ct. 1782 (1977), and *International Assn. of Machinists v. Street*, 367 U.S. 740, 6 L.Ed. 2d 1141, 81 S. Ct. 1784 (1961). These decisions involved the First Amendment rights of employees in closed or agency shops not to be compelled, as a condition of employment, to support with financial contributions the political activities of other union members with which the dissenters disagreed.

Street and *Abood* are irrelevant to the question presented in this case. In those cases employees were required, either by state law or by agreement between the employer and the union, to pay dues or a "service fee" to the exclusive bargaining representative. To the extent that these funds were used by the union in furtherance of political goals, unrelated to collective bargaining, they were held to be unconstitutional because they compelled the dissenting union member "to furnish contributions of money for the propagation of opinions which he disbelieves. . . . '' *Abood, supra*, 431 U.S. at 235 n.31, 97 S. Ct. 1799 (Thomas Jefferson as quoted in I. Brant, James Madison: The Nationalist 354 [1948]).

According to the majority, stockholders simply are not ''compelled'' in any relevant sense:

The critical distinction here is that no shareholder has been ''compelled'' to contribute anything. Apart from the fact, noted by the dissent, that compulsion by the State is wholly absent, the [shareholder] invests in a corporation of his own volition and is [free to withdraw his investment at any time and for any reason.] A more relevant analogy, therefore, is to the situation where an employee voluntarily joins a union, or an individual voluntarily joins an association, and later finds himself in disagreement with its stance on a political issue. The *Street* and *Abood* Courts did not address the question whether, in such a situation, the union or association must refund a portion of the dissenter's dues or, more drastically, refrain from expressing the majority's views. In addition, even apart from the substantive differences between compelled membership in a union and voluntary investment in a corporation or voluntary participation in *any* collective organization, it is by no means an automatic step from the remedy in *Abood*, which honored the interests of the minority without infringing the majority's rights, to the position adopted by the dissent which would completely silence the majority because a hypothetical minority might object. 435 U.S. at 794 N.34

The Court also alluded to the power of stockholders to determine through bylaw provisions whether the corporation should engage in debate on public issues and to prevent speech inconsistent with the views of the majority by the election of different directors. With respect to the dissenting minority of stockholders, the Court pointed to the availability of derivative suits to challenge corporate disbursements alleged to have been made for improper corporate purposes or merely to further the personal interests of management. Therefore, even assuming that the protection of shareholders constituted a compelling interest, the Court found ''no substantially relevant correlation between the governmental interest asserted and the State's effort to prohibit'' the bank from speaking, 435 U.S. at 795.

Curiously, several of the Court's most vigorous advocates for a broad interpretation of the First Amendment—Justices Brennan and Marshall, for example—dissented in *Bellotti*. The dissenters pointed out that the majority did not reject the notion that undue influence on the outcome of ballot issues might justify similar restrictions but held only that there was insufficient factual foundation to infer such a danger in Massachusetts. The dissenters disagreed. The dissent also gave greater weight to the minority protection rationale. They correctly observed that ''the analytical framework employed by the Court clearly raises great doubt about the Corrupt Practices Act,'' 435 U.S. at 821, and stated:

If the corporate identity of the speaker makes no difference, *all the Court has done is to reserve the formal interment of the Corrupt Practices Act and similar state statutes for another day*. As I understand the view that has now become part of First Amendment jurisprudence, the use of corporate funds, even for causes irrelevant to the corporation's business, may be no more limited than that of individual funds. Hence, corporate contributions to and expenditures on behalf of political candidates may be no more limited than those of individuals. Individual contributions under federal law are limited but not entirely forbidden, and under *Buckley v. Valeo*, expenditures may not constitutionally be limited at all. Most state corrupt practices acts, like the federal act, forbid *any* contributions or expenditures by corporations to or for a political candidate. (emphasis added)

Although what the dissenters pointed out with respect to the vulnerability of blanket restrictions on corporate contributions may be debated, the constitutional vulnerability, after *Bellotti*, of federal and state prohibitions on corporate expenditures to advocate the election or defeat of clearly identified candidates is surely correct.

The constitutionality of the prohibition against corporate political contributions contained in 2 U.S.C. § 441b and its predecessors has been upheld in a number of cases, which did not involve the expenditure provision, *Federal Election Commission v. Weinstein*, 462 F.Supp. 243 (S.D.N.Y. 1978); *United States v. Chestnut*, 394 F.Supp. 581 (S.D.N.Y. 1975); *aff'd*, 533 F.2d 40 (2d Cir. 1976); *Federal Election Commission v. Lance*, 635 F.2d 1132 (5th Cir.), *appeal dismissed*, 453 U.S. 917 (1981).

The Supreme Court has also upheld the $5,000 limit on the amount of contributions by an unincorporated association to its political action committee, *California Medical Association v. Federal Election Commission*, 453 U.S. 182 (1981).

The expenditure limitations have encountered greater difficulty. In *Republican National Committee v. Federal Election Commission*, 616 F.2d 1 (2d Cir. 1979), the Court upheld the limitations on expenditures by presidential candidates who accept federal funds, and the Supreme Court affirmed that result without opinion, 445 U.S. 955 (1980). But in *Common Cause v. Harrison Schmitt*, 512 F.Supp. 489 (D.D.C. 1980), *aff'd, by an equally divided court*, 455 U.S. 129 (1982), the courts held unconstitutional the limitation of independent expenditures in a presidential election campaign to $1,000 per political committee, 26 U.S.C. § 9012(f).

In *Democratic Party of the U.S. v. National Conservative Political Action Committee*, 578 F.Supp. 797 (E.D. Pa. 1983), *aff'd in part rev'd in part*, 105 S. Ct. 1459 (1985), a three-judge court struck down the $1,000 limitation on expenditures by political committees in a presidential general election in 26 U.S.C. § 9012(f).

The general question of corporate expenditures for expressing views on ballot issues has generated a number of decisions that parallel *Bellotti, see, Pacific Gas & Electric Co. v. Berkeley*, 60 Cal. App. 3d 123, 131 Cal. Rptr. 350 (1976) (city ordinance against corporate contributions or expenditures for ballot measure held unconstitutional); *Schwartz v. Romnes*, 495 F.2d 844 (2d Cir. 1974) (New York statute construed narrowly to exclude referenda from scope of law prohibiting corporate contributions for political purposes); *Corrigan v. Cleveland-Cliffs Iron Co.*, 169 Ohio St. 42, 157 N.E.2d 331 (1959); *C&C Plywood Corp. v. Hanson*, 420 F.Supp. 1254 (D.Mont. 1976), *aff'd*, 583 F.2d 421 (9th Cir. 1978); *Frias v. Board of Trustees*, 584 S.W.2d 944 (Tex.Civ.App. 1979), *cert. denied*, 444 U.S. 996 (1979); *Anderson's Paving, Inc. v. Hayes*, 295 S.E.2d 805 (W.Va. 1982) (statute unconstitutional); Anno., "Power of Corporation to Make Political Contribution or Expenditure Under State Law," 79 A.L.R. 491. In *Citizens Against Rent Control v. Berkeley*, 454 U.S. 290 (1981), the Supreme Court invalidated a local ordinance placing a $250 limitation on contributions to committees formed to support or oppose ballot measures.

In *Consolidated Edison Co. v. Public Service Commission*, 447 U.S. 530 (1980), the Supreme Court applied the principles established in *Buckley* and *Bellotti* to invalidate a New York Public Service Commission order that prohibited regulated, privately owned utilities in New York from utilizing material inserted in bills rendered to customers as a mechanism for the dissemination of the utility's position on "controversial matters of public policy." The Court rejected the PSC's contention that the order was simply a content-neutral "time, place and manner" regulation, pointing out that this prohibition of discussion concerning "controversial matters of public policy" was not content-neutral in the required sense. The First Amendment's hostility to content-based regulation of speech, the Court wrote, extends also "to prohibition of public discussion of an entire topic."

The Court held that a governmental restriction on non-commercial speech may be upheld "only if the government can show that the regulation is a precisely drawn means of serving a compelling state interest," 447 U.S. at 541. The Court failed to identify such a compelling interest and, citing *Bellotti* and Meiklejohn's essay (447 U.S. at 534, 544), invalidated the PSC order.

REMEDIES AND CORPORATE POLITICAL EXPENDITURES

So far this chapter has dealt with the constitutionality of governmental restrictions on corporate expenditures for political purposes. Read together, *Buckley v. Valeo, First National Bank of Boston v. Bellotti*, and *Consolidated Edison* raise a serious doubt whether any flat prohibition on corporate expenditures for political speech is consistent with the First Amendment. That issue is one that turns on the questions whether the government's rather attenuated interest in eliminating the possibility of a quid pro quo for public political support in advertising constitutes a compelling interest when weighed against the right of the public to have access to information and viewpoint concerning candidates for public office.

Putting to one side the constitutionality of governmental restrictions on corporate political spending, what potential remedies exist for corporate stockholders who disagree with the corporation's expenditures for such purposes? In *Cort v. Ash*, 422 U.S. 66 (1975), the Supreme Court unanimously held that a stockholder has no private right of action for violations of what is now 2 U.S.C. § 441(b) (previously codified as 18 U.S.C. § 610). In *Cort*, the Supreme Court suggested that state law remedies might exist for waste of corporate assets or for breach of fiduciary duty, or for *ultra vires* conduct by corporate directors. The question of the power of a corporation to make expenditures for political purposes would appear to turn on the subsidiary question whether the particular expenditure is reasonably connected to the best interests of the corporation. This, in turn, often involves application of the corporate "business judgment" rule, which vests a considerable degree of discretion in the directors of a corporation to determine in a particular case what is in the corporation's best interests. Although express statutory prohibitions against corporate contributions and expenditures exist in a number of jurisdictions—and where they exist allegations that corporate expenditures are *ultra vires* might ordinarily be expected to succeed—statutory restrictions on expenditures for corporate speech on the qualifications of political candidates are open to serious constitutional question.

NOTES

1. By way of illustrating how influential they have been, the views of Alexander Meiklejohn, or Justice Brennan's discussion of them in his Alexander Meiklejohn Lecture at Brown University on April 14, 1965, later published as "The Supreme Court and the Meiklejohn Interpretation of the First Amendment," 79 Harv. L. Rev. 1 (1965–1966), have been cited or quoted in either the majority, concurring, or dissenting opinions in the following forty-six Supreme Court and United States Court of Appeals decisions: Board of Education, Island Trees Union Free School District v. Pico, 457 U.S. 853 (1982); Richmond Newspapers, Inc. v. Virginia, 448 U.S. 555 (1980)(concurring opinion); Carey v. Brown, 447 U.S. 455 (1980); Consolidated Edison Corp. v. Public Service Commission, 447 U.S. 530 (1980); Herbert v. Lando, 441 U.S. 153 (1979)(dissenting opinion); Houchins v. KQED, 438 U.S. 1 (1978)(dissenting opinion); First National Bank of Boston v. Bellotti, 435 U.S. 765 (1978); Virginia Pharmacy Board v. Virginia Consumers Council, 425 U.S. 748 (1976); Hynes v. Mayor of Oradell, 425 U.S. 610 (1976)(concurring opionion); Time, Inc. v. Firestone, 424 U.S. 448 (1976) (dissenting opinion); Gertz v. Robert Welch, Inc., 418 U.S. 323 (1974) (dissenting opinion); Saxbe v. Washington Post Co., 417 U.S. 843 (1974)(dissenting opinion); Pittsburgh Press Co. v. Pittsburgh Commission of Human Relations, 413 U.S. 376 (1973)(dissenting opinion); Columbia Broadcasting System, Inc. v. Democratic National Committee, 412 U.S. 94 (1973); Gravel v. United States, 408 U.S. 606 (1972)(dissenting opinion); Branzburg v. Hayes, 408 U.S. 606 (1972)(dissenting opinion); Police Department v. Mosley, 408 U.S. 92 (1972); Red Lion Broadcasting Co. v. Federal Communications Commission, 395 U.S. 367 (1969); New York Times Co. v. Sullivan, 376 U.S. 254 (1964)(concurring opinion); Kimm v. Rosenberg, 363 U.S. 405 (1960); Yates v. United States, 354 U.S. 298 (1957) (dissenting opinion); Dennis v. United States, 341 U.S. 494 (1951)(concurring opinion); Kunz v. New York, 340 U.S. 290 (1951)(dissenting opinion); Wymbs v. Republican State Executive Committee, 719 F.2d 1072 (11th Cir. 1983); McGehee v. Casey, 718 F.2d 1137 (D.C. Cir. 1983); Association of Community Organizations for Reform Now v. Frontenac, 714 F.2d 813 (8th Cir. 1983); Litton Systems Inc. v. AT&T,

700 F.2d 785 (1983); Int. Society for Krishna Consciousness v. N.J. Sports and Exposition Authority, 691 F.2d 155 (3d Cir. 1982); Fehlhaber v. State of North Carolina, 675 F.2d 1365 (4th Cir. 1982)(dissenting opinion); CBS, Inc. v. Federal Communications Commission, 629 F.2d 1 (D.C. Cir. 1980); Hirschkop v. Snead, 594 F.2d 356 (4th Cir. 1979)(concurring opinion); Community Service Broadcasting v. FCC, 593 F.2d 1102 (D.C. Cir. 1978); Pierce v. Capital Cities Communication, Inc., 576 F.2d 495 (3d Cir. 1978); Herbert v. Lando, 568 F.2d 974 (2d Cir. 1977); Dellums v. Powell, 566 F.2d 167 (D.C. Cir. 1977); Home Box Office v. FCC, 567 F.2d 9 (D.C. Cir. 1977); Mississippi Gay Alliance v. Goudelock, 536 F.2d 1073 (5th Cir. 1976)(dissenting opinion); Glasson v. City of Louisville, 518 F.2d 899 (6th Cir. 1975); Hobbs v. Thompson, 448 F.2d 456 (5th Cir. 1971); Guzick v. Drebus, 431 F.2d 594 (6th Cir. 1970); Machesky v. Bizzell, 414 F.2d 283 (5th Cir. 1969); Edwards v. Habib, 397 F.2d 687 (D.D.Cir. 1968); Wolin v. Port of New York Authority, 392 F.2d 83 (2d Cir. 1968); Powell v. McCormack, 395 F.2d 577 (D.C. Cir. 1968); United States v. Miller, 367 F.2d 72 (2d Cir. 1966).

The works of Meiklejohn most frequently cited in the Supreme Court and the courts of appeals are *Political Freedom* (Oxford University Press, 1965), including the important book *Free Speech and Its Relation to Self-Government*, and his article, "The First Amendment Is an Absolute," 1961 Supreme Court Review 245 (Kurland, ed.).

2. This is a passage from Alexander Meiklejohn's *Free Speech and Its Relation to Self-Government* (1948), as reprinted in his book, *Political Freedom: The Constitutional Powers of the People*, Oxford University Press (1965), at pp. 24–25.

3. Ibid., pp. 25–27.

4. Ibid., pp. 27–28.

5. Act of January 26, 1907, ch.420, 34 Stat. 864.

6. Report of the Joint Committee of the Senate and Assembly of the State of New York appointed to Investigate the Affairs of Life Insurance Companies 397 (1906).

7. Act of March 4, 1909, c. 321, sec. 83, 35 Stat. 1103; Act of February 25, 1925, c. 368, 43 Stat. 1070; Act of June 25, 1943, c. 144, § 9, 57 Stat. 167–168; Act of June 23, 1947, c. 120, Title III, § 304, 61 State. 159, as well as by the Federal Election Campaign Act of 1971, and more recent amendments.

8. 43 Stat. 1070, 1074 (repealed 1948).

9. Act of June 25, 1943, ch.144, § 9, 57 Stat. 163, 167–168 (repealed 1948), *amending* Act of February 28, 1925, ch. 368, tit. III, § 363, 43 Stat. 1070, 1974.

10. See Hearings Before a Subcommittee of the Committee on Labor, House of Representatives, 78th Cong. 1st Sess., on H.R. 804 and H.R. 1483, May, 1943, pp. 2, 4.

11. Act of June 23, 1947, ch. 120, § 304, 61 Stat. 136, 159 (codified at 18 U.S.C. § 610).

See also, 6A *Fletcher Encyclopedia of the Law of Corporations* § 2940; Annot., *Power of Corporation to Make Political Contribution or Expenditure Under State Law*, 79 A.L.R. 3d 491; Annot., *Construction and Application of Provisions of Corrupt Practices Act Regarding Contributions by Corporations*, 125 A.L.R. 1029; Annot., *Power of a Business Corporation to Donate to a Charitable or Similar Institution*, 39 A.L.R. 2d 1192; Fletcher, *Corporate Political Contributions*, 29 Business Lawyer 1071 (1974); Garrett, *Corporate Contributions for Political Purposes*, 14 Business Lawyer 365 (1959); Comment: Civil Responsibility for Corporate Political Expenditures, 20 UCLA L. Rev. 1329 (1973); Brudney, *Business Corporations and Stockholders' Rights Under the First Amendment*, 91 Yale L.J. 235 (1981).

Bibliography

BOOKS

Alston, William, *The Philosophy of Language*, Englewood Cliffs, N.J.: Prentice-Hall, 1964.

Austin, J. L., *How To Do Things with Words*, J. O. Urmson, ed.; Oxford: Oxford University Press, 1965.

———, *Philosophical Papers*, Oxford: Oxford University Press, 1961.

Barron, Jerome A., and C. Thomas Diener, *Handbook of Free Speech and Free Press*, Boston: Little, Brown and Co., 1979.

Blackstone, W., *Commentaries on the Laws of England 151* (lst ed. 1765–1769), facsimile reprint, Chicago: University of Chicago, 1979.

Chafee, Zechariah, Jr., *Free Speech in the United States*, New York: Atheneum, 1969.

Cox, Archibald, *Freedom of Expression*, Cambridge: Harvard University Press, 1981.

Dorsen, Norman, Paul Bender, Burt Neuborne, Sylvia Law, *Emerson, Haber and Dorsen's Political and Civil Rights in the United States*, Boston: Little, Brown and Co., 1980.

Elliot, Jonathan, *Elliot's Debates* (2nd edition) Philadelphia: J. B. Lippincott, 1937.

Emerson, Thomas I., *The System of Freedom of Expression*, New York: Random House, 1970.

———, *Toward a General Theory of the First Amendment*, New York: Vintage Books, 1967.

Fletcher, William Meade, *Cyclopedia of the Law of Private Corporations*, Willamette, Illinois: Callaghan & Co., 1983.

Haiman, Franklyn S., *Speech and Law in a Free Society*, Chicago: University of Chicago Press, 1981.

Kairys, David, ed., *The Politics of Law: A Progressive Critique*, New York: Pantheon, 1982.

Lyons, John, *Semantics*, Cambridge: Cambridge University Press, 1977.

Meiklejohn, Alexander, *Free Speech and Its Relation to Self-Government*, New York: Harper and Row, 1948.

————, *Political Freedom: The Constitutional Powers of the People*, New York: Oxford University Press, 1965.

Mill, John Stuart, *On Liberty*, World Classics Edition, Oxford: Oxford University Press, 1974.

Milton, John. *Prose Works*, New York: Yale University Press, 1959.

Nowak, John E., Ronald D. Rotunda, and J. Nelson Young, *Constitutional Law*, St. Paul: West Publishing Co., 1978.

Nozick, Robert, *Anarchy, State and Utopia*, New York: Basic Books, 1974.

Paul, Jeffrey, ed., *Reading Nozick: Essays on Anarchy, State and Utopia*, Oxford: Basil Blackwell Publishing Co., 1982.

Searle, John R., *Speech Acts: An Essay in the Philosophy of Language*, Cambridge: Cambridge University Press, 1969.

Source Book on Corporate Image and Corporate Advocacy and Advertising, compiled by the Subcommittee on Administrative Practice and Procedure of the Committee on the Judiciary of the U.S. Senate, Washington, D.C.: U.S. Government Printing Office, 1978.

Tribe, Lawrence H., *American Constitutional Law*, Mineola: The Foundation Press, Inc., 1978.

Tuerck, David G. *Political Economy of Advertising*, Washington, D.C.: American Enterprise Institute for Public Policy Research, 1978.

COMMERCIAL SPEECH

Articles

Agthe, Dale R., *Private Residences: Validity and Construction of Ordinances Prohibiting or Restricting Distribution of Commercial Advertising to Private Residences—Modern Cases*, 12 American Law Reports 4th 851–855 (1983).

Alexander, Lawrence and Daniel A. Farber, *Commercial Speech and First Amendment Theory: A Critical Exchange*, 75 Northwestern University Law Review 307–315 (1980).

Appleton, Peter M. and Edwin K. Marzec, *Advertisers, Too, Have Constitutional Rights*, 19 Publishing, Entertainment, Advertising and Allied Fields Law Quarterly 393–403 (Spring 1981).

Baker, C. Edwin, *Commercial Speech: A Problem in the Theory of Freedom*, 62 Iowa Law Review 1–56 (1976).

————, *Scope of the First Amendment Freedom of Speech*, 25 U.C.L.A. Law Review 964–1040 (1978).

Barrett, Edward L., *The Unchartered Area—Commercial Speech and the First Amendment*, 13 University of California at Davis Law Review 175–209 (Spring 1980).

Bell, Griffin T., *Remarks before the Harvard Law Review, March 19, 1977*, 806 Antitrust Regulation and Trade Reporter F-1.

Blumoff, Theodore Y., *After Metromedia: Sign Controls and the First Amendment*, 28 St. Louis University Law Journal 171–199 (1984).

Boyce, David S., *Commercial Speech: First Amendment Protection Clarified—Bigelow v. Virginia*, 28 University of Florida Law Review 610–620 (1976).

Brennan, William J., *The Supreme Court and the Meiklejohn Interpretation of the First Amendment* 79 Harvard Law Review 1–20 (1965–6).

Brosnahan, Roger P. and Lori B. Andrews, *Regulation of Lawyer Advertising: In the Public Interest?* 46 Brooklyn Law Review 423–436 (Spring 1980).

Burnett, Barbara A. *Protecting and Regulating Commercial Speech: Consumers Confront the First Amendment*, 5 Comm-Ent 637–680 (1983).

Caldwell, Kirk, *Metromedia, Inc. v. City of San Diego: The Conflict Between Aesthetic Zoning and Commercial Speech Protection; Hawaii's Billboard Law Under Fire* (case note) *Metromedia, Inc. v. City of San Diego*, 5 University of Hawaii Law Review 79–111 (1983).

Canby, William C., *Commercial Speech of Lawyers: The Court's Unsteady Course*, 46 Brooklyn Law Review 401–422 (Spring 1980).

Carnes, Nancy L., *Zoning—Billboards—Exercise of Police Power for Aesthetic Purposes—Metromedia, Inc. v. City of San Diego*, 47 Tennessee Law Review 901–918 (1980).

Carulli, Thomas G., *Regulation of Advertising and Promotional Practices of Public Utilities Under the First Amendment*, 8 Fordham Urban Law Journal 373–403 (1980).

Childress, Steven Alan, *The Commercial Speech Doctrine Under the First Amendment* (case note) *Central Hudson Gas & Electric Corp. v. Public Service Commission*, 13 University of West Los Angeles Law Review 297–305 (1981).

Cohen, Jane C., *Ban on Advertising Promoting Energy Usage Violates First Amendment* (case note) *Central Hudson Gas and Electric Corp. v. Public Service Commission of New York*, 21 Natural Resources Journal 177–180 (January 1981).

Cox, Archibald, *Freedom of Expression in the Burger Court* 94 Harvard Law Review 1–73 (1980).

Davis, R. D., *Price, Validity and Construction of Statute or Ordinance Requiring or Prohibiting Posting or Other Publication of Price of Commodity or Services*, 89 American Law Reports 2d 901–952 (1963).

Denbow, Stetania A., *Commercial Speech and the First Amendment—Continuing Uncertainty After Six Years*, 12 Capital University Law Review 115–141 (1982).

Eclavea, Romualdo, *Identification of Jobseeker by Race, Religion, National Origin, Sex, or Age in 'Situation Wanted' Employment Advertising as Violation of State Civil Rights Laws*, 99 American Law Reports 3d 154 (1980).

Elliot, Eugene Burton, *A First Amendment Analysis of Governmental Suppression of Speech*, 60 Denver Law Journal 105–117 (1982).

Elman, Philip, *New Constitutional Right to Advertise*, 64 American Bar Association Journal 206–10 (1978).

Esposito, Joseph P., *First Amendment Rights: Freedom of Speech*, 1978 Annual Survey of American Law 135–159 (1978).

Farber, Daniel A., *Commercial Speech and First Amendment Theory*, 74 Northwestern University Law Review 372 (Oct. 1979).

Feldman, Mark B., *Commercial Speech, Transborder Data Flows and the Right to Communicate Under International Law*, 17 International Lawyer, 87–95 (Winter 1983).

Field, Laurence, *The New Commercial Speech Doctrine and Broadcast Advertising*, 14 Harvard Civil Rights–Civil Liberties Law Review 385–484 (1979).

Foster, Wayne F., *Validity, Construction, and Application of State Criminal Statute Forbidding Use of Telephone to Annoy or Harass* 95 A.L.R. 3d 411–44 (1979).

Franks, James B., *The Commercial Speech Doctrine and the First Amendment*, 12 Tulsa Law Journal 699–730 (1977).

Fuchsberg, Jacob D., *Commercial Speech: Where It's At*, 46 Brooklyn Law Review 389–399 (1980).

Heller, Francis H., *The End of the "Commercial Speech" Exception—Good Riddance or More Headaches for the Courts?* 67 Kentucky Law Journal 927–946 (1978–79).

Jackson, Thomas H. and John Calvin Jeffries, Jr., *Commercial Speech: Economic Due Process and the First Amendment*, 65 Virginia Law Review 1–41 (1979).

Jones, R. Steven, *Electric and Gas Utility Advertising: The First Amendment Legacy of Central Hudson*, 60 Washington University Law Quarterly 459–505 (1982).

Kalven, Harry Jr., *The New York Times Case: A Note on the General Meaning of the First Amendment*, 1964 Supreme Court Review 191–221.

Kaplan, Marilyn R., *Commercial Speech and The Right to Privacy: Constitutional Implications of Regulating Unsolicited Telephone Calls*, 15 Columbia Journal of Law and Social Problems 277–315 (Spring 1980).

Karmel, Roberta S., *The Tension Between The First Amendment and the Federal Securities Laws*, 521 Securities Regulation and Law Report, Sep. 26, 1979, A16–17.

Klushner, James A., *Freedom to Hear: The First Amendment, Commercial Speech and Access to Information*, 28 Wayne Law Review 137–179 (1981).

Knapp, Susan J., *Commercial Speech, the Federal Trade Commission and the First Amendment*, 9 Memphis State University Law Review 1–56 (1978).

Kohn, Bruce A., *The First Amendment and Scalping by a Financial Columnist: May a Newspaper Article be Commercial Speech?* 57 Indiana Law Journal 131–161 (1982).

Landis, Debra T., *Advertising as Ground for Disciplining Attorneys*, 30 American Law Reports 4th 742 (1983).

LeBrun, M. David, *Validity, Construction, and Effect of Statutes, Ordinances, or Regulations Prohibiting or Regulating Advertising of Intoxicating Liquors*, 20 American Law Reports 4th 600 (1983).

Lohmann, Paul M., *Recent Decisions: Protection of Commercial Speech—Virginia Board of Pharmacy v. Virginia Citizens Consumer Council, Inc.*, 60 Marquette Law Review 138–152 (1976).

Long, Joann E., *The Constitutionality of Oklahoma's Prohibition on Liquor Advertising*, 16 Tulsa Law Journal 734–782 (1981).

Luten, Susan Burnett, *Give Me a Home Where No Salesmen Phone—Telephone Solicitation and the First Amendment*, 7 Hastings Constitutional Law Quarterly 129–164 (Fall, 1979).

Maginess, C. R., *Exchange of Price Information as a Restraint of Trade: Reassessing Per Se Rules in Light of First Amendment Protection of Commercial Speech*, 48 Fordham Law Review 1005–1026 (1980).

Meeks, Thomas J., *Commercial Speech: Foreclosing on the Overbreadth Doctrine*, 30 University of Florida Law Review 479–490 (1978).

Meiklejohn, Donald, *Commercial Speech and the First Amendment*, 13 California Western Law Review 430–455 (1977).

Merrill, Thomas W., *The First Amendment Protection for Commercial Advertising: The*

New Constitutional Doctrine, 44 University of Chicago Law Review 205–254 (1976).

Neuborne, Burt, *A Rationale for Protecting and Regulating Commercial Speech*, 46 Brooklyn Law Review 437–462 (Spring, 1980).

Newton, Sally, *The Commercial Speech Doctrine: Bigelow v. Virginia*, 12 Urban Law Annual 221–232 (1976).

O'Connor, James J., *Issue Advertising on Television*, 107 Public Utilities Fortnightly 103–104 (April 1981).

Perry, Michael J., *Modern Equal Protection*, 79 Columbia Law Review 1023-1084(1979).

Pitofsky, Robert, *Beyond Nader: Consumer Protection and the Regulation of Advertising*, 90 Harvard Law Review 661–701, (1977).

Platt, Neal Robert, *Commercial Speech and the First Amendment: An Emerging Doctrine*, 5 Hofstra Law Review 655–671 (1977).

Preston, Paul, *Purely Commercial Speech and Its Relationship to the First Amendment*, 37 Louisiana Law Review 263–270 (1976).

Redish, Martin H., *Self-Realization, Democracy, and Freedom of Expression: A Reply to Professor Baker*, 130 University of Pennsylvania Law Review 678–688 (1982).

———, *The Value of Free Speech*, 130 University of Pennsylvania Law Review 591–645 (1982).

Reich, R. B., *Consumer Protection and the First Amendment: A Dilemma for the FTC?* 61 Minnesota Law Review 705–741 (1977).

———, *Preventing Deception in Commercial Speech*, 54 New York University Law Review 775–805 (1979).

Roberts, Barry S., *Toward A General Theory of Commercial Speech and the First Amendment*, 40 Ohio State Law Journal 115–152 (1979).

Rosedale, Eric L., *A Bifurcated Approach to Billboard Regulation and the First Amendment*, 3 Cardozo Law Review 327–356 (1982).

Rotunda, Ronald D., *The Commerical Speech Doctrine in the Supreme Court*, 1976 University of Illinois Law Forum 1080–1101 (1976).

St. Pierre, Michael A., *Narrowing the Scope of First Amendment Protection for Commercial Expression: Friedman v. Rogers*, 13 Suffolk University Law Review 1503–1523 (1979).

Schelling T., "Note", American Economic Review, May 1969, pp. 488–493.

Schiro, Richard, *Commercial Speech: The Demise of a Chimera*, The Supreme Court Review 45–98 (1976).

Shenefield, John H., *Antitrust and Evolution: New Concepts for New Problems* (Remarks before the Eleventh New England Antitrust Conference, Boston, Massachusetts, November 18, 1977).

———, *The Future Is Now* (Remarks before the Federal Bar Association, Washington, D.C., March 10, 1978).

Sheridan, David, *Commercial Speech: The Supreme Court Sends Another Valentine* 425 Buffalo Law Review 737–751 (1976).

Smith, Timothy G., *Recent Developments and New Directions in Antitrust: An Antitrust Division Perspective*, (Remarks before Annual Antitrust Symposium, Lewis and Clark Law School, Portland, Oregon, February 24, 1978).

Sullivan, E. Thomas, *First Amendment Defenses in Antitrust Litigation*, 46 Missouri Law Review 517–76 (1981).

Swope, William E., *Current Trends in Antitrust Enforcement: "A Prosecutor's Per-*

spective'' (Remarks delivered at the Southeastern Corporate Law Institute, Point Clear, Alabama, April 22, 1978.)

Thompson, Stephen G., *Antitrust, the First Amendment and the Communication of Price Information*, 56 Temple Law Quarterly 939–982 (1983).

Thompson, Stephen Lee, *Restricting the Application of the Commercial Speech Doctrine*, 79 West Virginia Law Review 274–292 (1977–78).

Travers, Timothy E., *Validity and Construction of State or Local Regulation Prohibiting Off-Premises Advertising Structures*, 81 American Law Reports 3d 486 (1977).

Tribe, Lawrence H., *The Supreme Court 1972 Term—Prohibition of Newspaper's Sex-Designated Help-Wanted Advertising Classification System*, 87 Harvard Law Review 1–302 (1973).

Watson, Kirk P., *Regulating Commercial Speech: A Conceptual Framework for Analysis*, 32 Baylor Law Review 235–246 (1980).

Woglom, Susan Stark, *Jury Award Advertising—Political Speech or Commercial Speech?* 15 Connecticut Law Review 273–301 (1983).

Young, James L., *Professional Trade Names: Unprotected Commercial Speech—Friedman v. Rodgers*, 59 Nebraska Law Review 482–506 (1980).

Notes

Advertisements for Contraceptives as Commercial Speech in the Broadcast Media, 31 Case Western Reserve Law Review 336–362 (1981).

Advertising Restrictions on Health Care Professionals and Lawyers: The First Amendment Limitations, 50 UMKC Law Review 82–98 (1981).

Application of the Fairness Doctrine to Ordinary Product Advertisements: National Citizens Committee for Broadcasting v. FCC, 20 Boston College Law Review 425–438 (1979).

Attorneys—Solicitation of Business: Modern Status of Law Regarding Solicitation of Business by or for Attorney, 5 American Law Reports 4th 866 (1981).

Big Brother's War on Television Advertising: How Extensive Is the Regulatory Authority of the Federal Trade Commission, 33 Southwestern Law Journal 683–701 (1979).

Billboard Advertising Still up in the Air (case note) *Metromedia, Inc. v. City of San Diego*, 11 Capital University Law Review 855–873 (1982).

Commercial Speech and the Limits of Legal Advertising, 58 Oregon Law Review 193–219 (1979).

Commercial Speech Falls Within the Protection of First Amendment—Virginia State Board of Pharmacy v. Virginia Citizens Consumer Council, 10 Creighton Law Review 362–377 (1976).

Commercial Speech—Linmark Associates, Inc. v. Township of Willingboro, 24 New York Law School Law Review 225–246 (1978).

Competitive Torts, 77 Harvard Law Review 887–978 (1964).

Constitutional Law: Billboards, Commercial Speech and the First Amendment (case note) *Metromedia, Inc. v. City of San Diego*, 21 Washburn Law Journal 672–678 (1982).

Constitutional Protection of Commercial Speech (case note) *Central Hudson Gas & Electric Corp. v. Public Service Commission*, 82 Columbia Law Review 720–750 (1982).

Corrective Advertising and the Limits of Virginia Pharmacy, 32 Stanford Law Review 121–142 (1979).

"Corrective Advertising" Orders of the Federal Trade Commission, 85 Harvard Law Review 477–506 (1971).

Fair Trial v. Unfair Advertising After Bates (Bates & Osteer v. State Bar of Arizona), 14 Forum 938–961 (1979).

"The First Amendment and Legislative Bans of Liquor and Cigarette Advertisements" 85 Columbia Law Review 632 (1985).

First Amendment Protection for Commercial Advertising: The New Constitutional Doctrine, 44 University of Chicago Law Review 205–254 (1976).

First Amendment Protection for Commercial Speech: An Optical Illusion? (Friedman v. Rogers), 31 University of Florida Law Review 799–814 (1979).

Freedom of Speech—Commercial Speech—Consolidated Edison; Central Hudson Gas, 66 American Bar Association Journal 1118–1122 (1980).

Group Vilification Reconsidered, 89 Yale Law Journal 308–332, 1450-1 (1979).

Legislative Choice and Commercial Speech (case note) *Central Hudson Gas and Electric Corp. v. Public Service Commission*, 1981 Utah Law Review 831–842.

Limitation of the Commercial Speech Exception to First Amendment Protection, 51 Tulane Law Review 149–156 (1976).

The Media Win the Billboard Battle, but Metro Wins the War (case note) *Metromedia, Inc. v. City of San Diego*, 15 University of California at Davis Law Review 493–520 (1981).

Municipal Billboard Regulation and the First Amendment (case note) *Metromedia, Inc. v. City of San Diego*, 23 Urban Law Annual 361–381 (1982).

The New Commercial Speech and the Fair Credit Reporting Act, 130 University of Pennsylvania Law Review 131–160 (1981).

New Commercial Speech Doctrine and Broadcast Advertising, 14 Harvard Civil Rights Law Review 385–484 (1979).

Professional Trade Names: Unprotected Commercial Speech, 59 Nebraska Law Review 482–506 (1980).

Reuniting Commercial Speech and One Process Analysis: The Standard for Deceptiveness in Friedman v. Rogers, 57 Texas Law Review 1456–1488 (1979).

Scope of Protection for Commercial Speech, 94 Harvard Law Review 159–168 (1980).

Since the Meadowlands Sports Complex Is not a Public Forum, the Prohibition of all Literature Distribution and Fund Solicitation by Outside Organizations Does Not Violate the First Amendment (case note) *International Society for Krishna Consciousness v. New Jersey Sports and Exposition Authority*, 28 Villanova Law Review 741–764 (1983).

State Constitution May Guarantee Broader Rights of Free Speech and Expression Than Those Rights Protected by the Federal Constitution, 1979 Washington University Law Quarterly 1161–1168 (1979).

Township Ordinance Prohibiting Distribution of Advertising Materials by Depositing Them on Premises Without Homeowner's Consent Violates the First and Fourteenth Amendments (case note) *Ad World, Inc. v. Township of Doylestown*, 28 Villanova Law Review 765–785 (1983).

Trade Names Are Not a Protected Form of Commercial Speech, 11 Texas Tech Law Review 717–727 (1980).

Unsolicited Commercial Telephone Calls and the First Amendment: A Constitutional Hangup, 11 Pacific Law Journal 143–167 (1979).

What Happened to the First Amendment: The Metromedia Case (case note) *Metromedia,*

Inc. v. City of San Diego, 13 Loyola University Chicago Law Journal 463–488 (1982).

Yes, FTC, There Is a Virginia: The Impact of Virginia State Board of Pharmacy v. Virginia Citizens Consumer Council, Inc. on the Federal Trade Commission's Regulation of Misleading Advertising, 57 Boston University Law Review 833–863 (1977).

CORPORATE POLITICAL SPEECH

Articles

Alderman, Richard M., *Commercial Entities Non-Commercial Speech: A Contradiction in Terms*, 1982 Utah Law Review 731–761 (1982).

Ator, Lloyd G., *The Federal Tax Consequences of Political Activity*, 3 American Law Institute–American Bar Association Course Materials Journal No. 2 101–112 (Oct. 1978).

Baker, C. Edwin, *Realizing Self-Realization: Corporate Political Expenditures and Redish's The Value of Free Speech*, 130 University of Pennsylvania Law Review 646–677 (1982).

Baldwin, Fletcher N., Jr., and Kenneth D. Karpay, *Corporate Political Free Speech: 2 U.S.C. 4416 and the Superior Rights of Natural Persons*, 14 Pacific Law Journal 209–241 (1983).

Beeken, Scott H., *A Tax Practitioner's Primer on Grassroots Lobbying, Taxes—59* The Tax Magazine 93–96 (February 1981).

Bettes, Marjory L., *First National Bank of Boston v. Bellotti: The Constitutionality of Government Restrictions on Political Spending by Corporations*, 16 Houston Law Review 195–208 (1978).

Biernbaum, Roy B., *The Constitutionality of the Federal Corrupt Practices Act After First National Bank of Boston v. Bellotti*, 28 American University Law Review 149–175 (1979).

Biggs, Linda Newman, *Corporations Right to Free Speech in Referendum Elections: First National Bank v. Bellotti*, 32 Southwestern Law Journal 1359–1373 (1979).

Blakely, Bruce W., *Public Utility Bill Inserts, Political Speech, and the First Amendment: A Constitutionally Mandated Right to Reply*, 70 California Law Review 1221–1262 (1982).

Blasi, Vincent, *The Checking Value in First Amendment Theory*, 3 American Bar Foundation Research Journal 521–649. (1977).

Boggs, Thomas Hale, Jr., *PAC's: Business Political Renaissance*, 14 Trial 5–7 (Jan. 1978).

Bolton, John R., *Constitutional Limitations on Restricting Corporate and Union Political Speech*, 22 Arizona Law Review 373–426 (1980).

Bostick, George H., *Proposed Regulations on Grass Roots Lobbying: Analysis of the Area and Special Problems Involved*, 54 The Journal of Taxation 332–338 (June 1981).

Brudney, Victor, *Business Corporations and Stockholders' Rights Under the First Amendment*, 91 Yale Law Journal 235–295 (1981).

Calhelha, Moacyr R., *The First Amendment: Political Speech and the Democratic Process*, 24 New York Law School Law Review 921–941 (1979).

Clyde, Hal Michael, *Corporate and Union Political Contributions and Expenditures Under 2 U.S.C. 441b: A Constitutional Analysis*, 1977 Utah Law Review 291–314 (1977).

Davis, Downie M., *Freedom of Expression—When May the Government Regulate the Public Expression of Ideas*, 25 Loyola Law Review 395–405 (1979).

Ely, John H., *Flag Desecration: A Case Study in the Rules of Categorization and Balancing in First Amendment Analysis*, 88 Harvard Law Review 1482–1508 (1975).

Falls, Harold Neill, Jr., *First Amendment Vagueness and Overbreadth: Theological Revisions by the Burger Court*, 31 Vanderbilt Law Review 609–637 (1978).

Fletcher, Stephen H., *Corporate Political Contribution*, 29 Business Lawyer 1071–1089 (1974).

Fox, Francis H., *Corporate Political Speech: The Effect of First National Bank of Boston v. Bellotti Upon Statutory Limitations on Corporate Referendum Spending*, 67 Kentucky Law Journal 75–101 (1978–79).

Garrett, Ray, *Corporate Contributions for Political Purposes*, 14 Business Lawyer 365–378 (1959).

Goldberg, The Honorable Arthur J., *The First Amendment and its Protections*, 8 Hastings Constitutional Law Quarterly 5–10 (1980).

Gray, John A., *Corporate Identity and Corporate Political Activities*, 21 American Business Law Journal 439–461 (1984).

Green, Thomas B., *Prohibition of Corporate Political Expenditures: The Effects of First National Bank v. Bellotti*, 1979 Utah Law Review 95–106.

Guiggey, John B., *Free Speech and Public Utilities: Consolidated Edison Co. v. Public Service Commission*, 44 Albany Law Review 515–531 (1980).

Hall, Leslie W., *The First and Fourteenth Amendments Preclude a State Public Utility Commission's Blanket Suppression of a Utility Company's Billing Inserts Discussing Controversial Issues of Public Policy*, 58 University of Detroit Journal of Urban Law 531–544 (1981).

Harrison, Jeffrey L., *Public Utilities in the Marketplace of Ideas: A Fairness Solution for a Competitive Imbalance*, 1982 Wisconsin Law Review 43–74 (1982).

Hart, Senator Gary, and William Shore, *Corporate Spending on State and Local Referendums: First National Bank of Boston v. Bellotti*, 29 Case Western Reserve Law Review 808–829 (1979).

Hazen, Thomas L., and Bren L. Buckley, *Models of Corporate Conduct: From the Government Dominated Corporation to the Corporate Dominated Government*, 58 Nebraska Law Review 100–135 (1978).

Henkin, Louis, *The Supreme Court, 1967 Term—Forward: On Drawing Lines*, 82 Harvard Law Review 63–92 (1968).

Kalven, Harry J., *The Concept of the Public Forum: Cox v. Louisiana*, 1965 Supreme Court Review 1–32.

Karnezis, Kristine Cordier, *Power of Corporation to Make Political Contribution or Expenditure Under State Law*, 79 American Law Reports 3d 491 (1977).

Karst, Kenneth L., *Equality as a Central Principle in the First Amendment*, 43 University of Chicago Law Review 20–68 (1975).

Keane, Paul R., *Political Speech, Inc.: The Bellotti Decision and Corporate Political Spending*, 13 Suffolk University Law Review 1023–1064 (1979).

Kiley, Thomas R., *PACing the Burger Court: The Corporate Right to Speak and the Public Right to Hear After First National Bank v. Bellotti*, 22 Arizona Law Review 427–443 (1980).

Krauskopf, Anne M., *Influencing the Public: Policy Considerations Defining the Tax Status of Corporate Grassroots Lobbying*, 28 Catholic University Law Review 313–357 (1979).

Maloney, John P., *From Marketplace to Ballot Box: The Corporate Assertion of Political Power*, 12 Connecticut Law Review 14–61 (1979).

Mancino, Douglas M., *Lobbying by Public Charities*, 11 Tax Adviser 452–462 (August 1980).

Marticelli, J. J., *Power of a Business to Donate to a Charitable or Similar Institution* 39 American Law Report 2d 1192 (1955).

Mastro, Randy M., Deborah C. Costlow, and Heidi P. Sanchez, *Taking the Initiative: Corporate Control of the Referendum Process Through Media Spending and What to Do About It*, 32 Federal Communications Law Journal 315–369 (1980).

Mayton, William T., *Politics, Money, Coercion, and the Problem with Corporate PACS*, 29 Emory Law Journal 375–394 (1980).

Mazo, Mark Elliot, *Impact on Corporations of the 1976 Amendments to the Federal Election Campaign Act*, 32 Business Lawyer 427–450 (January 1977).

Meiklejohn, Alexander, "The First Amendment Is an Absolute," 1961 Supreme Court Review, 245–266.

Mickenberg, Ira, *The Constitutionality of Limitations on Contributions to Ballot Measure Campaigns*, 2 Southwestern University Law Review 527–558 (1981).

Miller, Arthur S., *On Politics, Democracy, and the First Amendment: A Commentary on First National Bank v. Bellotti*, 38 Washington and Lee Law Review 21–41 (1981).

Mueller, John E., and James R. Paerinello, *The Constitutionality of Limit on Ballot Measure Contributions*, 57 North Dakota Law Review 391–426 (1981).

Murdock, Margaret Maize, and J. Nicholas Murdock, *Corporate Expression in Wyoming Ballot Issues, Referendum and Initiatives: A Political and Legal Dilemma*, 14 University of Wyoming Land and Water Review 449–489 (1979).

Nicholson, Marlene Arnold, *The Constitutionality of the Federal Restrictions on Corporate and Union Campaign Contributions and Expenditures*, 65 Cornell Law Review 945–1010 (1980).

O'Kelley, Charles R., *The Constitutional Rights of Corporations Revisited: Social and Political Expression and the Corporation after First National Bank v. Bellotti*, 67 Georgetown Law Journal 1347–1383 (1979).

Patton, William, and Bartlett Randall, *Corporate "Persons" and Freedom of Speech: The Political Impact of Legal Mythology*, 1981 Wisconsin Law Review 494–512.

Prentice, Robert A., *Consolidated Edison and Bellotti: First Amendment Protection of Corporate Political Speech*, 16 Tulsa Law Journal 599–657 (1981).

Ratner, David L., *Corporations and the Constitution*, 15 University of San Francisco Law Review 11–29 (1980–81).

Redish, Martin H., *The First Amendment in the Marketplace: Commercial Speech and the Values of Free Expression*, 39 George Washington Law Review 429–473 (1971).

Richman, Steven M., *Election Law—Political Expression by Artificial Persons in Referendum Campaigns*, 1979 Annual Survey of American Law 285–300 (1979).

Shaw, Bill, *Corporate Speech in the Marketplace of Ideas*, Winter 1982, 7 The Journal of Corporation Law 265–283 (1982).

Notes

All the Free Speech Money Can Buy: Monopolization of Issue Perception in Referendum Campaigns, 35 University of Miami Law Review 157–164 (1980).

Billing Inserts: A Unique Forum for Free Speech (case note) *Consolidated Edison Co. v. Public Service Commission*, 30 DePaul Law Review 705–719 (1981).

Comment: Civil Responsibility for Corporate Political Expenditures, 20 UCLA Law Review 1327 (1973).

The Constitutionality of Municipal Advocacy in Statewide Referendum Campaigns, 93 Harvard Law Review 535–563 (1980).

Constitutional Law—Corporate Freedom of Speech—First National Bank of Boston v. Bellotti, 13 Suffolk University Law Review 124–137 (1979).

Construction and Application of Provisions of Corrupt Practices Act Regarding Contributions by Corporations, 125 American Law Reports 1029 (1940).

Corporate Advocacy Advertising: When Business Right to Speak Threatens the Administration of Justice, 1979 Detroit College of Law Review 623–675 (1979).

Corporate Free Speech: First National Bank of Boston v. Bellotti, 20 Boston College Law Review 1003–1024 (1979).

Corporate Identity of Speaker Does Not Deprive Corporate Speech of Its Entitlement to First Amendment Protection, 28 Emory Law Journal 183–214 (1979).

The Corporation and the Constitution: Economic Due Process and Corporate Speech, 90 Yale Law Journal 1833–1860 (1981).

Elections: Corporate Free Speech—The Right to Speech and Contribute, the Right to Influence and Dominate (case note) *Winn Dixie Stores v. State*, 12 Stetson Law Review 236–249 (1982).

First Amendment Overbreadth Doctrine, 83 Harvard Law Review 844–927 (1970).

First National Bank v. Bellotti: First Amendment Protection for Corporate Speech, 48 UMKC Law Review 96–107 (1979).

First National Bank of Boston v. Bellotti: Corporate Political Speech in Ballot-Measure Campaigns, 8 New York University Review of Law and Social Change 63–86 (1978–79).

First National Bank of Boston v. Bellotti: The Reopening of the Corporate Mouth—The Corporation's Right to Free Speech, 21 Arizona Law Review 841–869 (1979).

Freedom of Expression in a Commercial Context, 78 Harvard Law Review 1191–1211 (1965).

From Dartmouth College to Bellotti: The Political Career of the American Business Corporation, 6 Ohio Northern University Law Review 392–430 (1979).

Massachusetts Statute Forbidding Corporate Contributions or Expenditures for Non-Partisan Political Advertising Violates the Speech Clause, 47 Cincinnati 661–669 (1968).

Municipal Corporations—Zoning Sign Ordinance Violating First Amendment Right to Political Expression Ruled Unconstitutional (case note) *State v. Miller*, 11 Seton Hall Law Review 345–347 81980).

Note (Consolidated Edison Co. v. Public Service Commission), 1981 Wisconsin Law Review 399–418.

Note, 1983 Detroit College Law Review 1613.

The Regulation of Union Political Activity: Majority and Minority Rights and Remedies, 126 University of Pennsylvania Law Review 386–424 (1977).

Suppression of Public Utility's Bill Inserts Discussing Controversial Public Issues Infringes the Freedom of Speech Protected by the First and Fourteenth Amendments (case note) *Consolidated Edison Co. v. Public Service Commission*, 30 Emory Law Journal 893–926 (1981).

Tax Subsidies for Political Participation, 31 Tax Lawyer 461–482 (1977–78).

Index of Cases

Index

About the Author

EDWIN P. ROME is partner in the Philadelphia law firm of Blank, Rome, Comisky and McCauley. He has addressed the Association of General Counsel on First Amendment issues pertaining to corporate speech and is co-author of *Pennsylvania Trial Handbook* for Pennsylvania lawyers. He is a member of the American College of Trial Lawyers and the International Academy of Trial Lawyers.

WILLIAM H. ROBERTS is also a partner in the Philadelphia law firm of Blank, Rome, Comisky and McCauley. Messrs. Rome and Roberts have been involved in several landmark Supreme Court cases in the field of commercial and corporate free speech, including *Cort v. Ash, Central Hudson Gas & Electric Corp. v. Public Service Commission,* and *Consolidated Edison Co. v. Public Service Commission.*